Out of Time

Oxford Studies in Gender and International Relations

Series editors: J. Ann Tickner, American University, and Laura Sjoberg, University of Florida

Windows of Opportunity: How Women Seize Peace Negotiations for Political Change
Miriam J. Anderson

Women as Foreign Policy Leaders: National Security and Gender Politics in Superpower America
Sylvia Bashevkin

Gendered Citizenship: Understanding Gendered Violence in Democratic India
Natasha Behl

Enlisting Masculinity: The Construction of Gender in U.S. Military Recruiting Advertising during the All-Volunteer Force
Melissa T. Brown

The Politics of Gender Justice at the International Criminal Court: Legacies and Legitimacy
Louise Chappell

Cosmopolitan Sex Workers: Women and Migration in a Global City
Christine B. N. Chin

Intelligent Compassion: Feminist Critical Methodology in the Women's International League for Peace and Freedom
Catia Cecilia Confortini

Complicit Sisters: Gender and Women's Issues across North-South Divides
Sara de Jong

Gender and Private Security in Global Politics
Maya Eichler

This American Moment: A Feminist Christian Realist Intervention
Caron E. Gentry

Troubling Motherhood: Maternality in Global Politics
Lucy B. Hall, Anna L. Weissman, and Laura J. Shepherd

Breaking the Binaries in Security Studies: A Gendered Analysis of Women in Combat
Ayelet Harel-Shalev and Shir Daphna-Tekoah

Scandalous Economics: Gender and the Politics of Financial Crises
Aida A. Hozić and Jacqui True

Rewriting the Victim: Dramatization as Research in Thailand's Anti-Trafficking Movement
Erin M. Kamler

Equal Opportunity Peacekeeping: Women, Peace, and Security in Post-Conflict States
Sabrina Karim and Kyle Beardsley

Gender, Sex, and the Postnational Defense: Militarism and Peacekeeping
Annica Kronsell

The Beauty Trade: Youth, Gender, and Fashion Globalization
Angela B. V. McCracken

Global Norms and Local Action: The Campaigns against Gender-Based Violence in Africa
Peace A. Medie

Rape Loot Pillage: The Political Economy of Sexual Violence in Armed Conflict
Sara Meger

From Global to Grassroots: The European Union, Transnational Advocacy, and Combating Violence against Women
Celeste Montoya

Who Is Worthy of Protection? Gender-Based Asylum and US Immigration Politics
Meghana Nayak

Revisiting Gendered States: Feminist Imaginings of the State in International Relations
Swati Parashar, J. Ann Tickner, and Jacqui True

Gender, UN Peacebuilding, and the Politics of Space: Locating Legitimacy
Laura J. Shepherd

A Feminist Voyage through International Relations
J. Ann Tickner

The Political Economy of Violence against Women
Jacqui True

Queer International Relations: Sovereignty, Sexuality and the Will to Knowledge
Cynthia Weber

Bodies of Violence: Theorizing Embodied Subjects in International Relations
Lauren B. Wilcox

OUT OF TIME

The Queer Politics of Postcoloniality

Rahul Rao

OXFORD
UNIVERSITY PRESS

Oxford University Press is a department of the University of Oxford. It furthers
the University's objective of excellence in research, scholarship, and education
by publishing worldwide. Oxford is a registered trade mark of Oxford University
Press in the UK and certain other countries.

Published in the United States of America by Oxford University Press
198 Madison Avenue, New York, NY 10016, United States of America.

Library of Congress Cataloging-in-Publication Data
Names: Rao, Rahul, 1978– author.
Title: Out of time : the queer politics of postcoloniality / Rahul Rao.
Description: New York, NY : Oxford University Press, [2020] |
Includes bibliographical references and index.
Identifiers: LCCN 2019047243 (print) | LCCN 2019047244 (ebook) |
ISBN 9780190865511 (hardback) | ISBN 9780190865528 (paperback) |
ISBN 9780190865542 (epub) | ISBN 9780190865559
Subjects: LCSH: Gay rights—Uganda. | Gay rights—India. |
Gays—Uganda—Social conditions—21st century. | Gays—India—Social
conditions—21st century. | Homosexuality—Law and legislation—Uganda. |
Homosexuality—Law and legislation—India. | Homophobia—Uganda. |
Homophobia—India. | Postcolonialism. | Great Britain—Colonies—Social conditions.
Classification: LCC HQ76.8.U33 R45 2020 (print) | LCC HQ76.8.U33 (ebook) |
DDC 323.3/264096761—dc23
LC record available at https://lccn.loc.gov/2019047243
LC ebook record available at https://lccn.loc.gov/2019047244

for Naina

CONTENTS

ACKNOWLEDGEMENTS

Sometime after Bangalore's Sirsi flyover was built in 1999 but before I had graduated from National Law School of India University in 2001, Arvind Narrain asked me—as we whizzed over K. R. Market on his bike—'How do you identify?' I'm not sure I understood the question. 'I don't know. Marxist? It depends on the context,' I replied evasively, shouting over the wind and the din of traffic. I don't know if it was the answer Arvind was looking for, but to his credit he accepted it without demur. In the years since that delightfully failed exchange, he has become a friend and trusted interlocutor. Sometime in 2008–2009, Arvind and other members of the queer law collective that edited *Law like Love* invited me to contribute a chapter, setting me off on a journey of which this book is one result.

Although I've had doubts about whether International Relations offered the most hospitable disciplinary terrain for that journey, Cynthia Weber has persuaded me otherwise. I am grateful for her friendship, scholarship, and mentorship, which have made place in the discipline for something that we are now beginning to call queer IR. Like countless others, I have been inspired by the work of Jasbir Puar. *Terrorist Assemblages* gave us a formidable theoretical arsenal with which to make sense of what was, till then, an inchoate sense of disquiet with queer liberalism. Jasbir's friendship and support have been invaluable in bringing this project to fruition. My thanks also to my doctoral supervisor Andrew Hurrell, who has remained a steadfast source of encouragement.

David Kato was the first person with whom I made contact in Uganda when I began to research controversies around homosexuality in the country. I will never forget the shock of hearing about his murder in 2011, especially as I had received one of his characteristically energetic emails only a few days before. His loss is irreparable, but I'm moved by the courage and resolve that his comrades have demonstrated in its aftermath. I am grateful for the time that Frank Mugisha has given me over the last nine years. Geoff Ogwaro's friendship enlivened my time in Kampala. Parts of this research would not have been possible without the translation assistance of Ambrose Barigye. My thanks are due to all the kuchu activists who took time to share their views with me. Kevin Ward has taught me more about religion in Uganda than anyone else. Revd. Michael Ssentamu and Stephen Ssenkaaba provided helpful orientation to the worlds of Ugandan Anglicanism and Catholicism, respectively. I was fortunate to have met Olive Melissa Minor while in Kampala, and have benefited tremendously from reading her work. Sutapa Choudhury, Michael Collins, Robin, and Manu welcomed me into their home for parts of my stay. I cannot exaggerate the importance for me of conversations with Sylvia Tamale and Stella Nyanzi, both of whom provided advice and affirmation at a crucial juncture. Having followed Stella's life and work, I have come to think of her as offering one of the most original, provocative, and powerful examples of what a queer theorist can do in the world. I hope my admiration for her is evident in these pages.

I am grateful to the Leverhulme Trust for funding this project through a Research Fellowship that gave me time for research and writing. Thanks also to the British Institute in Eastern Africa and SOAS University of London for timely small grants that funded research trips to Uganda and India.

This book could only have been written at SOAS, where I have worked since 2008 and for which my love is, frankly, irrational. Early conversations with Phil Clark and Stephen Chan equipped me with indispensable practical advice. I am grateful to successive heads of the Department of Politics and International Studies who supported research-led teaching while also giving me time and space in which to engage in intensive research and writing. A special thanks to colleagues in the International Relations, Comparative Political Thought, and South Asia clusters for their intellectual comradeship and collegiality. It's difficult to overstate my debt to the Centre for Gender Studies, which has given me an additional institutional home. I am especially grateful to Gina Heathcote, whose brilliantly organised writing weeks contributed in a very tangible way to the completion of this book. I am grateful to all my teaching assistants over the years, whose enthusiasm for their work despite the precarious conditions in which it is carried out is humbling. My most profound debt is to my students, particularly those who signed up for our impossibly ambitious course on 'Queer Politics in Asia, Africa and the Middle East.' If parts of this book seem familiar to you, this is because your scepticism and affirmation have shaped its arguments. I have learned a great deal from my doctoral students, especially Hila Amit, Jacquelyn Strey, Hinni Aarninsalo,

Lars Aaberg, and Shikha Dilawri. I owe additional thanks to Jacquelyn and Ueli Staeger for timely research assistance.

Nothing has helped my writing more than the pressure of having to think of things to say on The Disorder of Things. Huge thanks to Paul Kirby, Meera Sabaratnam, and our fellow bloggers for creating this scintillating corner of the Internet. I'm grateful to my colleagues in the Radical Philosophy collective with whom I have enjoyed sharing the labour of producing a journal. Both these communities have taught me the value of curating open access non-disciplinary venues for the publication of incisive and timely critique.

I have specific debts to a number of people who generously read earlier drafts of chapters in this book: Reem Abou-El-Fadl, Anna Agathangelou, Grietje Baars, Victoria Browne and the RP collective, Rohit De, Nikita Dhawan, Maria Elander, Sameen Gauhar, Neve Gordon, Aeyal Gross, Aggie Hirst, Kimberly Hutchings, Emily Jones, Laleh Khalili, Nivi Manchanda, Akanksha Mehta, Matt Nelson, Stella Nyanzi, Jordan Osserman, Di Otto, Chris Rossdale, Robbie Shilliam, Akshi Singh, Mayur Suresh, Charles Tripp, Kevin Ward, and Cynthia Weber. Arvind Narrain and Clare Hemmings read the entire manuscript in record time and helped me to see the wood where previously there had been only trees. For help with specific queries as much as for giving me their sense of the world, I am grateful to Daniel Baer, Rochana Bajpai, Gautam Bhan, Michael Bronski, Eddie Bruce-Jones, Sonia Corrêa, Catriona Drew, Mark Gevisser, Kapil Gupta, akshay khanna, Hagar Kotef, Scott Long, Akanksha Mehta, Kavya Murty, Arvind Narrain, Divya Rao, Danish Sheikh, Akshi Singh, Nikita Sud, Adriaan van Klinken, and friends on Facebook. Sita Balani, Sarah Keenan, and Alyosxa Tudor gave me reading suggestions that improved the theoretical scaffolding of particular chapters. I am grateful for numerous invitations to give talks and seminars about my work, and to the audiences at these events whose questions and comments enriched it. Few of these have been more formative than Shamira Meghani's brilliantly organised 2010 conference 'Dissident Citizenship'.

Early versions of some chapters appeared elsewhere as follows: Chapter 2 as 'The Locations of Homophobia', *London Review of International Law* 2, no. 2 (2014): 169–199; Chapter 3 as 'Re-membering Mwanga: Same-Sex Intimacy, Memory and Belonging in Postcolonial Uganda', *Journal of Eastern African Studies* 9, no. 1 (2015): 1–19; Chapter 4 as 'A Tale of Two Atonements', in *Queering International Law: Possibilities, Alliances, Complicities, Risks*, edited by Di Otto, 15–34 (London: Routledge, 2018); and Chapter 5 as 'Global Homocapitalism,' *Radical Philosophy* 194 (Nov/Dec 2015): 38–49. I am grateful for permission to revise this material.

At Oxford University Press, I have been fortunate to work with Angela Chnapko, who has been a patient and supportive editor. My thanks also to the series editors, J. Ann Tickner and Laura Sjoberg, to three anonymous readers for helpful comments and feedback at various stages of the project, to Alexcee Bechthold for assistance with the submissions process, to Dorothy Bauhoff for copyediting the manuscript, to Suganya Elango for overseeing the production process, and to the rest of the team behind the production of this book.

I have many friends to thank: Antara Datta and Saranya, Samvid, and Samar Sridhar for forcing me to play the violin, Sameen Gauhar for her companionship (self and others), Paul Kirby and Aggie Hirst for photo booth shenanigans, Yuka Kobayashi for IDGAFA solidarity, Alex Luck and Mayur Suresh for gay times, Neel Mukherjee for laughs and letters, Tamson Pietsch and Ruth Higgins for a conversation that drew us closer just through the having of it, Akshi Singh for provincialising Bengal, and Alice Wright and Lenny Stillman for themselves and all the people, places, and animals they bring in their wake. Tanya Singh will recognise her role in precipitating key moments in this book. Devina Sivagurunathan went further than anyone in declaring her queer affiliation with me. On some days, I only wanted to talk to Akanksha 'darkest of times' Mehta. Jordan Osserman found me through the first draft of the first chapter and has stuck around till the end—this makes me happy. I love Conor Ryan's eye for things both very small and very large. He reminds me every day of how vast and exhilarating the world is.

I'm grateful to my sister Nitya and brother-in-law Venks for their love and hospitality. I hope to be meeting them at the cutlery station for a long time to come. My mother Gayatri lives the richest and most public-spirited life of anyone I know. Her curiosity and love keeps us going as a family. My father Ashok was, in the words of one of his friends, 'the nicest man'. His love for me was total even when he was most anguished about my life choices. This book is for him.

ABBREVIATIONS

ABVP	Akhil Bharatiya Vidyarthi Parishad (All India Student Council)
ACB	Anglican Church in Brazil
ACNA	Anglican Church in North America
AHA	Anti Homosexuality Act
AHB	Anti Homosexuality Bill
APPG	All Party Parliamentary Group
ATS	Alien Tort Statute
BJP	Bharatiya Janata Party
CANA	Convocation of Anglicans in North America
CARICOM	Caribbean Community
CHOGM	Commonwealth Heads of Government Meeting
CMS	Church Missionary Society
COU	Church of Uganda
CPI(M)	Communist Party of India (Marxist)
FBO	faith-based organisation
GAFCON	Global Anglican Future Conference
GILRHO	Global Index on Legal Recognition of Homosexual Orientation
HDT	Human Dignity Trust
HRC	Human Rights Council
IBEAC	Imperial British East Africa Company
ICG	International Crisis Group
IFI	international financial institution
ILGA	International Lesbian, Gay, Bisexual, Trans and Intersex Association
IMF	International Monetary Fund
IPC	Indian Penal Code
JNU	Jawaharlal Nehru University

KSBCC	Karnataka State Backward Classes Commission
LABIA	Lesbians and Bisexuals in Action
LGBTI	lesbian, gay, bisexual, transgender, intersex
NALSA	National Legal Services Authority
NRM	National Resistance Movement
OBC	Other Backward Class
OBE	Order of the British Empire
PCC	Pentecostal Charismatic Church
PEPFAR	President's Emergency Plan for AIDS Relief
QC	Queen's Counsel
SC	Scheduled Caste
SMUG	Sexual Minorities Uganda
SOGI	sexual orientation and gender identity
ST	Scheduled Tribe
TEC	The Episcopal Church
VHP	Vishwa Hindu Parishad (World Hindu Council)

PROLOGUE

In the *Prison Notebooks* Gramsci says: 'The starting-point of critical elaboration is the consciousness of what one really is, and is "knowing thyself" as a product of the historical process to date, which has deposited in you an infinity of traces, without leaving an inventory.' The only available English translation inexplicably leaves Gramsci's comment at that, whereas in fact Gramsci's Italian text concludes by adding, 'therefore it is imperative at the outset to compile such an inventory.'[1]

—Said, Orientalism, 25

I came out in the autumn of 2002 after watching a production of Caryl Churchill's *Cloud 9*. I suppose many things had brought me to the point where I could be interpellated as gay, but the play must have been the last straw. It comprises two acts, the first of which takes place in an unnamed British colony in Victorian Africa, and the second in London in 1979 (which is also the year in which the play was first performed). In Act One, Clive, the white paterfamilias, attempts to impose his ideals on his family and on the 'natives' of the colony in which he is stationed. Churchill's stage directions inform us that Betty, Clive's wife, is played by a man because she wants to be what men want her to be. Edward, their son, is played by a woman to underscore Clive's authoritarian attempts to impose masculine behaviour on the effeminate boy. Victoria, their daughter, is played in this act by a

---

1. This omission is rectified in editions of the Quintin Hoare and Geoffrey Nowell Smith English translation of the *Prison Notebooks* issued after the one that Said must have consulted. Said's observation reminds us that intellectual traditions differ in their view of the wisdom of placing oneself in the text. We have come to expect reflections on personal experience from feminists and queer theorists ('the personal is political'), but there is something bracing about recalling that some Marxists and most postcolonial theorists have also encouraged this.

doll. Joshua, a black servant, is played by a white man because he wants to be what white people want him to be. Other members of the household include Betty's mother Maud, who takes it upon herself to enforce the petty but rigid status distinctions of settler colonial society, and the sullen and unfulfilled governess Ellen. Two visitors quickly become implicated in the life of the family—Mrs Saunders, the proverbial 'merry' widow, who seeks out the company of her fellow-settlers when trouble begins to brew in the colony; and Harry Bagley, an explorer modelled on the Victorian adventurer Richard Burton.

Clive struggles through the first act to administer his family and the territory of which he is in charge. Offstage, the natives are restless. He and the other white men flog the 'stable boys' and set a village on fire as punishment for acts of insubordination. Onstage, gender trouble is everywhere, in a bad way. Characters appear to be trapped in bodies in which they are uncomfortable and in relationships of unacknowledged, unreciprocated, or thwarted desire. Clive lusts after the fiercely independent Mrs Saunders but seems to have trouble appreciating that no means no, even if she once said yes. Betty desires Harry, but Harry wants a woman who will pine for his return at a safe distance. His libidinal energies are directed elsewhere—at Joshua, Edward, and, in a spectacularly ill-judged moment, Clive. Disgusted by the vice that is never named—'a disease more dangerous than diphtheria'[2]—Clive urges Harry to marry. Anyone will do. Ellen is conscripted for this purpose, her desire for Betty remaining invisible and unthinkable. On learning that his parents were killed in the suppressed rebellion, Joshua, who has hitherto played the obsequious servant to the hilt, shoots at Clive while he is in the midst of proposing a wedding toast.

When Act Two opens in 1970s London, the characters are twenty-five years older, but a hundred years have passed. The sun has mostly set on the British Empire, although a glancing reference to the killing of a soldier in Belfast reminds us that it limps grimly on. Now middle-aged, Betty has left Clive and is beginning to enjoy the freedom that comes with having work and an independent source of income. Rediscovering the pleasures of masturbation, she feels a guilt-laced triumph in her recovery of selfhood. Victoria, a socialist feminist, is married to Martin, whose zealous efforts to play the supportive husband seem ironically self-defeating. Victoria moves in with her lesbian lover Lin, who has a daughter, Cathy. Edward is in a relationship with Gerry, but they seem to want different things. Edward enjoys playing house, but Gerry prefers the carnal offerings of the sauna and the

2. Churchill, *Cloud 9*, 40.

cruising ground. Later Edward feels both an attraction to women and a desire to be one, eventually moving in with Victoria and Lin. Betty picks up Gerry in a park. Clive, cipher for white patriarchy, is utterly defeated.

If this sounds confusing, that may be precisely the point. Written over a decade before the 1990 publication of Judith Butler's *Gender Trouble*, *Cloud 9*'s cross-casting of characters in terms of gender and race demand an enactment of Butler's suggestion that drag and trans performativity undermine the notion of gender as having an 'abiding substance'.[3] As the bleak comedy of Act One demonstrates, if gender appears to have such a substance, this is the effect of the never entirely successful regulation of attributes along culturally established lines of coherence,[4] here supplied by the discourses of God, Queen, and country, and enforced through the institution of the family. In contrast, Act Two offers us a glimpse of the possibility that the repetitious performance of gender need not always consolidate norms but might sometimes subvert them, making gender trouble 'not through the strategies that figure a utopian beyond, but through the mobilization, subversive confusion, and proliferation of precisely those constitutive categories that seek to keep gender in its place by posturing as the foundational illusions of identity.'[5]

In a foreword to *Cloud 9*, Churchill writes that all the characters in the second act change a little for the better.[6] But the play is hardly straightforward about this, dodging the temptation to evangelise. Victoria seems paralysed by the array of personal and professional choices now apparently available to her. Martin's fumbling attempts at a progressive masculinity are curiously overbearing. Lin's sexual identity politics don't seem to have dislodged much else about her worldview ('I've changed who I sleep with, I can't change everything').[7] The brave new childcare arrangements through which Cathy and Tommy are being raised are precarious and constantly threatening to unravel. Gerry and Edward might be able to fuck with abandon in post-Wolfenden England, but their relationship is strained by the incompatibility of their perversions.[8] And yet with the exception of Cathy, who is played by a man to dramatise the coercive socialisation into girlhood of children gendered female at birth, for the most part, the characters in the second act seem to inhabit genders of their choice. Gender

3. Butler, *Gender Trouble*, xxiii.
4. Ibid., 32–33.
5. Ibid., 44.
6. Churchill, *Cloud 9*, [ii].
7. Ibid., 66.
8. I borrow this expression from Nelson, *The Argonauts*, 27, 69.

is still disorderly in Act Two, but in ways that feel more agential, experimental, and open-ended.

At its heart, *Cloud 9* is premised on a parallel between colonial and sexual oppression that Churchill acknowledges finding in the work of Jean Genet.[9] Mining a set of well-worn stereotypes in the colonial archive in which the European penetration of the Orient is expressed in floridly sexual terms, Churchill frequently has her characters express erotic interest in one another through metaphors of exploration and conquest (Clive to Mrs Saunders: 'Caroline, you smell amazing. You terrify me. You are dark like this continent. Mysterious. Treacherous.')[10] As the natives are flogged offstage, white characters allude to sadomasochistic fantasies of being beaten.[11] In its evocation of the homology between colonial and sexual domination, *Cloud 9* anticipates a central argument of Ashis Nandy's *The Intimate Enemy* and of the field of postcolonial studies more generally.[12] Crucially, the abrupt transition between the two acts seems to imply that the sexual liberation, such as it is, of postwar Britain is indissociable from the struggles that forcibly divested it of its empire. As such, the play evinces a deeply Fanonian awareness of the essential truth that colonialism also oppresses the coloniser.[13]

But it was galling to think, as I watched the play in 2002, that while decolonisation had in some powerful way loosened sexual and racial strictures in the former imperial metropolis, it had hardly had the same effect elsewhere. Even as the audience in whose midst I watched the play laughed in appreciation of its biting satire, I felt something more like anger as it brought into relief for me the gap between my enjoyment of a public and political freedom that I had come to take for granted as a postcolonial Indian citizen with a great deal of gender, class, caste, and religious privilege on the one hand,[14] and what I was beginning to think of as the coloniality of my sexuality on the other.[15] (You might say that I felt the rage

9. Churchill, *Cloud 9*, [i].
10. Ibid., 13–16.
11. Ibid., 15, 32.
12. Critics of the play have charged that it fails to do justice to both dimensions of this homology, focusing more on the sexual than the racial. Amoko, 'Casting Aside', points out that despite being set in colonial Africa, the first act limits its representation of African men to the figure of the collaborationist native informant and fails to represent African women and children at all, while the second act makes little reference to race and empire. This is true, but it seems to demand that a play that is centrally about sexuality and whiteness in Britain discharge a representational burden it never took up in the first place.
13. Fanon, *Black Skin*.
14. Rao, 'Before Bandung'.
15. Lugones, 'Coloniality of Gender'.

of the entitled.) Almost certainly, as a graduate student who had recently arrived in Oxford from India and had thereby acquired a sudden and astonishing access to the ostensible freedoms that gay liberation had won in a putatively more advanced West, the discourse of what Jasbir Puar would call 'homonationalism' had some role to play in interpellating my gayness.[16] And yet as I sat in the theatre watching *Cloud 9*, more destabilising than the differences between places was the sense that my own political and sexual liberation had not marched in step with one another, so that it was as if some parts of myself had been marooned in Act One even as others had been carried away by the surge of time into Act Two. Coming out felt like a way of catching up, less with other places than with other parts of myself.

I'm hardly the first person to speak of coming out as an attempt to reconcile a divided self. It would take me a little longer to appreciate the naiveté of straightforward analogies between sexual liberation, or at least this particular manifestation of it, and political decolonisation. To come out is to purport to reveal a hitherto secret truth about one's sexual identity. The structure of secrecy and disclosure at work here presupposes the existence of something called 'sexuality' that describes an aspect of a hidden interiority that we think of as the 'self'. It is to suppose, as akshay khanna explains, that 'who I fuck or am attracted to says something about the type of person I am.'[17] Michel Foucault famously locates the emergence of the homosexual as a type—or as he puts it, 'a species'—in biomedical and legal discourses that were circulating in Europe in the latter half of the nineteenth century.[18] But more fundamentally, the very notion of the self to which sexuality attaches is itself an artefact of the colonial encounter. Among the most profound effects of colonial governmentality was a tendency on the part of native modernising elites to increasingly understand their 'selfhood' and bodies, their relationship with the environment, health and illness in the same terms as their colonisers, in part by privileging biomedical discourses over local idioms and practices.[19] In seeking to win recognition for a diversity of sexual identities to which individual selves might have access, contemporary LGBT activism is both enabled by and further entrenches ontologies of personhood originally forged in conditions of colonial modernity. Thus notwithstanding the respite from compulsory heterosexuality that it can bring, to swap one sexual orientation for another,

16. Puar, *Terrorist Assemblages*.
17. khanna, 'Us "Sexuality Types"', 167.
18. Foucault, *Will to Knowledge*, 43.
19. khanna, 'Us "Sexuality Types"', 167.

as coming out purports to do, is still to play by the rules of the empire of sexuality.[20]

So there is something ironic, maybe even embarrassing, about beginning a book that has postcolonial pretensions with a story about coming out. And yet perhaps it is the very parochialism inherent in thinking of coming out as a liberatory gesture that, in the wake of queer theory, necessitates a coming out about coming out. Still, what interests me about this moment in my life is less the fact of my coming out than the sensations of temporal lag and rupture that impelled it—an experience that suggested to me in the most visceral way that temporal movements could have dramatic psychic and political consequences. *Cloud 9*'s first act ends with Clive desperately trying to uphold the gendered order of things by having Harry marry Ellen. The opening lines of the second act amplify his failure with a graphic description by Gerry of having his dick sucked by a man on a local train. Something quite dramatic has happened to the imagined community that is the nation in the interval between the two acts. But we are left to fill in the blanks ourselves.

20. Not everyone plays by these rules. Much of khanna's work seeks to provincialise the ontologies of personhood that mainstream LGBT activism speaks to as being meaningful only to those it describes, mockingly but evocatively, as 'us evolved, English-speaking, urban, etc. people who have, inter alia, heard of the Kinsey Report' or, more pithily, 'us, sexuality types' (ibid.). In contrast, through ethnographic work outside this milieu, khanna encounters a range of people for whom the erotic and the sexual do not speak to a sense of self or enter into the definition of self at all. Here, people might have non-normative sex without thinking of themselves as different. khanna suggests that what is at stake here is 'a "sexualness" that escapes the frame of sexuality, [a] desire and eroticism that flows through people without constituting them as subjects' (khanna, *Sexualness*, 12). For early critiques of the paradigm of sexuality and its tendency to valorise coming out as the sine qua non of sexual liberation, see Puar, 'Transnational Sexualities'; Massad, 'Re-Orienting Desire'; Gopinath, *Impossible Desires*, 14.

CHAPTER 1

Introduction

The queer politics of postcoloniality

Ever since Hegel mapped time onto space so that Africa was imagined as Europe's past and Europe as everyone else's future, time has been central to the politics of imperialism and anti-imperialism. The violence of colonial and postcolonial projects of conquest and expropriation could be justified through the claim that the temporally primitive were being 'civilised' and, later, 'developed' to the point where in a distant future, they might—if they were deserving—be entitled to think of themselves as human.[1] In Johannes Fabian's influential formulation, imperialism consists in the 'denial of coevalness'—in the denial that all human societies are 'of the same age'.[2] Neville Hoad tells us that like the 'primitive', the figure of the sexual deviant or pervert—the queer—emerged in the annals of sexology, psychoanalysis, and anthropology as an instance of arrested development, retardation, degeneracy, and decadence.[3]

The experience of being relegated to what we might think of as positions 'out of time' is a deeply ambivalent one, promising both marginalisation and the prospect of release from the iron cage of hegemonic time. Indeed,

---

1. Chakrabarty, *Provincializing Europe*.
2. Fabian, *Time and the Other*, 31, 159.
3. Hoad, 'Arrested Development'. See also Weber, *Queer International Relations*, 47–71, for an account of the figuration of the queer as underdeveloped and undevelopable in international relations discourses.

Out of Time. Rahul Rao, Oxford University Press (2020). © Oxford University Press.
DOI: 10.1093/oso/9780190865511.001.0001

Fabian proposes an important distinction between the denial of coevalness as a condition of domination and the refusal of coevalness as an act of liberation.[4] Queer theory complicates this dichotomy by taking seriously the possibility that denial might be transmuted into refusal. That is to say, we are urged to transform the abjection of exclusion into a repudiation of inclusion. Much of the queer theoretical literature on temporality celebrates alienation from what Elizabeth Freeman calls 'chrononormativity',[5] expressing hostility toward a mainstream LGBT politics that is perceived as seeking assimilation into hegemonic straight time. Salutary as its critiques have been, we need to consider the extent to which queer theory's determination to stand askew to the progressive march of time has been shaped by its geopolitical provenance in the contemporary United States and its opposition to what David Eng has described as 'queer liberalism'.[6] We can see how this matters in Jasbir Puar's helpful summation of her intellectual project, which she sees as addressing 'what happens after certain liberal rights are bestowed, certain thresholds or parameters of success are claimed to have been reached: What happens when "we" get what "we" want?'[7]

I wrote this book in the shadow of struggles around the decriminalisation of queer sex in places where it seemed to me that people had not got what they wanted, or had only just got what they wanted, or felt implicated in the fact of others not having what they wanted. Rather than offering critique in the smug afterlife of victory, I am interested in critique in contexts in which people cannot not want things that they do not have. Moreover, the contexts in which I encountered these affective modes of dissatisfaction—not having, tenuously having, feeling guilty about others not having—all had something to do with the experience of British colonialism. This book investigates the temporalities of the kinds of queer politics that become possible in the aftermath of colonialism. In it, I ask how time matters differently in the queer postcolony.

QUEER POSTCOLONIALITY AND ITS DISCONTENTS: THREE THUMBNAIL SKETCHES

In October 2009, a little known member of the Ugandan Parliament named David Bahati introduced an Anti Homosexuality Bill (AHB) that has been

4. Fabian, *Time and the Other*, 154.
5. Freeman, *Time Binds*, 3.
6. Eng, *Feeling of Kinship*.
7. Puar, *Right to Maim*, xviii.

described as 'the most egregious piece of legislation to emerge out of post-independence Uganda'.[8] Sections 145 and 146 of the Uganda Penal Code Act 1950, much of which is a legacy of British colonial penal law, already criminalised homosexuality. The AHB sought to intensify and expand the realm of prohibition, creating a range of new offences related to the practice and 'promotion' of homosexuality out of a professed desire to protect the 'traditional family' and 'culture of the people of Uganda' from the putatively alien scourge of queer sex. At one end of a spectrum of proposed offences stood the oddly named crime of 'aggravated homosexuality', defined as a same-sex sexual encounter, the moral depravity of which was deemed exacerbated by a number of factors. If the 'victim' were disabled or a minor, or if the 'offender' were HIV positive, in a position of parental or other authority, a recidivist, or found to have manipulated the 'victim' into having sex through the use of drugs, the penalty would be death.[9]

Faced with the claim that they were 'unAfrican', Ugandan LGBTI[10] activists responded by pointing to the remarkable internationalism of the AHB itself. In March 2009, the Ugandan capital Kampala had been host to a widely reported 'Seminar on Exposing the Homosexual Agenda' attended by three visiting US evangelical Christian pastors—Scott Lively, founder of Abiding Truth Ministries and Defend the Family International and better known for coauthoring *The Pink Swastika*, which peddles the claim that homosexuals were responsible for the Nazi Holocaust; Caleb Lee Brundidge, a self-described ex-gay man affiliated with the Extreme Prophetic Ministry in Phoenix, Arizona; and Don Schmierer, a board member of the US ex-gay organisation Exodus International.[11] The seminar was organised by Stephen Langa, director of the US-backed Uganda-based organisation Family Life International, and attracted an audience of thousands, including prominent members of the Ugandan political establishment, clergy, and media.[12] The initial draft of the AHB was substantially informed by the key themes

8. Kintu, *Ugandan Morality Crusade*, 15.
9. The full text of the Anti Homosexuality Bill, 2009, can be found at https://drive.google.com/file/d/0B7pFotabJnTmYzFiMWJmY2UtYWYxMi00MDY2LWI4NWYtYTVlOWU1OTEzMzk0/view?ddrp=1&hl=en, accessed 21 June 2016.
10. Sub-Saharan African queer activists tend to use the acronym 'LGBTI' to describe the constituency for whom they work, suggesting a greater integration of intersex politics here than is apparent elsewhere. In switching between 'LGBT', 'LGBTI', and other signifiers of sexual and gender non-normativity, I aim to mirror the usage of the activists I am discussing in any given context. For a discussion of the theoretical issues implicated in the choice of these terms, see 'Notes on "Queer"' later in this chapter.
11. Mukasa, 'Spreading Lies'. Audio recordings of the seminar are available at http://publiceye.org/multimedia/public/kapya-audio-files.zip.
12. Kaoma, *Globalizing the Culture Wars*, 14–15.

of the seminar, which had explored the putative threat that homosexuality posed to marriage and family life, and the propensity of homosexuals to 'recruit' children into their 'lifestyle'.[13] In addition, Bahati's sponsorship of the AHB was reportedly influenced by his membership of the Fellowship, a caucus of born-again Ugandan parliamentarians linked to the powerful and secretive US evangelical movement of the same name that is sometimes also referred to as the Family.[14]

Mirroring the internationalism of their opponents, Ugandan LGBTI activists mobilised condemnation of what Western media dubbed the 'Kill the Gays' Bill.[15] A number of states and institutions, including the United States, the United Kingdom, Canada, and the European Parliament, were publically critical.[16] Sweden threatened to cut development assistance, worth about $50 million at the time.[17] Mindful of Uganda's reliance on in-ternational aid, President Yoweri Museveni sought to restrain enthusiasm for the AHB amongst members of his National Resistance Movement (NRM), which has ruled Uganda since 1986. In January 2010, he warned that the Bill had become a 'sensitive foreign policy issue' and manoeuvred behind the scenes to ensure that it remained bottled up in parliamentary and cabinet sub-committees for long periods.[18] Over the next four years, the AHB became something of a political football in the complex domestic and international politics of Uganda. Museveni maintained a studied am-bivalence towards the Bill, sometimes appearing to support its objectives and at other times viewing it as unnecessary, in an attempt to court both an evangelical Christian constituency opposed to homosexuality and an international donor community committed to LGBTI rights. As Deborah Kintu has argued, intermittent discussion of the AHB and a number of other morality laws, including an Anti Pornography Bill, usefully distracted the Ugandan public from the regime's increasingly dismal record of gov-ernance as well as Museveni's determination to hold on to his presidency for life.[19] The AHB came to be championed periodically by a succession of more minor political and religious figures seeking to enhance their profile within the NRM and in the fiercely competitive and fragmented landscape

13. Gettleman, 'Americans' Role'.
14. Sharlet, 'Straight Man's Burden'.
15. See, for example, *Advocate*, 'Maddow Uganda'.
16. Eleveld, 'White House Condemns'; Watt, 'Fury at Uganda Proposal'; European Parliament, *Resolution on Uganda*.
17. Kincaid, 'Sweden Responds'.
18. Ssebaggala, 'Straight Talk'.
19. Kintu, *Ugandan Morality Crusade*.

of Ugandan Christianity.[20] The Bill was eventually passed in December 2013 at the urging of the Speaker of Parliament, Rebecca Kadaga, then rumoured to be a potential successor to Museveni. After further prevarication on Museveni's part, this time purportedly on account of his need for a definitive opinion from the Ugandan and international scientific community on the 'causes' of homosexuality,[21] the law received presidential assent in February 2014. In an attempt to deflect the criticism that the AHB had incurred, the Anti Homosexuality Act (AHA) was marginally less draconian. Amongst other things, it replaced the death penalty for 'aggravated homosexuality' with a sentence of life imprisonment.

Once again, condemnation was swift and forceful. A number of donors signalled their intention to delay, redirect, or cancel aid, with the World Bank following through on this threat with the indefinite postponement of a $90 million loan to Uganda on the grounds that the AHA would adversely affect health programmes that the money was to have supported.[22] Ugandan LGBTI and human rights organisations came together in a Civil Society Coalition on Human Rights and Constitutional Law, which pursued a multipronged campaign against the Act. In March 2014, a group of petitioners challenged the constitutionality of the AHA. Without addressing the substantive grounds of challenge, the Constitutional Court struck down the Act in August 2014 on the procedural ground that it had been passed without the requisite parliamentary quorum.[23] Museveni is thought to have had a hand in this outcome. Commentators suggested that the judgement was intended to rehabilitate his image in the eyes of the donor community in time for his attendance at the US-Africa Leaders Summit in Washington, D.C., a few days later.[24]

While the tabling of the first draft of the AHB in 2009 and the striking down of the AHA in 2014 offer convenient markers with which to bookend this story, the discourses that underpinned and challenged these legislative initiatives continue to circulate. Homosexuality remains criminalised, while the state uses other legal and extra-constitutional means to crack down on the 'promotion' of homosexuality.[25] Ugandan queers continue to suffer stigmatisation and harassment and fear the prospect of renewed

20. Nyanzi and Karamagi, 'Social-Political Dynamics'; Bompani and Valois, 'Sexualizing Politics'; Valois, 'Scandal Makers'.
21. Rao, 'Staying Positivist'.
22. Yukhananov, 'World Bank Postpones'.
23. *Prof. J. Oloka-Onyango and others v. Attorney General*, [2014] UGCC 14.
24. Nyanzi and Karamagi, 'Social-Political Dynamics', 31.
25. Rodriguez, *Economics of Queer Inclusion*, 47–49.

efforts to pass the AHA or some variant thereof, even as they find ways to live and thrive in conditions of precarity.[26]

In the same period that anti-homosexuality legislation was under consideration in the Ugandan parliament, the Indian anti-sodomy law became the subject of intense public scrutiny as a result of a long-running campaign waged in opposition to it, primarily in the courts. Enshrined in section 377 of the Indian Penal Code (IPC), which criminalised 'carnal intercourse against the order of nature',[27] this provision was also a legacy of what had originally been a British colonial penal law. Just as Ugandan conservatives derided homosexuality as 'unAfrican', anti-homosexuality discourses in India—particularly among the Hindu Right— also harped on the putative cultural inauthenticity of queer sex.[28] And just as Ugandan activists had responded to these discourses by pointing to the foreign provenance of anti-homosexuality activism, the Indian queer movement made much of the origins of section 377 in what it frequently referred to as the 'Judaeo-Christian morality' of British colonial administrators.[29]

Although Indian activists had first challenged section 377 in 1994, the first judicial affirmation of their position came in July 2009, when the Delhi High Court ruled in *Naz Foundation v. Government of NCT of Delhi* that the provision violated constitutional entitlements to dignity, privacy, equality, and freedom from discrimination. The decision had the effect of 'reading down' section 377 so that it no longer criminalised private, consensual sex between adults of the same sex. In December 2013, the Supreme Court of India overturned this decision on appeal in *Suresh Kumar Koushal v. Naz Foundation*,[30] effectively recriminalising same-sex conduct. Dismissing the petitioners' claims about the putative unconstitutionality of section 377, the Court expressed its powerlessness to amend the law to keep pace with shifting social perceptions. Four months later, a different bench of the same court hearing *National Legal Services Authority (NALSA) v. Union of India*,[31] filed by a group of trans petitioners, contradicted the *Koushal* decision by finding that discrimination against trans persons on the basis of sexual orientation or gender identity violated their fundamental rights.[32]

26. SMUG, *From Torment to Tyranny; 'That's How I Survived'*.
27. Section 377, IPC, provides that 'Whoever voluntarily has carnal intercourse against the order of nature with any man, woman or animal, shall be punished with imprisonment for life, or with imprisonment of either description for a term which may extend to ten years, and shall also be liable to fine'.
28. Bacchetta, '(Hindu) Nation Exiles Its Queers'.
29. 160 Delhi Law Times 277 (hereafter *Naz*), para. 7.
30. (2014) 1 SCC 1 (hereafter *Koushal*).
31. (2014) 5 SCC 438 (hereafter *NALSA*).
32. *NALSA*, paras. 55, 77.

The issue was finally settled in September 2018, when the Supreme Court overruled the *Koushal* decision in *Navtej Singh Johar v. Union of India*,[33] holding that section 377 was unconstitutional insofar as it criminalised consensual, adult homosexual activity.

Navtej settles constitutional questions around the legality of homosexuality. In elite (predominantly gay male) circles in which the legalisation of sodomy has represented the horizon of aspiration, this perhaps opens up the very question that Puar is interested in: 'what happens when "we" get what "we" want?' In contrast, my interest in this book insofar as India is concerned is in the temporalities of trans politics as expressed in the demands of the *NALSA* petitioners. Reflecting the overwhelmingly working class and subordinate caste composition of the trans community, these petitioners sought state recognition as a category of 'socially and educationally backward' citizens in an attempt to access constitutional guarantees of affirmative action in public employment and education made available to those deemed 'backward'.[34] The Court endorsed this demand, but its directives to this effect have been ignored by the executive and legislature in successive attempts to implement the ruling through enabling legislation, perhaps precisely because of its potentially momentous redistributive implications for trans citizens.[35] Moreover, state discourse around the *NALSA* case revealed an enduring tendency to read 'trans' through the figure of the hijra, to whom connotations of criminality cemented in colonial discourse continue to attach.[36] This too, then, remains an unfinished struggle marked by the shadow of coloniality.

One link between the otherwise distinct contexts of Uganda and India is their inheritance of anti-queer laws from colonial legislation to which they were subject while under British rule. Legal histories of anti-sodomy law inform us that while sodomy was sporadically prosecuted in England under the common law, its first codification in the British Empire as 'carnal intercourse against the order of nature' occurred in section 377 of the IPC, which was enacted in 1860.[37] The IPC was exported to other colonies and

33. WP (Crl) No 76 of 2016 (hereafter *Navtej*).

34. See Chapter 6 for an extensive discussion of the language of backwardness, which has been deployed and resignified in the long history of Dalit political and legal struggle against caste subordination in the Indian context, but also sits uncomfortably with postcolonial critiques of the temporal claims of orientalist colonial discourse.

35. For a detailed critique of the Transgender Persons (Protection of Rights) Bill 2019, which is the most recent attempt at such enabling legislation at the time of writing, see Sampoorna, 'SPWG Statement'. See also http://orinam.net/resources-for/law-and-enforcement/the-transgender-persons-protection-of-rights-bill-2019/.

36. Dutta, 'Contradictory Tendencies', 230.

37. Human Rights Watch, *This Alien Legacy*, 15.

also influenced codification in England itself, with section 377 providing the model for the reformed punishment of 'buggery' in the 1861 Offences Against the Person Act. The 1899 criminal code of the Australian colony of Queensland provided a second influential model in the empire. Reflecting legislative changes that had taken place in England in the intervening period, its anti-sodomy provision was more expansive than section 377 in criminalising passive and active partners, as well as attempts to commit the offences it defined. The Queensland model was exported to Britain's African colonies, including Nigeria, Kenya, Tanzania, and Uganda.[38]

Colonial discourse frequently imagined the colonies as opening up non-normative sexual possibilities for desiring white male subjects. The putative licentiousness of these spaces was attributed variously to the climate, the savagery of the natives, and the paucity of European women.[39] The spectre of unbridled sexual opportunity generated considerable anxiety, compelling the introduction of policies intended to curtail it. Ann Stoler has shown how an overriding concern with 'degeneracy' in colonial contexts sutured racial and sexual anxieties to construe unconventional sex as a danger to the body politic.[40] The criminalisation of sodomy was one element in a broader biopolitical apparatus of colonial regulation animated by a range of concerns including the sexual relations of prostitution and concubinage, the control of venereal disease, the proper rearing of children and management of the household, and the 'improvement' of the population through the use, among other things, of eugenicist practices of selective sterilisation.

Prompted by forceful reminders from queer activists in the global South, the increasing awareness in British LGBT circles that anti-sodomy laws in many former British colonies are a remnant of their colonial experience has generated a curious discourse of atonement for colonialism. This discourse has also become audible at the highest levels of British government, in debates in both houses of Parliament[41] as well as in statements from leading politicians, including most recently former Prime Minister Theresa May, who opened the 2018 Commonwealth Heads of Government Meeting (CHOGM) in London with a statement of regret for the British colonial imposition of anti-sodomy laws in the empire, and for 'the legacy of discrimination, violence and even death that persists today' as a result of them.[42]

38. Ibid. See also Han and O'Mahoney, *British Colonialism*, 24–26.
39. Hyam, *Empire and Sexuality*; Lane, *Ruling Passion*; Bleys, *Geography of Perversion*; Aldrich, *Colonialism and Homosexuality*.
40. Stoler, *Race and the Education of Desire*.
41. I discuss these debates in Chapter 4.
42. Duffy, 'Theresa May'.

This discourse of atonement is remarkable in emanating from sections of the British political establishment not known for their eagerness to acknowledge the ravages of empire, and it sits uncomfortably with their continuing unwillingness to reckon with monumental imperial crimes such as slavery. Far from effecting closure, reconciliation, or healing, these halting attempts at reckoning with the past open up deeply discomfiting questions about contemporary understandings of 'sexuality' and 'race' and of the forms of injury associated with them.

WHAT THIS BOOK IS ABOUT: THREE THEORETICAL THREADS

In marking the shadow of coloniality that hangs over these scenes of queer postcolonial discontent, it is not my intention to offer a simple and satisfying colonial origin story of anti-queer animus. Instead, I am interested in the manner in which contemporary struggles over queer freedoms return to the scene of the colonial and in the work that such 'returns' seek to accomplish. I am sceptical of some of these returns, given the manner in which they seem to offer the postcolonial state an alibi for its perpetuation and promulgation of anti-queer laws. If postcolonial critique is to continue to remain meaningful in the contemporary world, it must do more than simply remind us of the enduring legacies of colonialism. It cannot avoid wading into the messy critical task of determining how responsibility for ongoing oppressions must be apportioned between colonial and postcolonial regimes. It must be attentive to shifts in power, including those that enable formerly colonised states to become colonial in their own right. In the particular contexts that this book investigates, it must allow for the possibility that the project of decoloniality might itself become a vehicle for the politicisation of 'homophobia'.

The book is constructed around three interrelated strands of argument. First, it provides a critical historical account of the global skirmishes occasioned by the Ugandan AHA that were to have profound consequences for the development of global governmentality in relation to LGBTI rights. Second, in its examination of these skirmishes, as well as related struggles in India and Britain, the book illuminates the tendency of queerness to mutate in different configurations and fields of power to become a metonym for other categories such as nationality, religiosity, race, class, and caste. Revisiting the notion of intersectionality, the book argues that these mutations tell us something important about the foundational political grammars of the states and social institutions in which queer difference struggles to make space for itself. Queerness serves as an analytic here, bringing into relief the originary and ongoing violence in which these institutions were forged and are reproduced. Third, by paying attention to the dialectic between colonial and postcolonial power, the book offers a distinctive account of the politics of time in the queer postcolony. Whereas much of the queer theoretical literature on time and temporality, produced as it is in the global North, sees its task as a critique of the progressive triumphalist temporalities of queer liberalism, this book addresses a different question: less 'what is to be done' than 'what is being done' temporally in queer postcolonial struggles. In this register, the book demonstrates how queer postcolonial presents are marked by the shadow of both past and future, with these temporal zones offering distinct resources and terrains for struggle.

The Global Frictions of Homosexuality and Anti-homosexuality

Uganda was not the only place in the world experimenting with anti-queer legislation in the period under consideration. Nonetheless, the AHA attracted attention for a number of reasons, placing the country at the vortex of global arguments over LGBTI rights. The first draft of the AHB, which proposed the death penalty for 'aggravated homosexuality', drew attention for the sheer ruthlessness of its provisions. As reports of its sponsors and backers began to circulate, it quickly became implicated in the politics of transnational evangelical Christianity. Additionally, the aid dependency of the Ugandan state made it a feasible target for international advocacy (in comparison to, say, oil-rich Nigeria, which passed a law prohibiting same-sex marriage, or Russia, which passed a law to 'protect' children from exposure to homosexual 'propaganda' in the same period, without attracting the same degree of international sanction). International reactions to the AHA from donor states, the Bretton Woods institutions, and the UN system, among other actors, set new precedents and institutionalised new forms of global governmentality in relation to LGBTI rights. The crisis constructed around the AHA is therefore worthy of study as a moment that has been generative for the international regime dealing with LGBTI rights.[43]

There has been a great deal of scholarship on various aspects of the Ugandan crisis, including its domestic politics,[44] media discourse,[45] the role

43. Here I follow Amar, *Security Archipelago*, in viewing the global South as the locus of innovation of norms of global governance.
44. Tamale, 'Out of the Closet'; Tamale, *Homosexuality*; Ssebaggala, 'Straight Talk'; Nyanzi and Karamagi, 'Social-Political Dynamics'; Kintu, *Ugandan Morality Crusade*.
45. Cheney, 'Locating Neocolonialism'; Sadgrove et al., 'Morality Plays'.

of different Christian denominations,[46] the history of gender and same-sex relations,[47] and the politics and everyday life of the LGBTI community.[48] Scholars have also analysed the global politics of homophobia[49] and the Christian Right.[50] Working across these different bodies of literature, I am interested in what might be called, following Anna Tsing, the global 'frictions' of the AHA. In her work on the destruction of Indonesian forests, Tsing offers a fascinating account of the global connections at the heart of processes of deforestation and their contestation, without resorting to the global/local dichotomy. She argues that the universal aspirations of capital, knowledge, and political alliance must travel across distance and become practically effective through friction: 'the awkward, unequal, unstable, and creative qualities of interconnection across difference.'[51] As she explains, it is through 'contingent and botched encounters' that the universal comes to be both effective and limited.[52] A number of the chapters that follow in this book explore the 'frictions' that presaged, produced, and were precipitated by the AHA—in 'contingent and botched' encounters between the precolonial kingdom of Buganda and British colonialism, between the Church of Uganda and its sister provinces in the Anglican Communion, between the aid-dependent Ugandan state and its international donors, and between LGBTI activists in the global South and North.

Central to these encounters is the interpellative force of what Puar has influentially theorised as 'homonationalism,' whereby the acceptance of liberal LGBT rights has become a barometer of a nation's fitness for sovereignty, a new element in the contemporary standard of civilisation in international relations.[53] Drawing on my reading of Uganda's encounters with international financial governmentality in the wake of the AHA, I argue that the civilisationalist logic of homonationalism must be supplemented

46. Ward, 'Same-Sex Relations'; Hassett, *Anglican Communion*; Oliver, 'Transnational Sex Politics'; Ward, 'Anglican and Catholic Churches'; Bompani, '"For God"'; Valois, 'Scandal Makers'.

47. Hamilton, 'Flames of Namugongo'; Nannyonga-Tamusuza, *Baakisimba*; Nannyonga-Tamusuza, 'Female-Men'; Guma, 'Narratives of "Saints"'.

48. Nyanzi, 'Dismantling Reified African Culture'; Nyanzi, 'Queer Pride'; SMUG, *From Torment to Tyranny*; Peters, '*Kuchus* in the Balance'; SMUG, *That's How I Survived*; Lusimbo and Bryan, '*Kuchu* Resilience'; Bryan, 'Kuchu Activism'; Rodriguez, *Economics of Queer Inclusion*.

49. Weiss and Bosia, eds., *Global Homophobia*; Picq and Thiel, eds., *Sexualities in World Politics*; Altman and Symons, *Queer Wars*.

50. Kaoma, *Globalizing the Culture Wars*; Anderson, 'Conservative Christianity'; Kaoma, *Colonizing African Values*; Bob, *Global Right Wing*.

51. Tsing, *Friction*, 3.

52. Ibid., 271.

53. Puar, *Terrorist Assemblages*; Puar, 'Citation and Censorship', 139.

with the political economy logic of what I call 'homocapitalism.' While sharing key discursive features with homonationalism, homocapitalism operates in accordance with a distinct set of imperatives. Holding out the prospect of a rosy future redolent with growth and productivity should a state embrace LGBT rights, homocapitalism is arguably more significant than homonationalism in certain contexts. In drawing on the hegemonic logic of neoliberal reason, it offers an apparently more consensual strategy of persuasion than homonationalism with its coercive tropes of civilisation and barbarism. The promise of futurity inherent in homocapitalism may prove to be more seductive where the chastisement of homonationalism has not 'yet' succeeded in drawing recalcitrant states into its embrace or, worse, has raised their anti-imperialist shackles. Indeed, precisely as a result of the intellectual, even if not political, success of the *critique* of homonationalism, homocapitalism may be emerging as the weapon of choice wielded by a global queer liberalism.

Queer Mutations: or, Intersectionality Revisited

As the scenes of encounter in this book shift from one chapter to the next, queerness seems to become a signifier for different things—anti-imperialism *and* imperialism (Chapter 2), paganism *and* Christianity (Chapter 3), whiteness (Chapter 4), embourgeoisement (Chapter 5) and subordinate caste status (Chapter 6). In illuminating this shape-shifting quality of queerness, the book is centrally preoccupied with demonstrating how gender and sexuality are co-constituted by a host of other categories including (but not only) nation, religion, race, class, and caste. In this sense, its analysis may be understood as intersectional, albeit in a way that is somewhat different from the manner in which this term is typically deployed.

In an important critique of intersectionality, Puar has lamented the tendency of intersectional analyses to presume that 'components' of identity are 'separable analytics' that can be disassembled. She makes a case for the notion of assemblage as being 'more attuned to interwoven forces that merge and dissipate time, space, and body against linearity, coherency, and permanency.'[54] Puar detects a representationalist impulse in intersectional work that compels a stabilisation of identity across space and time and works 'to still and quell the perpetual motion of assemblages, to

54. Puar, *Terrorist Assemblages*, 212.

capture and reduce them, to harness their threatening mobility.'[55] While these tendencies are indeed characteristic of much 'intersectional' scholarship that has been produced in the three decades since the concept was first articulated, and perhaps more so of casual deployments of the term in everyday political speech and praxis, a close reading of the work that generated it reveals that this need not be the case.

In the 1989 article that is typically credited with coining the notion of intersectionality, Kimberlé Crenshaw is concerned with the manner in which black women in the United States are ill served by mainstream anti-discrimination doctrine.[56] Surveying cases in which courts disallowed the claims of black female plaintiffs, Crenshaw finds that while sex discrimination was being understood in terms of the experiences of race- and class-privileged white women, race discrimination was being understood in terms of the experiences of sex- and class-privileged black men. In both cases, the paradigmatic beneficiaries of protection against discrimination were those who were privileged *but for* their embodiment of the protected characteristic. Partly the singularity of the basis of their disadvantage gave their cases the sort of epistemic clarity that was absent in the case of persons disadvantaged simultaneously on multiple grounds, although the brute fact of greater privilege no doubt also smoothed their access to legal remedy. The crucial point here is that far from treating sex and race as 'separable analytics', in demonstrating that dominant understandings of sex and race discrimination were defined respectively by the experiences of bourgeois white women and black men, Crenshaw in effect reveals the purportedly singular 'axes' of sex and race to be always already 'invisibly intersectional'.[57] In doing so, she throws the presumed separateness of these categories into crisis. Indeed in a later article, she would explicitly declare this to be her intention.[58]

If the axes are understood in this way—not as (unmarked) gender intersecting with (unmarked) race, but as the set of 'white women' in relation to the set of 'black men'—their intersection becomes a mathematical

<hr />

55. Ibid., 213.
56. Crenshaw, 'Demarginalizing the Intersection'. Although Crenshaw is credited with coining the term 'intersectionality', the spirit of her argument has a long genealogy. Crenshaw herself cites Sojourner Truth's famous 'Ain't I a Woman?' speech delivered in 1851. More immediate antecedents include the Combahee River Collective statement, as well as interventions in black British feminism (see, for example, Amos and Parmar, 'Challenging Imperial Feminism'), and Third World feminisms (see, for example, Mohanty, 'Under Western Eyes'). For a useful historical account, see Carastathis, *Intersectionality*, chapter 1.
57. Carastathis, *Intersectionality*, 53.
58. Crenshaw, 'Mapping the Margins', 1244.

impossibility. Crenshaw is keen to point out that black women *cannot* be represented by some combination of dominant anti-discrimination doctrines that privilege the experiences of white women and black men. This is why she describes the (impossible) intersection, not as the place where black women's experiences can be named, but as a site of 'erasure',[59] 'burial',[60] as 'a location that resists telling',[61] and as a void.[62] Thus, against Puar's characterisation of intersectionality as representationalist, I find myself more in agreement with Anna Carastathis's view of it as a critique of representational politics. As she puts it, 'the intersection reveals the institutionalised failure to hear Black women's representational claims, but it does not disclose the content of their experience.'[63]

I suspect that intersectionality has been widely taken up in the simplistic 'additive' mode that Puar is rightly critical of—whereby the combination of categories imagined to be separable is thought to illuminate positionalities—because of a misreading of the metaphor of the traffic intersection that Crenshaw deploys.[64] Crenshaw introduces the metaphor to make a limited point, namely, that in a context in which an accident is the result of a collision at the intersection of cars travelling from different directions (read: multiple forms of discrimination), the availability of remedy should not be contingent on being able to identify precisely which driver is at fault since it may be impossible to make this determination. Nonetheless, the close correspondence between image and concept, not least in the word that describes them both, has resulted in the metaphor overpowering its referent. Moreover, the overwhelming tendency to visualise the traffic intersection as a crossroads produced by the approach of two roads *that have nothing to do with one another prior to or after their crossing* has reinforced the tendency to think of intersectionality in terms of 'separable analytics'.

How might we conceive of these 'roads' as inseparable? Scholars have experimented with a range of alternative formulations, including mutual constitution, co-constitution, interlocking, intermeshing, and interweaving, although all of these seem ultimately unsatisfactory in their implication of distinct analytics coming together for a time. In a discussion of caste in South Asia, Dalit intellectual and visionary B. R. Ambedkar offers

---

59. Crenshaw, 'Demarginalizing the Intersection', 139, 140, 146.
60. Ibid., 160.
61. Crenshaw, 'Mapping the Margins', 1242.
62. Ibid., 1282.
63. Carastathis, *Intersectionality*, 118; see also Lugones, 'Heterosexualism', 193.
64. Crenshaw, 'Demarginalizing the Intersection', 149.

a strikingly different way in which to think about relationships between categories. Having surveyed a number of different definitions of caste, he concludes that 'prohibition, or rather the absence of intermarriage—endogamy, to be concise—is the only [characteristic] that can be called the essence of Caste when rightly understood.' Accounting for the institutions of sati, compulsory widowhood, and child marriage as different means to the end of endogamy and, thereby, caste, he reiterates that 'they create and perpetuate endogamy, while caste and endogamy, according to our analysis of the various definitions of caste, are one and the same thing. Thus the existence of these means is identical with caste and caste involves these means.'[65] By collapsing the distinction between ends and means, Ambedkar takes us away from the base-superstructure imagery of orthodox Marxism. The relationship between caste and gender cannot be visualised as the separate layers of base/superstructure, as the separable axes of a crossroads, or even as the mutual constitution produced by the strands that make up a rope, each of which takes its contours from the other. Instead, rather like a Mobius strip, caste *is* the regulation of gender, which *is* caste. The philosopher Elizabeth Grosz uses the image of the Mobius strip to point to the ways in which 'while there are disparate "things" being related, they have the capacity to twist one into the other.'[66]

It is in this sense that I think of queerness as *becoming* anti-imperialism and imperialism, paganism and Christianity, whiteness, bourgeoisness, and subordinate caste status in the various frictions that I explore. To conceive of queerness as becoming materialised in these ways is to read it less as being crosshatched by other categories than as becoming a metonym for those categories, rather like one surface of the Mobius strip becomes the other. In tracking these queer metonymic mutations, I am inspired by a range of approaches including queer theology,[67] queer of colour critique,[68] queer Marxism,[69] and queer Dalit perspectives.[70] But where each of these approaches tends to centre an analytical category such as religion, race, class, or caste in order to explore its reproduction through queerness, the categories that are central to my analysis shift from one scene of friction to

65. Ambedkar, 'Castes in India'.
66. Grosz, *Volatile Bodies*, 209–210.
67. Hamilton, 'Flames of Namugongo'.
68. Ferguson, *Aberrations in Black*; Muñoz, *Disidentifications*; Gopinath, *Impossible Desires*; Puar, *Terrorist Assemblages*.
69. Hennessy, *Profit and Pleasure*; Floyd, *Reification of Desire*; Rosenberg and Villarejo, 'Queer Studies and the Crises of Capitalism'.
70. Vidya, '(Trans)gender and Caste'; Kang, 'Casteless-ness'; Kang, 'Queering Dalit'; Baudh, 'Invisibility'.

another, betraying not only the versatility and plasticity of queerness but also—as I will suggest in conclusion—the foundational grammars of the states and social institutions in which queer difference struggles to make space for itself.

Time Travel in the Queer Postcolony

The construction of the queer as a temporally primitive figure has generated a rich literature on the consequences of what we might think of as its emplacement out of time. Queer theory has dwelt on the ambivalence of this emplacement, noting its potentially marginalising and liberatory effects. Much of the impetus for its reflections on temporality has come from an antipathy towards mainstream LGBT movements in the West, which are perceived as striving to overcome queer marginalisation by seeking assimilation into the hegemonic temporal trajectories of homonormativity or 'chrononormativity'.[71] Unsurprisingly, a remarkably consistent feature of this literature has been the clarion call—articulated in different ways—to turn away from the progressive linearity of straight time.

For example, concerned that in the effort to move seamlessly from shame to pride, queer movements might be in danger of repressing or inadequately reckoning with the past, Heather Love wonders whether staying with the very affects that we seek to leave behind—melancholia, depression, pathos, shame—or what she calls 'feeling backward' might better channel individual grief into collective grievance.[72] In a similar vein, Freeman jettisons what she sees as an avant-garde understanding of queer critique as having always anticipated and solved problems ahead of time, suggesting instead that queer potential might 'trail behind actually existing social possibilities . . . in the tail end of things, willing to be bathed in the fading light of whatever has been declared useless.'[73] These turns toward the past are broadly resonant with Lee Edelman's disavowal of the future. Unmasking the ideology of what he calls 'reproductive futurism'— understood as the pervasive inability to imagine politics without a fantasy of a future constructed around a figural Child who is persistently invoked to deny queers their enjoyment of liberty in the name of safeguarding this Child—Edelman urges queers to embrace the role ascribed to them by the political right as destroyers of the social fabric and to renounce the fantasy

71. Freeman, *Time Binds*, 3.
72. Love, *Feeling Backward*, 28.
73. Freeman, *Time Binds*, xiii.

that good behaviour will secure for them a place in the future. As he puts it, 'there are no *queers* in that future as there can be no future for queers, chosen as they are to bear the bad tidings that there can be no future at all. . . .'[74] While Edelman's antipathy toward the anti-libertarianism of chrononormativity is widely shared, his disavowal of the future has been criticised as a potentially depoliticising move, most available—ironically— to those for whom the future is most secure.[75] José Muñoz suggests that the anti-relationality of Edelman's polemic is achieved at the expense of viewing sexuality as a singular trope of difference, uncontaminated by gender, race, and other particularities.[76] Poignantly reminding us that re- productive futurism never sacralises children of colour, he argues that for those most oppressed in the past and present, hope can only ever lie in the future—'the future is queerness's domain.'[77]

What interests me about this literature is less the particular temporal reorientations advocated by its key figures than that they are keen to ad- vocate such reorientations at all, even if only negatively. We are urged to think and feel our way backward, forward, or sideways[78] in time, or at least *not* to march forward, if we are to mine our queer potential. Even as this literature has enriched our understanding of the relations be- tween time, psychic life, and political transformation, the manifesto-like quality of these pronouncements is symptomatic of its reaction against the chrononormativity of mainstream Western LGBT politics in the pre- sent moment, and of its desire to intervene in this present. In this, it demonstrates an aspiration to what Kimberly Hutchings calls 'timeli- ness'—the enduring post-Kantian belief (that, she argues, persists even in many anti-historicist thinkers) that the theorist of time might be able to 'read' the trajectory of the present and intervene in it in a timely fashion in order to redirect the arrow of time.[79] Disrupting the linear trajectories of chrononormativity with its avowedly untimely gestures—feeling back- ward, anti-futurism, critical utopianism—queer theoretical work on tem- porality ironically stages *timely* interventions in a chrononormative present in which the seductions of progressivist queer inclusion within state and market grow increasingly powerful. Moreover, the confidence with which some of its key figures advocate temporal reorientations—evident, for

74. Edelman, *No Future*, 29–30.
75. Halberstam, *Queer Art of Failure*, 106–110, 118.
76. Muñoz, *Cruising Utopia*, 94–95.
77. Ibid., 1, 11.
78. Stockton, *Queer Child*.
79. Hutchings, *Time and World Politics*, 154–155.

example, in the polemical tone adopted by Edelman and others[80]—is enabled by a narrowing of the spatial frame of inquiry to the terrain of the geopolitical West or, even more narrowly, the United States.[81] I want to suggest that if we were to widen the spatial frame to take seriously the disparate trajectories of queer politics outside these locations, it would be more difficult to read in any singular fashion what might more appropriately be thought of as the heterotemporality of the global queer political present, much less to advocate equally singular reorientations of political temporality.

Methodologically, this would require us to take space and place more seriously in our investigations of time. Indeed I will attempt to show, especially in Chapter 2, which theorises place formation as a temporal process, that these considerations are inextricable from one another. Much of this book is concerned with the dialectical opposition between two statements that commonly frame scenes of queer postcolonial contestation—'homosexuality is Western' and 'homophobia is Western'. By way of preface, I want to note how these apparently spatial claims also stake out temporal positions on the question of 'homosexuality'. This might begin to allow us to see how the temporal imaginaries of queer liberation in the formerly colonised world are forced to grapple with a quite distinct set of preoccupations from those in the West.

The claim that 'homosexuality is Western', typically voiced by queerphobic conservatives in the global South, has mobilised activist archival efforts seeking to demonstrate the existence of same-sex desire in non-Western locations. Much of this work evinces a particular interest in searching for signs of such desire in a precolonial past, with which it might effectively refute conservative claims about the putatively alien and specifically Western provenance of such desire. Thus, a temporal quest becomes central to the effort to demonstrate spatial belonging within the 'nation' (even if the nation itself did not exist in the earlier time that is being excavated for this purpose). For example, explicitly framing their effort to compile evidence of 'same-sex love in India' as being intended to counter the 'homophobic myth that homosexuality was imported', Ruth Vanita and Saleem Kidwai argue that 'at most times and places in pre-nineteenth century India, love between women and between men, even when disapproved of, was not actively persecuted.'[82] Stephen Murray and Will Roscoe conclude an

80. See, for example, Schotten, *Queer Terror*.
81. Mikdashi and Puar, 'Queer Theory', 218, remind us that much of what passes for Queer Theory comes out of American Studies.
82. Vanita and Kidwai, *Same-Sex Love*, xviii, xxiii.

influential survey of 'African homosexualities' with the claim that 'there are no examples of traditional African belief systems that singled out same-sex relations as sinful or linked them to concepts of disease or mental health—except where Christianity and Islam have been adopted.'[83] Positioning their work in opposition to the hate speech of some contemporary African leaders who condemn homosexuality as 'unAfrican' in addition to being unnatural and sinful, Ruth Morgan and Saskia Wieringa similarly seek to recover 'female same-sex practices in Africa' that were put under duress by the combined forces of Christianity and colonialism.[84]

Notwithstanding the tactical value of this scholarship as a riposte to queerphobic claims about the cultural inauthenticity of queer desire, its activist usefulness is premised on a reification of the precolonial past into a spatiotemporal location that is constructed as entirely indigenous, uncontaminated by contact with the West or indeed any other external influence. These activist imperatives allow, perhaps even encourage, a certain incuriosity about the possibility that non-normative desire might have been stigmatised in the precolonial past, even if in ways that were distinct and less institutionalised than those introduced by colonial modernity. It may not be going too far to suggest that the imperatives of struggle against colonially imposed sodomy laws have induced an implicit 'pinkwashing' of the precolonial past, occasionally made explicit in the bald claim that 'homophobia is Western'. Above all, postcolonial claims and counterclaims about the spatiotemporal provenance of 'homosexuality' seem to have bought into a common nativism, whereby forms of desire and prohibition that cannot be shown to have existed within the boundaries of the nation are ipso facto illegitimate.

The tensions between the imperatives of critical historiography and political victory have generated critiques of the instrumentalisation of the archive for activist purposes. Anjali Arondekar has been critical of the manner in which the archive has become freighted with hope, as if it contained the secret whose revelation might effect transformation.[85] To approach the archive in this way is to know in advance what we expect to find in it. It is to risk the temptation of filling in its blanks by ventriloquising its inaudible subalterns, notwithstanding Gayatri Spivak's warning against this tendency.[86] Arondekar seeks to 'redirect attention from the frenzied

83. Murray and Roscoe, *Boy-Wives*, 270.
84. Morgan and Wieringa, *Tommy Boys*, 17.
85. Arondekar, *For the Record*.
86. Spivak, 'Can the Subaltern Speak?'. For an example of such ventriloquism, see Narrain and Gupta, 'Introduction', xix–xxi. In a section entitled 'the voice of the queer subaltern', the authors read the 1884 case *Queen v. Khairati*, an early precedent in the

"finding" of new archival sources to an understanding of the processes of subjectification made possible (and desirable) through the very idiom of the archive.'[87] She argues that without attention to how archives segregate and constitute objects of study such as 'sexuality'—without asking what archives *do* rather than simply what they *have*—the turn to the archive risks consolidating rather than interrogating these constructions. Disavowing the 'lexicon of "resisting silences" and "liberation"' that has been grafted onto archival research, she describes her own project as an 'archival hermeneutics that assembles reading practices adequate to the writing and survival of a robust and ethical queer/colonial historiography.'[88]

But the reference to ethics, as well as the evident inspiration that Arondekar draws (albeit in a rather obscure endnote) from the idiom of 'reparative criticism'[89] practised by scholars such as Eve Sedgwick, suggests that for all her suspicion of 'liberation', she holds fast to the possibility of a scholarship not completely dissociated from a politics of reparation and indeed hope.[90] At any rate, rather than resolving the tension that Arondekar brings into relief, I want to try to navigate it in this book. What if we were to decide *not* to resign ourselves to the irreconcilability of queer liberation and scrupulous scholarship? Might it be possible to draw on the potentially reparative possibilities of a turn towards the past without succumbing to the temptations of vulgar empiricism, ventriloquism, and anachronism? Do the triumphalist trajectories of chrononormativity exhaust the possibilities of a turn to futurity? In short, what sorts of time travel can postcolonial queers undertake that might be both 'robust and ethical'?

archive of judicial interpretation of section 377, which is also incidentally the subject of chapter 2 of Arondekar, *For the Record*. After recounting the facts of the case and the judge's decision, the authors go on to speculate about what Khairati's gender might have meant to her. Invoking Ranajit Guha (rather than Spivak's criticism of Guha and the larger subaltern studies project of which they were both part), Narrain and Gupta argue that 'tracing a queer legal history is . . . not only about studying the colonial roots of homophobia; it is equally about recovering the voices of its victims. More often than not, the victims have been rendered voiceless and a queer legal history has to read into what has not been said, and "dignify [the silence] . . . as the textual site of a struggle to reclaim for history an experience buried in the forgotten crevice of our past."'

87. Arondekar, *For the Record*, 3.

88. Ibid., 8, 20.

89. Sedgwick famously distinguishes 'reparative criticism' from the 'hermeneutics of suspicion' that characterises what she calls 'paranoid criticism'. As she explains, '[t]he desire of a reparative impulse . . . is additive and accretive. Its fear, a realistic one, is that the culture surrounding it is inadequate or inimical to its nurture; it wants to assemble and confer plenitude on an object that will then have resources to offer to an inchoate self.' Sedgwick, *Touching Feeling*, 149.

90. Arondekar, *For the Record*, 25.

ORGANISATION OF THE BOOK

The chapters in this book are organised as responses to the last three questions, with Chapters 3 and 4 turning towards the past and Chapters 5 and 6 turning towards the future. Or perhaps more accurately, while the first set of chapters explores the past-in-the-present, the second looks to the future-in-the-present. Because the book is invested in a conception of past, present, and future as temporal states that inflect and infect one another, rather than as following in chronological succession, these chapters can be read in any order. In what follows, I explain what is at stake in mining memory and futurity for queer political possibility.

Queer Memory

In his influential critique of the Eurocentrism of social theory, Dipesh Chakrabarty calls for modes of engaging with the past that do not rely solely on the categories of conventional historiography. Chakrabarty argues that when the history of political modernity outside the West is told through the master category 'capital', it always delivers a narrative of failure, lack, and deficit. A history 'posited by capital' (which he calls History 1) offers a reductive view of the past in focusing on what turn out, in retrospect, to have been the preconditions of capital.[91] Chakrabarty calls for an interruption of History 1—which he regards as 'at once both indispensable and inadequate'[92]—with histories that pay attention to lifeworlds that do not contribute to the self-reproduction of capital (which he places under the sign History 2). In the nearest that he comes to a programmatic statement, he explains:

> The point is to ask how this seemingly impervious, all-pervasive code [History 1] might be deployed or thought about so that we have at least a glimpse of its own finitude, a glimpse of what might constitute an outside to it. To hold history, the discipline, and other forms of memory together so that they can help in the interrogation of each other, to work out the ways these immiscible forms of recalling the past are juxtaposed in our negotiations of modern institutions, to question the narrative strategies in academic history that allow its secular temporality the appearance of successfully assimilating to itself memories that are,

91. Chakrabarty, *Provincializing Europe*, 63–64.
92. Ibid., 16.

strictly speaking, unassimilable—these are the tasks that subaltern histories are suited to accomplish.[93]

I take seriously Chakrabarty's suggestion here that memory might offer a vantage point from which to interrogate the claims of a dominant history. Prompted by the claim—voiced in Uganda, India, and elsewhere—that 'homosexuality is Western', I am drawn in Chapter 3 to Namugongo, a pilgrimage site on the outskirts of Kampala where hundreds of thousands of pilgrims gather every June to commemorate the founding myth of Christianity in Uganda. Textual missionary accounts of the late nineteenth-century events that give this site its significance inform us that Mwanga, the last precolonial ruler of the Buganda kingdom, executed a number of his courtiers here in 1885–1886. We are told that Mwanga was antagonised by their conversion to Christianity, under the influence of which they refused to indulge his 'unnatural' desires.[94] Nearly eighty years later, the 'Uganda martyrs', as they would come to be known, would be canonised by the Catholic Church, formalising a tradition of veneration that continues to this day. I am curious about the extent to which contemporary popular memory of the martyrdoms echoes the textual sources in remembering 'sodomy' in a time before the advent of Christianity in Uganda. How does such remembering coexist with the claim that 'homosexuality is Western'?

Prompted by the counterclaim, articulated by embattled queer activists in the global South, that 'homophobia is Western', I am drawn in Chapter 4 to Westminster—these days less the mother of parliaments than the authoritative national repository of Britain's postcolonial melancholia.[95] I am curious about the introspection, if any, that angry denunciations of British colonial legacy elicit. To the extent that it is forthcoming, such introspection is typically the outcome of complex interactions—some cosy, some conflictual—between parliamentarians and activists of various kinds. Parliamentary debates on colonial responsibility are few and far between, but their staging offers rare opportunities for the spectres of the victims of British colonialism to haunt the highest echelons of government. Yet a juxtaposition of such occasions suggests that spectres differ in their capacity to haunt. In this chapter, I suggest that British parliamentarians seem more attuned to the spectres of the victims of colonial anti-sodomy laws than to those of the millions enslaved by British colonial capital. I ask what

93. Ibid., 93–94.
94. Faupel, *African Holocaust*.
95. Gilroy, *After Empire*.

this might imply about the racialisation of queerness and the sexualisation of slavery in contemporary British public consciousness.

In turning to memory, I hope to avoid some of the problems that queer activist historical ventures encounter, while remaining alert to its potential for catalysing political change. Memory, and haunting in particular, does not pretend to provide an authoritative account of the past, but offers instead what Avery Gordon calls a 'way of knowing' that understands 'the constellation of connections that charges any time of the now with the debts of the past and the expense of the present.'[96] Moreover, in attending to the public memory of pilgrims and parliamentarians, rather than looking for secrets concealed by the archive I am interested in the open secrets that hide in plain sight in practices of intense memorialisation. My intuition here is that attending to stories about the past that people are already telling themselves might offer opportunities for dissidence and for expanding our conceptions of liberation in ways that are less didactic than those that emerge from the pronouncements of professional historians or human rights activists. By paying attention to the contradictions in these stories and amplifying dissident possibilities, we might heed Walter Benjamin's call to 'take control of a memory, as it flashes in a moment of danger' by 'setting alight the sparks of hope in the past.'[97] Benjamin's reference to danger is salutary because, as we shall see, the process of igniting memory is deeply conflictual. What becomes evident is that memory is less a treasure trove of stories than a battleground on which competing accounts joust for hegemony. The point of the turn to memory is not that it promises an end to conflict, but that it sometimes offers queers a more hospitable terrain for it.

But memory does not always serve. As Pierre Nora observes in his account of what he tellingly calls *les lieux de mémoire*, 'memory takes root in the concrete, in spaces, gestures, images, and objects.'[98] The concrete embeddedness of memory is the source of both its power and limits. It gives memory a certain finitude, which brings risks. Temporal turns toward the past, whether in the register of history, memory, or something else, are fundamentally conservative in their impulse to recover something that was present that now appears absent, and especially so when the space of remembrance is geographically circumscribed by the boundaries of the nation or other political community. What if this spatially circumscribed past contains nothing available for retrieval to serve the contemporary

96. Gordon, *Ghostly Matters*, 142.
97. Benjamin, 'Concept of History'.
98. Nora, 'Between Memory and History', 9.

need for legitimation? In an early intervention in queer historiographical debates, Nayan Shah warns of precisely this danger, arguing that 'we may trap ourselves in the need of a history to sanction our existence. [Queers] are present now. On that alone we demand acknowledgement and acceptance.'[99] How might postcolonial queer movements leverage the 'now' and 'hereafter' in their quest for liberation?

Queer Futures

When past and present seem unpromising as vehicles for liberation, it can be tempting to turn towards the future. Yet the future is not an empty slate, easily amenable to the inscription of our deepest desires. It can sometimes rise unbidden, presenting us with its own spectres from which we feel compelled to seek respite. In his essay on 'The Uncanny', Sigmund Freud describes unexpectedly encountering his own image as a paradigmatically uncanny experience. He recalls sitting in a train compartment that is suddenly jolted, whereupon the door of an adjoining washing-cabinet swings open and an elderly man in a dressing gown and traveling cap comes in. Thinking that the man had mistakenly ventured into his compartment, Freud gets up to redirect him, only to realise to his dismay that the intruder is none other than his reflection in the mirror on the open door. He recalls thoroughly disliking his appearance.[100] Stephen Frosh reads Freud's reaction as one of aversion to 'the truth of getting old and shabby', which he would rather be without.[101] In temporal terms, Freud receives an intimation of the future that he does not like. Here, it is the future that haunts the present. The more general point that Frosh draws out of this is that 'what should be the present is in fact infected both by the past and by the future.'[102]

The famous opening words of *The Communist Manifesto* attest to the work that spectres of futurity do in the present. Marx and Engels declare that 'a spectre is haunting Europe—the spectre of Communism.'[103] This spectre propels 'the Powers of old Europe' into an alliance held together by the sole purpose of exorcising the spectre. In their hands, the spectre of Communism becomes a stick with which to beat their opponents (for

99. Shah, 'Sexuality', 123.
100. Freud, 'Uncanny'.
101. Frosh, *Hauntings*, 22; see also Segal, *Out of Time*, 21–23.
102. Frosh, *Hauntings*, 34.
103. Marx and Engels, *Communist Manifesto*, 2.

'Communism' read 'Islamic terrorism' as the spectral sign of early twenty-first century geopolitics). Yet it is also clear from their brief preface that, in the view of Marx and Engels, at the time that they are writing very little has happened to justify the paranoia with which this spectre is invoked. Indeed they urge Communists to make real what has hitherto been a 'nursery tale' by coming together behind the *Manifesto* to make manifest the worst fears of the bourgeoisie. Thus, futurity is no less a battleground than memory, providing the stage for struggles to ward off foreboding spectres and to bring preferred futures into being.

If queer movements are haunted by a spectre, it is the spectre of abjection. In Chapters 5 and 6, I explore two kinds of futural responses to this spectre. The first takes the form of what I call homocapitalism, an ideology forged in interaction between elite LGBT activists and technocrats in international financial institutions (IFIs) such as the World Bank and the International Monetary Fund (IMF). Denied belonging within the nation, some activists have turned to making the case for inclusion, not in a language of justice or human rights, but through a refiguration of the queer as model capitalist subject whose inclusion promises a future of growth and economic dynamism. This argument has been embraced by IFIs eager to rehabilitate themselves in a time of capitalist crisis by brandishing an image of progressiveness. While the logics of inclusion and exclusion at work in homocapitalism mirror those identified in analyses of homonationalism, they operate in a distinct geotemporal context. Homocapitalism names a strategy of persuasion operative in a moment in which the postcolonial nation has not 'yet' or has only ambivalently accepted the case for queer inclusion in the face of the overwhelming pressure of a modernity represented by the homonationalist hegemon. It offers a shift of argumentative register in which the language of the market is deployed to repress an unresolved moral argument about the acceptability or desirability of queerness in the nation. As I will show, this apparently materialist strategy for queer inclusion relies on a spurious understanding of 'homophobia' as 'merely cultural'[104] that obscures the ways in which global capitalism engenders the forms of material precarity in which homophobic moral panics flourish.

If homocapitalism aspires to upward mobility, Chapter 6 explores the futures opened up by queer identification with those relegated to the bottom of the social hierarchy. Queer theorists have drawn attention to the association of the queer with temporal primitiveness,[105] but have paid

104. Butler, 'Merely Cultural'.
105. Hoad, 'Arrested Development'; Weber, *Queer International Relations*, 47–71.

less attention to the specifically *temporal* responses of those relegated to states of primitiveness. The crucial question here is one that Lucinda Ramberg asks in a reflection on the geopolitics of queer theory and the sexual politics of Dalit studies: 'How is asynchronicity inhabited by those deemed backward?' More particularly, what do 'backward futures' look like?[106] The Indian Supreme Court's *NALSA* decision forms the point of departure for my inquiry here. The trans community's demand for state recognition of its 'backward class' status in this case sought to avail of a legal framework that has accreted over several decades as a result of Dalit and subordinate caste assertion, with a view to ameliorating the condition of what is formally referred to in the Indian political lexicon as 'backwardness'. Moving beyond the element of pragmatism in this demand—in which respect it is not different from the clamour of many groups in India for state recognition of their 'backwardness'—I take it as an invitation to explore convergences between Dalit and trans articulations of futurity by speculating on what it might mean to view the futural politics of Ambedkar through a trans lens and vice versa. I contextualise this inquiry in light of the configuration of political forces in contemporary India, where a ruling neoliberal Hindu Right faces off against a tenuously linked array of oppositional groups, with a view to posing a broader set of questions about how queer/trans/Dalit futures relate to the imagination of the future of the nation itself.

In sum, rather than offering a temporal manifesto, the chapters that follow might be read as a series of investigations into what Anna Agathangelou and Kyle Killian describe as 'the political function of time as a limit, a resource, a site of exploitation and ultimately antagonism.'[107] Situated in the interstices between international relations, political theory, and queer studies, the book joins a body of literature that is concerned with the temporality of the international.[108] The project of the more normatively inclined of these works is twofold—first, to provincialise the time of Western modernity,[109] and second, to make visible the manner in which subjects and populations placed in positions of temporal belatedness, or outside of time altogether, have 'defied, deflected and appropriated' their temporal emplacement.[110] The second of these objectives effectively asks

106. Ramberg, 'Backward Futures', 223.
107. Agathangelou and Killian, 'Introduction', 14.
108. See, for example, Hutchings, *Time and World Politics*; Ogle, *Global Transformation of Time*; Hom et al., *Time*; Younis, 'Race'; Rao, 'One Time'.
109. Chakrabarty, *Provincializing Europe*.
110. Kumarakulasingam, 'Introduction', 758.

what it might mean to live 'out of time'. Without attempting an exhaustive inventory, I think of being out of sync with time, of running out of time, of making up for lost time, of being ahead of or behind one's time, of taking time out, of passing time (or timepass, as we South Asians would say), of outing oneself time after time.

NOTES ON 'QUEER'

In using the term 'queer' to signify sexual and gender non-normativity, I take my cue from scholar-activists in India[111] and Uganda,[112] who have argued that the term can be appropriated and resignified to do useful work in their respective contexts, despite its originally Anglo-American provenance. In many of these usages, 'queer' has functioned somewhat contradictorily as both an umbrella term for a range of identity categories, and as a critique of identity politics itself. This latter connotation emerged from a prominent, if marginal, leftist tendency in queer liberation movements in the global North. As Michael Warner pointed out in the early days of what would come to be called queer theory, because the sex/gender order blends with a wide range of institutions and ideologies—the family, state, market, 'culture', religion, 'race', biomedical and other regimes of the body—to challenge it is to encounter these other institutions as problems and to struggle with them as well. 'Being queer means fighting about [all] these issues all the time.'[113] The open-ended nature of this definition, besides making 'queer' available for appropriation and resignification, also makes possible a broader objective of this book, namely a demonstration of the co-constitution of gender and sexuality by other categories such as nation, religion, race, class, and caste. Needless to say, the queer insistence on 'fighting about [all] these issues all the time' is not universally shared, distinguishing it from a more single-issue oriented liberal LGBT politics that seeks inclusion within, rather than the deconstruction of, hegemonic structures of state, nation, and market.[114]

---

111. Narrain, *Queer*; Narrain and Bhan, *Because*; khanna, *Sexualness*, 28–33; Kang, 'Queering Dalit'.

112. Nyanzi, 'Dismantling Reified African Culture'; Nyanzi, 'Queer Pride'; see also Ekine and Abbas, *Queer African Reader*; Currier and Migraine-George, 'Queer Studies' for discussions of 'queer' in other Sub-Saharan African contexts.

113. Warner, 'Introduction', xiii.

114. For accounts of how the split between queer and LGBT approaches manifests in the queer IR literature, see Richter-Montpetit, 'Everything You Always Wanted'; Rao, 'State of "Queer IR"'.

Yet even scholars sympathetic to a queer deconstructive agenda have been sceptical about the feasibility and/or desirability of its appropriation in other locations.[115] Ashley Tellis argues that in its travels to India, 'queer' has shed its radical, militant connotations, forged in the confrontational politics of ACT-UP activists incensed by the Reagan administration's murderous disregard for people living with HIV/AIDS, to become a bland signifier for a multitude of sexual minority groups constituted and governed by a transnational non-profit industrial complex to which only the most elite activists have access.[116] In his words:

> Without an interrogation of the discourse of global governance, the global cir-culation of the term 'queer', the politics of international funding, the politics of NGOisation, the power of colonialism, the poison of nationalism, the no-longer new economic order, the unquestioning faith in the law, the unstated inhabitation of Brahminism, the easy slide into patriarchalism and the heady jolt of utopian rhetoric that enables one to simply vault over all of this into a 'queer' paradise, there can be no 'queer movement' in India and the one that claims to exist is not asking any of these questions.[117]

Bracketing for now the matter of whether the 'queer movement' is asking these questions, note that the critique is not that 'queer' *cannot* travel, only that it *has* not. Indeed one might read Tellis's argument as a demand for a *more* thoroughgoing importation of queer critique and praxis—one that is more faithful to the spirit of Warner's insurrectionary understanding of the term.

Scholars of gender and sexuality in Sub-Saharan Africa have also expressed reservations about the relevance of queer theory to their work. Morgan and Wieringa refuse to describe as 'queer' the female same-sex practices that they catalogue, because many of these aim to reinforce nor-mative sexual and gender performance rather than to subvert them.[118] Keguro Macharia has criticised the tendency of queer scholarship on Africa to shoehorn 'evidence' gathered from the continent into Eurocentric categories while neglecting African conceptual and intellectual frameworks in the shaping of analytical agendas.[119] Indeed the persistent refrain that

---

115. Dutoya, 'Defining the "Queers"'.
116. Tellis, 'Disrupting the Dinner Table'. This observation applies equally in 'queer's' original home, suggesting that the description of the fate that it has allegedly suffered has less to do with geographical provenance than with more global processes of leftist decline and co-optation.
117. Ibid., 155.
118. Morgan and Wieringa, *Tommy Boys*, 310.
119. Macharia, 'Being Area-Studied'; see also Epprecht, *Heterosexual Africa?*, 12–16.

'homosexuality is Western'—notwithstanding its elisions—has rendered doubly urgent the task of decolonising knowledge production around non-normative genders and sexualities.

One manifestation of attempts at decolonisation has been the search for, or invention of, indigenous terms that name personal truths and histories of non-normative desire. Yet as Aniruddha Dutta and Raina Roy explain in a discussion that focuses on the category 'transgender' in India but has wider implications, dominant centres of knowledge production and funding provincialise vernacular categories (such as hijra, kothi, kinnar, aravani, tirunangai/tirunambi) while reinforcing the use of 'trans' as an overarching signifier for gender non-normativity.[120] Dutta and Roy's concern is not with the putative inauthenticity of trans—which, as many have pointed out, has come to be adapted and inhabited by gender nonconforming people in a variety of locations[121]—but with the conceptual baggage of the term such as the homo-trans and cis-trans binaries that it erects, which do not always reflect the lived realities of gender nonconformity in the contexts in which it is deployed.

In Uganda, the term 'kuchu', meaning 'same' in Swahili, has emerged as an umbrella signifier for sex and gender nonconformity.[122] But linguistic indigeneity does not easily resolve questions around inclusion and decolonisation. In her pioneering ethnographic work on the kuchu community, Stella Nyanzi notes that 'despite its wide circulation as the preferred label for sexual minorities in Uganda, [she] encountered same-sex loving individuals who strongly disassociated from the label *kuchu* because it was highly politicised, connotated militant activism or radical "in-your-face" advocacy for sexual minority rights' and who preferred to identify as some element of LGBTI (or, in some cases, to not identify at all).[123] The adoption of kuchu as an identity may well have broadened in the time since Nyanzi made this observation. Nonetheless, I am struck by the fact that the occasional disidentification from the category that she witnessed tracks the same fault lines and aversions produced by the term 'queer'. The inadequacies of both queer and kuchu as comprehensive placeholders for gender and sexual non-normativity point to the limits of language and

120. Dutta and Roy, 'Decolonizing Transgender'.
121. Mohan et al., *Towards Gender Inclusivity*, 30.
122. Peters, '*Kuchus* in the Balance', 38–39, 174; Lusimbo and Bryan, '*Kuchu* resilience'. Importantly, the connotation of 'sameness' in 'kuchu' has not restricted its application to same-sex desiring persons, with heterosexual trans and gender nonconfirming persons also embracing the term.
123. Nyanzi, 'Dismantling Reified African Culture', 959.

signification itself, suggesting that we ought to be more interested in the work that such placeholders do than in conjuring unimpeachable signs for them.

On this question, too, there is much disagreement among 'queer' theorists. Robyn Wiegman and Elizabeth Wilson have challenged queer theory's allegiance to anti-normativity, arguing that this effectively views norms as always and only restrictive and excluding, missing the ways in which they are productive of the very proliferation of difference that anti-normativity seeks.[124] Relatedly, Saba Mahmood has steered our understanding of agency away from a reductive focus on the consolidation and subversion of norms, urging us to take account of 'the variety of ways in which norms are lived and inhabited, aspired to, reached for, and consummated.'[125]

Given my interest in the criminal law, the norms with which I am most concerned in this book *are* paradigmatically restrictive and excluding, even if this is not the only kind of work that norms do. But there is a different sense in which anti-normativity cannot tell the full story of what it means to be queer. Subjects who do not think of themselves as deviant might nonetheless be queered by the law. And as much as some respond to the experience of being queer or queered with proud gestures of defiance and ownership, others wish to conform, to stay out of trouble, to keep heads below parapets. How can we do justice to queer desires for normativity as a means toward a liveable life without always and everywhere levelling the charge of homonormativity?[126] Butler reminds us that 'a liveable life does require various degrees of stability', making it crucial to distinguish between 'norms and conventions that permit people to breathe, to desire, to love, and to live, and those norms and conventions that restrict or eviscerate the conditions of life itself.'[127] Indeed we might think of this task as constitutive of the space of contemporary queer politics.

(DIS)POSITIONALITY

When I embarked on this project, I had hoped to use my positionality as an Indian living in Britain to bring a different kind of sensibility to the work

124. Wiegman and Wilson, 'Introduction'.
125. Mahmood, *Politics of Piety*, 23.
126. I have been pushed to think about this question by Strey, 'Queer Moments'.
127. Butler, *Undoing Gender*, 8.

that I was trying to do in Uganda than might be typical of researchers based in the West. Having been shaped politically and intellectually by the work of comrades in the queer movement in India, I engaged with my Ugandan interlocutors as a citizen of another former British colony that was also grappling with the entanglements of gender, sexuality, and imperial legacy. I fantasised about leveraging the money and resources of the global North institution in which I work to facilitate horizontal connections between global South locations. This is not always how my project or presence in Uganda was perceived. On one of my many days at the Anglican Uganda Martyrs shrine in Namugongo, a priest with whom I had spent several hours turned to me and said, in an attempt to be helpful, 'be careful with your things. When people see a muzungu like you, they will try to steal your phone and camera.' The word 'muzungu' can refer to all foreigners, but is more typically used to refer to people racialised as white. Literally translated, it means 'one who roams around'—a more apposite description of 'fieldwork' than any other that I have come across. Indeed the term is supposed to have first been used in the African Great Lakes region to refer to eighteenth-century European explorers.

Although most Ugandans would identify me as a muyindi (Indian)—which comes with its own baggage—being called a muzungu jolted me out of the naiveté with which I had been thinking about my positionality. In his resolutely anti-nostalgic 'Reflections on Exile', Edward Said suggests that for all its miseries, the experience of displacement might enable a 'plurality of vision . . . an awareness of simultaneous dimensions' that he calls 'contrapuntal'.[128] And elsewhere, reflecting on his positionality as 'an Arab with Western education' living in the US—a country from which he remained politically estranged on account of its treatment of much of the rest of the world—he writes that 'belonging, as it were, to both sides of the imperial divide enables you to understand them more easily.'[129] Being called a muzungu made me think more pessimistically about my diasporic location as threatening to bring with it the worst of 'both sides'—the loss of local knowledges and the internalisation of imperial epistemes. I began to worry that whatever the colour of my skin or passport, a project conceived around sexuality would mark me out as a muzungu in the eyes of many.

And yet imperialism has strange afterlives that yield unexpected forms of connection across space and time. On another day, just as I was about to enter Namirembe Cathedral, the main Anglican church in Uganda, an

---

128. Said, *Reflections on Exile*, 186.
129. Said, *Culture and Imperialism*, xxx.

elderly woman inquired 'are you an Anglican?' 'Sort of,' I wanted to respond, thinking of the fourteen years that I had spent in Church of South India schools originally established by Anglican missionaries and the seven years that I had spent, later in life, in two Oxford colleges.[130] So I was not untruthful, even if evasive, when I mumbled in response that I had studied in Anglican schools. I might have added that as an inveterate member of my school choir, I had been steeped in Anglican liturgy since before a time when anything like sexuality was remotely intelligible to me. And so, fortified by the knowledge that I could sing the Nicene Creed, I entered the church.

130. I was following a well-worn itinerary. George Uglow Pope (1820–1908), Anglican missionary and Tamil scholar, was principal of Bishop Cotton School in Bangalore before taking up a lectureship at Balliol College, Oxford.

CHAPTER 2

The Location of Homophobia

Two discursive constructions of homophobia in Uganda constitute the
focus of this chapter. In the first, Uganda is imagined to be a gay 'heart
of darkness', a construction that is aided by its geographical contiguity
with that original heart of darkness seared in the Western literary imagination by Joseph Conrad's eponymous novel.[1] In this account, homophobia
in Uganda is seen as deep rooted, pervasive, and normative. As countless
media reports purporting to analyse attitudes towards sexuality inform us,
'homophobia is rife in Africa.'[2] Contrasted with the queer freedoms of the
West, such discursive constructions of Uganda and Africa produce what
Jasbir Puar has described as 'homonationalism'—an assemblage in which
LGBT rights have come to be mobilised as new markers for an old divide between the civilised and the savage.[3] Drawing on evidence of links between
Ugandan and US-based Christian evangelicals, the second discursive construction of homophobia in Uganda locates responsibility for anti-queer
sentiment in the country almost entirely in the hands of Western anti-gay
activists. While tactically useful in deflecting claims about the foreignness
of queer subjectivities, this relocation of homophobia evacuates the agency
of Ugandans or interprets their agency reductively as being manipulated or
instrumentalised by external actors. I describe this alternative construction as 'homoromanticism' because it views Ugandans as blameless pawns
in an essentially Western 'culture war' that has been displaced onto Africa.

1. Conrad, *Heart of Darkness*.
2. See, for example, Bunting, 'African Homophobia'; Smith, 'Why Africa Is the Most
Homophobic Continent'; for a critique, see Macharia, 'Homophobia in Africa'.
3. Puar, *Terrorist Assemblages*.

Out of Time. Rahul Rao, Oxford University Press (2020). © Oxford University Press.
DOI: 10.1093/oso/9780190865511.001.0001

Although antithetical to homonationalism in differently locating responsibility for homophobia, homoromanticism is complicit in reiterating a view of Africans as lacking the agential capacity necessary to function as authors of innovative and indigenous forms of queer and anti-queer affect. Underpinning both discourses are practices of mapping affect so as to produce a tight linkage between sexuality, place, time, and legitimacy such that particular attitudes towards sexuality (and indeed particular sexualities) become markers of belonging to particular places. In this chapter I survey such mapping practices before asking how we might account for political 'homophobia' in Uganda in a way that navigates between the Scylla of homonationalism and the Charybdis of homoromanticism. Drawing on the work of critical geographers as well as postcolonial, feminist, and queer theorists, I argue that we might do this by complicating our understanding of 'place' as a temporal process constituted by transnational relations and flows that unfold over time. I deploy this framework to account for the contemporary construction of 'Ugandan culture' by focussing on two key historical junctures at which attitudes towards sexuality appear to have shifted in crucial ways. In doing so, I hope to account for the transnational production of homophobia in Uganda in a manner that acknowledges the agency of Ugandan elites without lapsing into orientalist narratives of 'African homophobia'.

The terms 'homophobia' and 'transphobia' remain inadequate signifiers for the forms of anti-queer affect that I want to understand in this book. 'Phobia' suggests a fear or aversion that is often articulated with, but also distinct from, cognate affects such as anger, hatred, disgust, shame, and envy that might underpin acts of violence towards queers. The theorisation of such affects as phobias tends to individualise and pathologise a social hostility that maintains the structural maldistributions of heteronormative patriarchy. 'Phobia', in other words, lets society off the hook. 'Homo' and 'trans' are differently inadequate in that they do not capture the array of subjectivities without heteronormative and cisgender privilege against which such hostility is expressed, or the variety of reasons for which it may be expressed. These are not reducible to an antipathy to same-sex attraction or gender transgression, but may have more to do with class, caste, ethnicity, race, religion, disability, and other markers of (un)belonging or some intersection thereof. Ryan Thoreson additionally points to the historically contingent etymology of the term 'homophobia', which evolved in the global North to become a flexible signifier for different forms of anti-queer affect which emerged out of Victorian notions of sexual morality, psychoanalytic understandings of development, and pseudoscientific and psychological theories. Such preoccupations may be distinct from those animating anti-queer affect in postcolonial global South contexts such as anxieties about the preservation of family, custom, or sovereignty in the face of global North hegemony. Thoreson therefore suggests 'anti-queer animus' as a more expansive signifier for the affects that are typically placed under the sign of 'homophobia'.[4]

I agree with much of Thoreson's critique, but continue to use the terms 'homophobia' and 'transphobia', despite their limitations, for two reasons. First, they remain the shorthand of choice for kuchu activists to describe the structures and affects that they struggle against. I want to recognise the agency of these activists in refashioning these terms into more capacious and flexible signifiers that might better accommodate the virulent affects against which they struggle. While the dominant discourse surrounding the AHA has been directed against 'homosexuality', trans people have disproportionately suffered its effects on account of the visibility of their perceived non-normativity. Moreover, as I will go on to show, a historical account of the institutionalisation of homophobia in Uganda reveals that it has been imbricated with misreadings of gender identity. As such, while I use the term 'homophobia' to reference the dominant discourse, I sometimes employ the term 'queerphobia' as a more inclusive signifier to gesture at the ways in which homophobia and transphobia interact with and reinforce one another while remaining distinct affects. Second, Thoreson's reading of the geographical provenance of 'homophobia' does not imply that the concept cannot travel. Indeed, the extensive links between Ugandan and US conservatives and the appearance in Uganda of a 'family values' discourse that borrows heavily from the playbook of US anti-gay activists would seem to suggest exactly this. Drawing on her work in Southeast Asia, Meredith Weiss argues that homophobia is increasingly expressed in *anticipation* of the emergence of LGBTI movements in gestures of pre-emptive mobilisation.[5] This is also visible in parts of Sub-Saharan Africa, where conservatives have sometimes legislated against same-sex marriage without it being demanded by local LGBTI movements. The phenomenon of anticipatory queerphobia challenges the temporal assumption that queerphobia is always a reaction to queer mobilisation. More fundamentally, it challenges the presumption that queerphobias must be ontologically commensurate with the forms of erotic expression and desire that they contest. Instead, queerphobias have sometimes become unmoored from actually existing expressions of desire and identity, so that it can

4. Thoreson, 'Troubling the Waters', 25.
5. Weiss, 'Prejudice before Pride'.

sometimes make sense to speak of homo/trans/queerphobia in contexts where homosexual and transgender subjectivities are unintelligible.

'THE WORLD'S WORST PLACE TO BE GAY': THE SPACETIMES OF HOMONATIONALISM

Every year, the International Lesbian, Gay, Bisexual, Trans and Intersex Association (ILGA) publishes a report assessing the global extent of 'State Sponsored Homophobia'.[6] The report is accompanied by a series of maps, the most comprehensive of which provides an overview of laws governing sexual orientation. The map adopts a traffic light system of coding. It depicts states that criminalise same-sex relations with death sentences or imprisonment in shades of red; states that have decriminalised or never criminalised such relations and that offer protection against discrimination in yellow; and states that accord varying degrees of recognition to same-sex unions and adoption of children by same-sex parents in shades of green. Like the bull's eye on a dartboard, it is the red and reddish states of (mainly) Anglophone Sub-Saharan Africa and the Caribbean, North Africa, and West, South, and Southeast Asia that grab the viewer's attention.

Three features of this map are noteworthy. First, like all political maps, the ILGA map privileges the state as the basic unit of spatial analysis. This is apparent not only in the lines on the map that demarcate states from one another, but also in the accompanying report, the bulk of which comprises country-specific entries that summarise the law in each state. The state-centric ontology of the exercise reinforces the common-sense assumption that 'state-sponsored homophobia' is most appropriately understood with reference to acts of commission or omission of the state being investigated. This occludes the possibility that transnational actors and processes may be more germane to understanding the contemporary production of homophobia in a number of places. Legal scholar Anne Orford has demonstrated that liberal international projects have long been underpinned by an imaginative geography in which the attribution of problems to local factors allows a sanitised view of the international as the domain of solutions.[7]

Second, the map depicts a hegemonic progress narrative that Robert Wintemute has described as the move from 'basic rights' to 'sex rights' to 'love rights'.[8] The adoption of this narrative as a yardstick with which

6. ILGA, 'Maps'.
7. Orford, *Reading Humanitarian Intervention*, 85.
8. Wintemute, 'From "Sex Rights"'.

to judge progress on rights concerning sexual orientation is dubious on a number of grounds. Aeyal Gross questions whether such a narrative can be understood as progressive in the sense of being cumulative. He points out, for example, that conventional legal definitions of marriage (a 'love right') as an exclusive relationship between two persons curtail the very liberty that is the object of supposedly prior struggles for 'sex rights'.[9] In addition, the ILGA report's implicit premise that decriminalisation, protection, and recognition are chronologically successive stages reflects a North Atlantic experience that may not be mirrored elsewhere. Courts in Uganda, for example, have repeatedly affirmed the equal enjoyment of constitutional rights by queer persons, effectively protecting them from some forms of discrimination in a context in which homosexuality is criminalised.[10] This in no way obviates the need for decriminalisation; rather, it compels us to question whether it is necessarily a condition precedent to the enjoyment of other rights and freedoms.

Third, in purporting to chart progress, the map offers a spatial representation of time, most arrestingly through its choice of colours. If the red in the traffic light palette connotes stoppage or stasis, the green conveys the impression of dynamism and movement. More profoundly, the banality of red-yellow-green as an integrated system of signalling suggests that we are all on a road, *the same road*, governed by a common set of rules. In his account of the evolutionary narratives that have suffused understandings of 'homosexuality' since the inception of that term in the 1870s, Hoad argues that evolutionary narratives are distinguished by three assumptions: first, that the narrative must culminate in an ultimately unified subject—in this context, what Dennis Altman has theorised as the 'global gay';[11] second, that the manifold others of this subject are perceived as already incorporated into and transcended by this subject; third, that this incorporation and transcendence is achieved by the temporalisation of space.[12] As Hoad explains, 'the rest of the world is understood as equivalent to the past of the now dominant form of male homosexuality in the western metropolis: we were like them, but have developed, they are like we were and have yet to develop.'[13] Thus the temporalisation of space manages heterogeneity by promising the eventual subsumption of difference into the forms of

9. Gross, 'Sex, Love, and Marriage', 243–249.
10. See, for example, *Mukasa and Oyo v. Attorney-General* (2008) AHRLR 248 (UgHC 2008); *Kasha Jacqueline, David Kato Kisule and Onziema Patience v. Rolling Stone Ltd. and Giles Muhame*, Miscellaneous Cause No. 163 of 2010.
11. Altman, 'Global Gaze'.
12. Hoad, 'Arrested Development', 133.
13. Ibid., 148.

subjectivity currently existing in what claim to be the most advanced parts of the world, while hierarchising that difference in the interim. In mapping the world in terms of its progress along an itinerary already traversed by Euro-America, the ILGA map offers a spatial representation of the evolutionary narratives that inform much contemporary global queer activism. In this, it is neither unique nor especially blameworthy, but representative of a hegemonic sensibility.[14]

If maps hierarchise difference through the spatialisation of time, league tables do this more bluntly through the device of ranking. A 2016 ILGA survey of attitudes towards 'LGBTI people' in fifty-three states across the major continental regions ranks Sub-Saharan African respondents as expressing the highest levels of hostility to LGBTI people. On the crucial question of whether 'being LGBTI should be a crime', for example, it reports the highest levels of endorsement from Africa (45%) and, within the continent, singles out Nigeria, Uganda, and Ghana as being the only countries in the world where support for criminalisation exceeds 50%.[15] Again, such ranking exercises are now a familiar feature of media coverage and global advocacy in relation to LGBTI rights.

My interest here is less in questioning the methodologies used to conduct these surveys (although we might do that, too) than in asking what affective labour such advocacy materials are intended to perform. As with other hierarchical indices of global governmentality, the ranking impulse of these materials is intended to mobilise the competitive jouissance of international relations, applauding states that move in the direction of progress and shaming those that do not. Crucially, the production of the appropriate affects (shame at being left behind or at the bottom, determination to improve) presupposes a consensus on the meaning and direction of progress. But where value disagreements are at stake—when one state's 'progress' is another's 'moral decay'—the motivational potential of such advocacy is less straightforward. Here the substantive issues at stake have to be translated into another category whose value *is* apparent to all—'modernity', perhaps—with the result that shame is mobilised less through a cultivation of empathy with the pain of queer subjects than through an arousal of the anxiety that attends being stranded on the wrong side of modernity. This is why, despite the novelty of sexual orientation and gender

14. See, for example, the interactive map on the home page of Human Dignity Trust, accessed 3 July 2016, http://www.humandignitytrust.org/; 'Towards a Free and Equal World', UNAIDS, accessed 3 July 2016, http://www.unaids.org/en/resources/infographics/20140108freeequal/.
15. ILGA, 'ILGA-RIWI 2016', 5.

identity as salient categories in international politics, their discussion evokes long-standing divides between the civilised and the savage.

Orientalist strategies of mobilising shame are often internalised by those anxious to cross these divides. To see this we have to look at a map produced by Indian LGBT activists that, while predating the ILGA maps that I have been discussing, shares their spatial imaginary. This map was published in 2006 as part of a set of advocacy materials intended to mobilise public opinion in favour of the decriminalisation of homosexuality at the time that the Delhi High Court was considering a petition on this matter. It colours in orange those countries that criminalised sodomy at the time (mainly Sub-Saharan Africa, a few states in the Caribbean, and West, South, and Southeast Asia) with the rest of the world coloured white. The map is captioned with a rhetorical question: 'Only the Countries coloured in orange continue to criminalize sodomy. To which world must India belong?'[16] The question is posed in the knowledge that it will only ever be answered in one way by an elite Indian audience anxious to break away from what used to be called the Third World to assert India's status as a great power-in-waiting. It presents the decriminalisation of sodomy as a means by which India might signal its readiness for this transition. In doing so, it identifies the criminalisation of sodomy as a signifier of belonging to the underdeveloped world and its opposite as a means of escape from this category.

Spatially centre-stage in the maps I have been discussing, and historically the repository for Western anxieties about backwardness and savagery, Africa occupies a prominent place in contemporary cartographical and other depictions of homophobia. Within Africa, Uganda has acquired a certain notoriety in these discussions since the advent of the AHB in 2009. Its hyper-visibility, produced through the mapping and measuring techniques I have discussed earlier, has been reinforced by a series of sensationalist media narratives that purport to journey into the vortex of its homophobia. Two documentaries aired on the BBC relatively early in the life of this story are illustrative of this trend. The first, produced by gay British DJ Scott Mills, is rhetorically titled *The World's Worst Place to Be Gay?*[17] The second follows the visit of gay British writer, actor, and presenter Stephen Fry to Uganda for his documentary series *Out There*, which explores what it means to be gay in 'difficult' places.[18]

16. See the map in Open Letter Against Sec 377 by Amartya Sen, Vikram Seth and others, 16 September 2006, http://orinam.net/377/background-of-sec-377/.
17. Mills, *World's Worst Place*.
18. Fry, *Out There*.

While professing to explore homophobia in Uganda, both documentaries are bookended by comparisons with Britain, which is constructed as a haven of gay freedom. Fry's documentary opens with scenes from a gay civil partnership ceremony in London. Mills's film begins in a pub in London's gay Soho district where, pictured in amiable conversation with friends, Mills vigorously denies that he has ever encountered homophobia. Ritualistic caveats about the relative novelty of Britain's gay friendliness are followed by the assertion that 'compared to elsewhere, we're a model of tolerance.' Recalling Chandra Mohanty's critique of the gaze of white Western feminism,[19] the remark reminds us that such cross-cultural comparisons are deployed to construct hierarchies in which the Western self finds proof of its emancipation in the shackles of its non-Western other. When John Bosco Nyombi, a gay Ugandan exile in Britain, narrates his experience of persecution in Uganda, Mills can only reply: 'our experiences are completely different, 'coz I had a really easy time growing up, being gay. It wasn't an issue for me at all.' Nyombi responds incredulously: 'It looks like we are on different planets.'[20] Unmentioned in Mills's film is the story of Nyombi's struggles with the British Home Office in his long and arduous quest for asylum in the United Kingdom.[21]

Both films feature a set of stock characters. On the one hand, both give considerable airtime to the most vociferous spokespersons for homophobia in Uganda, who expound at length on their belief that homosexuals are paedophiles, that anal sex is unnatural and physically debilitating, and so on. The interviews are confrontational, although it isn't clear what purpose these confrontations serve beyond yielding sensationalist sound bytes that cater to a voyeuristic desire for comedy and horror. Both are provided in abundant measure by pastors Martin Ssempa, founder of Makerere Community Church and a self-proclaimed crusader against homosexuality, and Solomon Male, executive director of Arising for Christ. Ssempa's inspired attempt to arouse the antipathy of his congregants by screening gay fetish pornography featuring fisting and scat play quickly went viral, before becoming the subject of vicious parodies that have immortalised him as the whistle-blower on the alleged homosexual propensity to 'eat da poo poo.'[22] Male's views, featured on both documentaries, do not appear to

19. Mohanty, *Feminism Without Borders*.
20. Mills, *World's Worst Place*.
21. Neumann, *Getting Out*.
22. For the original talk, see 'Eat Da Poo Poo', accessed 4 July 2016, https://www.youtube.com/watch?v=jjnrLt3VuSM; for the parodies see for example http://knowyourmeme.com/memes/eat-da-poo-poo.

have changed in the two and a half years that separate them, suggesting that the 'homophobes'—unmoved by the arguments of their journalistic interlocutors—exploit these global televisual opportunities to broadcast and exaggerate their views on ever larger stages. Absent any semblance of analysis, 'homophobia' in these spectacles appears inexplicable, irrational, unmoveable.

On the other hand, the films also feature members of Kampala's kuchu community—often the same ones, which is perhaps understandable given the reluctance of many to out themselves, with a decided preference for the most abject stories. For example, both filmmakers speak to Stosh Mugisha, a transman, who narrates his experience of being raped as a fourteen-year-old, and of becoming pregnant, HIV positive, and suicidal. Fry follows this harrowing account with the observation that '[Stosh's] life encapsulates almost every detail of the gay experience in Uganda.'[23] The claim is staggeringly reductive, revealing a disinterest in, or an inability to explore, the complexity and richness of kuchu lives.

In her extraordinary doctoral thesis on the everyday lives of Kampala's kuchus, Melissa Minor Peters does just this. While acutely attentive to the violence, poverty, and stigmatisation that kuchus suffer, through a praxis that draws as much on friendship as on her ethnographic skills as an anthropologist, Peters maps practices of kuchu consumption, leisure, pleasure, and activism as they unfold in a variety of spaces, including homes, neighbourhoods, churches, malls, markets, and bars. The portraits of kuchus that emerge from her work describe lives that are at once vulnerable and empowered, sometimes finding acceptance in unlikely places. In a remarkable vignette about one of her interlocutors Gerald(ine), Peters describes how the efforts of two men to have Gerald(ine) expelled from her neighbourhood on account of being a 'homosexual' were countervailed by the protests of a group of older women who regarded her as their daughter, culminating in an order by the village chairman that the use of the term 'homosexual' as an epithet would incur a punishment of compulsory social service. As Peters remarks, 'here, in an impoverished neighbourhood in the "world's worst place to be gay", a village by-law now states that residents may not call the neighborhood's most flamboyant homosexual a homosexual, or face cleaning a garbage-strewn slum.'[24] Peters is alive to the representational double bind in which kuchus find themselves. Stories of violence and atrocity are central to making human rights claims and

23. Fry, *Out There*.
24. Peters, '*Kuchus* in the Balance', 113–114.

accessing the support needed for survival in conditions of precarity. At the same time, the ceaseless reiteration of these narratives risks fetishising injury as identity, making queer subject positions constitutively abject and unliveable.[25]

What is striking about hegemonic narratives of homosexuality and violence surrounding the AHA is their assignment of Ugandan actors to positions of savagery, abjection, or martyrdom, with the politics of the country being flattened into a morality play featuring the Western journalist, human rights activist, or academic as speaker of truth to homophobic power. In this, they offer a paradigmatic illustration of Makau Mutua's claim that the contemporary human rights regime is constituted by the subject positions of savages, victims, and saviours.[26] Western actors have related to Uganda through this triadic frame with astonishing regularity. Take, for example, the documentary film *Kony2012*, produced by the charity Invisible Children with the ambition of mobilising a global grassroots campaign to demand the arrest and trial of Joseph Kony, leader of the guerrilla Lord's Resistance Army (LRA) in northern Uganda.[27] Viewed over 100 million times on YouTube within six days of its release, making it, in the words of *Time* magazine, 'the most viral video of all time',[28] the film provides a grossly oversimplified view of the conflict. Depicting northern Uganda as a territory populated by warlords, child soldiers, and sex slaves, and infantilising its audience quite literally through a narrative device whereby the director purports to explain the conflict in terms comprehensible to his five-year-old son, the film offers a deceptively and dangerously simple solution. Likening Kony to Hitler and Osama bin Laden, it urges viewers to lobby the US government to dedicate military resources to his pursuit and capture, effectively building popular pressure for the US militarisation of East Africa.[29]

As noteworthy as the film itself was the news, ten days after its release, of the psychotic breakdown suffered by its director Jason Russell, who was caught on film wandering the streets of San Diego naked. Attempting to account for his behaviour, Russell explained: 'I literally thought I was responsible for the future of humanity. It started to get into the point where my mind finally turned against me and there was a moment that click [*sic*], I wasn't in control of my mind or my body.'[30] In an odd coincidence, Fry

25. Ibid., 197–98.
26. Mutua, 'Savages, Victims, and Saviors'.
27. Invisible Children, *Kony2012*.
28. Carbone, 'Top 10'.
29. Mamdani, 'Kony'.
30. Williams, 'Kony 2012'.

described attempting to commit suicide after filming the Ugandan episode of *Out There*. Following his interview with the Ugandan Minister for Ethics and Integrity Simon Lokodo, whom he describes as a 'foaming, frothing homophobe of the worst kind', Fry recalls his state of mind: 'I paced around trying to analyse what it was that disappeared from me and it seemed that the whole essence of me had disappeared.'[31] Staring into the abyss that is Uganda, these moral crusaders—rather like Conrad's Kurtz—appear to be in danger of losing themselves.

The AHA thus provided a modern pretext for the expression of a recurrent Western horror, fascination, and even attraction, towards the fecundity and corruption of tropical Africa. Anticipating the thesis of Said's *Orientalism*, in a 1975 lecture indicting *Heart of Darkness* as a racist text, Chinua Achebe attributes this tendency to 'the desire—one might say the need—in Western psychology to set Africa up as a foil to Europe, as a place of negations at once remote and vaguely familiar, in comparison with which Europe's own state of spiritual grace will be manifest.'[32] In the narratives I've been discussing, Uganda becomes metonymous with Conrad's Africa—'the antithesis of Europe and therefore of civilisation, a place where man's vaunted intelligence and refinement are finally mocked by triumphant bestiality.'[33]

HOMOROMANTICISM AND THE ELUSIVENESS OF AFRICAN AGENCY

In promoting the AHA as a means of defending the 'culture of the people of Uganda' from Western corruption and thereby reproducing a spatial imaginary that locates queerness in the West, Ugandan conservatives comfortably inhabit the homonationalist assemblage. Queer activists and scholars have tended to respond to their claims with the reminder that the impetus for strengthening anti-queer laws originally imposed by British colonial authorities came from US evangelical Christians. Despite being antithetical to one another, both sets of claims—that 'homosexuality' *and* 'homophobia' are imports from the West—are historically plausible. But they are also evasive in obscuring landscapes of queer desire and phobia that have little to do with imported ontologies of sexuality.

31. Williams, 'Stephen Fry'.
32. Achebe, *Hopes and Impediments*, 2–3.
33. Ibid., 3.

At one level, the claim that homosexuality is—or at least was originally—Western is scrupulously Foucauldian. Foucault locates the emergence of homosexuality as a category characterised 'less by a type of sexual relations than by a certain quality of sexual sensibility' in biomedical and legal discourses circulating in Europe in the 1870s.[34] Historical materialists have attributed the emergence of non-normative sexualities at this time to the shifts wrought by industrial capitalism, urbanisation, and the advent of wage labour. As John D'Emilio explains, these processes weakened the centrality of the family as the primary unit of material subsistence, enabling the emergence of ideologies of individuality and the refusal of compulsory heterosexuality.[35] Drawing on one or both of these logics, queer postcolonial scholars have accounted for the emergence of queer sexualities in the global South with reference to a range of vectors and processes including the globalisation of capital,[36] human rights discourses,[37] and HIV/AIDS funding.[38] Common to these accounts is a diffusion narrative in which sexualities that were first expressed in the West come to be articulated in other locations, albeit in locally specific ways. Yet Foucauldian accounts of the transnational diffusion of a politics of sexuality in no way deny the ubiquity of same-sex desire across time and space. Conservative proclamations that 'homosexuality is Western', on the other hand, are usefully ambiguous on the question of whether they are referring to sexual identities or acts. The suggestion that their objection is to novel sexual identities rather than familiar, if disagreeable, acts is muddied and rendered disingenuous by the fact that the laws against 'carnal intercourse' of which they are such vociferous defenders focus squarely on acts.

The claim that 'homophobia is Western' is similarly evasive without being untrue. 'Homophobia' presumes the existence of something called 'homosexuality' to which it is antithetical. This is true even if, as in the case of anticipatory homophobia, it temporally precedes the appearance of 'homosexuality' in a particular location. Whether it comes before or after 'homosexuality' or blooms alongside it, contemporary 'homophobia' seems to take tellingly similar forms in different places, betraying its movement—one might say its 'importation'—across borders. This is the story that activists are trying to tell by pointing to the transplantation of colonial penal codes across borders and to the transnational organising of

34. Foucault, *Will to Knowledge*, 43.
35. D'Emilio, 'Capitalism and Gay Identity'.
36. Altman, *Global Sex*.
37. Massad, 'Re-orienting Desire'.
38. Seckinelgin, 'Global Activism'.

contemporary anti-gay activists. At the same time, if 'homophobia' is tied to an imported ontology of sexuality, it may be too narrow and novel a category to encompass indigenous affective aversions toward non-normative sex and gender that predate and persist alongside this ontology. The disinclination to contemplate the possibility of such affects romanticises the indigenous precolonial as a spacetime of unmitigated tolerance, generating the discourse of what I am calling homoromanticism. Indeed, such a discourse may encourage a flawed understanding of even what is appropriately called homophobia. For while the import narrative is persuasive as an account of the origins of homophobic law, it fails to account for the embrace and resignification of colonial laws by postcolonial elites or indeed the promulgation of new laws such as the AHA. Let us see how these problems play out more specifically in the Ugandan context.

Most commentators trace the immediate impetus for the AHA to the virulent anti-queer sentiments expressed at the March 2009 seminar held in Kampala and, more generally, to the close relationships between Ugandan politicians and clergy and the US-based Christian Right.[39] Kapya Kaoma has argued that the activities of US evangelical Christians in Africa should be understood as 'collateral damage' from the US culture wars.[40] Having lost domestic battles around issues such as the ordination of women and queers as bishops, or the blessing of same-sex unions, conservatives within mainline Episcopal, Methodist, and Presbyterian churches in the West have begun to establish transnational alliances with what they take to be the more socially conservative branches of their denominations, principally in Sub-Saharan Africa, Latin America, and Southeast Asia. Forged through the distribution of funds via evangelical development and humanitarian charities, these alliances serve two purposes from the point of view of their US participants. First, they empower conservatives to dominate the governing bodies of these denominations, enabling them to block progressive reforms such as the consecration of women and queers as bishops or the recognition of same-sex marriage. In doing so, they are acutely attentive to a politics of scale, hoping to win at a global level the battles that they have lost at national and local levels. Tsing reminds us that 'scale is not just a neutral frame for viewing the world; scale must be brought into being: proposed, practiced, and evaded, as well as taken for granted.'[41] As

---

39. Mukasa, 'Spreading Lies'; Gettleman, 'Americans' Role'; Sharlet, 'Straight Man's Burden'.

40. Kaoma, *Globalizing the Culture Wars*; Kaoma, *Colonizing African Values*. The narrative in this paragraph is substantially informed by these two reports, as well as Hassett, *Anglican Communion*.

41. Tsing, *Friction*, 58.

I shall discuss later in this chapter, the 'scaling up' of controversies over homosexuality to the level of the decennial Lambeth conference, a key global deliberative forum for Anglican Christians, has proved to be a crucial move in the struggle to renegotiate central tenets of the faith. Second, such relationships also provide spiritual refuge for dissident conservative evangelical Christians in the United States. This has become evident in a series of moves visible within the Anglican Communion, the constitutionality of which remains controversial. Dissatisfied with liberalising attitudes in the Episcopal Church (TEC)—the US 'province' of the Anglican Communion—some conservative parishes in the United States have broken ties with it and have placed themselves under the 'spiritual oversight' of bishops in Nigeria, Rwanda, Kenya, and Uganda. Simultaneously, some African churches have severed their relationship with TEC and announced themselves to be in communion with a rival entity—the newly formed Anglican Church in North America (ACNA). Central to these complex constitutional moves has been the decision of conservatives not to leave the Communion, which would have ceded ground to liberals, but to legitimate their dissidence with the blessing of conservative bishops in global South provinces.

What emerges from Kaoma's meticulous research is a transactional relationship in which US conservatives supply money in return for the political and spiritual support of their African allies. Homophobia, in this analysis, remains an essentially US preoccupation—a reaction to the advance of LGBT rights in the United States that, beleaguered on its home turf, sustains itself through international alliances by capitalising on the demographic strength and financial weakness of African churches. Indeed Kaoma emphatically recommends that we might better challenge the myth that human rights advocacy is Western neocolonialism 'by exposing the *Americanness* of the recent politicization of homosexuality and abortion in Africa.'[42] On the one hand, such an explanation provides a salutary corrective to homonationalist narratives of a primordial 'African homophobia' by offering a radically different geographical account of the construction of homophobia that also accounts for the timing of its salience at a particular historical juncture. On the other hand, Kaoma's largely instrumentalist account of the transnational politics of the US-based Christian Right begs questions about the political and theological values, beliefs, and agency of African clergy who are central to the relationships that underpin the ongoing institutionalisation of homophobia in Uganda.[43] Indeed, US

---

42. Kaoma, *Colonizing African Values*, viii (emphasis in original).
43. Anderson, 'Conservative Christianity', 1597; Lee, 'Extraversion', 139.

conservatives reject liberal criticisms of their relationships with African churches as racist in their portrayal of African clergy as pliant instruments of American will. In more recent work, Kaoma has been careful to acknowledge that Africans are primary agents in the sexual politics of the continent, with their allies in the North playing a secondary role. Yet the substance of his argument remains largely unchanged, for this acknowledgement is immediately followed up with the claim that African sexual politics 'involves transfer of resources, ideologies and tactics from the like-minded global North activists to African players' on both the queerphilic and queerphobic sides of the debate, implying that African sexual politics is largely derivative of analogous debates in the West.[44]

Kuchu activists have been complicit in co-producing the narrative that homophobia is a Western import, not least because of its tactical utility in deflecting the charge that homosexuality is Western. Nonetheless, some Ugandan writers have expressed discomfort with the manner in which such a narrative minimises the agency of Ugandans in their own politics. Voicing scepticism of the import narrative, Sylvia Tamale quotes a proverb in Luganda 'Kyewayagaliza embazzi kibuyaga asude', which she translates literally as 'the tree you wanted to chop down has been uprooted by a thunderstorm.' Tamale interprets this as implying that 'chance favours a prepared mind.'[45] This demands a reframing of our inquiry. Even if homophobia were 'imported' into Uganda from elsewhere, we need to ask why it found fertile soil in which to thrive there.

PLACE *AS* TIME: A QUEER POSTCOLONIAL MATERIALIST VIEW

Underlying discourses of homonationalism and homoromanticism is a modular view of queer and anti-queer affect as transportable from one place to another and as bearing a kind of stamp of origin. Such a view also presupposes a conception of places as discrete, bounded entities endowed with distinctive essences that can be conceived of in isolation from one another and juxtaposed against each other. Yet critical geographers have long pushed back against such understandings of place. Rejecting the common-sense equation of space with stasis, feminist geographer Doreen Massey begins from the premise that space is constructed out of social relations that are inherently dynamic.[46] This leads her to think of place 'as

44. Kaoma, 'African or un-African', 126.
45. Tamale, 'Politics of Nonconforming Sexualities', 34.
46. Massey, *Space, Place and Gender*, 2.

a particular articulation of those relations, a particular *moment* in those networks of social relations and understandings.'[47] For Massey, the mix of social relations that constitute a place are not all included within its boundaries, with many stretching well beyond what are thought to be its confines. This means that the particularity of any place is constructed 'not by placing boundaries around it and defining its identity through counter-position to the other which lies beyond it, but . . . through the specificity of the mix of links and interconnections *to* that "beyond." '[48] Thus, Massey's conceptualisation of place foregrounds its temporal and relational character. As she puts it, 'places can be conceptualized as processes.'[49]

In a survey of the literature on place, Marxist geographer David Harvey takes issue with Massey's view. While sympathetic to her political critique of static and exclusivist understandings of place, Harvey regards her more dynamic and porous conceptualisation as sacrificing much of what the concept was intended to capture analytically (specificity, uniqueness) and politically. Place, Harvey says, cannot both be open and function in the way that left localist critiques of neoliberal globalisation want it to—as an incubator of alternatives to global hegemonies.[50] But one might make a distinction here, as Massey does, between the way places *are* currently seen and the ways in which they *might* be seen.[51] As she explains, views of place that appeal to its putative essence are typically referring to a particular moment when the character of that place and the social relations dominant within it were to the advantage of the groups advancing these claims.[52] Crucially, the success of such claims relies on a mystification of their temporal character. Those asserting a particular definition of place not only offer an account that is frozen at a convenient moment in time, but also mask the act of freezing so as to convey the impression of timelessness.

Not unrelatedly, Harvey refers us to Alfred Whitehead's understanding of places as entities that achieve relative stability for a time in their bounding and internal ordering, occupying a piece of space in an exclusive way for that time. Describing such entities as 'permanences', Whitehead understood place-formation as the process of 'carving out "permanences" from a flow of processes.' Yet 'permanences', in Whitehead's view, are not eternal but always subject to time, undergoing 'perpetual perishing'.[53] Such

47. Ibid., 5 (emphasis added).
48. Ibid.
49. Ibid., 137.
50. Harvey, *Cosmopolitanism*, 189.
51. Massey, *Space, Place and Gender*, 121.
52. Ibid., 169.
53. Harvey, *Cosmopolitanism*, 190.

a view mediates some of the tensions described earlier by acknowledging the temporal, processual, and relational character of place, while paying attention to the politics of its attempted stabilisation in the form of 'permanences'. This avoids the overly voluntarist belief that places might be easily reconstituted by new flows once they have achieved a certain stability in their bounding and internal ordering.

Postcolonial theory complicates this view of place by reminding us of the role of power in its (re)constitution. Through what he calls 'contrapuntal reading', Said argues that cultural identities ought to be conceived not as essentialisms, but as ensembles in which identities exist in relation to an array of opposites.[54] By way of illustration, he reads a number of ostensibly metropolitan texts in ways that reveal the constitutive role of colonial peripheries in their production, reconceiving the imperial encounter as one that produces 'overlapping territories' and 'intertwined histories'. We are reminded, for example, that it is Australian wealth that enables the *Great Expectations* that Pip entertains, that the order and civility of Jane Austen's *Mansfield Park* are enabled by surpluses from slave plantations in Antigua, and that Giuseppe Verdi's *Aida* was commissioned by the Khedive of Egypt to celebrate the inauguration of his new opera house in Cairo— itself intended as a symbol of a modernising Egypt's entry into international society. Core and periphery are constituted by movements of people, commodities, money, and ideas; but importantly, movement takes place in both directions, with consequences for both places, making imperative a recognition of the agency of the periphery in constituting the modern world.[55]

Homophobia and the Black Postcolony

Equipped with these more complex ways of understanding 'place', we can now return to the question of how the meaning of place becomes stabilised in ways that incorporate or disavow queer desire. Frantz Fanon's reflections on the relationship between sexual desire and racial antipathy have long provided an important albeit vexatious entry point into this question insofar as the black postcolony is concerned. Fanon's account of what Kobena Mercer calls the 'libidinal economy of Negrophobia' is shot through with what many queer theorists have read as 'homophobia' as a result of his

54. Said, *Culture and Imperialism*.
55. Barkawi and Laffey, 'Postcolonial Moment'.

tendency to explain racism as a concomitant of sexual 'perversion'.[56] Fanon describes the white supremacist imaginary as reducing the black body to the sexual and the biological: 'In relation to the Negro, everything takes place on the genital level.'[57] 'Negrophobia', then, becomes an expression of both fear of, and desire for, rape by the black man. As Fanon puts it, 'the Negrophobic woman is in fact nothing but a putative sexual partner—just as the Negrophobic man is a repressed homosexual.'[58] Fanon is deeply insightful here about the nature of racial and sexual hatred, understanding both forms of hatred less as straightforward 'phobias' than as unstable and explosive amalgams of desire and antipathy (including the self-hatred that comes from desiring what one is supposed to disavow). Diana Fuss usefully situates Fanon's observations as responses to the anti-blackness of a colonial sexual economy that exploited the sexual services of black people, used sexual humiliation and torture as instruments of subjugation, and endlessly reproduced the myth of the black man as violent, oversexed rapist to justify its own unrelenting violence. Fanon would also have been aware of, and reacting against, the then common equation of the homosexual 'invert' and the non-white 'primitive' in Freudian sexology.[59]

Nonetheless, when Fanon turns his attention (all too briefly) to same-sex desire, his argument acquires two troubling features. First, he seems to associate homosexuality with whiteness. In a footnote in *Black Skin, White Masks*, Fanon claims not to have observed 'homosexuality' in his native Martinique, but acknowledges the presence of gender-transitive individuals who, he insists, 'lead normal sex lives.'[60] The only Martinicans who become homosexuals, in his view, are those who travel to Europe, but even they do so under duress, as a means of eking out a living in a society that will offer them few opportunities. Homosexuality here is a function of white exploitation. Second, outside these limited circumstances, Fanon seems unable to imagine a same-sex encounter that is not cross-racial rape, with the result that he tends to read the violent cultural relations of colonial occupation under the sign of 'homosexuality' rather than the more appropriate 'homophobia'. As Lee Edelman has pointed out: 'where it is "given" that white racism equals castration and "given" that homosexuality equals castration, then it is proper to conclude that white racism equals (or expresses through displacement) homosexuality and, by the same token, in a reversal

56. Mercer, 'Decolonisation and Disappointment', 124.
57. Fanon, *Black Skin*, 157.
58. Ibid., 156.
59. Fuss, 'Interior Colonies', 31–32.
60. Fanon, *Black Skin*, 180.

of devastating import for lesbians and gay men of color, homosexuality equals white racism.'[61] In other words, the association of homosexuality with the castration effected by white racism marks out black queers as appropriate objects of antagonism for black liberation movements. Scholars of African sexualities have traced precisely these antagonisms in important strands of black liberation politics in Zimbabwe[62] and South Africa.[63]

I have long been struck by how black feminist and queer thinkers have not been content to leave the argument here. While acknowledging that 'Fanon had fucked up opinions about the homosexual', Keguro Macharia is profoundly disturbed by how the dismissal of Fanon as 'homophobic' has enabled 'white queer studies' to disengage with the conceptual problems posed by black and postcolonial studies in an attempt to 'protect its foundations in a West defined as white.'[64] He argues that 'if, following Fanon, the Negro represents genitality within colonial modernity, and if the term "homosexual" names a desire for genitality, then desire itself must be directed toward—or routed through—blackness understood as that which incarnates desire for/as genitality.'[65] As such, Fanon remains enduringly useful for queer studies in theorising 'how blackness comes to figure within and as desire, as the portal to homosexuality as desire' in conditions of colonial modernity, which is also the only kind of modernity we have known.[66] bell hooks is likewise candid in her criticism of Fanon, observing that his tendency to represent the psychic wounds of colonialism through the gendered metaphors of emasculation and castration effectively narrates colonialism as the violence of white men inflicted upon black men. Black women disappear in this paradigm, which presumes that 'all will be well when men are able to reach a level of homophilia: a quality of love for one and another that precludes the possibility of domination and dehumanisation so central to the maintenance of the coloniser/colonised relationship.'[67] Nonetheless, in an intensely personal meditation that insists on her profound debt to Fanon, she likens her relationship with him to her feelings of love and rebellion vis-à-vis her father:

> Already a resisting reader whenever I heard the sound of my father's own voice, I knew how to let go every sound he uttered that was destined to limit

61. Edelman, *Homographesis*, 55.
62. Epprecht, 'Black Skin'.
63. Stychin, *Nation by Rights*.
64. Macharia, 'Frantz Fanon'.
65. Ibid.
66. Macharia, 'Queer Genealogies'.
67. hooks, 'Feminism', 82–83.

and confine me as surely as I learned to cling to every word that brought me closer to a freedom that enabled me to leave my father's house—to leave home. It was the practice of being a resisting reader that enabled me to hear in Fanon's theories of decolonisation, paradigms I could use constructively in order to liberate myself.[68]

My own attempt at resistant reading refuses to take for granted the articulations between sexuality, racism, imperialism, and nationalism, which I suspect are more historically contingent, shifting, and amenable to rearticulation than Fanon might have supposed or his interpreters allowed. Here I am also mindful of recent queer scholarship that has warned against Africa-wide generalisations,[69] or what Chimamanda Ngozi Adichie has described as 'the danger of a single story.'[70] The story I tell in the remainder of this chapter tries to take seriously the specificity of the Ugandan experience. Taking its cue from the processual, temporal, and relational accounts of place in feminist, historical materialist, and postcolonial geography, it seeks to account for the role of claims about sexuality in the construction and stabilisation of 'Ugandan culture'. I focus on two key moments of transnational friction separated by over a century, both of which feature significant power shifts that opened up opportunities for Ugandan elites to redefine place. While focused on Uganda, the argument could have wider implications. One unfortunate consequence of the Fanonian reading of queer desire as a concomitant of white racism is that anti-queer animus becomes tethered to—indeed an expression of—anti-imperialism, which furnishes its legitimacy. In contrast, the Ugandan story reveals 'homophobia' to be more opportunistic, sometimes functioning in the service of imperial collaboration and at other times expressing a decolonial impulse. Unmasking this shape-shifting versatility might weaken the link between homophobia and anti-imperialism in Fanonian queer postcolonial discourse, opening up possibilities for the delegitimation of anti-queer affect.

'Homophobia' as Imperial Collaboration

The modern state of Uganda takes its name from Buganda, the largest and most powerful of the precolonial kingdoms that were merged to constitute

68. Ibid., 81. See also Muñoz, *Disidentifications*, 8–9.
69. Macharia, 'Homophobia in Africa'; Bennett, 'Subversion and Resistance'; Awondo, Geschiere and Reid, 'Homophobic Africa?'; Thoreson, 'Troubling the Waters'.
70. Adichie, 'Danger'.

it. Outsiders were first drawn into the affairs of the kingdom in the mid-nineteenth century, lured by the promise of ivory and slaves, as well as its strategic location at the headwaters of the Nile. They brought with them cloth, guns, and two of the major 'world religions'. Islam came first via Swahili-speaking Arab traders from Zanzibar and the East African coast, followed by the Anglican Church Missionary Society (CMS) in 1877 and the French Catholic White Fathers in 1879.[71] Historians remain divided over why the Kabakas (kings) of Buganda permitted their subjects to convert to the new religions. Some read the invitation that Mutesa I (1857–1884) extended to the missionaries as an expression of his desire for external ties that would facilitate the modernisation of his kingdom. He might have hoped that new belief systems would undermine the authority of the traditional gods, who had become too independent and subversive of royal power.[72] Or he might have calculated that the European great powers, which invariably followed on the heels of missionaries from their countries, could be useful in balancing the threat that he perceived from Egypt in the north.[73] Others suggest that the appeal of the new religions was primarily ideological, answering the deep spiritual yearnings of a Baganda[74] elite whose worldview had been shattered by a series of inexplicable disasters— epidemics, drought, famine, and military defeat—provoking a search for new ways of making sense of the world.[75]

Whatever the reason, by the time Mwanga II ascended the throne in 1884 at the age of eighteen, he inherited a kingdom whose elites were fractured along religious lines. Each faction was patronised by one of the many external powers encroaching on Buganda in the ongoing scramble for Africa: the Protestants were close to the British, the Catholics to the Germans, and the Muslims to the sultan of Zanzibar. Traditionalists in the court viewed all three groups with suspicion. Less adept than his father at balancing these rivalries, Mwanga responded erratically. The first signs of crisis were evident in a decree forbidding the Baganda from working for foreigners. Under its authority three Protestant converts at the CMS mission were executed in January 1885. Even so, traditionalists in the court led by the Machiavellian Katikkiro (Prime Minister) Mukasa, perceiving Mwanga as being too close to the Christian converts with whom he had

71. Ward, 'History of Christianity'.
72. Low, 'Converts and Martyrs', 154; Reid, 'Images', 282–283.
73. Oliver, Missionary Factor, 67.
74. The Baganda (singular: Muganda) are the largest ethnic group in the kingdom of Buganda and in the state of Uganda as a whole. Their language is Luganda. The adjectival form is Kiganda.
75. Brierly and Spear, 'Mutesa', 603, 609.

spent much of his youth, mounted a coup against him in February 1885. The coup was thwarted, in part because of intelligence received from some of the Christians, who were then rewarded with high office. Fearing a loss of favour, the Katikkiro and his allies worked to discredit the Christians, pointing to their links with external powers as evidence of their treachery. When news of the imminent arrival of the new CMS Bishop Hannington coincided with reports of German annexation of the port of Bagamoyo on the Tanganyika coast, they persuaded Mwanga to order the killing of the bishop in October 1885. The next victim, a month later, was Joseph Mukasa Balikuddembe, leader of the Catholic pages in the court, who had had the temerity to remonstrate openly with Mwanga over the murder of Hannington.

Balikuddembe's clash with Mwanga was sharpened by another more personal disagreement, of which the Catholic theologian J. F. Faupel provides what is still the most widely cited account.[76] Relying on missionary writings,[77] Faupel alludes darkly to the 'unpleasant vice', 'unnatural passion', 'works of Sodom', 'unwelcome attentions', 'shameful proposals', 'unnatural lust', 'shameful demands', 'unnatural vice', 'evil purpose', 'shameful treatment', but also more specifically to 'the vice of homosexuality', 'the vice of sodomy', and 'the practice of homosexuality' to which the young king was allegedly devoted, suggesting in culmination that it was the 'abominable vice' that provided the most proximate reason for Mwanga's conflict with the missionaries.[78] Balikuddembe had enraged Mwanga by going to great lengths to protect his wards from the Kabaka's solicitations. Notwithstanding his efforts to assert authority through the executions of 1885, Mwanga was filled with a sense of foreboding in the early months of the following year, interpreting a series of events—a fire in the royal enclosure, a lightning strike on the Katikkiro's house, the public conversion to Christianity of his own sister Nalumansi—as evil omens. Returning from an unsuccessful hunt towards the end of May 1886, he searched in vain for his favourite page Mwafu, only to be told that the boy was praying at one of the missions. In a rage, Mwanga ordered the execution of all Christian pages who refused to renounce their allegiance to the Anglican and Catholic missions. On 3 June 1886, thirty-two people were burned to death at the execution site at Namugongo (near present-day Kampala). While attentive to the broader geopolitical tensions of the moment, Faupel insists that

76. The narrative in this section is substantially drawn from Faupel, *African Holocaust*.
77. See, for example, Ashe, *Two Kings*, 101.
78. Faupel, *African Holocaust*, 47, 82, 83, 86, 91, 110, 125, 130, 137. The more specific references to 'homosexuality' or 'sodomy' are at 5, 9, 10, 68, 74, 137.

[t]o gloss over the unpleasant vice to which Mwanga was addicted would be to disregard the decisive factor in the story of the persecution. True enough, there was in Buganda sufficient hatred of Christianity and all that it stood for to produce an outbreak of persecution at any time, but this hatred could never have had free rein without the consent of the Kabaka. As Mwanga was himself attracted towards Christianity, it seems unlikely that he would ever have given his consent had it not been for the constant thwarting of his unnatural passion by the Christian pages.[79]

The killings continued sporadically until March 1888, galvanising the formation of a coalition of Muslims, Catholics, and Protestants that succeeded in deposing Mwanga in September that year. In the civil wars that ensued when the victors fell out amongst themselves, the Protestants eventually gained the upper hand with the assistance of the Imperial British East Africa Company (IBEAC), paving the way for the establishment of the British Protectorate of Uganda in 1894. Meanwhile, the White Fathers initiated proceedings for the canonisation of the murdered Catholic pages.[80] In 1964, Pope Paul VI recognised as saints the twenty-two Catholics who had been executed at Namugongo.

The story of the 'Uganda martyrs', or at least this version of it, places an instance of thwarted same-sex intimacy at the heart of what is essentially the founding myth of both the Ugandan state and Ugandan Christianity. Unsurprisingly, queer theorists have seized on this story to reflect on the irony of present-day African politicians and clergy disavowing queer bodily intimacies as a corruption introduced by Western human rights 'imperialism', when it was earlier waves of Western imperialism that appear to have delegitimised such practices in the first place.[81] In this vein, Hoad brilliantly reads Mwanga as a queer anti-imperialist patriot 'who fucked (with the full and bizarre semantic range of that verb) both Christianity and imperialism and ultimately lost.'[82] I want to suggest that we need to do more than simply register the remarkable reversal of the articulations of queerness with imperialism and anti-imperialism evident in the temporal gap between this moment and our own, through a more careful tracing of how, when, and why attitudes toward something that comes to be called 'sexuality' change in ways that have implications for belonging

79. Ibid., 82.
80. Thoonen, *Black Martyrs*, 282–291.
81. Hamilton, 'Flames'; Hoad, *African Intimacies*; Parkinson, 'Mwanga's Ghost'; Guma, 'Narratives of "Saints" and "Sinners"'.
82. Hoad, *African Intimacies*, 19–20.

and for the definition of place. In telling this story, it becomes evident that the martyrdoms occasioned a moment of tremendous flux in which newly empowered elites seized the opportunity to redefine 'place' to their advantage, in ways that profoundly implicated sexuality.

Hoad's reading of the martyrdoms offers a useful starting point, not least for its caution against imposing a modern sexual identitarian interpretation on the narrative, notwithstanding the rhetoric of abomination with which the missionary sources are replete. Beginning from a position of uncertainty about the way in which Mwanga's contemporaries viewed his intimacies with his pages, Hoad speculates that practices that might have served ritual, religious, initiatory, fealty-producing, and/or other public functions may have been recorded and re-coded by nineteenth-century European missionaries as 'sex', steeped as *they* were in discourses about perverse sexualities that were beginning to be articulated in Europe.[83] But might it be possible to say something more definitive about how nineteenth-century Baganda viewed the bodily intimacies of their Kabaka, and about how their attitudes might have shifted in this moment?

A key impediment to answering this question lies in the fact that most of the textual sources that are contemporaneous with these events were produced by European missionaries and heavily shaped by their investments. Subaltern studies historiography has long had to grapple with the challenge of 'reading' subaltern consciousness from archives that record the perspectives of elites. Exemplary in this regard is Ranajit Guha's technique of teasing a rebel insurgent consciousness out of the prose of counterinsurgency that documents its suppression.[84] Something similar might be done with the prose of canonisation, the quasi-judicial process for which leaves behind an extensive documentary record that, while produced and managed by church authorities, sometimes admits discrepant voices, particularly in the statements of witnesses attesting to the suffering and the miraculous powers of the martyrs. It is here that the first glimpses of Kiganda attitudes toward Mwanga's corporeal proclivities come into view.

In his account of the beatification of the martyrs in 1920 (a step precedent to canonisation), J. P. Thoonen records an important discrepancy between native witness depositions at a first tribunal hearing convened in November 1887, and those made before a second tribunal in 1913–1914. The first depositions by the native witnesses say nothing about Mwanga's bodily intimacies, although introductory statements by the missionaries

83. Ibid., 13.
84. Guha, *Elementary Aspects*, 15.

give much importance to his 'shameful passions'. In contrast, all the witnesses appearing before the second tribunal cited this as a cause of Mwanga's hostility to the Christians.[85] While these discrepancies do not shake Thoonen's faith in the centrality of 'sodomy' to the martyrdoms, they beg several questions. Does the lack of reference to Mwanga's bodily intimacies by the native witnesses appearing before the first tribunal imply that they found them to be unremarkable? Or were they too frightened to be seen to be testifying against their king? Could the shift in the nature of testimony given by the witnesses between the two tribunals suggest a process of tutoring by the missionaries with a view to improving the martyrs' prospects for canonisation? Or did it reflect a more widespread shift in the norms governing 'sexuality', in the course of which the Baganda might have internalised a sense of shame inculcated in them by the missionaries with respect to corporeal practices that had been unremarkable till the arrival of Christianity?

Some Baganda *did* produce textual accounts of the events they had witnessed, their ability to do so invariably being a mark of their elite status. Both Faupel[86] and Thoonen[87] insist that sodomy was not only unchristian, but also abhorred by the Baganda. In making this claim, both rely on a text on the customs of the Baganda by Apolo Kagwa, widely considered to be Buganda's first native historian and ethnographer.[88] Prefiguring the modern import/export discourse around sexuality, Kagwa observes in a chapter on marriage that Arab visitors to the court were responsible for the introduction of sodomy into Buganda.[89] This claim can be found even earlier in the autobiography of Ham Mukasa, whose illustrious career began in the court of Mutesa I and culminated in his service as Kagwa's secretary when the latter was Katikkiro of Buganda.[90]

The claim that sodomy was endemic amongst Arabs but unknown in Sub-Saharan Africa is a recurring trope in the colonial archive. The most notorious exposition of this thesis can be found in the 'Terminal Essay' of Richard Burton's translation of *The Arabian Nights*. Burton maps what he calls a 'Sotadic Zone' (named after the classical Greek poet Sotades whose verses dealt with homoerotic themes) stretching through the Mediterranean, West Asia, the northern half of the Indian subcontinent,

85. Thoonen, *Black Martyrs*, 168.
86. Faupel, *African Holocaust*, 9.
87. Thoonen, *Black Martyrs*, 6–7, 30–31, 53, 102.
88. Reid, 'Ghosts', 356–357.
89. Kagwa, *Customs of the Baganda*, 98.
90. Mullins, *Wonderful Story*, 176.

East Asia, and the Americas, where sodomy was reportedly endemic, while insisting that it was unknown amongst the 'negro and negroid races' except where imported by foreigners. Although he purports to explain the prevalence of sodomy with reference to climatic factors that allegedly induce a blending of masculine and feminine temperaments, this apparently geographically deterministic thesis is contradicted by numerous instances in the essay where he attributes variations in behaviour to racial, religious, and demographic factors, and indeed to the 'import' or transmission of sodomy from one place to another as a result of migration.[91] Burton would have been known to elites in Buganda in the 1880s, having claimed credit alongside John Hanning Speke for the (European) 'discovery' of the source of the Nile in Lake Victoria between 1857–1859.[92] So it is not inconceivable that the missionary and Kiganda accounts on which Faupel and Thoonen rely were informed by Burton's speculations on sexual geography, which happened to be published in the year of the executions at Namugongo (albeit initially only for private circulation). While Kagwa played the role of elite native informant to a number of colonial writers on Buganda,[93] the relationship between colonial European and early Kiganda writing was mutually reinforcing, with each informing and deriving legitimation from the other.[94]

What explains this peculiar mapping of sexual practice in colonial discourse? Rudi Bleys describes the complex ways in which imperial discourses of race and sexuality were articulated simultaneously and in analogy with one another. 'Racial' groups were gendered by being assigned positions along a scale of masculinity, even as sexual deviants within the metropolis were analogised with racial inferiors.[95] In part, this reflected threat assessments and the differential success of the imperial project in different parts of the world. The feminisation of the Americas, Asia, and the Pacific had much to do with the relative ease with which these spaces were penetrated by Western imperialism. In contrast, the Arab world, which successfully resisted colonisation for long periods, was masculinised in

91. Burton, 'Terminal Essay'. The climatological explanation is given at 207–208, 210. It is contradicted in references to Turks and to urban-rural variations in Asiatic Turkey (232), in claims about variation amongst Hindus, Muslims, and Sikhs in the Indian sub-continent (236), and in the incorporation of vast territories encompassing many different climatic conditions, such as China and the Americas (238, 240), within the so-called Sotadic Zone.
92. Kennedy, *Highly Civilized Man*.
93. See, for example, the 'Preface' in Roscoe, *Baganda*.
94. Reid, 'Ghosts', 356.
95. Bleys, *Geography of Perversion*, 45, 90.

orientalist discourse. Within this colonial sexual imaginary, Sub-Saharan Africa occupied a peculiar position as a place that was masculinised but conquered, and, in addition, as a place where the sexual perversions that Burton and others had mapped so attentively were thought to be absent. Bleys speculates that the demand for black slave labour aroused a European desire for black hypermasculinity, which seemed unable to contemplate the possibilities of black male effeminacy or same-sex desire. Even when colonial anthropologists began to report observations of same-sex behaviour, the discursive imperatives of the slave economy made it impossible to offer more comprehensive representations of African sexualities.[96]

Marc Epprecht suggests that the association of homosexuality with 'advanced' civilisations, exemplified in Edward Gibbon's writing on the decadent sexual morality of a declining Roman empire, produced the contrary stereotype of an exclusively heterosexual Africa. In this symbolic economy, Africa was regarded as too primitive and its people too close to nature to be capable of exhibiting the unnatural sexualities that were thought to be characteristic of more advanced societies. *Their* problem was a lack of control over their heterosexual instincts, an excess of natural virility, and a heterosexual lasciviousness that the civilising mission would have to tame. Where African same-sex conduct was undeniable, the sophistication that such behaviour was thought to embody was attributed to contact with more advanced outsiders such as Arabs, whose sordid reputation in orientalist discourse was already firmly entrenched.[97]

Sylvia Nannyonga-Tamusuza offers an important critique of Kagwa's claim that sodomy had been unknown in Buganda till its introduction by the Arabs. She suggests that there is something disingenuous about the claim, given the taboo on public discussion of matters related to gender or sexuality at the time. She points out that the Baganda did indeed have a word for sodomy—*bisiyaga*—which first finds mention in the Luganda Bible, prepared by European missionaries with Kiganda assistance. In her view, the claim about the Arab origins of sodomy originated with European missionaries who considered the Arabs their chief rivals in matters of proselytisation. Drawing on work in linguistics, she speculates that the term *bisiyaga* may have been adapted from the Arabic root *siag*, meaning 'against nature'. She reasons that even if the Baganda had practised homosexuality before the arrival of the Arabs, they were hardly likely to confess this to their European interlocutors in a context where such an admission

96. Ibid., 35, 46, 172.
97. Epprecht, *Heterosexual Africa?*, 39–42.

would incur severe condemnation.[98] This politico-linguistic analysis raises the possibility that the European-influenced Arabic-derived etymology of the Luganda word for sodomy might have offered nineteenth-century Christianising Baganda a moral alibi enabling a disavowal, through displacement onto others, of practices that their new religion considered sinful.

More significantly, Nannyonga-Tamusuza reconstructs the gender landscape of nineteenth-century Buganda in a way that allows us to see how differently gender was understood by Baganda at the time.[99] Drawing on oral history, she reveals how gender in precolonial Buganda was imbricated with considerations of status and space. Within the palace, *balangira* (princes) and *bambejja* (princesses) were gendered male, while *bakopi* (commoners) were gendered female regardless of anatomical sex. Outside the palace, *bakopi* assumed genders that tended to align with anatomical sex, although masculine women, feminine men, and celibates were assigned distinct genders. These shifting but highly regulated gender possibilities had a number of social implications. As men, *bambejja* were addressed as 'ssebo' (sir), initiated sexual liaisons, proposed marriage to *bakopi*, paid bride price, and did not bear children. The Kabaka was addressed as 'Ssaabasajja' ('Man among men'). All *bakopi* were his 'wives', with both anatomically male and female *bakopi* referring to the Kabaka by terms typically used for a husband— *nnanyinimu, omufumbo, bbaffe*.[100] These insights allow us to bring more specificity to Hoad's speculation that European missionaries might have misunderstood what they saw in Mwanga's court. Even if Mwanga's corporeal intimacies with *bakopi* in the palace amounted to 'sex' in the eyes of the Baganda, the ritualised fluidity of gender suggests that they might have regarded as heterosexual what nineteenth-century Europeans read as 'homosexuality'. This remarkable possibility also alerts us to the ways in which misreadings of gender identity might have underpinned the emerging 'homophobia' of European missionaries.

To understand why none of this finds mention in Kagwa's otherwise detailed inventory of Kiganda customs, we have to recall his political investments and allegiances. Barely escaping Mwanga's purges, he emerged

98. Nannyonga-Tamusuza, *Baakisimba*, 212–218.
99. Nannyonga-Tamusuza, 'Female-Men'. Her work might be located within a tradition of African feminist scholarship that has demonstrated how categories such as 'woman' and 'man', that are taken for granted in Western gender discourses, either did not exist (Oyěwùmí, *Invention of Women*) or did not definitively assign all social roles (Amadiume, *Male Daughters*) in a number of African societies prior to sustained contact with Western colonialism and Christianity.
100. Nannyonga-Tamusuza, 'Female-Men'.

as leader of the Protestant faction before going on to become a key collaborator with the IBEAC and its agent, Frederick Lugard, whose bluster and firepower were crucial to the eventual triumph of the Protestants and their British backers in the civil wars that followed Mwanga's ouster. Kagwa manoeuvred himself into the position of Katikkiro, holding the office from 1889 to 1925, well into the period of the British Protectorate. In a recent revisionist biography of Mwanga that seeks to rehabilitate him as an anti-imperialist patriot, Ugandan historian Samwiri Lwanga-Lunyiigo offers a damning indictment of Kagwa's collaborationist role in the advent of British rule over Uganda: 'just as Queen Elizabeth I had bestowed a knighthood on a notorious pirate, Francis Drake, so had King Edward VII bestowed a knighthood on Apolo Kagwa . . . Francis Drake delivered stolen Spanish gold and silver bullion and Apolo Kagwa delivered Buganda's sovereignty.'[101] In other words, the key ethnographic source on which the most authoritative accounts of the martyrdoms rely to claim abhorrence of sodomy in Kiganda culture was produced by a figure deeply invested in Mwanga's downfall.

The earliest written accounts of Kiganda culture were produced by a generation of ambitious, male modernising elites such as Kagwa, who were anxious to transform their societies in ways that better equipped them to deal with the onslaught of colonial modernity. Placed by force of circumstances in the influential position of being able to define 'culture', their ethnographic works ought to be read less as straightforward inventories of extant cultural repertoires than as political opportunities to redefine and stabilise the meaning of place in ways that they believed might better meet the political exigencies of the moment. In her account of the gendering of modernity in Iran, Afsaneh Najmabadi demonstrates how that country's nineteenth-century encounter with Europe elicited a number of different responses, many of which took the form of an embarrassed dissimulation or disavowal around practices that modernising Iranian elites were beginning to realise were considered barbaric by their putatively more advanced European interlocutors.[102] One result of this process, in Buganda as in Iran, was the effacement of indigenous gender performances judged to be sinful or deviant in the eyes of the colonial civilising mission, which many native modernisers embraced. Consequently, as Sylvia Tamale argues in the

<hr />

101. Lwanga-Lunyiigo, *Mwanga II*, 2. For a more ambivalent view of elites such as Kagwa and (Ham) Mukasa that regards them as seeking good relations with the British in order to secure colonial assistance in the development and modernisation of Buganda, see Kahyana, 'Shifting Marginalities'.
102. Najmabadi, *Women with Mustaches*, 32–54.

African context, notions of 'culture' articulated in the writings of these early modernisers, which cast a long shadow over contemporary debates around gender and sexuality, were effectively collaborative constructions by colonial and native male patriarchs.[103]

And yet, these concerted elite efforts at redefining place and culture cannot fully contain the contradictions and contingencies that marked engagement with the outside world. Buried in the pages of James Miti's unpublished history of Buganda is a tale of the contrasting fortunes of two allegedly Arab 'imports': sodomy and gonorrhoea. Miti writes that when Mutesa I contracted gonorrhoea, it

> became no longer a shameful thing to be infected with gonorrhoea; on the other hand, people foolishly prided themselves on having been infected with it. The disease was praised; and people encouraged it, just because it was a novel introduction and was so well spoken of. Gonococcal infection then came to be regarded as a mark of great daring and a means of earning respect from one's fellow men. Lines such as
> *He is a fool who hath no gonorrhoea*
> *He is a coward who this disease should fear*
> were frequently quoted and used by the people, and were even sung in public.[104]

Miti has harsher words for sodomy, which he condemns in two sentences as an 'immoral habit', a 'sin against nature', and a 'dirty game', making no further mention of the practice in an otherwise detailed description of the events culminating in the executions of 1886. If gonorrhoea could become fashionable through its association with Mutesa despite its alleged foreign provenance, why did sodomy not enjoy the same repute on the strength of its practice by Mwanga? And why does sodomy simply drop out of Miti's account altogether, following his terse condemnation of it? Like Kagwa, Miti spent the early years of his life as a page in Mwanga's court. He too escaped the purges of the early Christian converts, before going on to enjoy a career as an official in the government of the British Protectorate and as a chief in the Bunyoro kingdom. His account of escaping the purges is shot through with ambivalence. He speaks of returning to the scene of persecution because 'we felt rather ashamed of ourselves in running away from and leaving our fellows to suffer death alone.'[105] And he pre-empts accusations of

103. Tamale, 'Researching and Theorizing Sexualities', 20.
104. Miti, *Short History*, 131–132.
105. Ibid., 272.

cowardice with the insistence that the survivors 'suffered more by mental agony and apprehension by being left behind while all their fellows were taken away to the end of the sorrowful journey along which they had all travelled.'[106] His account is infused with an anxiety that history will judge the survivors of the purges to have been less devout than those who perished on account of their refusal to abandon their faith. Perhaps he feared that dwelling on the sexual shenanigans of Mwanga's court would invite unwelcome speculation about the reasons for which survivors had been pardoned or had managed to escape. Writing one of the earliest authoritative histories of his country as a member of the collaborationist native elite, Miti can scarcely bring himself to acknowledge rumours of the 'abominable vice' in the momentous events that he had lived through.

In contrast, the autobiography of Ham Mukasa offers a strikingly candid admission of participation in the 'vilest customs' that 'Arabs and Turks' brought to the court of Mutesa I.[107] More remarkably, Mukasa speaks of the 'evil lads' who frequented his father's house, getting drunk, smoking and trying to teach him 'other sins'—suggesting that these customs spilled out of the precincts of the royal palace.[108] He writes of the impression that the biblical story of the destruction of Sodom had on him, of the fear and mental distress that it caused him, of his dreams of Mengo Palace burning down and of being unable to run away.[109] The writing is leaden with guilt and self-flagellation in the repeated references to lusting after 'evil things'[110] and longing 'to get drunk, and to commit other sins'[111]—temptations avoided only thanks to lack of opportunity rather than fear of God. Mukasa's exhausting battle with himself is brought to an end in June 1896, when God sends him the Holy Spirit.[112] And it is here that we can begin to understand the candour of this narrative. Adopting what would later come to be the familiar idiom of the 'born again' Christian life story, Mukasa's public confession of sin operates both to check his own potential lapse back into wickedness and to offer the possibility of redemption to others still mired in the swamp of evil.

106. Ibid., 287.
107. Mullins, *Wonderful Story*, 176.
108. Ibid., 181.
109. Ibid., 187.
110. Ibid., 202.
111. Ibid., 203.
112. Ibid., 206–207.

One way or another—through silence, displacement, confession, and disavowal—Buganda's first historians and ethnographers refused sodomy a place in the inventories of Kiganda culture. So successful were these efforts that, as we shall see in the next chapter, for most of Uganda's post-colonial history, the events precipitating the martyrdoms were rarely seen to pivot on questions of gender and sexuality. The question for us here is how and why the effacement of queer corporeal intimacies has gone from being a concomitant of imperial collaboration in the late nineteenth century to an expression of anti-imperialism in our time.

It is widely agreed that 'homosexuality' was not a matter of public concern in Uganda till 1997–1998, when senior figures in the Anglican Church of Uganda (COU) began to articulate theological positions on the issue in the run-up to the 1998 Lambeth conference.[113] Although Catholics constitute the largest religious denomination in Uganda's overwhelmingly Christian population,[114] it is the Anglican Church that has historically been the most powerful religious institution in the country, owing to its close association with British colonial power.[115] Eight of Uganda's nine presidents have been Anglican, the only exception being Idi Amin, who was Muslim. The global politics of Anglicanism has therefore had considerable impact on Uganda; but as one of the largest provinces in the Anglican Communion, Uganda also influences the worldwide Communion. As such, it is to developments in the Communion that we must look in order to account for the timing of the emergence of rhetoric around homosexuality as a salient issue in Ugandan political life.

In the mid-1990s, the Communion was rocked by a number of controversies around the ordination of non-celibate homosexuals as priests and bishops in TEC. In 1996, a TEC ecclesiastical court dismissed charges against Revd. Walter Righter, the assistant bishop of Newark, who had been accused of heresy on account of his decision to ordain as a deacon a gay man living in a sexual relationship with another man.[116] In

---

113. Hassett, *Anglican Communion*, 84; Ward, 'Anglican and Catholic Churches', 135; Kintu, *Ugandan Morality Crusade*, 7.

114. The 2014 Census reported that Catholics constituted 39.3% of the population, followed by Anglicans (32%), Muslims (13.7%), and a category labeled 'Pentecostal/Born Again/Evangelical' (11.1%). This last category recorded the single largest increase in adherents, up from 4.7% in 2002, mostly at the expense of the Catholic and Anglican shares of the population. Source: Uganda Bureau of Statistics, *Census 2014*, 19.

115. Oliver, *Missionary Factor*; Gifford, *African Christianity*.

116. See 'The Trial of Bishop Walter Righter', accessed 3 August 2016, http://anglicansonline.org/archive/news/articles/1997/righter.html.

1997, Frank Griswold, who as Bishop of Chicago had ordained openly homosexual candidates to the priesthood, was elected presiding bishop of TEC. Both moves suggested an emerging consensus within TEC on the legitimacy of such ordinations. Anticipating that sexuality would figure prominently on the agenda of the 1998 Lambeth conference, disgruntled conservative Episcopalians convened a series of preparatory meetings at Kuala Lumpur, Dallas, and Kampala in 1997–1998, in an attempt to forge common positions with likeminded colleagues from global South provinces.[117] Kaoma is therefore correct to point to the role of US conservatives in initiating attempts to establish global conservative alliances against homosexuality.[118] He is less helpful in accounting for the receptiveness of African clergy to the American advance in anything other than material and instrumentalist terms.

Miranda Hassett helps us to understand this receptiveness by drawing attention to a dramatic reframing of Africa's position in the Anglican Communion at this time.[119] Long portrayed as a troubled continent mired in poverty and corruption, Africa was now courted by US conservatives as the solution to the problems that bedevilled the Communion. By way of example, Hassett cites a speech delivered by Stephen Noll, a key Episcopalian dissident, at the Dallas meeting in September 1997. Attempting to persuade African clergy to take seriously an issue to which they had hitherto devoted little attention, Noll says:

> when America sneezes, the whole world catches a cold. In the case of the sexuality virus, it has already spread to most Western churches of the Communion, and Southern hemisphere churches will be exposed more and more because of the financial, educational, and media influence of the West . . . it is crucial for the rest of the Anglican Communion to take notice and 'come over and help us'. It has frequently been said in recent years that Third World Anglicans are in a much stronger place spiritually than Westerners and that re-evangelization of the original colonizing nations is called for.[120]

Noll makes some interesting moves in these remarks. First, he cautions Anglicans in the global South that although homosexuality might not currently be high on their list of priorities, it ought to be, even if only to preempt the spread of the 'sexuality virus'. Second, in a remarkable reversal of

117. Hassett, *Anglican Communion*, 47–70.
118. Kaoma, *Globalizing the Culture Wars*.
119. Hassett, *Anglican Communion*.
120. Noll, 'Handwriting on the Wall'.

the imaginative geography of secular discourses of humanitarian intervention in which, typically, the affluent West intervenes in a benighted Third
World, Noll calls for the opposite. Third, this Third World rescue mission,
in Noll's rendering of it, carries the libidinal promise of a reversal of the colonial civilising mission: those who were once at the receiving end are now
charged with penetrating the darkness of a disenchanted world.

Noll's biography reveals an interesting circularity of influence that
attests to the mutual constitution of core and periphery in the Anglican
Communion. At the time of his 1997 intervention, Noll had been based at
the Trinity (Episcopal) School for Ministry in Ambridge, Pennsylvania.[121]
As Kevin Ward explains, the Ambridge seminary espoused an explicitly
evangelical and charismatic brand of Anglicanism more akin to that of the
COU than the Anglo-Catholicism of TEC. This was due in no small part to
the influence of its first Principal, the Australian bishop Alfred Stanway,
who had worked in East Africa where he had been deeply influenced by
the spirit of Balokole, a revivalist movement notable for its puritanical
sexual ethics that began in the COU in the late 1920s. In 2000, in a further
deepening of these links, Noll was recruited by the then Archbishop of the
COU, Livingstone Mpalanyi Nkoyoyo, to serve as the first Vice Chancellor
of Uganda Christian University. This gave him an ideal vantage point from
which to continue to shape dissident Episcopalian positions on the future
of the Anglican Communion while also giving the COU a high profile role
in this endeavour.[122]

Hassett describes well the many ironies inherent in the position of the
conservative US Episcopalians:

> [The] newly developed global-mindedness of the conservative Episcopal
> camp is surprising to many other Americans, who do not generally expect so-
> cially conservative white people to think, talk, and work in terms of greater
> relationships with the global South across racial and cultural boundaries. Social
> and moral conservatism in the United States tends to correlate with American
> exceptionalism, a view of the United States as a special nation with a unique
> global role—usually one of leading, teaching, and intervening in other nations.
> In contrast, Episcopal conservatives in the late 1990s were increasingly arguing
> that the Episcopal Church, and the United States in general, had a problem that
> needed intervention and correction from other nations—and not just any other
> nations, but the poor and marginalized nations of the global South.[123]

121. https://contendinganglican.org/about-stephen-noll/, accessed 2 December 2018.
122. Ward, 'Anglican and Catholic Churches', 136.
123. Hassett, *Anglican Communion*, 65.

Conservative overtures to African clergy must have seemed a refreshing contrast to liberal Episcopalian criticisms of African positions on sexuality, which tended to come across as condescending or even racist. Recalling their 'appalling proposal . . . to approve of homosexuality as an alternative lifestyle', Nkoyoyo, who was Archbishop of the COU at the time of the 1998 Lambeth conference, offers the following recollection of the meeting:

> [S]ome bishops from western countries had a patronising attitude towards the African Church. On the one hand, they believed that Africans were incompetent in theological reflection and, therefore, not qualified to contribute to the development of Anglican theology. An impression was being made that in the same way the African church received the faith from western churches, they were obliged to endorse the compromises that the western church had, in many places, taken on board against the teaching of the Holy Bible [. . .] there was also a general feeling that the African church was severely impoverished, and largely dependent upon western aid for her development activities. It was believed that this dependency did not give her the authority to take a strong stand in defence of the scriptures [. . .] The main question . . . was whether the belief and practice of the Anglican Communion would be based upon the teaching of the scriptures or whether it would be determined by the practices that had come to be accepted in western culture.[124]

Nkoyoyo and the other Ugandan bishops were convinced that 'although the western Missionaries had planted the initial seed of the gospel, the seed had grown and matured to a status where the African church could state her own position and challenge any teaching that conflicted with the Holy Bible.'[125] In the event, delegates at Lambeth made clear that they were 'rejecting homosexual practice as incompatible with Scripture', while promising in a more conciliatory vein to minister to all persons regardless of sexual orientation.[126]

The resolution did little to heal the rifts in the Communion. In 2003, liberal Episcopalians were seen to have upped the ante when the openly gay and non-celibate Gene Robinson was consecrated as Bishop of New Hampshire, triggering an unprecedented rupture in relations between

124. Mbabazi, *Leadership Under Pressure*,143–144.
125. Ibid., 144.
126. Lambeth Conference 1998, Section I.10—Human Sexuality, accessed 4 August 2016, http://www.anglicancommunion.org/resources/document-library/lambeth-conference/1998/section-i-called-to-full-humanity/section-i10-human-sexuality?author=Lambeth+Conference&subject=Human+sexuality&year=1998.

several Anglican provinces and TEC. In 2006, Nkoyoyo's successor as Archbishop of the COU, Henry Luke Orombi, formally broke communion with TEC.[127] Orombi directed much of his ire at the then Archbishop of Canterbury, Rowan Williams, for his failure—in his capacity as symbolic head of the Anglican Communion—to hold TEC to account for its perceived departures from the 1998 Lambeth resolutions. Justifying his intention to boycott the 2008 Lambeth conference, Orombi bemoaned the obsolescence of the very architecture of the Communion, deriding Canterbury's position of spiritual leadership as 'a remnant of British colonialism'[128] and declaring elsewhere that 'the long season of British hegemony is over.'[129] In both Nkoyoyo and Orombi, we can hear a desire to assert the theological maturity of a postcolonial African church within a more egalitarian Communion. Reflecting on the meaning of Anglicanism, Orombi suggests that this project of decolonisation requires delinking Anglican belief and practice from British culture. Orombi seeks to disembed scripture from its historical context, insisting on its 'primacy, clarity, sufficiency, and unity' in an attempt to protect Christian life from the vicissitudes of cultural change.[130]

Read in this way, sexuality seems almost incidental to these debates. Although profoundly consequential for the sexual lives of millions of people, the affective investment of African clergy in these debates seems driven as much by an anti-colonial impulse as by convictions about the merits of an issue to which they had not devoted considerable attention before this moment. In much the same way that Lata Mani reads the position of Indian widows in debates over sati abolition between British officials and male Indian nationalists in colonial India,[131] one might say that queer bodies become the terrain on which the antagonists contend. This view of sexuality as a terrain or ground of struggle, rather than a substantive value integral to the essence or identity of place, might also account for the apparent ease with which 'homophobia' switches positions in relation to the imperialism/anti-imperialism binary over the course of Uganda's postcolonial history.

Curiously, Hassett retreats from such a conclusion, despite adducing a rich discursive archive that would appear to support it. In her view, the attribution of anti-homosexuality sentiment at Lambeth 1998 to

127. Ward, 'Anglican and Catholic Churches', 136.
128. Orombi, 'Church Cannot Heal'.
129. Orombi, 'What Is Anglicanism?'.
130. Orombi, 'Church Cannot Heal'.
131. Mani, *Contentious Traditions*.

postcolonial revanchism effectively absolves the Southern churches of any fundamental blame by conceding the legitimacy of their reaction.[132] She might say that such an attribution is another manifestation of what I have been calling homoromanticism, insinuating as it does that the global South can do no wrong because it has been so oppressed. But this would be true only if one had difficulty accommodating the possibility that the position of the COU is *both* decolonial *and* homophobic—a stance that demands a more complex moral reaction than has typically been forthcoming from either liberal Episcopalians or their secular LGBTI allies. To recognise the possibility of a decolonial homophobia is to understand that decolonisation promises only a more democratic way of making decisions; it does not presuppose that those decisions will necessarily have emancipatory outcomes. Political theorists have long recognised the possibility of 'illiberal democracy', in which democratically made decisions deliver non-liberal outcomes.[133] One can applaud the long overdue power shifts underway in the Anglican Communion while bemoaning the manner in which some newly empowered actors have chosen to exercise voice within it.

Perhaps even decolonisation is too simple a lens through which to understand the positions adopted at Lambeth by a number of African clergy. For many, the re-evangelisation of the former colonising nations that originally brought Christianity to Africa is a pressing imperative, seeing as they now appear to have lost their way. Orombi's counterpart in the Church of Nigeria, Peter Akinola, who was similarly critical of TEC and Canterbury for failing to enforce Anglican doctrine, was especially proactive in this respect. He established the Convocation of Anglicans in North America (CANA) as a missionary body to which disaffected TEC parishes could affiliate themselves under the oversight of the Church of Nigeria. CANA has its own bishops, who are consecrated by the Church of Nigeria to minister to conservative Episcopalians in the United States. (It is difficult to think of parallels in secular life, where US entities have seceded from US-based lines of authority to place themselves under the jurisdiction of an African counterpart.) Criticised for intervening in the affairs of another Anglican province, Akinola retorted that he was 'simply doing what Western churches had done for centuries, sending a bishop to serve Anglicans where there is no church to provide one.'[134] Elsewhere, he has complained of the double standards by which practices of intervention are judged:

132. Hassett, *Anglican Communion*, 110.
133. Zakaria, 'Rise of Illiberal Democracy'.
134. Polgreen and Goodstein, 'Axis of Episcopal Split'.

When America invades Afghanistan it is in the name of world peace. When Nigeria moves to Biafra it is an invasion. When England takes the Gospel to another country, it is mission. When Nigeria takes it to America it is an intrusion. All this imperialistic mentality, it is not fair.[135]

In Mary-Jane Rubenstein's reading of these theopolitical disputes, 'Akinola is not criticizing imperialism so much as he is defending his own right to exercise it alongside everyone else.'[136] She traces this impulse to what she considers the Communion's 'original sin': 'founded upon a strategy of socio-political imposition, every move it makes seems to one party or another a colonizing gesture. This being the case, the only available strategy seems to be reciprocation: England colonized Nigeria, which is looking to counter-colonize the very communities now threatening to re-colonize it.'[137] While Rubenstein is keen to think through other modes of community that might better enable living together in difference, her diagnosis of the Communion's contemporary predicament seems astute. It is also a salutary reminder that the desire for redress lives in close proximity to the drive for revenge.

While these readings add greater nuance to our understanding of the affective politics underpinning the expression of homophobia in the COU and the Anglican Communion more broadly, it is vital not to overstate the degree to which power has shifted within the Communion. The size and vitality of churches in the global South, contrasted with shrinking church attendance in the North, certainly give the former the demographic advantage, but the brute realities of international political economy mean that wealth remains disproportionately concentrated in the North. Moreover, Hassett's careful ethnographic work in the conservative TEC parishes reaching out to African churches reveals the endurance of troubling racial stereotypes. Far from portending a new egalitarianism in global Anglican relations, Hassett found that for many white conservatives in these parishes the attractiveness of African Christianity lay in its perceived primitiveness, which was thought to better guarantee its fidelity to the revealed Word.[138] Thus, to speak of 'homophobia' as expressing a decolonial impulse is not necessarily to imply the achievement of decoloniality.

There is more to say about the manner in which debates over homosexuality have deepened rifts within the Anglican Communion, but my focus

135. Gledhill, 'For God's Sake'.
136. Rubenstein, 'Anglicans in the Postcolony', 149.
137. Ibid., 152–53.
138. Hassett, *Anglican Communion*, 167–207.

here has been on the role of the COU in these debates. Antagonised by the liberalisation of TEC and some other Anglican provinces on matters of sexual morality, conservative dioceses and parishes continue to withdraw from their provinces and create new ones, such as ACNA and the Anglican Church in Brazil (ACB), which remain unrecognised by Canterbury as provinces of the Communion. At a global level, the Global Anglican Future Conference (GAFCON) has become the deliberative forum of choice for conservative Anglicans in preference to the Lambeth conferences. The COU has led the way in threatening to boycott Lambeth 2020 and other meetings convened by Canterbury unless 'Godly order is restored', which in practical terms entails the invitation of ACNA and ACB and the disinvitation of liberal churches such as TEC that are seen to have gone rogue.[139] Meanwhile, the Communion as a whole teeters on the brink of schism, held together for now by painful and tenuous compromise. In January 2016, in a move that was widely seen as a victory for conservative Anglicans, TEC was suspended for a period of three years from key voting positions in the Communion's organisational structures as a mark of censure for its endorsement of same-sex marriage.[140]

DIS/ORIENTING HOMOPHOBIA

In this chapter, I have tried to offer an account of the transnational production of homophobia in Uganda that navigates between the perils of homonationalism and homoromanticism. Against the homonationalist tendency to map (in)tolerance of queer desire onto place, I have attempted to demonstrate how unstable these associations have been over time. Much of the argument has rested on a temporal account of the construction of place that reveals the shifting status of same-sex desire in the national imaginary at different historical junctures, sometimes becoming a signifier of resistance to imperialism and at other times being seen to be an expression of it. At the same time, it is crucial not to assume that the relations between sexuality and nation are easily rearticulated. As I have tried to show, such realignments become possible in moments of political flux, when powerful social groups find it advantageous to redefine and stabilise the meaning of place. But 'place' by its very nature is sticky, and such opportunities do

139. Archbishop Stanley Ntagali Statement at Jerusalem 2018, accessed 3 December 2018, https://www.youtube.com/watch?v=ZBJdnafCfCY&feature=youtu.be.
140. 'Statement from Primates 2016', accessed 3 December 2018, https://www.anglicannews.org/news/2016/01/statement-from-primates-2016.aspx.

not come often. Against the homoromanticist tendency to absolve African actors of responsibility for the production of homophobia, I have tried to foreground their agency. If place is (re)constituted by transnational flows between places, we must think of those places as being in mutually constitutive relations with one another, notwithstanding the differences in power that might exist between them. In attempting to demonstrate the agency of the 'weak' in such processes of mutual constitution, I have tried to move beyond narrowly instrumentalist accounts that insist on measuring agency in the materialist currencies that generate the very hierarchies by which they are judged as weak, to take seriously the values and beliefs that inform their agency.

In attempting to unsettle orientalist practices of locating homophobia, I have also been inspired by the geographies of resistance of kuchu activists. In March 2012, the kuchu umbrella organisation Sexual Minorities Uganda (SMUG) sued the anti-gay activist Scott Lively in a US court. Filed under the US Alien Tort Statute (ATS), which allowed US non-citizens to sue in US courts for violations of customary international law or a treaty to which the United States is party, the suit alleged Lively's participation, in collaboration with a number of prominent Ugandans, in a conspiracy to persecute sexual minorities in Uganda on a scale sufficiently widespread and systematic to constitute a crime against humanity. In June 2017, the court affirmed that Lively's actions in 'aiding and abetting efforts to demonize, intimidate, and injure LGBTI people in Uganda' violated international law, but dismissed the case on jurisdictional grounds following a 2013 US Supreme Court decision that had limited the extraterritorial application of the ATS.[141] Quite apart from the practical reliefs that may or may not follow from this decision, the very fact of SMUG's suit against Lively offers the possibility of a different kind of humanitarian intervention—one in which the putative objects of liberal international humanitarian benevolence intervene, in their own interest, in the politics of their putative rescuer/oppressor. One of the unremarked-upon ironies of US-Uganda interactions over the AHA is that the US executive, intensely preoccupied with the question of how it might pressure the Ugandan government into withdrawing this draconian legislation, felt itself to be precluded from restricting the transnational anti-gay activism of figures like Lively by its constitutional obligation to respect the right to free speech of its citizens. Indeed, the Obama administration's Ambassador-at-Large for International Religious

---

141. *Sexual Minorities Uganda v. Scott Lively*, accessed 3 December 2018, https://ccrjustice.org/home/what-we-do/our-cases/sexual-minorities-uganda-v-scott-lively.

Freedom, David Saperstein, made it a point to defend the First Amendment rights of US religious figures who support anti-LGBTI initiatives abroad, despite their divergence from the stated gender priorities of the administration, 'so long as they [did] so peacefully.'[142] Although SMUG tended to have warm relations with Obama administration officials, the case against Lively wisely abandoned reliance on the ambivalent executive branch of government. Taking matters into its own hands, SMUG's intervention in the US legal process also offers an ironic counterpoint to the interventions of African Anglicans in the troubled internal affairs of TEC.

What are we doing when we compare places? In *The Book of Mormon*, a savage parody—appropriately enough, for the subject of this chapter—of the activities of US Mormon missionaries in northern Uganda, one of the missionary protagonists, Elder Price, prays that he will be assigned to his favourite place in the world: Orlando, in the US state of Florida. To his dismay, he is paired up with the bumbling Elder Cunningham and sent to a village in northern Uganda whose inhabitants struggle with poverty, famine, drought, AIDS, and a fundamentalist warlord who considers the clitoris to be an abomination that has brought the wrath of God upon the country. Despite the stereotypical frames through which northern Uganda is presented—or perhaps because they are wildly exaggerated to the point of parody—throughout the musical, the joke is very firmly on the missionaries. With the exception of the lead Ugandan character Nabulungi, whose interest in Mormonism is overdetermined by fantasies of love and emigration to the United States, for the most part the Ugandan characters are portrayed as sceptical of the promises of conversion, taking up their new faith with an ironic detachment born of long experience with the incursions of foreign religions. Traumatised by his first encounter with Uganda, Elder Price returns to Orlando—or rather thinks he has, till the vision of Orlando, in what turns out to be a nightmare, segues into a bizarre Dantean 'Spooky Mormon Hell' in which Price is brought face to face with the likes of Genghis Khan and Adolf Hitler as punishment for having failed in his mission. Out of his reverie, he is forced to confront the failure of his childhood utopia: 'Orlando . . . / Orlando . . . / I loved you Orlando / Your Bright Lights / Your Big Dreams / Your Promises You Couldn't Keep. / Orlando, Orlando, / Without You, Orlando. / I'm just a Guy. / Who Will Die. / And Never Go Back to / You.'[143]

142. Lavers, 'US Official Declines'.
143. Parker, Lopez and Stone, *Book of Mormon*, 97.

There is something uncanny about watching the show, as I did, in the aftermath of Omar Mateen's devastating attack on the queer Pulse nightclub in Orlando in June 2016.[144] Mateen killed forty-nine mostly Latinx queer people and injured scores of others in what was immediately described as the deadliest terrorist attack in the United States since those of September 11, 2001. Suddenly, the juxtaposition of Orlando and Uganda as epitomising pleasure and pain, respectively, looked less secure. Days after the massacre, kuchus held a vigil in Kampala in solidarity with the victims, which they tweeted under the hashtag 'UgandaisOrlando'.[145] For a brief moment, Orlando had shattered the illusion that queers could take their safety for granted anywhere. Perhaps out of that grim realisation might be born a more egalitarian solidarity.

144. See 'GLQ Forum/Aftereffects: The Pulse Nightclub Shootings', *GLQ: A Journal of Lesbian and Gay Studies* 24, no. 1 (2018).
145. Nyanzi, 'LGBTIQ Ugandans Mourn Orlando'.

CHAPTER 3

Re-Membering Mwanga, Mourning the Martyrs

Every June, hundreds of thousands of pilgrims congregate at Namugongo, the site of the execution of the Uganda martyrs on the outskirts of Kampala. They come from all over Uganda and further afield—Kenya, Tanzania, Rwanda, the Democratic Republic of Congo, and elsewhere. Some walk from their places of origin, sometimes for several weeks. On June 3, the anniversary of the execution of most of the martyrs, the road to Namugongo is a river of humanity. The visitor approaching from Kampala encounters the Catholic shrine first, where pilgrims await admission in endless, snaking queues. The atmosphere is festive. Hawkers line the street, selling food, clothes, footwear, religious books, CDs, posters, and souvenirs. Music, devotional and profane, blares from huge sound systems. Banners proclaim greetings from prominent political and religious figures and from the various dioceses to which the pilgrims belong. In recent years, the presence of security personnel has become more obtrusive.[1]

The Catholic shrine is dominated by its church, which the Vatican has designated a minor basilica. An immense, conical structure, the apex of which is visible from miles away, the building is a sleek, modernist interpretation of an African hut. Clad in a metallic grey material on the outside and wood panelled on the inside, the cone has twenty-two facets, each of which represents one of the Catholic martyrs. Twenty-two rods radiating out of the centre support the roof and are visible on the outside like a giant

---

1. These observations are drawn from three visits to Namugongo in 2010, 2012, and 2016—the latter two at the time of Martyrs' Day in early June.

Out of Time. Rahul Rao, Oxford University Press (2020). © Oxford University Press.
DOI: 10.1093/oso/9780190865511.001.0001

exoskeleton. Each facet of the cone rests on a wall fitted with a beautiful stained glass window depicting one of the martyrs. A short distance from the church is an artificial lake with an island pavilion in the centre, which is reached by a number of walkways laid across the water. This is the venue for the large outdoor mass that takes place on Martyrs' Day, watched by pilgrims assembled on the tiered seating constructed around the lake. The grounds begin to fill up several days before the climactic celebrations on June 3, as pilgrims arrive in groups and settle themselves and their belongings on the grassy slopes of the campus for the duration of their stay. People talk, sing, cook, pray, wash and dry clothes, or make confession to one of the many priests on hand. The mood is relaxed, as it might be at a picnic or a leisure outing, but the spiritual fervour of many of the pilgrims is unmistakeable. Around the Marion grotto and the statues of martyrs near it, pilgrims can be seen on their knees with eyes closed and rosaries in hand, or bent low, foreheads touching the ground. Some kiss the statues and relics or read from Bibles. Many take photographs on their mobile phones. All attend one or more of the services taking place in several different languages in the basilica.

A short walk down the road stands the Anglican shrine dedicated to the memory of the twenty-three Anglican martyrs who perished in the 1886 purges. Because the Anglican Church does not recognise saints, the theological focus here is on remembrance, rather than worship. Despite the smaller size of the services conducted here, the Anglicans pride themselves on the fact that their memorial is constructed on the site where all but one of the martyrs were killed. The focal point here is a small chapel whose altar stands over the mass grave in which the remains of the martyrs— both Catholic and Protestant—are buried (a guide informed me that they were buried together because it was impossible to tell the Catholic ashes from the Protestant ones). Till recently, the chapel stood outdoors and was surrounded by a number of exhibits: a life-size model of the martyrs awaiting their burning on a pyre, the executioner standing by to carry out his orders, and the remains of a tree to which the martyrs are believed to have been tied and then tortured before their deaths. In 2015, a museum was opened to house many of these structures. This is a large double-domed building that now incorporates the chapel as well as a new exhibit featuring highly graphic sculptural representations of the martyrdoms. Very little is left to the imagination by the figures of martyrs being disembowelled or dragged on their backs to their executions. The Anglican premises also house the Namugongo Martyrs' Seminary, comprising a library, dining hall, classrooms, and accommodation. The land slopes down gradually towards a grassy hollow, on the rim of which stands a larger church. At the bottom of the hollow lies 'Mukajanga's well'—named after the chief executioner—the waters of which are believed to be holy because the executioners are said to have used it to wash the blood of the martyrs off their implements. Pilgrims queue to collect the holy water in plastic jerry cans. On Martyrs' Day, the main Anglican service is held outdoors in the hollow for a congregation of several hundreds.

Across the road from the Anglican shrine, hidden behind a row of shops, stands the Namugongo mosque. It is a small, single-storey structure built on the site where over seventy Muslims were executed in 1875–1876 on the orders of Mutesa I. His early encouragement of Islam had turned to antipathy when the new converts began to insist on observance within the palace of dietary rules and corporeal practices such as circumcision.[2] A foundation stone laid by Idi Amin in the 1970s offers a reminder of a time in which commemoration of the Muslim martyrs was encouraged. The local imam lives in a cluster of huts to one side of the structure. In comparison with the grandeur and popularity of the Catholic and Anglican sites, the deserted air of the mosque—at least on the days I visited—and the evident poverty in which its caretakers live seem like metaphors for the relative positions of the different communities in Ugandan history and politics.

How does commemoration of the martyrdoms, the most authoritative accounts of which pivot around the practice of 'sodomy' by Kabaka Mwanga with pages in his court, coexist with the claim that same-sex intimacy is alien to Ugandan culture? As I mentioned in the previous chapter, queer theorists have revisited this story in a variety of ways to explore whether and how it might be claimed by sexual minority activists to rebut the suggestion that their corporeal intimacies are culturally inauthentic. Criticising a tendency among postcolonial African historians to downplay the sexual and emotional content of Mwanga's decisions in favour of more sanitised political readings, Kenneth Hamilton offers an avowedly sex-positive rendering of the story that seeks to restore the centrality of sexual desire in moving the political and historical narrative.[3] In contrast, Neville Hoad scrupulously avoids a sexual identitarian reading of the dramatis personae on the ground that this would be anachronistic; he nonetheless argues that whatever Mwanga's corporeal intimacies meant to his contemporaries, they were read by missionaries and colonial authorities as a mark of defiance against Christianity and Western imperialism.[4] By recasting Mwanga as queerer or more patriotic than the standard narrative

2. Brierly and Spear, 'Mutesa', 602; Low, 'Converts and Martyrs', 155–156.
3. Hamilton, 'Flames of Namugongo', 196.
4. Hoad, *African Intimacies*, 19–20.

allows, these interpretations seek to revise hegemonic renditions of the martyrdoms as a tale of persecution of innocent Christians by a predatory sodomite.[5]

Subversive as they may be, these readings essentially take the form of a deconstructive excursus through a textual archive in which the theorist uses critical approaches to prise open the story at points of ambiguity in order to admit counter-hegemonic readings. Yet these alternative readings lack any grounding in the popular. Most queer theoretical engagements with the martyrdoms seem oblivious to the scale of their popular commemoration, not only in the annual celebrations on Martyrs' Day, but also through a more quotidian circulation of the story in the form of pamphlet hagiographies, school history curricula, dramatic and cinematic representations, and so on. In other words, they have not been very interested in contemporary Ugandan memory of the events of the late nineteenth century and in the way this might shape views about the perceived indigeneity or foreignness of same-sex intimacy. I ask whether everyday memory of the Uganda martyrdoms places 'sodomy' at the heart of the narrative in the way that the most popular textual accounts do. If so, what possibilities for contemporary sexual dissidence lurk within public memory? If not, what genealogies of amnesia (perhaps even 'homophobia') might we extract from a study of public memory?

MEMORY AND HISTORY

Rather than seeking to excavate something that is buried or to recall what has been forgotten, my interest here is in exploring the possibilities for sexual dissidence immanent within practices of intense memorialisation. My interest in memory was provoked by the intuition that it might offer possibilities for immanent critique that were less didactic, and therefore more democratic, than those that might emerge from discourses of history or human rights. Because a strategy that relies on memory seeks to activate resources that are always already available in public discourse rather than to inject new ideas into a discursive context in which newness is stigmatised as inauthentic, it carries the promise of greater political effectiveness. I use the verb 'activate' in the spirit of Walter Benjamin's exhortation to 'take control of a memory, as it flashes in a moment of danger' with a view to 'setting alight the sparks of hope in the past.' Memory, for

---

5. See also Parkinson, 'Mwanga's Ghost'; Guma, 'Narratives of "Saints" and "Sinners" '.

Benjamin, did not purport to narrate '"how it really was"'; rather, to take control of memory entailed the effort 'in every epoch . . . to deliver tradition anew from the conformism which is on the point of overwhelming it.'[6]

Pierre Nora offers perhaps the most categorical statement of the distinction between memory and history when he says:

> Memory and history, far from being synonymous, appear now to be in fundamental opposition. Memory is life, borne by living societies founded in its name. It remains in permanent evolution, open to the dialectic of remembering and forgetting, unconscious of its successive deformation, vulnerable to manipulation and appropriation, susceptible to being long dormant and periodically revived. History, on the other hand, is the reconstruction, always problematic and incomplete, of what is no longer. Memory is a perpetually actual phenomenon, a bond tying us to the eternal present; history is a representation of the past.[7]

On this account, my discussion of the martyrdoms in the previous chapter is an intervention in the register of history, attempting as it does to reconstruct how Mwanga's contemporaries might have viewed his bodily intimacies. An investigation of memory, by contrast, would explore how these practices were remembered and made sense of by subsequent generations from the vantage point of their respective presents. Yet the distinction is far from straightforward. The term 'history' is itself ambiguous, as Michel-Rolph Trouillot reminds us, referring in its vernacular usage to 'both the facts of the matter and a narrative of those facts.'[8] Understood as the distinction between 'what happened' and 'that which is said to have happened', these different vernacular connotations seem to map onto what the professional historian, following Nora, might call 'history' and 'memory', respectively. But framing the distinction in this way raises weighty methodological questions. Anti-positivists would point out that there is simply no way of accessing 'what happened' except through *someone's* account of 'that which is said to have happened'. History, one might say, is simply memory with an army.[9]

Persuasive as this conflation is, as Trouillot explains, it leaves nonpositivists in a dilemma. While they can point to multiple versions of 'that which is said to have happened', they cannot give a full account of the

---

6. Benjamin, 'On the Concept of History'.
7. Nora, 'Between Memory and History', 8.
8. Trouillot, *Silencing the Past*, 2.
9. I am indebted to Sundhya Pahuja for this formulation.

production of any of these narratives without recourse to some notion of history, for the reasons why a specific story matters to a specific group of people are themselves historical.[10] The very act of unmasking a narrative as an instance of special pleading presupposes a truer, or at least larger, account of events. This presupposition admits that the historical process has some autonomy vis-à-vis the narratives that are constructed about it. At the same time, narratives are produced in particular historical contexts. These tensions lead Trouillot to insist on both the distinction and overlap between historical process and narrative. Attempting to navigate a course between the extremes of positivism and anti-positivism, he brackets the question of what history is to focus on how it works, concluding that

> history reveals itself only through the production of specific narratives. What matters most are the process and conditions of production of such narratives. Only a focus on that process can uncover the ways in which the two sides of historicity intertwine in a particular context. Only through that overlap can we discover the differential exercise of power that makes some narratives possible and silences others.[11]

In an important methodological contribution to feminist historiography, Victoria Browne is similarly attentive to the necessity and difficulty of distinguishing between what I have been calling history and memory. While acutely conscious of the pitfalls of a naively positivist historical realism, Browne finds herself unable and unwilling to jettison an interest in 'what really happened'. She reminds us that where claims of injustice and atrocity are concerned, a disavowal of interest in 'what really happened' can be irresponsible. Drawing on the work of Paul Ricoeur, among others, she argues that although present assumptions, perspectives, and preoccupations condition our understanding of the past, the traces of the past which provoke historical enquiry in the first place also impose constraints on the kinds of meanings with which the past can be imbued. This gives the 'time of the trace' a nonlinear 'two way' temporality. As she explains, 'traces of the past "spill forwards" into the present, yet the historical past is also "constituted backwards" when traces are taken up and configured within a historical narrative.'[12]

Thus, although my interest in memory was initially stirred by the sense that it might provide a more demotic and subversive alternative to history,

10. Trouillot, *Silencing the Past*, 13.
11. Ibid., 25.
12. Browne, *Feminism*, 50–51.

I have come to distance myself from both those who draw stark distinctions between memory and history and those who collapse them into one another. The investigations in this and the preceding chapter might productively be read together as exemplifying the 'two-way' temporality of the trace. If in the previous chapter, traces of the past as contained in elite texts 'spill forwards' into the present in ways that perplex and confound the contemporary reader, in this chapter I am more interested in the ways in which these traces come to be taken up in the politics of the present. Mindful of Trouillot's reminder that narratives about the past are shaped by their historical context, the first half of the chapter provides a historical account of the production of memory about the Uganda martyrdoms.

The second half of the chapter draws on ethnographic study of practices of commemoration of the martyrdoms to offer a snapshot of contemporary memory, in which the echoes of prior accounts and understandings coexist with newer ones. I have found Carol Gluck's typology of terrains of memory useful in identifying and assessing the relative significance of different sources of memory. Gluck delineates four terrains of memory: official memory, encompassing activities connected with the state including government rhetoric, commemorative rituals, public monuments and museums, and national textbooks; vernacular memory, dominated by popular culture and the mass media; individual personal pasts, which can themselves be understood as forms of vernacular memory, but are more private and less organised; and meta-memory, in which debates about memory themselves become another field of memory.[13] The discussion in this chapter moves between these different terrains. Rather than disentangling 'memory' from something that might be called 'history', I find that fragments of contemporary memory bear the impress of, but also do battle against, claims that travel under the sign of history.

A BRIEF HISTORY OF MEMORY OF THE UGANDA MARTYRDOMS

One wall of the dining hall of the Uganda Martyrs' Seminary at Namugongo bears a mural depicting the arrival and development of Anglican Christianity in Uganda. The work comprises a number of panels, each of which portrays a different moment in this story. It begins with an image of Mutesa addressing his pages in the presence of the explorer Henry Morton Stanley. There follows an excerpt of a famous letter written by Mutesa to

13. Gluck, 'Operations of Memory', 52–58.

Queen Victoria and published in the London *Daily Telegraph* in 1875, in which the Kabaka invites British missionaries to evangelise in his kingdom, lamenting 'I and my people are in total darkness.' We are then shown an image of CMS missionaries in England huddled around this letter, followed by the arrival in Buganda of one of their number and the baptism of the first native converts. Immediately below this is an image of Henry Wright Duta speaking to a group of these converts with the Bible that he was instrumental in translating into Luganda in his outstretched hand. The focal point of the painting is a depiction of the executions at Namugongo. In the lower half of this central scene, we see one of the executioners on the verge of spearing a page. Above this panel, the unfortunate condemned carry bundles of firewood to build the pyre on which they will burn. The flames from the pyre rise up into the air, merging almost seamlessly with the wings of angels who appear to lift the martyred pages to the heavenly abode for which they are destined.

The second half of the mural abruptly shifts register to depict the good works of the church, with people engaged in a range of productive activities such as agriculture, shoemaking, carpentry, and chemistry. Symbols of modernity and progress—an aeroplane, a ship, trucks carrying books, and a final scene depicting a light-skinned doctor and a black nurse ministering to a visibly malnourished black child—dominate this section of the mural. The abruptness of the transition in the mural between the historical and political narrative of the first half and depictions of the everyday benevolence of the church in the second is striking. If the first half opens up questions about the frictions between Uganda and the West, the Buganda monarchs and the church, or indeed religion and politics more generally, the second half appears to smooth them over.

Any account of Ugandan memory of the persecutions of 1885–1886 must begin with the production of a cult of martyrdom by the Catholic Church. In a study of martyrdom in early Christianity, Elizabeth Castelli argues that martyrdoms cannot be understood simply as historical occurrences, but are produced through processes of narrative interpretation and retelling directed at particular audiences. Central to these processes is the effort to infuse violence and suffering with meaning by drawing them into a broader narrative about justice and the right ordering of the cosmos. The production of martyrdom can be understood as a way of refusing the meaninglessness of death by avowing its contribution to the construction of this longed-for order.[14] But Castelli also supplements her account of the psychic

14. Castelli, *Martyrdom and Memory*, 34, 173.

impulses underpinning the production of martyrdom with a more socio-political reading. In this regard, Ronald Kassimir has argued that there is no evidence of the emergence of a spontaneous cult of reverence towards the 'Uganda martyrs'.[15] Rather than incorporating a popular movement, the Catholic Church has been deeply invested in creating one. It has done so primarily through the institution of sainthood, its control of the formal procedures for which have allowed it to dominate the production of knowledge about the 'martyrdoms'. One measure of Catholic hegemony in this respect is the fact that even Anglicans rely on Catholic sources for knowledge of the persecutions.[16]

Kassimir is particularly insightful about the political motivations for Catholic interest in claiming the martyrdoms. Despite securing greater numbers of converts, Buganda Catholics were ultimately defeated in the civil wars of the late 1880s, largely because the Anglicans had been able to call on the resources of the IBEAC. Allocated the province of Buddu and assigned a lower number of chieftainships in the postwar power-sharing arrangements, aggrieved Catholics found in the martyrs a potent symbol for the suffering of their community in the new Anglican-controlled dispensation. Insinuating that they had sacrificed more to bring Christianity to Buganda, the Catholics' discursive capture of the martyrdoms may have been part of an effort to claim equal status vis-à-vis the Anglicans.[17] In addition, Kassimir notes a crucial shift between two early influential Catholic narratives of the martyrdoms, both of which I have referred to in the previous chapter. At the time that Thoonen was writing in 1941,[18] the martyrs had not yet become a national symbol, and the Catholic presence in Buganda was divided between the White Fathers, the Mill Hill Fathers, and the Verona Fathers, who were mostly French, British, and Italian, respectively. Faupel effects a crucial reframing by describing the martyrs in his opening paragraph as 'men of Uganda',[19] despite the fact that most of them were of Kiganda ethnicity and all of them had been raised, converted, and killed in Buganda.[20] Published for the first time in 1962, the year of Uganda's independence from British rule, Faupel's text was an

15. Kassimir, 'Complex Martyrs', 370.

16. At one of the Anglican services that I attended at Namugongo in 2012, a celebrant read excerpts of descriptions of the suffering of the martyrs from the Catholic Faupel's *African Holocaust*.

17. Kassimir, 'Complex Martyrs', 372.

18. Thoonen, *Black Martyrs*.

19. Faupel, *African Holocaust*, 1.

20. Kassimir, 'Complex Martyrs', 375.

instrument in the Catholic Church's effort to establish a national church across ethnic lines.

How was Mwanga remembered? Leaving aside the textual missionary sources, Kevin Ward makes a striking claim about the communal memory of the churches when he writes that

> Ugandans have not focused on the homosexual issue in the ways they have recalled and appropriated the story of the martyrs for the life of the Christian community. Rather, political questions of power and the limits of obedience have been fundamental: whether one's first loyalty is to an earthly, possibly despotic, ruler, or to God, the King of the Universe.[21]

Even within this framing of the story as one about the conflict between temporal and spiritual authority, the normative coding of its central characters has not been static. Ward cites an open letter written to the president of Uganda by one Nuwa Sentongo in the early 1960s, in which the writer bemoans the endurance of a colonial historiography that condemns Mwanga—failing to recognise his role in resisting foreign domination—and lionises his disloyal pages. Ward remarks that such invocations of Mwanga as an African patriot and of the pages as imperial collaborators were not uncommon at the time of Uganda's independence. He argues that narratives of the martyrdoms shifted during periods of authoritarian rule, particularly under Amin, when the martyrs came to be celebrated as symbols of resistance to tyranny.[22] Amos Kasibante locates this shift more precisely in the 1977 assassination of the Anglican Archbishop Janani Luwum, reportedly on the orders of Amin.[23] The timing of this event, falling as it did on the centenary of the arrival of Anglican Christianity in Buganda and almost a century after the murder of Bishop Hannington on the orders of Mwanga, might have facilitated a belated demonisation of Mwanga in Ugandan eyes through a process of analogical linkage with the figure of Amin.

These analogies appear to be at work in the speech that President Museveni gave at the Anglican shrine at Namugongo in 1986, both the centenary of the martyrdoms and the year in which his NRM assumed power after its ouster of Milton Obote's second administration. Implicitly comparing the violence of the Amin and Obote II regimes to Mwanga's

21. Ward, 'Same-Sex Relations', 90.
22. Ibid.
23. Interview with Amos Kasibante (Anglican priest, St. Cyprian's Church), Leeds, UK, 20 April 2012.

despotic abuses, Museveni invoked the martyrs as national and non-denominational symbols of resistance to tyranny, in an attempt to inspire his people to rebuild their devastated country.[24] Two important points emerge from these successive shifts in public memory. First, memory is powerfully shaped by the imperatives of the present. Second, the 'sexual' dimension of the story, so prominent in the early missionary accounts, seems to have been strikingly insignificant in Ugandan public memory during this period. Even condemnatory invocations of Mwanga focused on what made him similar to more recent autocrats, rather than on his alleged sexual idiosyncrasies.

To trace more recent mutations in the remembering of the martyrdoms, I analysed coverage of the annual Martyrs' Day celebrations by the newspaper *New Vision*. As the leading state-run national daily, the paper might be regarded as a significant terrain of official memory. I examined issues from the first week of June over a twenty-year period from 1991 through 2011. During this period, lead stories on Martyrs' Day reported on the sermons and speeches delivered at the Anglican and Catholic shrines at Namugongo, which typically sought to link the lessons of the martyrdoms to pressing political themes of the day—postwar reconstruction, peace in northern Uganda and the neighbourhood, and corruption, to cite a few examples. Subsidiary stories on the inner pages of the newspaper took a more historical or human-interest angle, recounting stories of the martyrs and the numerous shrines, commemorative practices, and cultural productions that immortalise them,[25] or sketching portraits of some of the less well-known figures associated with them.[26] Still other stories covered more prosaic and logistical aspects of the commemorations, such as the arrangements that had been made for pilgrims, traffic restrictions in force, and so on. Editorials and opinion pieces frequently bemoaned the unexploited tourist potential of the event. For much of the period analysed, there is virtually no mention of sex or homosexuality in the coverage, either in the context of recounting the circumstances of the martyrdoms or

24. Kassimir, 'Complex Martyrs', 382; Ward, 'Same-Sex Relations', 91.
25. Bisiika, 'Namugongo'.
26. Recent issues have featured stories about the Muslims executed by Mutesa I (Kabuye, 'Did You Know'), Hannington (Bisiika, 'Bishop Hannington'), survivors of the persecutions and their descendants (Baguma, 'My Grandpa'; Kalibbala, 'Bravery'), the chief executioner and his descendants (Mugisa and Waiswa, 'Family'; Lukwago and Waiswa, 'Mukajjanga'), later candidates for sainthood from the region including former Tanzanian President Julius Nyerere (Nsambu, 'Acholi Boys'; Kajoba, 'Catholics Pray'; Baguma, 'Nyerere').

in a more contemporary sense, barring a few stray references to sermons urging marital fidelity or responsible sexual behaviour in the wake of AIDS.[27]

This changes abruptly in 2004, when the *New Vision* issue of 4 June reports on Martyrs' Day celebrations held the previous day under the head-line 'Fight Homos—Odoki,'[28] quoting then Chief Justice Benjamin Odoki as urging Christians to fight vices such as 'homosexuality, pornography and political intolerance'. It also quotes then Anglican Archbishop Orombi as preaching: 'We will never be shaken by any immoral teachings infiltrating our country. They (martyrs) never compromised their faith, we will not compromise ourselves.'[29] In 2005, Martin Ssempa, the Pentecostal anti-gay crusader, published an opinion piece on the eve of Martyrs' Day, in which he characterises Mwanga as 'a deviant homosexual who used his demigod status to appease his voracious appetite for sodomy by engaging in these unmentionable acts with his pages at court.'[30] Attributing Mwanga's execu-tion of the pages largely to their refusal to take part in the 'homosexual ac-tivities of the court', Ssempa then uses the story to discredit sexual rights activists, asking:

> how are we reacting to the gradual global Mwanga who daily increases his legal machinery over the whole world. Using the agencies of media, education and global state; out-of-control judges, homosexual activists Trojan horsing as human rights, women [sic] rights, stigma and AIDS/HIV rights? What does this mean for the people whose faith and culture is ma-liciously denigrated and labelled as hateful, homophobic, heterosexist and unsophisticated?[31]

Ssempa concludes the article with a dramatic confession of his own ex-perience of being propositioned, as a seventeen-year-old break-dancer looking for a job, by a prominent unnamed Ugandan television personality. Insisting that he 'refused to bend over and missed out on the job', Ssempa vows: 'I will not stop advocating for more young men and women who will refuse to bend over one more time to the Mwangas of this generation.'[32] We

27. 'Pope Set to Visit Uganda Early 1993', *New Vision*, 4 June 1992; see reporting of Martyrs' Day sermons in *New Vision*, 4 June 1993, 2.
28. Namutebi, 'Fight Homos'.
29. Ibid.
30. Ssempa, 'When Faith'.
31. Ibid.
32. Ibid.

are presented with an image of the teenage Ssempa as a Ugandan martyr, resisting the depredations of a contemporary Mwanga to his professional detriment, and urging fellow Ugandans to emulate his example. By the time Museveni warned of the dangers of sodomy in his 2010 Martyrs' Day address (in stark contrast to his 1986 speech), he was simply reiterating what had by then become a familiar theme.[33]

The timing in 2004–2005 of this sexual and specifically homosexual framing of the martyrdoms is unsurprising, coinciding as it does with the appearance of rifts in the Anglican Communion in response to the consecration of Gene Robinson in 2003, as discussed in the previous chapter. However, it is crucial not to overstate the impact of these new frames. Even as Ssempa and others sought to retell the story of the martyrdoms as a tale of homosexual predation, other articles in *New Vision* offered less jaundiced views of Mwanga. A 2004 piece suggested that he had been judged too harshly by history, reminding readers of his sense of restraint relative to the fearsome Mutesa and contextualising his actions in light of his youth and impressionability and his manipulation by wily courtiers such as the Katikkiro.[34] In both 2004 and 2005, the paper also carried less sexualised and more political accounts of the martyrdoms, with the martyrs described as 'forbears of rational consciousness, civil activism and political protest' who 'found themselves trapped in the dilemma of balancing the demands of the church (their conscience) and the state.'[35] Although anti-homosexuality rhetoric continued to feature in Orombi's Martyrs' Day remarks and coverage thereof in 2008–2009, accounts of these sermons are juxtaposed with non-sexual interpretations of the martyrdoms that occasionally subvert quite explicitly the hegemonic normative coding of the central characters. In a 2009 column in which six Ugandan lawyers were asked 'How would you have handled the martyrs' case today?' five of the six suggested that a case could be made for Mwanga on the basis that he had acted within the remit of his authority as it was understood in his time and that his actions could be rationalised as a defence of his political interests against the threat of rebellion.[36] An opinion piece in the same issue of the paper expresses puzzlement that the executed pages are remembered as martyrs, observing that Muslims challenging the political and social structures of

33. Kagolo, 'Museveni Warns'.
34. Ssejjengo, 'Mwanga Judged'.
35. 'Martyrdom Made Political Statement', *New Vision*, 3 June 2004, 29; see also Bisiika, 'Bishop Hannington'.
36. Baguma, 'How Would You'.

contemporary states on account of their faith are more likely to be branded terrorists and to incur the full wrath of the law even if they are considered martyrs by some Islamist groups.[37]

The reference to Muslims in the 2009 article coincides with other reframings of the martyrdoms—unrelated to sexuality—that were evident at the time. The martyrdoms were depicted in a film released in the same year named *Mukajanga*, after the title of Mwanga's chief executioner, who is its central character. The film places the Muslim pages executed by Mutesa alongside the Christian pages executed by Mwanga—anachronistically, given the decade that separated the two sets of killings—so that Muslims and Christians are portrayed as living, praying, and dying for their faith side by side in a show of ecumenical solidarity. While the Muslim struggle is admiringly described as a 'jihad', the film seems animated by a desire to draw Muslims into what has hitherto been a Christian but also a national narrative. Although there are few references to sexuality in the film, the attempt to insert into the narrative of the martyrdoms a group that has traditionally had little place in it anticipates more recent queer attempts to do something similar. The film is also interesting for its depiction of Mukajanga, who, despite wielding the terrifying power of an executioner, is portrayed as insecure, ambivalent, comical, and too faint-hearted for his profession. Mukajanga is plunged into a deep personal crisis when he discovers that his own son Bulwadda is one of the converts to Islam whose disobedience has occasioned the Kabaka's death sentence that he must now execute. Like Antigone, Mukajanga is torn between filial and political loyalty, a tension that is exacerbated by his professional obligations and his rivalry with a fellow-executioner, Senkoole, who has demonstrated *his* loyalty to the Kabaka by executing his own daughter. Mukajanga follows suit, but tragic as this outcome is, it is also necessary for the larger purpose of admitting Muslims into the glory of the martyrdoms.[38]

---

37. Ssemuwemba, 'Do the Uganda Martyrs'.

38. Simwogerere, *Mukajanga*. The Antigone dilemma surfaces in a different way, with the focus on a Creon-like figure in the 2012 play *Just Me, You and the Silence* written by Ugandan playwright Judith Adong, which explores the controversies occasioned by the AHB. Here, the central character Jacob Obina—a barely disguised version of David Bahati—must grapple with the personal and political fallout of his own son coming out as gay, obliging him under the terms of his proposed legislation to endorse the punishment (possibly even execution) of the latter. Although there are no references to the Uganda martyrdoms in the script, the play reprises the theme of intractable conflict between competing loyalties that is so central to the martyrdoms.

SEX IN CONTEMPORARY MEMORY OF THE
UGANDA MARTYRDOMS

The foregoing historical account of memory of the Uganda martyrdoms might convey the misleading impression that memory is any *one* thing at a given point in time. As I discovered during my fieldwork, this is unlikely to have ever been the case. I visited Kampala in 2010, 2012, and 2016, on the latter two occasions at the time of Martyrs' Day celebrations in June, to study how Ugandans remember the martyrdoms. My primary sites of interest were the Catholic and Anglican shrines at Namugongo, where I observed and participated in a number of religious services in the days leading up to the commemorations on 3 June. During this period, I conducted just over fifty semi-structured interviews with a range of people. These included pilgrims, priests, theology students, and others working at the shrines in various capacities; officials and guides working at sites of memorialisation associated with the Ugandan state (the National Museum, the Uganda Tourism Board) and the Buganda kingdom (the Kasubi tombs where the most recent Kabakas are buried, and Mengo Palace, the residence of the Kabaka); people more distant from official church and state memorialisation, including journalists, academics, and directors and actors associated with films about the martyrdoms; and kuchu activists.

Each interview revolved around a simple question: Why did Mwanga order the execution of his pages? Although I was particularly interested in the extent to which same-sex desire as a factor precipitating the martyrdoms was salient in public memory, I never brought up the subject of sex myself (except in interviews with writers and kuchu activists). If and when my respondents raised the subject of Mwanga's corporeal desires, I expressed curiosity about the sources of their knowledge, the degree to which this factor shaped their normative evaluation of the protagonists, and their views on the legitimacy of contemporary same-sex desire. I conducted interviews in English and, with the assistance of translators, in Luganda, Runyankole-Rukiga, Swahili, and French.[39] In what follows, I identify four modes in which sex figured (or did not) in the course of these interviews, which I describe as 'disinterest', 'displacement', 'denial', and '(dis)identification'. These modes of remembrance frequently bear the imprint of earlier historical narratives, many of which remain astonishingly durable, while also calling these narratives into question.

39. I observed no correlations between the language in which interviews were conducted and the kinds of responses obtained.

The overwhelming majority of pilgrims whom I interviewed at the Anglican and Catholic shrines at Namugongo narrated the story of the martyrdoms with no mention of Mwanga's sexual proclivities. Kaunda Wilson, a young Catholic man selling calendars and posters of the martyrs near the entrance to the Catholic shrine, offered me a version of the story that was typical of many of the responses I received. In Wilson's telling, upon hearing the pages recite the Lord's Prayer—'Thy Kingdom come, Thy will be done'— Mwanga was angered by the prospect that his courtiers were worshipping another king, 'the King of kings' as they called Him.[40] In a variation on this theme, theology students conducting guided tours for pilgrims at the Anglican shrine explained that Mwanga had been angered by the pages' preference for worshipping the 'one supreme God' rather than the pagan 'small gods' of Buganda.[41] Sometimes my interlocutors described the pages' rebellion against the king as both political and spiritual. As Anglican priest Revd. Cyprian Mugabe explained to me:

> The king . . . after realizing that these people believe in another King, he became jealous, that how can you call another person the King. And then he decided to look for everyone who is believing in that King. That King is Jesus Christ. So when he came across these martyrs, he decided to kill them. . . . Second to that, they were worshipping any other god. Not his god. Because he had god in his kingdom, that everybody can worship. . . . So now these people started worshipping other god, he became jealous and started killing one by one.[42]

I received substantially similar accounts from tourist guides at the Uganda National Museum and the Kasubi Tombs.[43] The leading secondary school history textbook, written in accordance with the requirements of the Uganda National Examinations Board history syllabus, describes the pages as 'disrespectful' in their refusal to renounce their new faith.[44] It lists practices condemned by Christianity, including polygamy, circumcision,

40. Interview with Kaunda Wilson (calendar seller), Uganda Martyrs' Shrine (Catholic), Namugongo, Uganda, 2 June 2012.
41. Interviews with Frank and Ngonbe Noah (theology students), Uganda Martyrs' Seminary (Anglican), Namugongo, Uganda, 2 June 2012.
42. Interview with Revd. Cyprian Mugabe (Anglican priest), Uganda Martyrs' Seminary (Anglican), Namugongo, Uganda, 2 June 2012.
43. Interview with Joseph (guide at Uganda National Museum), Kampala, Uganda, 6 June 2012; interview with Richard (guide at Kasubi Tombs), Kampala, Uganda, 7 June 2012.
44. Okello, *History of East Africa*, 211, 213.

human sacrifice, belief in shrines, killing of twins, witchcraft, and satanic activities, but makes no mention of homosexuality or gender transgression.[45]

Looking, as I was, for evidence of queer memory, I have to confess to a feeling of disappointment, even demoralisation, as I conducted interview after interview in which the story that I had travelled to Uganda to hear was simply not audible. My expectations, heightened by an immersion in the Catholic missionary writings on the martyrdoms and queer readings thereof, were simply not borne out by what I was hearing in the 'field'. The irrelevance of the putative sexual dimension of the martyrdoms to the vast majority of pilgrims I conversed with seemed to call into question my entire research project. If the very people most invested in perpetuating the memory of the martyrs were indifferent to the possible corporeal provocations for their execution, there simply was no 'memory' here for a queer politics to activate.

Scholars of memory have been equally interested in its opposite: forgetting, amnesia, silence. For Marc Augé, memory 'is the product of an erosion caused by oblivion. Memories are crafted by oblivion as the outlines of the shore are created by the sea.'[46] Trouillot takes an analogous view when he argues that 'mentions and silences are . . . active, dialectical counterparts of which history is the synthesis.'[47] Taking a view of silence as an active process, perhaps better conveyed by the verb 'to silence', Trouillot explains that silence can enter the process of historical production at four moments: the moment of fact creation (the making of sources); the moment of fact assembly (the making of archives); the moment of fact retrieval (the making of narratives); and the moment of retrospective significance (the making of history).[48] One way to make sense of the disappearance of 'sodomy' in the gap between textual European missionary sources and the vernacular Ugandan memory of the church is to think of it as the result of a process of silencing. Bridging this gap are the first written accounts of the martyrdoms produced by Baganda eyewitnesses to its dramatic events who, as we saw in the previous chapter, give short shrift to the question of sodomy or mention it only to attribute its practice to outsiders such as Arabs. This could be read as an instance of silencing at the moment of fact creation.

The problem with this interpretation of the omission of sodomy in these sources (or indeed in the contemporary remembrance of pilgrims)

45. Ibid., 212, 216–217.
46. Augé, *Oblivion*, 20.
47. Trouillot, *Silencing the Past*, 48.
48. Ibid., 25–26.

is that concepts such as silence, amnesia, omission, and forgetting presume that there is something about which to be silent, something that has been forgotten. On what basis can a critic presume to know, not only *that* something is missing, but also *what* that something is? What if, as some of my interlocutors challenged me, the missionaries had fabricated the claim that Mwanga was a sodomite? Bracketing this question for the moment, one conclusion that we might draw from the non-sexual narratives of the martyrdoms that most pilgrims offered is that the homophobic *re*sexualisation of the story that has been attempted by some elites beginning in 2004–2005 has been relatively unsuccessful in reshaping everyday communal memory of the martyrdoms.

Displacement

Priests and nuns were among the few respondents to offer a sexual account of the martyrdoms. This might be because they comprise the social group that is most steeped in the textual missionary sources and most invested in their continued authority. This is how Fr. Joseph Mukasa Muwange, Promoter of the Uganda Martyrs Devotion at the Catholic shrine, narrated the events culminating in the executions of 1885–1886:

> When the missionaries came, they came with Christian values. When they came here, they found people very much fond of their culture. But there were elements in the culture that could not cope up with the Christian values that were brought by the missionaries . . . at that time there used to be . . . between three hundred and four hundred young boys in the palace. And some of them had copied some elements from Arabs. And the missionaries were saying, 'No you should take this direction, this direction, this direction.' And Joseph Mukasa Balikuddembe got very much involved. He volunteered himself to help the boys. Now imagine a big number of boys, a big number of young people without anybody to guide them. Everything would have been very unfortunate. . . . So Joseph Mukasa Balikuddembe advised courageously, 'If you are called to such and such a place, by so and so, at such and such awkward hours, please do not go. Because that will lead to the violation of your chastity.'[49]

49. Interview with Fr. Joseph Mukasa Muwange (promoter of the Uganda Martyrs Devotion), Uganda Martyrs' Shrine (Catholic), Namugongo, Uganda, 21 June 2012. Fr. Muwange provides a verbatim account in his film *From Servants to Saints*.

Two things are interesting about this response. First, the peculiar combination of coyness and candour with which the love that dare not speak its name is clearly alluded to through a reference to the 'awkwardness' of the time and place of its consummation. This calls to mind Foucault's observation that 'silence itself—the things one declines to say, or is forbidden to name, the discretion that is required between different speakers—is less the absolute limit of discourse, the other side from which it is separated by a strict boundary, than an element that functions alongside the things said, with them and in relation to them within over-all strategies.'[50] Bridging the gap between the missionary texts and the everyday understanding of congregations, responses of this kind appear to mediate between the attention of the former and the indifference of the latter to the question of sodomy. Other clerical respondents were more forthcoming in naming 'homosexuality', or even the 'gay, lesbian' acts that the martyrs refused the Kabaka.[51] Still, I never heard the martyrdoms narrated in a sexually explicit fashion in the sermons and public messages that I listened to at Namugongo, suggesting that clergy were less inclined to offer this account from the pulpit than in the context of a private interview. It is worth underscoring that I am making a limited point here, drawn from my observations at Namugongo, because there have been no shortage of denunciations of homosexuality by preachers in Kampala's Pentecostal charismatic churches.

Second, having brought up conflicts with Christianity, Fr. Muwange hovers uncertainly between locating values contrary to Christianity in Kiganda culture and displacing responsibility for them onto the Arabs. This was a recurring feature of conversations in which respondents referenced Mwanga's thwarted sexual passions, and attests to the endurance of the tropes of African heterosexuality and Arab perversion that, as we have seen, saturated the colonial archive.[52] It also anticipates and parallels the tendency to displace contemporary queer practices onto Western influence. One corollary of displacement is the containment of vice within the person of Mwanga through the attribution of his corporeal intimacies to peculiarities of his circumstances and influences. Revd. Michael Ssentamu, an Anglican priest, told me that one reason for Mwanga's 'homosexuality'

50. Foucault, *Will to Knowledge*, 27.
51. Interview with a nun from the Congregation of the Daughters of Mary (Masaka Diocese), Uganda Martyrs' Shrine (Catholic), Namugongo, Uganda, 2 June 2016.
52. Interview with Isabirye David (theology student), Uganda Martyrs' Seminary (Anglican), Namugongo, Uganda, 30 May 2012; interview with Stephen Ssenkaaba (journalist, *New Vision*), Kampala, Uganda, 30 May 2012.

was his belief that he would die of syphilis, like his father Mutesa, if he had sexual intercourse with women.[53]

Two levels of displacement are evident here. First, the scapegoating of Mwanga cleanses the institution of the Buganda monarchy and wider Kiganda society from the taint of homosexuality. But second, the displacement of responsibility for Mwanga's behaviour onto the Arabs ultimately enables the rehabilitation of Mwanga and the reclamation of precolonial Kiganda culture, notwithstanding their departures from 'Christian values'. Many pilgrims were proud of the fact that Mwanga had been baptised later in life and died a Christian. Some evinced a complex moral attitude, seeing him as both the villain of the story and part of God's plan. As one pilgrim explained to me, 'maybe it was the will of God that used him to do this, like he used Judas to destroy Jesus Christ, so that people can discover themselves.'[54] The result is that, despite its role in the persecution of Christians in the founding moment of their religion in Uganda, the Buganda monarchy has been seamlessly integrated into Ugandan Christianity. The present Kabaka Ronald Mutebi II, great-grandson of Mwanga, is a frequent guest of honour at Martyrs' Day celebrations. Pictures of Mutebi's family are sold as souvenirs at the Anglican celebrations, and the Anglican service concludes with the singing of the anthems of Buganda and Uganda.[55]

Denial

Sometimes, an account of the martyrdoms that began without mentioning sex would, upon further questioning, morph into something ranging from scepticism to outright denial of the sexual angle. The most eloquent of these responses came from the historian Samwiri Lwanga-Lunyiigo, whose recent revisionist biography of Mwanga seeks to rehabilitate him as an anti-colonial patriot. Offering a political reading of the events leading up to the executions that emphasises the geopolitical manoeuvrings of external powers in East Africa and the ways in which different religious factions in Buganda were implicated in these moves, the book is keen to demonstrate that Mwanga was not hostile to Christianity and does not deserve the reputation for cruelty that mainstream historiography has bestowed on

53. Interview with Revd. Michael Ssentamu (Anglican priest), Uganda Martyrs' Seminary (Anglican), Namugongo, Uganda, 13 June 2012.

54. Interview with pilgrim, Uganda Martyrs' Shrine (Catholic), Namugongo, Uganda, 2 June 2016.

55. Participant observation at the Anglican Martyrs' Day service, Namugongo, Uganda, 3 June 2012.

him. Lwanga-Lunyiigo is especially critical of the suggestion that Mwanga engaged in sodomy and spends some time rebutting this assertion.[56] He reiterates the claim that homosexuality was abhorred by the Baganda, arguing that this made it an especially useful charge for the missionaries to level against Mwanga with a view to discrediting him in the eyes of his people. Even if British missionaries had got wind of the practice of sodomy in the palace, he argues, they could not credibly have been shocked by it given the extent to which British public discourse was infused with rumour and scandal around the homosexual exploits of contemporary public figures such as Oscar Wilde and General Gordon. For the same reason, he is sceptical of the missionary claim that sodomy had been learned from the Arabs, given that they would (or ought to) have known that sodomy was common in their own cultures. In an interview with me, Lwanga-Lunyiigo also argued that social practices in the court tended to be adopted by elite Baganda. Referencing evidence of the enthusiastic embrace of gonorrhoea once Mutesa had contracted the disease, he asks why there is no evidence of a similar enthusiasm for sodomy in Mwanga's time.[57]

More generally, Lwanga-Lunyiigo was scathing about recent interest (including perhaps my own) in Mwanga's 'homosexual' tendencies. Shrewdly observing that contemporary sexual minority movements had become interested in Mwanga because they were 'looking for pedigree', he insisted that there was no historical foundation for this quest. Towards the end of the interview, he remarked:

> They say you're not giving human rights to these [LGBTI] people. They must have their rights. But to me, if you practice that orientation, you have opted out of humanity, you are no longer human. So human rights should not apply to you. And that's the attitude [of] many of my generation.[58]

Despite the robust arguments in his book against the sodomy claim, I could not help wondering whether Lwanga-Lunyiigo's antipathy toward contemporary sexual rights claims played some role in shaping his view of the historical record, making his intervention as much an artefact of memory as the other responses surveyed here. Given the nature of contemporary mainstream Ugandan public discourse on homosexuality, perhaps an acknowledgement of Mwanga's corporeal practices would

56. Lwanga-Lunyiigo, *Mwanga II*, 83–84.
57. Interview with Samwiri Lwanga-Lunyiigo (historian), Kampala, Uganda, 26 June 2012.
58. Ibid.

impede Lwanga-Lunyiigo's larger project of rehabilitating him, so that heterosexualisation becomes the price of Mwanga's political rehabilitation.

I am intrigued by the attention that Lwanga-Lunyiigo devotes to the sodomy claim in his book, even if only to repudiate it. In its attempt both to account for the making of the sexual claim and to discredit it, denial is in striking contrast to the disinterest that everyday accounts of the martyrdoms evince towards the sexual angle. Indeed, rather than being characterised as denial, Lwanga-Lunyiigo's stance might better be described as 'negation', which Freud understood as the cognition, without acceptance, of something that is repressed.[59] In Freud's account, negation involves the separation of an intellectual function from an affective process, confirming the presence of what is negated while maintaining an affective aversion to it. This also recalls Foucault's classic account of how 'homosexuality' comes into being and becomes visible through the efforts made to repress it.[60] Something similar appears to be at work in the negating mode of remembrance, which brings up the question of Mwanga's homosexuality only to deny it and reiterate an affective aversion to it.

I was surprised to encounter denial in conversation with a senior figure in the COU. When I raised the question of Mwanga's reputed sexual behaviour with retired Archbishop Nkoyoyo, whom we encountered in the last chapter as the leading Ugandan voice at the 1998 Lambeth conference, he was quick to reply: 'That is a kizungu story which Ugandans do not believe!'[61] This is ironic because texts by bazungu such as Faupel and Thoonen are still the foundation of official church memory. Nonetheless, Nkoyoyo's response suggests anxiety within the church about continuing to rely on colonial sources. His response is additionally interesting because of his family connection with the martyrdoms as the grandson of a survivor of the purges. As the story goes, Nkoyoyo's grandfather Eriya Kagiri had initially been one of the condemned, but received a last-minute reprieve from Mwanga on account of his exemplary service in looking after the Kabaka's wives.[62] Nkoyoyo's version of the story, handed down from one generation to the next, is therefore in a manner of speaking an eyewitness narrative that might in its original iteration have contained the silences that I have suggested were common in such narratives. Perhaps what began as silence has hardened into denial in our own more explicitly homophobic times.

59. Freud, 'Negation'.
60. Foucault, *Will to Knowledge*.
61. Interview with Archbishop Livingstone Mpalani Nkoyoyo (former Archbishop of the COU), Kampala, Uganda, 13 June 2012.
62. Baguma, 'My Grandpa'.

Whether understood as denial or negation, this mode of remembrance in no way necessarily follows from either religiosity or homophobia—and it is worth underscoring, if it needs to be said at all, that religiosity and homophobia do not map neatly onto one another.[63] If Lwanga-Lunyiigo and Nkoyoyo participate, in different ways, in a homophobic discourse, this cannot be said of other respondents who were equally sceptical of the claim that Mwanga engaged in sodomy. James Onen, broadcaster and founder of the atheist group Kampala Freethought, was also dismissive of the putative sexual dimension of the story, suggesting—like Lwanga-Lunyiigo—that the sexual claims could have been a ploy to tarnish Mwanga's reputation prior to his deposition, with the martyrdoms themselves offering spectacularly useful propaganda for proselytisation.[64] In stark contrast to Lwanga-Lunyiigo and Nkoyoyo, Onen was a vocal critic of the AHB, drawing attention in his radio shows to what he saw as its prejudices and hypocrisies.[65] His denial of Mwanga's alleged sexual practices seems to emanate from a more generalised cynicism about religion and the politically interested claims of missionary sources.

Perhaps the only characteristic that links the three very different voices I've tried to describe in this section is a decolonial impulse—widespread amongst the Ugandan intelligentsia—that regards colonial historiography with a high degree of scepticism and seeks to break with it. This impulse manifests itself in a range of diverse and contradictory projects such as indigenisation of the church, revisionist history, and atheism—each of which, as we have seen, can have different implications for the more specific question of queer dissidence.

(Dis)Identification

Every so often during the course of my fieldwork, I was reminded that the precolonial Kiganda gender landscape that Nannyonga-Tamusuza describes remains a living memory.[66] Exhibit 1: while on a guided tour of the new Anglican museum at Namugongo in 2016, I expressed interest in a statue of Princess Nalumansi, a sister of Mwanga, who had also been killed on his orders after her conversion to Christianity. I had been aware of this,

---

63. See, for example, Van Klinken, *Kenyan, Christian, Queer*.
64. Interview with James Onen (broadcaster), Kampala, Uganda, 12 June 2012.
65. Onen, 'FBUP Episode 012'.
66. Nannyonga-Tamusuza, 'Female-Men'. I offer a summary description of this landscape in the previous chapter.

but had never seen any tangible commemoration of her death. Responding to my surprise at the memorialisation of a female martyr, my guide confirmed that Nalumansi was indeed considered a martyr but pointed out my gender error: 'a princess in Buganda is more he . . . because she was a royal.'[67] Exhibit 2: in March 2016, an imam named Sheikh Muzaata condemned homosexuality in the course of a sermon during Friday prayers at Kalitunsi mosque. Such denunciations have become so routine that this one might have escaped notice had he not made the extraordinary move of attributing the spread of homosexuality in Uganda to the Baganda, citing by way of evidence the practice of both male and female Baganda of referring to the Kabaka as *bbaffe* (husband).[68] At least one irate Muganda writer responded with a letter to *The Observer*, explaining that the title was simply a metaphor for power, demanding that the sheikh apologise for his statement, and affirming his own opposition to homosexuality.[69] The controversy illustrates both the persistence in public memory of older notions of gender, as well as the embarrassed disavowal that they generate when they interact with contemporary ontologies of gender and sexuality that might construe them as 'homosexuality'.

When I first began talking to kuchu activists about this project in 2010, I heard a range of different opinions on the fruitfulness of thinking about commemorative practices around the martyrdoms as a potential reservoir of queer memory. Some activists expressed tactical concerns, worrying that framing Mwanga as queer would antagonise the Baganda. The seriousness of this concern was underscored by the riots that had been provoked in 2009 by what many Baganda perceived as a slight to the authority of the Kabaka by the Museveni government on an unrelated matter.[70] Others were keener to engage with memory of the martyrdoms[71] or emphasised the importance of positionality, suggesting that Catholic Baganda were best placed to offer queer-positive interpretations.[72] There was also concern over the way the story lent itself to being framed as one about a predatory paedophilic king, given the ages of many of the executed pages, and

67. Interview with guide at Anglican museum, Uganda Martyrs' Seminary, Namugongo, Uganda, 31 May 2016.
68. I am indebted to Richard Lusimbo for drawing my attention to this story.
69. Kato, 'Sheikh Muzaata'.
70. Interview with Frank Mugisha (Executive Director, SMUG), Kampala, Uganda, 19 August 2010. For more on the riots, see ICG, *Uganda*, 13–18.
71. Interview with Kasha Jacqueline Nabagesera (Executive Director, Freedom and Roam Uganda), Kampala, Uganda, 25 August 2010.
72. Interview with Julius Kaggwa (Director, Support Initiative for People with Atypical Sex Development), Kampala, Uganda, 26 August 2010.

the tendency to forget that Mwanga was himself only a teenager when he ascended the throne. Such a framing would be particularly toxic in the current climate, given the associations between homosexuality and paedophilia that are frequently made in Ugandan public discourse.[73]

Nonetheless, from about the middle of the first decade of the 2000s, around the same time as the homophobic resexualisation of the martyrdom story, kuchu activists and allies had begun to claim Mwanga as a queer figure. In a 2003 article, Sylvia Tamale notes in passing, referencing Faupel, that 'it was an open secret . . . that Kabaka Mwanga was gay.'[74] The martyrdoms are referenced briefly in the 2011 documentary film *Getting Out*, produced by the Kampala-based Refugee Law Project, which investigates the plight of individuals fleeing persecution on account of sexual orientation or gender identity.[75] Another documentary entitled *Gay Love in Pre-colonial Africa: The Untold Story of the Uganda Martyrs*, produced by the Uganda Health and Science Press Association in 2012, attempts a more explicit reframing of the martyrdoms in a queer sex-positive way. The film refers to Mwanga as 'gay' and to the 'gay sex customs' in the courts of the Kabakas. An official palace guide explains that 'homosexual' activity took place in the palace and was tolerated so long as it was discreet. Most significantly, the film offers a political and sexual reading of the martyrdoms, reframing the executions as 'a clash of Western homophobia and African traditions' in an attempt to challenge claims that homosexuality is a Western import.[76] Recognition of Mwanga's queer corporeality has not been limited to kuchu activists. In December 2012, Morris Ogenga-Latigo, a former leader of the Opposition in the Ugandan Parliament, published a qualified critique of the AHB which notes in passing that 'the story of Kabaka Mwanga and his martyrdom of Christians has a homosexuality twist to it.'[77] Even Museveni, in less hostile moments, has acknowledged the presence of 'homosexual' kings in Ugandan history.[78]

Activist reclamations of Mwanga seek to 're-member' him in three senses: they remember him as a historical figure, they re-member him as a sexual being animated by queer desires, and they readmit him into membership of a political community whose founding myth sacrifices him on the altar of civilisation and moral progress. Although demonstrating the

73. Cheney, 'Locating Neocolonialism', 89.
74. Tamale, 'Out of the Closet'.
75. Neumann, *Getting Out*.
76. Kivumbi, *Gay Love*.
77. Ogenga-Latigo, 'Anti-homosexuality Bill'.
78. Feder, 'Ugandan President Denounces'.

indigeneity of same-sex desire by reclaiming same-sex loving historical figures is unlikely, by itself, to overcome antipathy towards such desire, it can still do useful work. The charge of cultural inauthenticity levelled by conservatives against queers, in questioning their very standing to engage in debate, is typically a ruse to avoid conversations about normativity that stand to alter power relations between social groups. Arguments about belonging may be a necessary prelude to more substantive conversations about normativity, even if they are by themselves insufficient in enabling queers to claim rights. We might think of them as conversations about what Hannah Arendt famously called 'the right to have rights.'[79]

Attempts to claim Mwanga as a queer ancestor are easily vulnerable to the historicist accusation of anachronism. Describing Mwanga as 'gay' ascribes to him a social identity that would have been unintelligible in his time. Carl Stychin recognises the intellectual force of the objection from anachronism, but suggests that it is beside the point because activist projections onto history seek to produce rhetoric that is politically salient rather than historically accurate.[80] Perhaps politically useful memory inescapably entails bad history. David Halperin's genealogical account of Western 'homosexuality' may allow a more ambitious response that is less resigned to the irreconcilability of these projects.[81] Following Sedgwick in tracing the historical accumulation of the different, irreducibly incoherent models of sex and gender deviance that now coexist under the sign of Western 'homosexuality', Halperin makes a distinction between identity and identification that is pertinent to our discussion:

> Just because earlier historical cultures may differ from modern ones in their organization of sex and gender, and just because Greek pederasty differs in a number of crucial respects from contemporary metropolitan gay identity, it doesn't follow that metropolitan gay men today cannot or should not identify with ancient Greeks. We don't only identify with those who are the same as us, after all; if other people weren't *different* from us, what would be the point of *identifying* with them? Identification gets at something, something important: it picks out resemblances, connections, echo effects. Identification is a form of cognition.[82]

79. Arendt, *Origins of Totalitarianism*, 296.
80. Stychin, 'Same-Sex Sexualities', 958.
81. Halperin, *How to Do*, 106–107.
82. Ibid., 15.

Indeed the gap between identity and identification may be visible in all operations of memory. Any study of memory has to pay attention to both what is remembered and who is doing the remembering. As Trouillot reminds us, it is often the case that 'the collective subjects who supposedly remember did not exist as such at the time of the events they claim to remember. Rather, their constitution as subjects goes hand in hand with the continuous creation of the past.'[83] This also means that the relationship between rememberers and the remembered is sometimes characterised by a non-reciprocity in which the former claim as ancestors those who might not recognise them as descendants.

Nowhere is this clearer than in the identification of pilgrims today with the Uganda martyrs. Kassimir reminds us that in Catholic doctrine and tradition, two criteria transform an execution into a martyrdom. First, the victims must have died because they were Christians. Second, they must have chosen to die, which is to say that they must have been killed not merely by virtue of being of their faith but *for* it.[84] Hagiographies of the martyrs anxiously reiterate evidence of both criteria, recounting the numerous instances in which the pages were given opportunities to recant their faith but refused to do so.[85] But as Kassimir points out, if, as many of the missionary sources claim, homosexuality was abhorred by Kiganda culture, then the precise motivation for the pages' resistance remains obscure. The fact that they had known Christianity for only a few years prior to their execution makes the prospect of their having died for it less plausible.[86] We simply don't know whether the pages died defending Kiganda or Christian values, or whether to take at face value the claim that these values were always already overlapping. The identification of pilgrims with the martyrs, then, may be as anachronistic as that of kuchus with Mwanga.

More importantly, identification is not the only mode of connection through which kuchus might relate to Mwanga, and the king may not be the only point of reference for them in the rich tapestry of the martyrdoms. Related to the notion of identification is the possibility of what José Muñoz calls 'disidentification'—a practice whereby minoritarian subjects reimagine dominant signs and symbols that are toxic to them, through engaged and animated modes of performance or spectatorship.[87] As he explains:

83. Trouillot, *Silencing the Past*, 16.
84. Kassimir, 'Complex Martyrs', 361.
85. Abdy, *Martyrs of Uganda*; Howell, *Fires of Namugongo*; Marion, *New African Saints*; Dollen, *African Triumph*; Malaba, *Story*.
86. Kassimir, 'Complex Martyrs', 364.
87. Muñoz, *Cruising Utopia*, 169.

Disidentification is about recycling and rethinking encoded meaning. The process of disidentification scrambles and reconstructs the encoded message of a cultural text in a fashion that both exposes the encoded message's universalizing and exclusionary machinations and recircuits its workings to account for, include, and empower minority identities and identifications. Thus, disidentification is a step further than cracking open the code of the majority; it proceeds to use this code as raw material for representing a disempowered politics or positionality that has been rendered unthinkable by the dominant culture.[88]

Understood in this way, disidentification might best describe the mode in which kuchus relate to Mwanga, allowing as it does for both the citation of his corporeal intimacies as evidence of the indigeneity of same-sex desire and a dissociation from the more venomous connotations of paedophilia and predation that, justifiably or not, cluster around him in public memory. Indeed, accompanying such disidentification with Mwanga may be a concomitant identification with the martyrs. I wonder if queer readings of the martyrdoms (including my own) have focused too much on Mwanga, neglecting possibilities for and perhaps even actually existing practices of kuchu identification with the martyrs. This is especially worthy of exploration because despite their subaltern status in history, the martyrs are immeasurably more powerful than their royal nemesis in devotional memory.

One exception to the queer scholarly tendency to neglect the martyrs might be Donald Boisvert's reading of them amongst other Catholic saints. Equal parts memoir, revisionist hagiography, and queer theoretical intervention, Boisvert's text stages a mutually contaminating encounter between gay and Catholic life, offering a queer reading of saints and a Catholic interpretation of gay icons. His project is premised on Catholicism's remarkable ability to negate the erotic while boldly affirming it in its art and ritual. Turning to the Uganda martyrs, Boisvert raises the tantalising possibility that 'before choosing to say "no," they had at some point earlier, said "yes".'[89] More profoundly, relying on Mark Jordan's interpretation of the remarkably similar story of the martyrdom of Saint Pelagius, he reads the story of the Uganda martyrdoms as a love triangle in which all the parties are male. In this reading, the martyrs do not deny same-sex love so much as vindicate it by choosing Christ as their lover. As Boisvert argues, 'their martyrdom is really only the story of a protracted and gracious seduction,

88. Muñoz, *Disidentifications*, 31.
89. Boisvert, *Sanctity and Male Desire*, 97.

one culminating in eternal union with their chosen lover and bridegroom,' making them 'truly iconic gay saints, in their spiritual grandeur as in their silent desires.'[90] Read in this light, the pilgrims I spoke to at Namugongo had been telling me a tragic love story in which the martyrs had died for a higher homoerotic love.

Fieldwork encounters also raised intriguing possibilities for queer identification with the martyrs that textual analysis had not yielded. The year 2016 saw the release of a new film about the martyrdoms called *Final Flames of Uganda Martyrs*. The film was written and produced by John Ssempebwa, deputy CEO of the Uganda Tourism Board—although this project was undertaken in a personal capacity. The film departs from the conventional view in which Mwanga or Mukajanga is held responsible for the executions. Instead, Mwanga is portrayed as a young and inexperienced king who made the mistake of retaining his father's Katikkiro, the crafty and ambitious Mukasa, as his prime minister, and fatally acting on his advice in killing the Christian converts. Ssempebwa has no interest in Mwanga's alleged sexual practices, finding it incomprehensible that a man with eighteen wives and numberless concubines could have had any interest in men.[91] As I spoke to Ssempebwa, I became more interested in his plans to develop the film in new directions, in particular his interest in telling the story of a relatively neglected martyr named Gyaviira. Ssempebwa explained to me that Gyaviira was the son of a chief named Ssemalago, who was a friend of the king and had been charged with maintaining the shrine of the god Mayanja, who took the form of a leopard. Ssemalago would communicate with Mayanja by making the sounds of a leopard, and trained his favourite son Gyaviira to do the same. But when Gyaviira entered the service of the Kabaka and was introduced to Catholicism by other converts in the court, he decided to leave the old ways behind.[92]

SSEMPEBWA: Do you know the worst punishment in our culture?
RAO: Being killed?
SSEMPEBWA: No, no, that's nothing. You see we're a warrior tribe . . . death is nothing. No, we're not afraid to die. The largest punishment here was being banished from your clan. Because

90. Ibid., 101–102.
91. Interview with John Ssempebwa (Deputy CEO, Uganda Tourism Board), Kampala, Uganda, 6 June 2016. This account of the film is based on this interview rather than a viewing of the film itself, which I was unable to obtain despite my best efforts.
92. See the official entry on Saint Gyaviira: http://www.munyonyo-shrine.ug/martyrs/other-uganda-martyrs/st-gyaviira/, accessed 12 December 2018.

clans lived like semi-families. So when you're banished from your clan, you had to wander and maybe try and find another clan. Now when you got there, people asked you your name. They're like, 'No, you don't belong here, please move on.' They gave you no food. So you had to walk the distance and go to another kingdom. You were a total misfit. The only martyr who got that punishment was this Gyaviira. He disassociated himself from his dad. Disassociated himself from barking like a leopard. And his dad banished him and told him to stop using his name. So they gave him this name Gyaviira, which means 'the place where the man comes from is feared'. He had no right to use anymore names like Musoke, which were his names.[93]

In the same year that *Final Flames* was released, SMUG compiled a report documenting 264 verified cases of persecution of LGBT individuals between May 2014 and December 2015, well after the Constitutional Court had nullified the AHA.[94] The forms of persecution documented include threats, violent attacks, torture, arrest, blackmail, press intrusion, legal prosecution, termination of employment, loss of property, harassment, eviction, mob justice, and perhaps most poignantly, 'family banishment'. Among the many stories that the report narrates is that of Muyomba, 20, who was beaten up and banished by his family after his father came across a Facebook profile that revealed his sexuality. The report quotes Muyomba at length:

He was so furious and called the whole family to tell them that he was very disappointed with me and would never allow his son to behave in such a disgusting manner. I was called before the whole family and very many embarrassing questions were asked to me. Some relatives wanted me taken to police for sometime so that I leave such an evil behavior. I was so scared and crushed by such attitude and pleaded and made all sorts of excuses—father to please forgive me, but he refused and instead threatened to beat me and kill me or have me arrested for such behaviour. He asked me to get my belongings and leave immediately. My world came crashing down because I had no idea where to go at this point. I cried and asked for mercy but no one listened. I thought that if I didn't pick my clothes my father would not chase me away for real—but no way. This time he asked me to leave his house immediately without carrying anything of

93. Ssempebwa interview.
94. SMUG, *'That's How I Survived'*, 5.

mine. I left home that day and went to a friend's place for a few days but all was really hard for me. Maybe as time passes my father will forgive me and let me be his son again but am just not sure right now.[95]

The story is both heartbreaking and banal in its familiarity. I think of Muyomba as a latter-day Gyaviira, banished by his father for departing from the old ways. And I find myself oddly moved by the predicament of fathers who sublimate their incomprehension of, and anguish at, the choices made by sons into the only affects that their own gendered subjectivities seem to permit—shame, denial, anger, rejection, 'homophobia'. Gyaviira is considered the patron saint of communication, traffic, and travellers, but it occurred to me that he could well be the patron saint of homeless kuchus.

Tragically, kuchus also have martyrs of more recent vintage. In January 2011, leading kuchu activist David Kato was bludgeoned to death in his home, only weeks after winning an injunction against the tabloid newspaper *Rolling Stone*, which had outed a number of kuchus, including Kato, and had called for them to be hanged.[96] Kato was the first kuchu activist with whom I had made contact at the start of my research and was the person through whom I met many of the other activists I know in Uganda. In my visits to the country since his death, I heard a number of conflicting accounts of his murder, not all of which pointed to the state. Still, most agreed that state-sponsored homophobia had, at minimum, created an atmosphere of impunity that had emboldened the assailant to the point of murder.

Notwithstanding these uncertainties, Kato has become the kuchu movement's first modern martyr[97]—a process that has been assisted in no small measure by the critically acclaimed biopic *Call Me Kuchu*, which documents his life and work.[98] Attending two screenings of the film in London, I was struck by the resemblance between affective responses to the film—grief, reverence, inspiration, resolve—and religious veneration of the Uganda martyrs that I had observed at Namugongo. Since 2012, an international advisory committee comprising sexual rights organisations has given an annual David Kato Vision and Voice Award to individuals who demonstrate courage and leadership in advocating for LGBTI rights,

95. Ibid., 19–20.
96. Rice, 'Ugandan Gay Rights'. The newspaper is unrelated to the US magazine with the same name.
97. For an excellent account of how the story of David's murder has been transformed into a powerful and simple morality tale despite its ambiguities, see Peters, 'Kuchus in the Balance', 193–228.
98. Wright and Zouhali-Worrall (dirs.), *Call Me Kuchu*.

particularly in difficult environments, effectively instituting a secular process for queer canonisation. On the second anniversary of Kato's death, SMUG issued a press release affirming that 'the martyrdom and the blood that David shed planted the seed of love that we all need to share, LGBTI to straight, straight to LGBTI, one to another.'[99]

The deeply religious, indeed Catholic, idioms of martyrdom and sainthood on which these forms of commemoration draw are by no means unique to the kuchu movement or the Ugandan context. Sociologists of the international have long recognised that secular projects have borrowed heavily from religious idioms of sacrifice and martyrdom to construct the foundations of their moral authority.[100] Few have done this more transparently than queer movements. On a visit to the Castro district in San Francisco, I found myself on a Harvey Milk Tour in the course of which walkers were invited to stop at the residence, the camera shop, and the campaign headquarters of the slain gay rights activist, like pilgrims tarrying at the Stations of the Cross. The Harvey Milk Plaza is invariably described as 'sacred ground' for the US LGBT movement. Yet the Ugandan context presents distinctive possibilities given the presence of a powerful martyr narrative that furnishes the founding myth of the nation itself, with which kuchus might (dis)identify. Perhaps this provides especially fertile soil in which the blood of martyrs might water the seeds of new churches.

99. SMUG, 'Remembering David Kato Kisule', press release, 26 January 2013, on file with author.
100. Hopgood, *Endtimes of Human Rights*; Hopgood, *Keepers of the Flame*.

CHAPTER 4

Spectres of Colonialism

The willingness to follow ghosts, neither to memorialize nor to slay, but to follow where
they lead, in the present, head turned backwards and forwards at the same time. To be
haunted in the name of a will to heal is to allow the ghost to help you imagine what was
lost that never even existed, really. That is its utopian grace: to encourage a steely sorrow
laced with delight for what we lost that we never had; to long for the insight of that moment in which we recognize . . . that it could have been and can be otherwise. . . . If you let
it, the ghost can lead you toward what has been missing, which is sometimes everything.
                                                    —Gordon, *Ghostly Matters*, 57–58

In October 2012, the British House of Lords provided the setting for an
unusual debate on the 'Treatment of Homosexual Men and Women in
the Developing World'. One speaker ventured that this might have been
the first debate on the global persecution and criminalisation of the 'LGBT
community' to be held in a national legislature.[1] The Conservative peer Lord
Lexden, who has been the official historian of the party since 2009, offered
a categorical statement of British responsibility for laws criminalising homosexuality in many parts of the world:

> we must remember where the laws criminalising homosexuals in many countries
> came from. They came from Britain, which alone among the European empires
> of the 19th century possessed a criminal code under which homosexuals faced
> severe penalties just for expressing their love and physical desire for one an-
> other. In India in the 1820s, Thomas Macaulay, later the greatest of all the Whig

---

1. HL Deb, 25 October 2012, vol. 740, col. 379.

Out of Time. Rahul Rao, Oxford University Press (2020). © Oxford University Press.
DOI: 10.1093/oso/9780190865511.001.0001

historians, devised a legal system which incorporated Britain's then firm and un-bending intolerance of homosexuality. The Indian penal code became the model for the legal systems of Britain's colonies in most of Africa and Asia. The love that had freely spoken its name and found expression in their native cultures be-came, in the definition of their new British-imported law, an unnatural offence.[2]

Lord Black of Brentwood, a gay Conservative peer and executive director of the Telegraph Media Group, affirmed this view by declaring simply: 'we caused this problem. That so many people around the globe still suffer from legal discrimination is one toxic legacy of empire. It is our duty to help sort that out.'[3] Lord Smith of Finsbury, a member of the Labour Party for most of his political career and the first British MP to come out as gay and later as HIV positive, described the continued existence of discrimination, vi-olence, and criminalisation in Commonwealth countries as 'shaming'. In his view, the fact that 'most laws in these countries have been inherited from us . . . gives us a special responsibility to do whatever we can to help to change things.'[4]

Similar sentiments were expressed in a debate on 'Global LGBT Rights' held in the House of Commons in October 2017. On this occasion, Lloyd Russell-Moyle, Labour MP for Brighton Kemptown, went further in thinking through the implications of this 'special responsibility'. Taking the view that the United Kingdom had an obligation to weigh in 'be-cause we were the ones that historically imposed some of these laws', he insisted that '[w]e cannot just wash our hands and say, "Well, we're anti-colonialists now, so we'll just let you get on with it." We have a duty to be proactive in our response.'[5] At the same time, recognising that it would not do to 'go into these countries again and to say, "Oh well, our old penal code was wrong. Reverse it",' he rowed back with the sug-gestion that 'our role is to stand shoulder to shoulder with other LGBT activists . . . around the world and to support them.'[6] Finally, Theresa May opened the 2018 CHOGM in London with a statement of regret for the anti-sodomy laws imposed by British colonial penal codes: '[t]hey were wrong then, and they are wrong now. As the United Kingdom's Prime Minister, I deeply regret the fact that such laws were introduced,

2. HL Deb, 25 October 2012, vol. 740, col. 378.
3. HL Deb, 25 October 2012, vol. 740, col. 389.
4. HL Deb, 25 October 2012, vol. 740, col. 391.
5. HC Deb, 26 October 2017, vol. 630, col. 539.
6. HC Deb, 26 October 2017, vol. 630, col. 540.

and the legacy of discrimination, violence and even death that persists today.'[7]

Remorse for British imperialism is rare and unexpected when it comes from the highest echelons of the Conservative Party and right-wing media. Indeed, analysts of imperial memory in contemporary Britain are more likely to draw attention to the amnesia that typically occludes a meaningful consideration of empire and its legacies.[8] So it is worth asking how and why the memory of empire has come to be invoked so pointedly in relation to the question of homosexuality. Does its invocation and sublimation into a discourse of 'special responsibility' express a kind of regret or atonement for colonialism? Why has this discourse become audible at this time and with respect to this issue? And what does it mean for these expressions of regret to be so categorical unlike the more ambivalent acknowledgements of responsibility for other manifestations of imperialism such as slavery?

In asking these questions, this chapter attempts to do two things. First, it brings the book's preoccupations with time, memory, and sexuality to bear on the erstwhile imperial metropolis to ask how perceptions of Britain's historic responsibility for anti-sodomy laws in the Commonwealth shape contemporary British activism. Second, juxtaposing conversations about what I will describe, somewhat reductively for now, as the 'sexual' and 'racial' legacies of colonialism, it reflects on the relative discursive power wielded by contemporary claims around 'sexual' and 'racial' justice. In doing so, I hope to trouble the separation of these analytics that their juxtaposition presumes. I argue that an implicit metonymy between queerness and whiteness in the imaginary of the British political elite fuels the discourse of atonement for colonial anti-sodomy laws that we now hear at the highest levels of government. In sum, I aim to make visible the historical structures and institutions through which sexuality comes to be read as 'race' in contemporary British politics.

BLAME GAMES

In recent years a number of studies have drawn attention to the colonial provenance of anti-sodomy laws, pointing out that former British colonies were more likely to have laws criminalising homosexuality.[9] French

---

7. Duffy, 'Theresa May'.
8. Gilroy, *After Empire*; Gopal, 'Redressing Anti-imperial Amnesia'.
9. Human Rights Watch, *This Alien Legacy*; Lennox and Waites eds., *Human Rights*; Han and O'Mahoney, *British Colonialism*.

colonies tended not to have such laws after the anti-sodomy provision was dropped from the Napoleonic Code in 1806. The revised Code influenced the law in other European powers and their colonies.[10] Introducing a collection of essays published in 2013, Corinne Lennox and Matthew Waites noted that 'the Commonwealth includes 42 (53.8%) of the 78 states which continue to criminalise same-sex sexual behaviour, and only 12 (10.6%) of 113 where it is legal,' concluding that 'the criminalisation of same-sex sexual behaviour by the British Empire . . . [has] had a lasting negative impact.'[11] The heightened awareness in the United Kingdom of the colonial provenance of anti-sodomy laws in much of the rest of the world has been the result of forceful reminders to this effect from global South activists. One of the earliest instances of this occurred in 2008, when activists in Mumbai, at the city's queer Pride that year, demanded an apology from the British government for the colonial imposition of anti-sodomy laws.[12] As I have already mentioned, reminders of the origins of anti-sodomy laws in colonially imposed penal codes are understandable tactical responses to the claim that 'homosexuality is Western', even if they remain inadequate explanations for the postcolonial persistence of these laws. Here I want to think about a different consequence of this reminder, namely its deployment by British actors to justify their assumption of a leading role in the struggle to decriminalise homosexuality in the global South.

British LGBT activist Peter Tatchell struck an early blow in this regard. In anticipation of the 2011 CHOGM in Perth, Tatchell called upon then British Prime Minister David Cameron to apologise for 'the homophobic persecution Britain has inflicted on the gay peoples of Africa, Asia, the Pacific and the Caribbean', suggesting that 'it would be a welcome gesture of contrition and moral leadership for our Prime Minister to acknowledge this terrible wrong and seek to atone for it.'[13] Under pressure, Cameron responded with an ill-advised comment suggesting that British aid would be linked to respect for LGBT rights in recipient countries.[14] Confronted with the suggestion of a new form of conditionality, leaders in Tanzania,[15] Uganda,[16] Ghana,[17] and elsewhere reacted with hostility. More significantly,

10. Kirby, 'Sodomy Offence', 64.
11. Lennox and Waites, 'Human Rights', 24. At the time of writing, 34 of the 72 countries that criminalise sodomy are in the Commonwealth.
12. Taylor, 'Gay Activists'.
13. Tatchell, 'David Cameron Urged'.
14. BBC News, 'Transcript'.
15. Mbuthia, 'Tanzania'.
16. BBC News, 'Uganda Fury'.
17. BBC News, 'Ghana Refuses'.

a number of African queer activists criticised Cameron's statement, warning that the refusal of Western aid on sexual rights grounds would reinforce perceptions of the Westernness of homosexuality, scapegoat queers for reduced aid flows, and entrench power disparities between donor and recipient countries.[18]

Two things became apparent in this moment. First, British elites seemed unusually receptive to the suggestion that they ought to recognise that anti-sodomy laws in the Commonwealth were a toxic legacy of British colonialism, which in turn especially obliged them to denounce such laws. Second, at least some of the modes in which they sought to discharge this obligation to undo the legacies of colonialism exposed them to charges, ironically, of neocolonialism. Nowhere was this clearer than in the manner in which Cameron had purported to act on the demand for apology through the mechanism of conditionality. This was of course a classic instance of state co-option and instrumentalisation of activist demands. But sometimes the activists themselves evinced delusions of neocolonial omnipotence. As the singer Elton John remarked in an interview with CNBC, 'These are old laws from the British Commonwealth and they need to be changed . . . the Queen could do that with one wave of her hand.'[19]

In a more credible vein, two London-based organisations—Kaleidoscope Trust and Human Dignity Trust (HDT)—have been prominent in urging the British government to play a more forceful role in advocating for the repeal of anti-sodomy laws globally. While Kaleidoscope focuses on lobbying and advocacy within the institutional structures of the Commonwealth, HDT's mission is to provide technical legal assistance in the form of funding and advice to lawyers and activists working to challenge the criminalisation of homosexuality through courts. It does this by bringing the resources of multinational law firms, who commit to working for the Trust on a pro bono basis, to support decriminalisation litigation by local human rights lawyers. It has supported litigation in Belize, Jamaica, Northern Cyprus, Singapore, and the European Union.[20] HDT's modus operandi attracted criticism at its very inception. Trinidad and Tobago activist Colin Robinson described its approach as 'unproductive', arguing that the Trust had 'muscled into a carefully planned constitutional suit by local and regional actors in Belize, daringly spun in the media as the Trust's global campaign kick-off.'[21] Indeed, early publicity for the organisation by its first Chief Executive

18. Pambazuka News, 'Statement'.
19. Mandell, 'Elton John'.
20. Human Dignity Trust, 'Legal Cases'.
21. Robinson, *Decolonising Sexual Citizenship*, 4.

Jonathan Cooper seemed to invite this impression. Speaking to *Guardian* columnist Zoe Williams in 2011, Cooper explained:

> I email our legal panel, asking: anyone have any experience of litigating in Belize? Someone comes back and says yeah, we'll represent you in this legal challenge. They bring in as their counsel [former Attorney General for England and Wales and for Northern Ireland] Lord Goldsmith, and the former attorney general of Belize, Godfrey Smith. We turn up as the international community, with a legitimate interest in the outcome of this case, but we do change the nature of the struggle because we have approached it on the basis that it's a major legal challenge. That is our intention. . . . We will fundraise, and there is something rather charming that you can say to somebody: 'If you give us £50,000, I can more or less guarantee that you will have decriminalised homosexuality in Tonga.' And actually, you know, that's great.[22]

The statement suggests a vision of legal and social transformation heavily mediated by external resources, expertise, and power and legitimated through a novel claim of legal standing ('we turn up as the international community'). These were precisely the elements of HDT's approach that antagonised Robinson, who explains:

> The chorus coming from the powers who gave us the sodomy laws in the first place has shifted to singing morality in a different key, often appealing more to righteousness than to shared values. And they have outshouted those of us working within our own nations to build ownership for a vision of postcolonial justice, national pride and liberty that includes sexual autonomy. . . . Global North advocates wanting the same changes often believe they have the answers but get in the way by taking the reins too often rather than following our lead. It is essential that those who genuinely support our equality listen to us, get behind where we are going, and push in the same directions.[23]

The constitutional challenge to Belize's anti-sodomy law, to which HDT was a party, succeeded in 2016.[24] Yet that same year, Cooper resigned from the Trust for reasons that appeared, ironically, to vindicate Robinson's criticisms. Citing disagreements with the HDT Board, Cooper justified his departure as a protest against the increasingly gatekeeping role that the Trust was beginning to play. Rather than simply providing legal advice to

22. Williams, 'Gay Rights'.
23. Robinson, *Decolonising Sexual Citizenship*, 6.
24. *Caleb Orozco v. The Attorney General of Belize*, claim no. 668 of 2010.

global South activists while leaving to them the crucial decisions about whether or not to pursue litigation, HDT had—in his view—played too heavy-handed a role by refusing to support litigation that it felt had little prospect of success.[25] Jason Jones, a British-based Trinidadian LGBT activist who pursued an ultimately successful challenge to anti-sodomy laws in Trinidad and Tobago, reiterated this criticism in a reflection on his legal struggle. Complaining that HDT had inexplicably reneged on a 2015 commitment to support his case, he credited his eventual success to a legal team comprising Trinidadian lawyers Rishi Dass and Antonio Emmanuel and former HDT consultant Peter Laverack, who had assisted in a personal capacity after dissociating himself from the Trust at the same time and for the same reasons as Cooper had.[26] Kaleidoscope was also criticised for gatekeeping when it first started. Matthew Waites observes that its creation of a Commonwealth Equality Network, a network of civil society organisations working to challenge inequality based on sexual orientation and gender identity, effectively sidelined other networks in which decolonial critiques of global LGBT organising from Southern activists had been prominent. Waites also notes that when Southern activists participated in early events organised by Kaleidoscope, they were invited to reflect on their local contexts rather than on global or transnational questions.[27] While the appointment of Phyll Opoku-Gyimah, trade unionist and co-founder of UK Black Pride, as Kaleidoscope's executive director from August 2019 powerfully signals the Trust's intention to take a decolonial representational politics seriously, it remains to be seen how this leadership change will transform its work.[28]

Besides becoming significant nodes in international activism, the new London-based transnationally oriented LGBT organisations have also sought to persuade the British government to play a more active role in advocacy against anti-sodomy laws. In 2015, HDT began to lobby for the creation of a UK Special Envoy to work towards ending LGBT persecution globally, analogous to the position established by the US State Department that same year.[29] In a briefing paper outlining the rationale for the post, citing the role of European courts in prompting decriminalisation in

25. Interview with Jonathan Cooper (former Chief Executive, Human Dignity Trust), London, 25 November 2016.

26. Jones, 'We Won'.

27. Waites, 'LGBTI Organizations', 652–654.

28. 'Phyll Opoku-Gyimah Appointed Executive Director of Kaleidoscope Trust', 15 May 2019, https://kaleidoscopetrust.com/news/159.

29. For an account of the US government's SOGI global advocacy, see Burack, *Because We Are Human*.

Northern Ireland, it argued that 'history shows that a helping hand from outside is needed to initiate the domestic protection of LGBT people' and that 'the UK, in particular, has the means and obligation to advocate for the repeal of criminalising and persecutory laws.' Unsurprisingly, the question of 'obligation' is tied to Britain's historic role in introducing anti-sodomy laws in its colonies. The paper framed the task of the proposed Special Envoy as being 'to help correct a historical wrong—not to impose an alien foreign agenda.'[30] The success of HDT's efforts is evident in the fact that a number of these themes are reflected in the April 2016 report of an All Party Parliamentary Group (APPG) on Global LGBT Rights. This report notes that while the colonial provenance of anti-sodomy laws 'offers a justification for British action to address the persecution faced by LGBT people . . . the same colonial history that impels action can also lead to accusations of neo-colonialism when that action fails to take into account local contexts.'[31]

In seeking to respond to anti-sodomy laws that are a legacy of colonial penal codes, Western activists struggle to strike a balance between two problematic even if antithetical tendencies. On the one hand, homonationalism names the tendency to construct the global South as a location of homophobia needing intervention from an enlightened North. On the other hand, and perhaps as a kneejerk response to critiques of homonationalism, we are beginning to witness the phenomenon that I described in Chapter 2 as homoromanticism—an affective stance in which the queer predicaments of the postcolonial world are attributed entirely to its colonial experience, with the agency of postcolonial elites in co-producing those predicaments being obscured. Some activists have ricocheted between both positions. Michael Kirby, former judge of the High Court of Australia and a leading international campaigner for LGBT rights, has spoken of sexual minorities being 'kept in legal chains by the enduring penal code provisions of the British Empire,'[32] describing such provisions elsewhere as 'a dear little legacy of the British Empire . . . a very special British problem.'[33] More recently he has affected a stroppier tone, observing that '[i]t is pathetic to blame this on British colonial administrators. Most Commonwealth countries have been independent for 50 years and the responsibility is theirs alone.'[34]

30. Human Dignity Trust, 'Should the UK Government', 5–6.
31. All Party Parliamentary Group on Global LGBT Rights, 'UK's Stance', 12–13.
32. Kirby, 'Sodomy Offence', 75.
33. Lauder, 'Commonwealth Leaders'.
34. Human Dignity Trust, 'Human Dignity Trust'.

Antithetical as these tendencies seem, they might be understood as different facets of orientalism in which, as Said explains, the 'Orient' is either denigrated for its backwardness or 'overvalued for its pantheism, its spirituality, its stability, its longevity, its primitivity, and so forth.'[35] In the context of contemporary discussions about LGBT rights, both dispositions buttress a claim about the indispensability of Western intervention, seen in the first as a civilising mission and in the second as an attempt to mitigate the damage wrought by earlier civilising missions. In attributing responsibility for the existence of postcolonial anti-sodomy laws mainly to their colonial imposition, contemporary metropolitan atonement discourses obscure the agency of postcolonial elites in retaining and resignifying such laws. Cameroonian LGBT activist Joel Nana describes the problem eloquently:

> If we truly believe that Africans are human, we should also be able to understand that they can make their own decisions. These decisions may be influenced by the need to protect or to violate rights, for real or perceived personal or collective good, but they remain African decisions. They are owned and defended. Denying them the agency that allows them to do that is similar to stripping them of their humanity.[36]

Viewed in this light, metropolitan 'atonement' for postcolonial anti-sodomy laws delivers insult in the same breath as it offers apology by sublimating an exaggerated sense of responsibility for these laws into a moral obligation to lead the struggle against them. How can atonement for imperialism end up looking so imperious?

SAYING 'SORRY'

In his novel *Atonement*, Ian McEwan offers a finely drawn portrait of the anatomy of atonement. Driven by a potent combination of ambition, passion, and jealousy, the young protagonist Briony Tallis commits an act for which she will later feel the need to atone. Convinced of her destiny as a writer, Briony weaves a series of events that she has witnessed from afar into a narrative of lust, betrayal, and violation, akin to the dark fairy tales that her precocious adolescent imagination favours. She levels

35. Said, *Orientalism*, 150.
36. Cited from Gevisser, 'Human Rights'.

an allegation that will prove unfounded, but will forever alter the lives of the other characters. As the consequences of her actions become apparent to her, Briony is wracked with guilt. Distancing herself from family and abandoning plans to go to university, she embraces the arduous life of a nurse in London during the Second World War, in penance for her act of falsehood. Her offer to recant her incriminating testimony is received with scepticism, with every expression of atonement on her part compromised by the self-interest of wanting to clear a conscience whose weight she can no longer bear. Towards the end of the novel, we realise that these scenarios of atonement have only ever played out in Briony's mind. Coming too late to make any difference in the lives that she has so drastically altered, it is the novel itself—it turns out that we have been reading *Briony's* novel— that is the act, or rather the speech act, of atonement. This places us as readers in the difficult position of having nothing but the self-justifying narrative of the wrongdoer as our sole record of events. As Briony herself wonders, 'how can a novelist achieve atonement when, with her absolute power of deciding outcomes, she is also God?'[37] In McEwan's rendering, far from being a simple act of contrition, atonement looks more like a voyage navigating the treacherous shoals of guilt, shame, resentment, self-pity, ambition, and egotism, across gradients of power.

Psychoanalytic perspectives may take us further in understanding atonement. Julia Gallagher has suggested that Melanie Klein's object relations theory may offer a particularly useful framework for understanding morality in international relations, given that relationships are central to her thought and practice.[38] Object relations theory explains the development of the psyche during early childhood through an account of how people relate to objects—both real objects in the world around them, and the internal objects that they build unconsciously to reflect the world and to help themselves make sense of it. As Gallagher explains, the child experiences external objects through projection, and mentally internalises these objects, which then constitute her personality. This in turn shapes further encounters with and internalisations of external objects. In this process, the child is both author of and subject to her internal objects, which are built on both positive and negative interactions with the world. At first, the positive and the negative seem separable, with 'good' objects fostering security and well-being and 'bad' objects bringing frustration and pain. But it is in the child's shocked realisation that both good and bad

37. McEwan, *Atonement*, 371.
38. Gallagher, 'Melanie Klein'.

are personified in the same object—the mother—that the reparative impulse is born as an attempt to attenuate the hateful feelings that the child experiences for the mother whom she also loves and needs.[39] Will Kaufman explains that for Klein, this reparative impulse is at the heart of psychic health, enabling a move from the destructive, psychotic, immature stage—the 'paranoid-schizoid position'—to the mature, integrated stage that she calls the 'depressive position'.[40] It is the experience of pain and guilt in the depressive position that fuels the reparative urge.

Yet guilt provides only a starting point—and a fraught one at that—for the reparative drive, which can take different trajectories. Even sympathetic commentators have criticised Klein's thinking about reparation as introverted, given its focus on making reparation to one's injured internal objects rather than to external ones. For C. Fred Alford, this kind of reparation is 'morally untrustworthy, as likely to be satisfied by painting a picture about the terrible deeds one has done as by making amends to actual victims.'[41] This is why Derek Hook is suspicious of reactions from guilt, which, despite the gestures of reparation that may flow from them, are often fundamentally self-serving in being motivated primarily by the need to alleviate the atoner's psychic discomfort. Hook questions whether a reparative act that is more concerned with salving one's own pain can constitute a genuinely ethical act.[42] Klein herself recognised that a subject overwhelmed by guilt may choose to deny or refuse it rather than to acknowledge and work through it, provoking gestures of what she called 'manic reparation'. As Hanna Segal explains:

> Manic reparation is a defence in that its aim is to repair the object in such a way that guilt and loss are never experienced. An essential feature of manic reparation is that it has to be done without acknowledgement of guilt. . . . The object in relation to which reparation is done must never be experienced as having been damaged by oneself. . . . The object must be felt as inferior, dependent and, at depth, contemptible. There can be no true love or esteem for the object or objects that are being repaired, as this would threaten the return of true depressive feelings.[43]

39. Ibid., 298–304.
40. Kaufman, 'Psychology of Slavery Reparation', 269.
41. Cited in ibid., 270.
42. Hook, 'White Privilege', 497.
43. Cited in Kaufman, 'Psychology of Slavery Reparation', 271.

Much of this is strikingly visible in the contemporary British discourse of atonement for anti-sodomy laws. This may sound paradoxical because, on the face of it, the discourse *does* acknowledge guilt in astonishingly categorical terms. Yet the guilt is easily displaced onto a historic self, separated from the contemporary United Kingdom by the temporal ruptures of decolonisation and of its own decriminalisation of sodomy. This means that, protestations of guilt notwithstanding, the object in relation to which reparation is made is not experienced as having been damaged by a recognisable self. British decriminalisation, albeit too late to benefit what were by then former colonies, fuels the sense of triumph and superiority vis-à-vis the object (we have progressed, they have stagnated).[44] The zealous assumption of British responsibility for anti-sodomy laws in the Commonwealth, blind to the complex postcolonial and transnational assemblages that perpetuate these laws, effectively constructs the objects of reparation as passive, inferior, and in need of a 'helping hand'. Cameron's incipient articulation of what we might think of as 'gay conditionality' betrays a desire for control and the delusions of omnipotence that are characteristic of manic reparation.[45] Perhaps this rare expression of atonement for colonialism at the highest levels of British government has been forthcoming precisely because it is thought to furnish the requisite standing for a moral crusade in which the United Kingdom can assert leadership.

We have been here before. In 2007, both houses of the British Parliament held debates to mark the bicentenary of the abolition of the slave trade in the British Empire. A striking characteristic of these debates was the frequency with which expressions of atonement for slavery, which should have been the focus of public attention, were upstaged by pride in Britain's putative leadership of the campaign for abolition. Yet this apart, the slavery debates stand in revealing contrast to parliamentary debates on homosexuality. In the remainder of this chapter, I juxtapose a reading of the slavery debates with the sentiments expressed in the homosexuality debates and in other attempts to grapple with the legacies of the state's self-avowed homophobic past. I want to think through contrasting treatments of the

---

44. For an illustration of this, see the speech of Crispin Blunt (Con) in HC Deb, 26 October 2017, vol. 630, col. 526: '. . . I am thinking of the role that we can play as parliamentarians. We should not underestimate the huge challenge that faces our parliamentary colleagues in other countries that, because of religious beliefs and the influence of religion in those societies, are in the same state as the United Kingdom in the 1950s when it comes to attitudes to LGBT people. . . . We should look our fellow parliamentarians in the eye when we have the opportunity to do so and get them to first base. People's sexuality is not something that they choose.'
45. Rao, 'On "Gay Conditionality"'.

spectres of colonialism evident in these engagements with the past, with a view to drawing out what is similar and different about these contexts, but also what is similar but construed to be different. By teasing out the contrasts in the way political elites speak of being haunted by the spectres of the 'racial' and 'sexual' legacies of colonialism, I hope to illuminate a troubling segregation of these analytics in the imaginary of the British state.

THE TEMPORALITY OF ATONEMENT

Many speakers in the slavery debates were unsparing in their description of the horrors of the slave trade and in acknowledging the extent to which Britain benefited from it, naming the royal family, the Church of England, the City, and their own predecessors in Parliament as beneficiaries of the trade and, more specifically, of the £20 million compensation that was paid to slave owners when the trade was abolished in 1807.[46] Nonetheless, the debates are saturated with discursive moves that seek to mitigate British culpability. These are evident at the very outset of the Commons debate, which was opened by then Labour Deputy Prime Minister John Prescott with a recitation of the lyrics of a slave chain re-enactment that he had reportedly seen performed by Ghanaian children: 'Not every black man was innocent. Not every white man was guilty.'[47] Words that in Ghana might open up a productive if painful debate about the complicity of some African elites in the slave trade become, in the mouth of a white British politician, a get-out clause that is unimpeachable given its attribution to children of colour.[48] A number of subsequent speakers took their cue from here, drawing attention to the involvement of Arab and African slave raiders in the trade, with one member describing slavery as 'a darker chapter in the development of every world civilisation.'[49]

Having de-exceptionalised the European slave trade, many speakers were keen to exceptionalise British virtue by framing the debate as a remembrance of abolition, rather than of the evil it was meant to end. Prescott described abolition as 'an historic moment for the United Kingdom, which

46. See, for example, the contributions of Chris Bryant (Lab), Vince Cable (LD), Diane Abbott (Lab), Dawn Butler (Lab), Jeremy Corbyn (Lab) and Claire Curtis-Thomas (Lab) to HC Deb, 20 March 2007, vol. 458.

47. HC Deb, 20 March 2007, vol. 458, col. 689.

48. For an insightful account of the divergent afterlives of slavery in Ghanaian and African American public cultures, see Hartman, *Lose Your Mother*.

49. HC Deb, 20 March 2007, vol. 458, col. 763 (see also cols. 704, 741–742). See also HL Deb, 10 May 2007, vol. 691, col. 1556–1559.

led the world in legislating against the vile trade in the slavery of human beings.'[50] Conservative William Hague, biographer of abolitionist William Wilberforce, described abolition as 'a moral benchmark of which other civilised societies rightly took note.'[51] Another Conservative, Malcolm Moss, ruled out an apology for the slave trade, asserting triumphantly that 'it was our country that produced the moral giants of their time.'[52] Obscuring the fact that one in two enslaved Africans crossed the Atlantic in a British ship, the debate became an exercise in 'remembering the abolition, forgetting the "trade".'[53]

Temporal tropes pervade the slavery debates. For many speakers, the apparently forward movement of time made it more important to speak about the present and future rather than the past. Large swathes of a debate that was supposed to be about the historic slave trade and its legacies segued into a discussion about contemporary forms of slavery and human trafficking. When Conservative MP Anthony Steen was rebuked by the Speaker for straying too far from the topic of the debate, he protested— quite reasonably—that 'at least 50% of hon. Members' speeches have concentrated on human trafficking and the new forms of slavery.'[54] Pressing as these issues are, their discussion had the effect of dimming the spotlight that the debate was intended to have shone on British culpability for the slave trade. For one thing, the geographies of contemporary human trafficking are different from those of the Middle Passage, enabling the old slave-owning powers to recast themselves as countries of refuge and rescue of trafficked persons rather than owning up to their sordid histories as perpetrators of enslavement. In addition, the discussion of contemporary slavery focused largely on 'sexual slavery', as if to insinuate that racial slavery was a thing of the past, while also obscuring the inseparability of sexual and racial oppression in historic and contemporary slavery.[55]

Many of the speeches suggested that the passage of time was the great obstacle to the offering of an apology for slavery. In some variants of the argument, time altered the moral status of the institution of slavery. Taking a view of morality as historically contingent, speakers argued that practices such as slavery that are considered crimes against humanity today were not

50. HC Deb, 20 March 2007, vol. 458, col. 687.
51. HC Deb, 20 March 2007, vol. 458, col. 696.
52. HC Deb, 20 March 2007, vol. 458, col. 742.
53. Waterton, 'Humiliated Silence', 131.
54. HC Deb, 20 March 2007, vol. 458, col. 728. See, for example, HC Deb, 20 March 2007, vol. 458, cols. 710, 714, 718, 728, 766.
55. For a critique of the use of the rhetoric of slavery in relation to contemporary forms of transactional sex, see Shah, Street Corner Secrets, 18–22.

morally wrong at the time of their commission, making their retrospective condemnation anachronistic.[56] But blithe assertions of the moral permissibility of slavery in the past typically ignore contrarian voices in those pasts. The writings of the sixteenth-century Spanish theologian Bartolomé de las Casas suggest that influential critiques of European conquest, genocide, and slavery emerged from within the ruling culture almost contemporaneously with the advent of these practices.[57] More pertinently, enslaved and formerly enslaved persons articulated powerful and eloquent objections to their subjection—figures such as Olaudah Equiano and Frederick Douglass were household names in their time.[58] To speak of slavery as a morally acceptable practice in its time is effectively to place contemporaneous opponents of slavery *out* of their time.

The more widely articulated temporal objection to apology underscored a putative lack of connection between those who committed morally heinous acts and those being called upon to apologise on their behalf. Liberal Democrat Vince Cable opined that 'in any sensible ethical system, one cannot apologise for things that happened ten generations ago.'[59] For Conservative Tobias Ellwood, the lack of any 'direct connection' between today's leaders and their predecessors made an apology unfeasible.[60] Emma Waterton astutely draws attention to the hypocrisy inherent in this stance, noting that 'paradoxically, while there is a strongly-held view that one cannot feel guilty about those things you did not commit, there is no such injunction against feeling pride in a temporally distant group's achievements.'[61] More fundamentally, gestures of temporal rupture that sever the present from the past undermine the ability of political communities to exercise agency. As Janna Thompson has argued, without a conception of intergenerational responsibility whereby present citizens accept responsibility for the actions and injustices perpetrated by their predecessors, it would be impossible for them to enter into commitments that bind future generations.[62]

Tellingly, the temporal objections to apology that were articulated so forcefully in the slavery debates have not precluded the British state from offering apologies in other contexts. Of particular interest for the purpose of this chapter are apologies related to the criminalisation of homosexuality. In December 2013, the computer pioneer and World War II

56. HC Deb 20, March 2007, vol. 458, cols. 741–742.
57. De Las Casas, *Brief Account*.
58. Equiano, *Interesting Narrative*; Douglass, *Narrative*.
59. HC Deb, 20 March 2007, vol. 458, col. 710 (see also cols. 773, 779).
60. HC Deb, 20 March 2007, vol. 458, col. 762.
61. Waterton, 'Humiliated Silence', 133.
62. Thompson, 'Apology'.

codebreaker Alan Turing was granted a posthumous royal pardon for a 1952 conviction for gross indecency.[63] Turing had been arrested for having sex with a nineteen-year-old man and was given a choice between chemical castration and imprisonment. He chose the former, but was dead within two years as a result of what was described as suicide. The 2013 pardon was the result of a campaign launched by a coalition of computer scientists, historians, and LGBT activists who were determined to honour Turing's memory for his contribution to the war effort and to science. It followed a 2009 apology from then Prime Minister Gordon Brown, who said, 'on behalf of the British government, and all those who live freely thanks to Alan's work, I am very proud to say: we're sorry. You deserved so much better.'[64]

In the Turing case the evident lack of connection between the authorities who had zealously enforced an unjust law against him and those called upon to apologise for this did not weaken the ability or resolve of the latter to take responsibility for the actions of their predecessors. Here, 'direct connection' was established by the continuous corporate personality of the state, rather than by an affinity between the individuals who committed the injustice and those who apologised for it. Moreover, the question of moral anachronism was never raised in respect of the Turing case, even though it might justifiably have been. After all, Turing was posthumously pardoned for an act that had been considered criminal at the time of its commission under a duly constituted law, and for which he had been convicted in accordance with due process. If anything, the enormously popular Turing pardon attested to a public appetite for morally anachronistic gestures that are seen to reverse historic injustices while also affirming the changed values of the community. Anachronistic judgements about the past trouble historians because they disrupt the effort to reconstruct the past with its meanings intact. But political communities demand a different relationship with the past. Insofar as identity is historically constituted, shifts in moral values as a result of political struggle must trigger an unending revisionism in moral judgements about the past, if only to allow an ever changing community to live with itself and its pasts.

A sceptic might distinguish the Turing apology from the slavery non-apology on a number of grounds, including the temporal. The sceptic might argue that the Turing case was more amenable to apology because a shorter period of time had lapsed between the commission of the injustice

63. BBC News, 'Royal Pardon'.
64. Brown, 'Gordon Brown'.

and the demand for apology. Britain's 'responsibility' for anti-sodomy laws in its former colonies might be dated, at the very latest, to the moment of decolonisation in the mid-twentieth century, roughly a century and a half after its abolition of the slave trade. But the putative temporal difference between these contexts is not a matter of brute chronology, for the duration of the institution of slavery cannot adequately be described with reference to the temporal markers of abolition and emancipation. In her account of the failure of Reconstruction in the post–Civil War United States, Saidiya Hartman demonstrates that emancipation was 'less the grand event of liberation than a point of transition between modes of servitude and racial subjection.'[65] Her argument resonates with a tradition of radical black scholarship that has traced the continuities between plantation slavery and contemporary institutions such as the prison industrial complex.[66] More significantly, Hartman cuts to the question of why the ghosts of slavery haunt the present with piercing clarity when she says:

> If slavery persists as an issue in the political life of black America, it is not because of an antiquarian obsession with bygone days or the burden of a too-long memory, but because black lives are still imperilled and devalued by a racial calculus and a political arithmetic that were entrenched centuries ago. This is the afterlife of slavery—skewed life chances, limited access to health and education, premature death, incarceration, and impoverishment. I, too, am the afterlife of slavery.[67]

To assert this, she clarifies, 'is not to deny the abolition of slavery or to assert the identity or continuity of racism over the course of centuries, but rather to consider the constitutive nature of loss in the making of the African diaspora and the role of grief in transatlantic identification.'[68] It is to recognise that 'the "time of slavery" negates the common sense intuition of time as continuity or progression; then and now coexist; we are coeval with the dead.'[69] Hartman's theorisation of the 'time of slavery' is profoundly relevant to the argument I am trying to make here in the way it exposes the hollowness of the insinuation that slavery is too temporally remote to be deserving of or amenable to the forms of historical redress that we might accord putatively more recent injustices.

65. Hartman, *Scenes of Subjection*, 6.
66. Davis, *Prison Industrial Complex*.
67. Hartman, *Lose Your Mother*, 6.
68. Hartman, 'Time of Slavery', 758.
69. Ibid., 759.

We need not look very hard to see how the time of slavery (and we might add, indentured labour) infuses contemporary British political life. Witness the everyday disposability of black and brown bodies, evident at the time of writing in a concatenation of atrocities including the Grenfell tower fire, the Islamophobia of 'anti-radicalisation' programmes such as Prevent, the state's production of a 'hostile environment' for migrants, and the perennial moral panic around refugees and asylum seekers. Nor is there reason to suppose that it is only the descendants of the dominated who are haunted by the spectres of past injustice. In the wake of the racist murder in 1993 of black British teenager Stephen Lawrence—a seismic event in the racial politics of contemporary Britain—a public inquiry headed by Sir William Macpherson famously concluded that the Metropolitan Police Service was 'institutionally racist'. Macpherson's ancestors—specifically a namesake who journeyed to the West Indies around 1800—were slave owners. Pointing to this genealogy, historian Catherine Hall wonders 'what part those imperial hauntings played in his understanding of the many failures attending the death of Stephen Lawrence?'[70] And yet haunting, or what Derrida calls 'hauntology', is an imprecise science, relying for its effects on the intersubjective relationship between the ghost and its host. Having slave owners in the family tree did not make David Cameron any more receptive to the claim for reparations with which he was confronted on a state visit to Jamaica.[71] If anything, Cameron demonstrated a remarkable tone deafness on the issue, urging his audience to 'move on' from such demands and attempting to soften his refusal with the promise of financial aid to build—of all things—a prison.[72]

THE MATERIALITY OF ATONEMENT

The British state has refused to apologise for slavery, presuming that such a gesture would bolster the case for reparations, now formally demanded by Caribbean Community (CARICOM) states.[73] This is why Tony Blair, prime minister at the time of the abolition commemoration debates, could bring himself to offer only an expression of 'deep sorrow' on the eve of the bi-centenary.[74] MPs expressed support for Blair's position across party lines,

70. Hall, 'Persons Outside the Law', 5.
71. Shepherd, 'David Cameron'. For an insightful account of the afterlives of slavery in the Jamaican context, see Shepherd, 'Slavery'.
72. BBC News, 'David Cameron'.
73. See http://caricomreparations.org/.
74. BBC News, 'Blair "Sorrow"'.

avoiding—in some cases explicitly refusing—an apology, and offering expressions of 'sincere regret', 'profound regret', and 'acknowledgement' instead.[75] Conversely, perhaps atonement for anti-sodomy laws appears to be more forthcoming because it is thought to be relatively costless. What costs it might incur in the form of diplomatic and monetary support to LGBT movements in the global South would be firmly within the discretion of a British government amenable to such assistance, and of a far lower order of magnitude than the sums that slavery reparations advocates typically discuss. To make a brutally obvious point, perhaps atonement is more contemplable in contexts in which it is seen to have no serious material repercussions.

Once again, the distinctions between these contexts are less clear-cut than they appear. The Turing apology and pardon have paved the way for a broader initiative that would pardon the nearly 50,000 men who were convicted under the same law as Turing was in the period during which it remained in force. In January 2017, a cross-party 'Turing's Law' came into effect, providing for posthumous pardons while also allowing those still living to apply to have their convictions deleted under a so-called disregard process. The application process was instituted in preference to a blanket pardon to prevent people from claiming to be cleared of offences that are still crimes, such as sex with a minor, sex in a public lavatory, and non-consensual sex.[76] Nearly 10,000 of the men convicted for 'gross indecency' are still alive. Activists have already begun to make the case for compensation owed to these men, citing the difficulties of unemployment, homelessness, family breakup, social stigma, and mental distress that many suffered as a result of their convictions.[77] Compensation would not be unprecedented, given the recent initiative of the German government to similarly quash convictions under its historic anti-sodomy law, Paragraph 175, and its allocation of 30 million euros to be paid as compensation to those victimised by it.[78] That the British government has opened the door to this possibility suggests that the Turing pardon and atonement for anti-sodomy laws more generally may not be entirely costless.

Still, in the case of slavery, the spectre of an infinitely larger transfer of resources to the descendants of the enslaved seems to have a chilling effect on even non-monetary expressions of atonement. In 2005, the theologian Robert Beckford produced a documentary featuring a

75. HC Deb, 20 March 2007, vol. 458, cols. 710, 741–742, 773.
76. UK Ministry of Justice, 'Press Release'.
77. Duffy, 'How Many People'.
78. Deutsche Welle, 'Germany to Pay'.

discussion between an economic historian, an actuary, and a workers' compensation lawyer who were invited to calculate the value of unpaid labour, unjust enrichment, and pain and suffering deriving from the enslavement of four million people. The experts came up with the staggering figure of £7.5 trillion, which amounted to six times the annual income of the United Kingdom at the time.[79] One guesses that the initiative was intended to underscore the enormity of the crime of transatlantic slavery and the weight of responsibility that former slave-owning powers bear for dismantling its legacies, with little expectation that its forensic calculations would compel an actual transfer of resources.

Indeed, many reparations activists are keen to deconstruct the popular understanding of reparations as a cash handout. The grassroots Pan-Afrikan Reparations Coalition in Europe (PARCOE) has criticised the focus on monetary reparations as misguided even if well-meaning, arguing that its narrow understanding of the debt owed sacrifices structural transformation for short-term gain.[80] Others have proposed a range of alternative measures by which reparations might be made, including the reframing of 'development' and 'debt forgiveness' as obligations of justice rather than charity owed by the global North to the South, and the imperative of a self-driven process of psychic repair.[81] Hartman declares herself to be agnostic on the question of reparations, arguing that there is something 'innately servile' about petitioning governments that are unwilling even to acknowledge that slavery was a crime against humanity.[82] For her, the ghosts of slavery demand something at once more autonomous from the state and more ambitious—nothing less than the reconstruction of society. As she puts it, 'I refuse to believe that the slave's most capacious political claims or wildest imaginings are for back wages or debt relief. There are too many lives at peril to recycle the forms of appeal that, at best, have delivered the limited emancipation against which we now struggle.'[83] I suspect that reparations denialists understand this. It is not the material infeasibility of reparations, even if we are constantly reminded of this, so much as the intransigence of white supremacy that undergirds denial.

79. Beckford and Mathur, *Empire Pays Back*.
80. Pan-Afrikan Reparations Coalition in Europe, 'PARCOE Position Paper'.
81. Chinweizu, 'Reparations'.
82. Hartman, *Lose Your Mother*, 166.
83. Ibid., 170.

In an insightful reading of Derrida's *Spectres of Marx*, Wendy Brown observes that 'while ghosts are "furtive and untimely," coming and going as they please, they can also be conjured and exorcised—solicited, beckoned, invoked, dismissed—and thus made to live in the present or leave the present in a manner that shapes both possibilities for and constraints on the future.'[84] The verbs in this sentence attest to the labour of what we might call a politics of spectres. As Brown explains, conjuring is 'a precise and deliberate activity paradoxically combined with pure hope.' More than simply figuring the presence of the past in the present, conjuring 'indexes a certain capacity to invoke and diminish it, to demand its presence on stage or to attempt to banish it to the wings.'[85] In juxtaposing distinct parliamentary reckonings with the spectres of colonialism, I have been trying to make visible the labour of conjuration, drawing attention to the efforts of political elites to beckon and solicit some spectres while burying and entombing others. What accounts for these preferences, and what might these spectral battles tell us about the politics of the present? If, as I have tried to suggest, time and money are red herrings in distinguishing between modes of reckoning with the 'homosexual' and 'racial' legacies of colonialism, why have British parliamentarians appeared so much more amenable to atonement for the former than the latter?

One answer lies in the very framing of this question, and the parliamentary debates that I have been reading, in terms that segregate analytics of sexuality and race. This segregation permits an imagination of the unmarked queer subject as white in ways that do interesting geopolitical work. I want to suggest that even as parliamentarians debate the 'Treatment of Homosexual Men and Women in the Developing World,' where the subjects of discussion are overwhelmingly people of colour, atonement for anti-sodomy laws is fuelled primarily by an elision of queerness with whiteness *at home* that operates on several levels. That is to say, we can only make sense of the otherwise inexplicable elite Conservative British mourning for the victims of colonialism in the developing world if we understand it as the runoff or remainder of tears shed for the injured white queer.

It is not incidental to the popularity of the campaign launched to pardon Turing that he was a middle-class white man of prodigious brilliance, who served the British state through his efforts to crack the Nazi Enigma code in a time of grave national peril.[86] Indeed, as historian Chris Waters has

84. Brown, *Politics Out of History*, 151.
85. Ibid.
86. Hodges, *Alan Turing*.

argued, Turing was exceptional even by the standards of 1950s Cheshire, where most men arrested for sexual offences were working class, unrepresented by private legal counsel, and not given the option of chemical castration to avoid a prison sentence, as Turing was.[87] While anti-queer laws and social attitudes ensnared people across lines of gender, race, and class, the knowledge that they also hurt white men with political, social, economic, and cultural capital—men like Oscar Wilde, Jean Genet, Harvey Milk, and of course Turing—elicits a visceral sense of horror amongst even the most powerful in contemporary public life. At a reception in the Chamber of the Speaker of the House of Commons marking the formation of the APPG on Global LGBT Rights in July 2015, I was struck by how a number of MPs in the group expressed joyful incredulity at the prospect of working to advance LGBT rights globally from within an institution where poignantly remembered and unnamed senior colleagues had been unable to be public about their sexualities in the not distant past.[88] In the 2017 British general election, forty-five queer MPs were elected to Parliament, reportedly giving it the highest level of out queer representation (7%) ever recorded in any legislature. All were white and none was trans—a fact that did not preclude this event from being reported as an 'LGBTQ' story.[89] Increasing queer representation of this kind in Parliament narrows the gap between the atoners and the atoned for, but may also circumscribe the imagination of atonement in particular ways.

British parliamentary interest in LGBT rights in the developing world and especially in the Commonwealth was the product of sustained engagement by the London-based organisations I discussed earlier in this chapter. Kaleidoscope led the way through the formation of the Parliamentary Friends of the Kaleidoscope Trust Group in 2013.[90] In this, it benefited from the high-level contacts of its co-founder Lance Price, who had been a media advisor to Tony Blair.[91] Not dissimilarly, in a candid interview with me after his departure from HDT, Cooper—an accomplished QC and a 2007 recipient of the Order of the British Empire (OBE) for services to human rights—was forthright about the degree to which his status as a 'posh white man' enabled him to facilitate access to the highest levels of British government for visiting activists from the global South.[92] Access

87. Waters, 'Turing in Context'.
88. Participant observation, House of Commons, London, 21 July 2015.
89. Reynolds, 'UK Just Elected'.
90. Kaleidoscope Trust, 'Kaleidoscope Trust'.
91. Waites, 'LGBTI Organizations', 649–650.
92. Interview with Jonathan Cooper (former Chief Executive, Human Dignity Trust), London, 25 November 2016.

was further eased by the fact that British LGBT activists were beginning to think globally at a time when political elites were increasingly keen to engage with their concerns. In the words of Alastair Stewart, formerly of Kaleidoscope and working with HDT at the time of writing, 'they had the keys to the door, but the door was already open.'[93] In Stewart's view, politicians were willing to discuss global LGBT rights, in part out of a perception that the domestic LGBT agenda had been more or less achieved. Moreover, the Conservative Party was keen to use LGBT rights, particularly support for same-sex marriage, as a means of detoxifying its image from 2010 onwards. Having been on the wrong side of many domestic LGBT battles over decriminalisation, equalisation of the age of consent, and the egregiously homophobic section 28, Conservative politicians viewed support for global advocacy of LGBT rights as an opportunity to burnish their queer credentials.

The history of battles over section 28 renders particularly ironic the segregation of sexuality from race in the elite political imaginary. The provision was inserted into the Local Government Act by the Thatcher government in 1988 to prohibit local authorities from 'promoting homosexuality' especially in schools, remaining in force till 2000 in Scotland and 2003 in the rest of the United Kingdom. By portraying local authorities as dangerously permissive, section 28 effectively fused homophobia with an attack on what were seen as bastions of leftist resistance to the central government. In her prescient account of the 'new right discourse' of Thatcherism, Anna Marie Smith demonstrates how the homophobic moral panic that produced section 28 drew a number of its discursive tropes—the threat of disease, foreign invasion, unassimilable others, dangerous criminals, subversive intellectuals, and excessive permissiveness—from earlier racist moral panics. Smith argues that (Enoch) Powellian and Thatcherite racism had become so normalised that subsequent demonisations tended to be shaped by the contours of its codes, tactics, and metaphors.[94] In Gianmaria Colpani's useful restatement, Smith provides an account of how racism structures the terrain on which homophobia installs itself.[95] That queerphobias might be path dependent on racism seems never to have occurred to today's elite political class who proclaim the queer friendliness of a Britain that is simultaneously convulsed by the anti-migrant discourse that fuelled the Brexit vote of 2016.

93. Interview (skype) with Alastair Stewart (former Acting Executive Director, Kaleidoscope Trust), 5 October 2016.
94. Smith, *New Right Discourse*, 22.
95. Colpani, 'Queer Hegemonies', 64.

In comparison with cosy interactions between elite LGBT activists and British parliamentarians, relationships between slavery reparations activists and their closest parliamentary interlocutors look somewhat different. In the parliamentary debates on the bicentenary of abolition, interventions by black MPs were crucial in underscoring the exceptionalism of transatlantic slavery,[96] in recognising the legacies of slavery,[97] and especially in offsetting the 'Wilberforcemania'[98] of white speakers with the reminder that enslaved persons emancipated themselves in insurrections like the Haitian revolution and countless lesser known rebellions.[99] Yet, with the exception of the late Bernie Grant, the Labour MP for Tottenham who co-founded and chaired the UK-based African Reparations Movement, black British politicians have not endorsed the call for reparations, even in the less-monetarily focused sense that many activists champion. (Interestingly, in her discussion of section 28, Smith singles out Grant as the only Labour politician who was willing to defend the introduction of queer positive images in local schools' sex education curricula—offering an example of political courage across a range of issues that remains unusual to this day.[100]) Grant's successor as Tottenham MP, David Lammy, went on record at the time of the abolition bicentenary as saying that he did not want to get into a 'blame fest' and commending Blair for having gone 'further than any other leader of any western democracy' in his expression of sorrow for the country's slave trading past.[101] Reading the 2007 British parliamentary debates, Barbadian historian and reparations advocate Hilary Beckles laments that 'it was a shameful sight to see and hear descendants of enslaved blacks singing the Blair song in and out of Parliament . . . the black group in the British Parliament did not support, even moderately, the notion of reparations as reconciliation.'[102]

Taking us back to the 2001 Durban Conference Against Racism, Racial Discrimination, Xenophobia and Related Intolerance, Beckles draws our attention to a broader and more disturbing response to the reparations agenda that might be described as white denial performed in blackface.

96. See the speech by Baroness Young of Hornsey (Crossbench) at HL Deb, 10 May 2007, vol. 691, col. 1570.
97. See the speech by Dawn Butler (Lab) at HC Deb, 20 March 2007, vol. 458, col. 719; see also the speech by Baroness Howells of St. Davids (Lab) at HL Deb, 10 May 2007, vol. 691, col. 1542.
98. Shepherd, 'Slavery', 13.
99. See the speech by Dianne Abbott (Lab) at HC Deb, 20 March 2007, vol. 458, cols. 698, 706. See also the speech by Jeremy Corbyn (Lab) at col 714.
100. Smith, New Right Discourse, 195.
101. BBC News, 'Blair "Sorrow"'.
102. Beckles, Britain's Black Debt, 197.

When the US delegation famously withdrew from the conference in protest against the equation of Zionism with racism and the appearance of the demand for slavery reparations on the conference agenda, its objections were voiced by two African Americans then serving in government: Secretary of State Colin Powell and National Security Advisor Condoleezza Rice. Analogously, the black Labour politician Baroness Valerie Amos (director of SOAS University of London, where I teach, at the time of writing) headed the British delegation and articulated its objections to the demand for slavery reparations. Beckles, who headed the Barbadian delegation to the conference, recalls that 'Amos was adamant that slavery and slave trading were not crimes because the British Parliament, and its colonial machinery, had made them legal.'[103] The delegations talked past each other, with British reliance on a strictly positivist interpretation of international law failing to engage with the Caribbean states' insistence that a moral global economy required acknowledgement and repair of the ravages that they had suffered as a result of transatlantic slavery.[104]

It is not difficult to appreciate the reasons for the hesitation that even progressive black politicians might feel in approaching the legacies of slavery through the idiom of reparation. The racism of mainstream white politicians and publics, the reductionist perception of reparations as a cash transfer, and a stubborn white leftist tendency to view all social justice concerns primarily through the prism of class make the issue a political non-starter.[105] In any case, it is less useful to focus on individuals, parties, or even governments than to think through the larger temporal and discursive structures that enable and disable the conjuring of particular spectres of colonialism at particular times. What is it about our historical moment that allows for the expression of atonement for the homosexual legacies of colonialism more easily than for its racial ones?

Framed in this way, the question becomes easier to answer. For some time now, queer theorists have tracked the manner in which 'LGBT rights' have come to function as a signifier of global modernity.[106] Yet 'civil rights'—those fragile achievements of anti-racist struggles—have never performed this role. As Paul Gilroy notes, 'the triumph over racism has not

103. Ibid., 195.
104. Du Plessis, 'Historical Injustice'.
105. Interview with Esther Stanford-Xosei (reparations activist), London, 14 October 2016. My requests for interviews were politely declined by the offices of David Lammy and Diane Abbott. Both expressed support for my interest in slavery and reparations, while citing time constraints in justification of their non-availability.
106. Hoad, 'Arrested Development'; Binnie, *Globalization of Sexuality*; Puar, *Terrorist Assemblages*.

been brought forward as a measure of modernization or an indication of national progress.'[107] This is not surprising when one recalls that it was the weakest members of international society—what Vijay Prashad evocatively calls 'the darker nations'—that championed international norms against racism, colonialism, and apartheid.[108] Little wonder, then, that anti-racism has rarely been an emblem of national prestige in the metropole. Instead, as Gilroy has persuasively demonstrated in the British context, the presence of black and brown immigrant bodies projects the ambivalences of empire into the national consciousness, reminding the white nation of its decline and thwarting the melancholic repressions of memory that are its preferred response to the loss of empire. As he explains, one strategy of escape from postcolonial melancholia has been a neurotic, compensatory attachment to the tribulations and triumphs of the anti-Nazi struggle which remains—undiminished by the passage of time—the nation's finest hour, perhaps because it provides the last moment of moral clarity and heroism before it commences its long decline.[109] We see the central tropes of this story being endlessly repurposed, particularly as Britain contemplates Brexit, in the context of which they are deployed to assuage the anxieties generated by a self-inflicted loneliness.

As I have shown in this chapter, a different response to the failures of melancholic repression that Gilroy calls attention to can be seen in the gestures of manic reparation that are sometimes made in a bid to snatch pride from the jaws of shame when the spectres of colonialism become too difficult to contain. While such gestures are visible in respect of the spectres of both the 'sexual' and 'racial' legacies of colonialism, this chapter has sought to bring into relief the divergent ways in which these spectres haunt contemporary British elites. Working through contradictions in the arguments that purport to justify these divergent reckonings with the past, I have argued that categorical expressions of atonement for the colonial imposition of anti-sodomy laws abroad are secured at the expense of a whitening of queer suffering at home.

SPECTRES OF THE QUEER ENSLAVED

In June 2016, a deeply divided UN Human Rights Council (HRC) voted to establish an Independent Expert on protection against violence and

---

107. Gilroy, *After Empire*, 136.
108. Prashad, *Darker Nations*.
109. Gilroy, *After Empire*, 95–98.

discrimination based on sexual orientation and gender identity. Five months later, the African Group of states in the UN General Assembly unsuccessfully attempted to challenge the legality of the independent expert's mandate.[110] The African resolution complained that 'non-internationally agreed notions such as sexual orientation and gender identity [were being] given attention, to the detriment of issues of paramount importance such as the right to development and the racism agenda.'[111]

There may be a legitimate discussion to be had about the relative priority accorded to struggles against discrimination on the basis of sexuality and race in the UN human rights system and, more profoundly, in our conceptualisation of modernity itself. Yet the juxtaposition of 'sexual orientation and gender identity' with 'the racism agenda', as if these had nothing to do with one another, reiterates the segregation of sexuality from race that I have been tracking in other arenas. If in the British Parliament this segregation allows the unmarked queer to masquerade as white, in the imaginary of the African Group the unmarked black subject of racism is straight. We might say, following Carastathis, that the very categories of 'sexuality' and 'race' come to be revealed in these deployments as 'invisibly intersectional'.[112] While this invisible intersectionality reflects hierarchies internal to the struggles that produce these analytical categories, it may also point to the limits of the spectres that they have conjured. What kinds of spectres lurk in the shadows, unattended and unimpressed by the erratic attempts to reckon with the past that I have explored in this chapter?

In June 1646, colonial authorities in the Dutch colony of New Netherland in present-day Manhattan sentenced an enslaved man named Jan Creoli to death for the crime of sodomy. Creoli was accused of having raped a ten-year-old boy, also enslaved, named Manuel Congo. Upon confessing to multiple instances of sodomy, Creoli was sentenced to be 'choked to death, and then burnt to ashes.' Court records suggest that Congo also confessed to the deed. Regarding him as a willing party but taking a more lenient view in light of his age, the court spared Congo the death sentence but ordered him to be flogged while watching Creoli's execution 'tied to a stake, [with] faggots piled around him, for justice's sake. . . .'[113] We only know what the court chooses to tell us, but the many gaps in this story have invited queer of colour theorists to commune with its ghosts. Refusing the reductively sexualising logic of sodomy law adjudication, Vincent Woodward asks us

110. Associated Press, 'African Nations'.
111. Statement of the African Group, 4.
112. Carastathis, *Intersectionality*, 53.
113. Van Zandt, *Brothers among Nations*, 159–163.

to consider the emotional and erotic hungers that might have driven Creoli and Congo to risk punishment in the pursuit of erotic pleasure and to think of 'their satiation, their momentary fulfilment, their pleasure as an index of survival praxis and cultural renewal.'[114] Kendall Thomas invokes the case to make the claim that 'in the US, the historical roots of the consistent conjuncture of homophobic and racist violence are older than the nation itself.'[115] And citing the case as the 'first mention of black queers in what were to become known as the United States,' elias farajajé-jones traces the conjunction of erotophobia and negrophobia that it embodies to the Bible itself.[116]

Working through a different archive, Omise'eke Tinsley evokes the queer relationships that emerge between women in the holds of slave ships crossing the Atlantic between West Africa and the Caribbean archipelago. Tinsley finds evidence of these relationships in historical, literary, and anthropological sources as well as in language itself. Studying relationships between women in Suriname, she explains that the term 'mati', which Creole women use to refer to their female lovers, comes from mate 'as in shipmate—she who survived the Middle Passage with me.'[117] For Tinsley, the relationships that the term conjures are queer, not necessarily in the sense of referring to same-sex love (although they may do that, too) but in the sense of disrupting the violence of normative order: 'connecting in ways that commodified flesh was never supposed to, loving your own kind when your kind was supposed to cease to exist, forging interpersonal connections that counteract imperial desires for Africans' living deaths.'[118]

Listening to the fitful attempts of the British political class to reckon with the legacies of colonialism, the spectres of what Tinsley calls the 'queer Atlantic' might well ask 'where are we in this?' It is an impossible question, for the queer enslaved are unimaginable within the terms of rubrics that segregate sexuality from race. But we evoke their spectres not simply

114. Woodward, *Delectable Negro*, 232.
115. Thomas, '"Ain't Nothin' Like"', 34.
116. farajajé-jones, 'Holy Fuck', 327. The book of Genesis (9:19–28) tells the story of the Curse of Ham, the son of Noah, who is regarded as the ancestor of all black peoples. When Ham chances upon his father lying drunk and naked outside his tent, he looks at his father, unlike his brothers Shem and Japheth who cover Noah with a blanket. Hearing of this after he awakes, Noah curses Ham's son Canaan and his descendants, ordering them to become the 'lowest of slaves' for Shem, Japheth, and their descendants in perpetuity. In some versions of the story, Ham's gaze on his naked father codes a more serious transgression such as castration or sodomy, linking Ham and all black peoples not only to slavery, but also to illicit sex.
117. Tinsley, 'Black Atlantic', 191.
118. Ibid., 199.

to correct a representational error, as if all would be well if the historical record were more complete and the apologies for colonialism more thoroughgoing. As Avery Gordon tells us, 'following the ghost is about making a contact that changes you and refashions the social relations in which you are located.'[119] To evoke the spectres of the queer enslaved is also to recall the structural dependence of racism and queerphobia on one another. It is to attend to the historical conjunctures through which queerphobias have installed themselves on a terrain structured by racism. And it ought to compel us to recognise the futility, but also the scandal, of segregated struggles against these oppressions.

119. Gordon, *Ghostly Matters*, 22.

CHAPTER 5

Queer in the Time of Homocapitalism

In February 2014, three days after President Museveni assented to the Anti Homosexuality Act (AHA), the World Bank announced that it was delaying a $90 million loan to Uganda that was to have funded maternal and infant care and family planning.[1] By early March, Norway, Denmark, and Sweden had followed suit, restricting the Ugandan state's access to another $20 million in aid. The Ugandan shilling was rattled by these announcements, forcing the central bank to intervene in the currency markets on three occasions within days of the bill receiving presidential assent.[2] While it appeared for a time that the Bank was considering approving the loan with conditions intended to safeguard access to healthcare for LGBT persons, Bank President Jim Kim confirmed in an interview in April 2015 that the loan had lapsed and that the Ugandan government had withdrawn its request for the funds.[3] By then, the Constitutional Court had struck down the AHA, although the narrow procedural basis of its ruling and continuing uncertainty over confidentiality in accessing public health services did little to assuage concerns for the safety of LGBT patients. In subsequent interviews, Kim noted that the Bank was the only donor to completely stop the flow of money to Uganda, implicitly suggesting that this had had much to do with the law's demise.[4]

The Bank's response to the AHA elicited mixed reactions, even from friends of LGBT rights. *The Economist*, typically an enthusiastic

1. BBC News, 'World Bank Postpones'.
2. Croome, 'Sweden Suspends'.
3. Feder, 'World Bank President'.
4. *Economist*, 'Pride and Prejudice'.

Out of Time. Rahul Rao, Oxford University Press (2020). © Oxford University Press.
DOI: 10.1093/oso/9780190865511.001.0001

proponent of a queer liberal agenda, was highly critical. Conceding that the decision was well-intentioned, the magazine nonetheless argued that it risked undermining the Bank's authority as a technocratic institution by embroiling it in political controversy, that it was capricious in singling out Uganda and LGBT rights for attention, and that it could be counterproductive if it drove borrowers into the hands of less scrupulous lenders.[5] LGBT activists disagreed, responding in its pages with the counterargument that discrimination on the basis of sexual orientation and gender identity (SOGI) was itself a cause of poverty, the elimination of which was central to the Bank's mission. They called for the inclusion of SOGI considerations in the mandatory 'social and environmental safeguards' that had long conditioned Bank lending.[6] Remarkably, while kuchu activists appear not to have been consulted by the Bank before it made its decision about the Uganda loan, they were broadly supportive of its approach, reflecting a subtle shift in their own positions on conditionality. Activists had been critical of public insinuations of conditionality such as those made by David Cameron in 2011 during the period in which the AHB was being discussed, preferring 'quiet diplomacy' at this time.[7] Yet as Clare Byarugaba explained to me, in the changed context produced by the legislative passage of the Bill, they were happy to see powerful institutions such as the Bank take a more public and punitive stand on their behalf. At the same time, they continued to insist that money intended for social expenditure ought to be disbursed with conditions or redirected to nongovernmental entities rather than withheld.[8]

The controversy over Uganda fuelled a broader conversation between the Bank and LGBT activists about the need for a more systematic integration of SOGI concerns in its work. Three developments around the time of the decision on the Uganda loan are noteworthy. First, in February 2014, the Bank released the results of a study estimating the cost of homophobia to the Indian economy at between 0.1% and 1.7% of its 2012 GDP.[9] At an April 2016 meeting with LGBT activists in Washington, DC, Kim announced that the Bank would fund analogous research in respect of other countries.[10] Second, activists had been pushing the Bank to incorporate SOGI anti-discrimination commitments into the environmental and

5. *Economist*, 'World Bank: Right Cause'.
6. Quesada et al., 'World Bank'.
7. Pambazuka News, 'Statement'.
8. Interview with Clare Byarugaba (Programme Coordinator, Chapter Four Uganda), Kampala, Uganda, 10 June 2016.
9. Badgett, 'Economic Cost of Homophobia'.
10. Sinani, 'World Bank Take Pride'.

social standards that regulate its lending. Kim hinted that the prospect of a SOGI safeguard policy had been opposed by Saudi Arabia, Russia, Kuwait, and 'many African countries'.[11] The Bank's revised safeguard standards, published in August 2016 after extensive consultation, made no mention of SOGI concerns. These were relegated to a separate and less authoritative 'directive' published alongside the safeguards.[12] Third, in October 2016, Kim announced the appointment of Clifton Cortez as the Bank's advisor on SOGI issues, a position charged with promoting LGBTI 'inclusion' throughout the work of the Bank while also serving as a point of liaison for external stakeholders.[13] Notwithstanding uncertainty around the depth of the Bank's commitment to SOGI issues, Uganda's AHA was therefore productive of new forms of international governmentality that sought to shape states' views on gender and sexuality through the instrumentality of capital.

In paying increasing attention to these issues, the Bank reflects broader trends in global capitalism. While LGBT organisations such as the US-based Human Rights Campaign and UK-based Stonewall have long evaluated corporations on the basis of their policies and practices relating to LGBT employees,[14] global multinational corporations have more recently begun to make a 'business case' for LGBT 'diversity and inclusion'. Open for Business, a coalition of leading global companies across a number of sectors, describes itself as having been formed in response to the spread of anti-LGBT sentiment in many parts of the world. It seeks to strengthen the evidence base for making 'the business and economic case for LGB&T inclusion' with a view to empowering dissenters—often located, in its view, in ministries of finance and commerce—in the LGBT-hostile markets in which its members operate.[15] Out Leadership, a network of senior business executives drawn from seventy companies, mainly in the fields of finance and law, aims to boost the presence of 'LGBT+' people at the most senior levels of corporate leadership with the argument that this is beneficial for business bottom lines; there is, in its words, a 'return on equality'.[16] And

---

11. Ibid.

12. See World Bank, 'Environmental and Social Framework' and World Bank, 'Directive'; see also Kadden, 'World Bank Releases'.

13. World Bank, 'World Bank Announces'.

14. See, for example, the Human Rights Campaign Corporate Equality Index 2017, http://www.hrc.org/campaigns/corporate-equality-index and the Stonewall Workplace Equality Index, http://www.stonewall.org.uk/get-involved/workplace/workplace-equality-index.

15. Open for Business, accessed 26 February 2017, https://www.open-for-business.org/about/.

16. Out Leadership, accessed 26 February 2017, http://outleadership.com/about/.

notwithstanding its criticism of the World Bank's forays into this area, *The Economist* has launched a major initiative of its own, titled 'Pride and Prejudice', comprising a website and a series of public events, which seeks to draw attention to the 'economic and business costs of LGBT discrimination and the profitable opportunities that lie in overcoming it.'[17] (As it turns out, Pride is expensive: the cheapest ('student rate') tickets to its 2019 Hong Kong event were priced at $150.[18])

I suggest that we think about the increasing proclivity of some activists to make a 'business case' for LGBT rights as a temporal and specifically futural response to the difficulties of using the past as a springboard for advocacy. Unable to occupy the moral high ground in a conversation oriented toward a past that is too laden with embarrassing 'ex-colonial baggage',[19] they reframe it as one about the future in which LGBT rights are hailed as harbingers of economic growth, productivity, and dynamism. By deploying arguments grounded in the self-interest of their interlocutors in better public health and stronger economic growth, rather than in the language of human rights or the redress of historic injustice, activists believe that they can avoid the appearance of moralising condescension.

This chapter proceeds in four parts. First, it asks why leading institutions of global capitalism have begun to take activist stances against homophobia at this time. Answering this question requires paying attention to the temporalities of global capitalist crisis, as well as to the promise of futurity that infuses neoliberal reason. Second, it unpacks the terms on which the figure of the queer has come to be recognised as a potential 'stakeholder' by the global development industry and in the strategic thinking of global businesses. Surveying research on the 'cost' of homophobia, I suggest—in an argument that mirrors Puar's analysis of homonationalism but is also distinct from it—that this embrace is a selective one, splitting off 'productive' from 'unproductive' queers with insidious implications for queer anti-capitalist struggle. Third, the chapter explores understandings of 'homophobia' that underpin the putative business case against it. I demonstrate that in an ironic convergence with an influential strand of Marxist feminism, the Bank in particular understands homophobia in the highly

17. *Economist*, 'Pride and Prejudice', accessed 26 February 2017, http://prideandprejudice.economist.com/. See Hooper, *Manly States*, for a reading of *The Economist* as the embodiment par excellence of an Anglo-American hegemonic masculinity that has been central to neoliberal capitalism.

18. http://eventsregistration.economist.com/events/pride-and-prejudice-2019/fees-20a88fd3e8e74d8fb4b06edef5fab353.aspx, accessed 14 January 2019.

19. Interview with Peter Laverack (barrister, former consultant with the Human Dignity Trust), London, 28 October 2016.

limited terms that Judith Butler has criticised as 'merely cultural'.[20] Such an understanding perpetuates the homonationalist tropes of cultural backwardness through which the attitudes of ordinary Ugandans are typically viewed, while absolving the Bank and other agents of global capital of complicity in the production of the material conditions in which homophobic moral panics thrive. I situate the expression of such panics in Uganda in the simultaneous and interrelated advent of neoliberal structural adjustment and charismatic Pentecostalism, the latter of which is widely regarded as a key vehicle for new conservative moral discourses around sexuality. Fourth, moving between the registers of theory, activism, and cultural production, the chapter concludes with some speculative reflections on how the incipient global homocapitalism that it describes might be resisted. I ask how we might reconceive the place of erotic desire in revolutionary struggle.

GENDER, SEXUALITY, AND CAPITALIST CRISIS

Sexuality has long been central to the development agenda, even if only implicitly. Andrea Lynch writes that the development industry has tended to frame sexuality as a problem driving phenomena such as 'overpopulation', disease, and violence, while ignoring its positive and affirmative dimensions.[21] Moreover, it has tended to neglect homoerotic desire, thinking about sex between men primarily in terms of HIV risk, ignoring sex between women, and viewing trans people largely through the lens of sex work. This may be a function of a widespread tendency among development workers to map queer desire onto class. In the cynical but revealing observation of Gilles Kleitz, 'The poor simply can't be queer, because sexual identities are seen as a rather unfortunate result of western development and are linked to being rich and privileged. The poor just reproduce.'[22]

But as the World Bank's recent attentiveness to LGBT rights suggests, this worldview has begun to shift. HIV/AIDS provided the initial impetus for development organisations to acknowledge gender and sexual diversity and to craft interventions targeted at communities deemed to be 'high risk' populations. More recently, gender and sexuality have acquired greater prominence on the development agenda as a result of legal and political reforms such as the decriminalisation of homosexuality, recognition of same-sex partnership and adoption rights, and access to

20. Butler, 'Merely Cultural'.
21. Lynch, *Sexuality*, 21–22.
22. Kleitz, 'Why Is Development', 2.

gender-affirming surgery in some places, alongside intensifying opposition to these developments. Aid agencies based in states that have witnessed such initiatives have tended to take greater cognisance of these issues in proportion to their salience in domestic politics. This has also been an effect of the greater propensity of employees in such agencies to openly identify as queer in their professional lives. Andil Gosine has described how the founding of the World Bank's LGBT staff association GLOBE was instrumental, first, in getting staff to come out at work and to lobby the Bank for better benefits, and later, in pushing the Bank to exercise political leadership on HIV/AIDS and to support LGBT advocacy in the global South.[23]

In trying to understand how and why global development and financial institutions have taken a greater interest in sexuality, we can learn something from their considerably longer engagement with (cisgender heterosexual) women. Central to this engagement has been a tendency to instrumentalise gender as a response to crisis. Kate Bedford has argued that gender was central to the Bank's reinvention of itself after the failure of its structural adjustment programmes in the 1980s.[24] Stung by criticism of the policies that comprised the 'Washington Consensus', which included liberalisation, deregulation, and privatisation in exchange for Bank assistance, the 'post-Washington Consensus' purported to recognise the importance of the state by abandoning conditionality, committing to borrowing country 'ownership' of policymaking, and partnering with civil society. It identified good governance, social safety nets, and targeted poverty reduction as key priorities. The family and especially poor women became crucial sites for the Bank in demonstrating its commitment to a kinder and more inclusive approach to economic growth.

Nonetheless, the terms on which women were drawn into Bank projects revealed an enduring commitment to neoliberalism. Previous Bank gender policy had been criticised for overlooking the double burden placed on women when they entered formal employment, and for ignoring men altogether. Still, the conviction that women were empowered by formal employment remained central to Bank lending. Simultaneously, Bank research on poor men purported to reveal that unemployment was fuelling a crisis in masculinity, which manifested itself in behaviours such as alcoholism, drug abuse, sexual violence, and child neglect. Bedford demonstrates how these insights produced a new model of intimate attachment that became pivotal to the post-Washington Consensus. If Bank projects had once been

23. Gosine, 'World Bank's GLOBE'.
24. Bedford, *Developing Partnerships*, 11.

informed by a breadwinner-housewife model of domesticity, now the Bank advocated a two-partner sharing model of love and labour in which women were encouraged to work more outside the home while men were urged to take on greater domestic caring responsibilities.[25] The new gender regime effectively reprivatised responsibility for social reproduction, privileging fatherhood promotion over state provision of childcare. Nonetheless, it appealed to a range of different constituencies because its benefits appeared unqualifiedly desirable. Greater sharing of the domestic labour of social reproduction was, after all, an unimpeachably feminist goal. Greater female employment in the market promised to disrupt traditional gender roles, and better gender relations promised a more efficient allocation of labour resources while also representing the Bank as a progressive agent.[26] Thus, gender relations were reimagined in ways that served neoliberal and feminist goals.

More generally, gender has been deployed in a variety of ways to reha-bilitate capitalism in the wake of the global financial crisis of 2007–2008. In one mainstream feminist reading, gender was seen to be constitutive of the crisis, which was diagnosed as the inevitable result of the aggressive, testosterone-fuelled culture of risk-taking that drove the unbridled pursuit of profit on trading floors. In this reading, women—imagined in essentialist ways as more prudent, risk-averse, inclusive, and compassionate—might have averted the crisis had they populated the upper echelons of business and finance in larger numbers. Emblematic of this view is journalist Ruth Sunderland's rhetorical question—'If Lehman Brothers had been Lehman Sisters, run by women instead of men, would the credit crunch have happened?'[27] Feminist scholars of international political economy have been critical of how such narratives have co-opted long-standing feminist demands for representation to obscure the structural causes of financial crises, as well as the tendency for their adverse effects to fall dispropor-tionately on women.[28] As Jacqui True observes, women became 'the silver bullet for the global financial sector, enabling corporations and states to redress perceptions of their risky and excessive behavior while avoiding major reform of the governance of markets.'[29] The championing of female capitalist leadership as a response to the crisis of capitalism also overlooks

25. Ibid., 22.
26. Ibid., 28–30.
27. Sunderland, 'Real Victims'.
28. Griffin, *Gendering the World Bank*; Elias, 'Davos Woman'; Hozić and True eds., *Scandalous Economics*.
29. True, 'Financial Crisis's Silver Bullet', 41.

how the elevation of some women is typically achieved at the expense of displacing the labour of social reproduction onto working class, racialised, and immigrant women. Indeed, Sara Farris accounts for the convergence of neoliberal, feminist, and xenophobic agendas in Western Europe in the ideological formation that she names 'femonationalism' by demonstrating how the facilitation of the entry of non-Western migrant and especially Muslim women into care and domestic work, while justified as a means of emancipating them from their oppressive 'cultures', operates to alleviate the crisis of social reproduction and to allow 'native-born' women to work outside the home.[30]

Sexuality has also come to be implicated in responses to capitalist crisis. Nicola Smith has usefully situated the advancement in the United Kingdom of a narrow gay agenda centred on same-sex marriage in the context of crisis-induced austerity that the country has endured for the last decade.[31] Although the push for marriage equality initially came from the centrist Liberal Democrats in 2010, the Conservative Party under David Cameron was quick to embrace the issue. Smith attributes this to its resonance with broader narratives articulated by British conservatives. On the one hand, the financial crisis and the resulting deficit were blamed on profligate welfare spending rather than the irresponsible lending of banks that had become 'too big to fail', thereby necessitating huge bailouts. Conservatives sought to shrug off the state's obligation to alleviate hardship by linking economic crisis to social decline, and calling for individual and familial responsibility by way of remedy. Cameron spoke of wanting to fix not only the budget deficit but also the 'responsibility deficit' apparently evident in 'troubled families' whom he described as being 'swamped with bureaucracy, smothered in welfare'.[32] Conservative support for same-sex marriage chimed perfectly with the drive to reprivatise social welfare through family promotion in a time of austerity. Thus, we need to make sense of the World Bank's initiatives in respect of gender and sexuality against the backdrop of a global financial crisis that was constituted and made sense of in a number of places through hegemonic narratives promoting austerity, state withdrawal, and the compensatory attachments of the family.

Until recently, gender research on the Bank has tended to portray it as a heteronormative institution.[33] While this claim is beginning to look dated, there are striking continuities in the Bank's understanding of the

30. Farris, *In the Name of Women's Rights*.
31. Smith, 'Queer Political Economy'.
32. Cameron, 'Troubled Families'.
33. Bedford, *Developing Partnerships*, 66; Griffin, *Gendering the World Bank*, 4–5, 204.

links between poverty and sexuality. Working through Bank research that suggests a relationship between poverty, masculinity, and misogyny, Bedford teases out an underlying belief that 'poor countries are more sexist than rich ones, and that markets transform gender relations in unequivocally more efficient and empowering directions.'[34] The analogous premise— that poor countries are more homophobic than rich ones—is on display in videos that staff at the Bank and the International Monetary Fund (IMF) produced as part of the viral *It Gets Better* campaign launched by US gay columnist Dan Savage to dissuade queer youth from committing suicide.[35] Both videos feature LGBT staff from the two institutions speaking about their struggles with growing up queer and being out in their personal and professional lives. On the Bank's video, one employee reflects that 'some [of his colleagues] had it easy coming out. But some others had it difficult. 'Specially those from developing countries.'[36] A speaker in the IMF video similarly elaborates, 'We have so many people from all over the world working here, and their ideas of sexuality, of orientation, of how things are supposed to be . . . it's all very different. You have anything from progressive Western countries to traditional Eastern countries. . . .'[37] Eliding 'culture' and capital, these narratives evoke central tropes of homonationalism, deploying queer tolerance to reproduce extant geopolitical hierarchies.

In a subversive reworking of the IMF video, parenthetically titled 'Pinkwashing version,' the Greek conceptual audiotextual performance duo FYTA draw attention to its conflation of the IMF's neoliberal project with an anti-homophobic civilising mission.[38] Employing humour, ridicule, and a dose of pseudo-psychoanalysis, the FYTA video is a viciously snarky deconstruction of the IMF's queer neoliberalism. Overlaying the IMF video with subtitled commentary, FYTA mock the coming out narratives of its overwhelmingly white, male, conventionally groomed, professional cast, drawing attention to the monotonously familiar and stereotypical elements in their narratives and deriding their excessive sentimentalisation in the video. FYTA scorn the narratives of personal trauma offered by each of the IMF staffers by juxtaposing their performances of suffering with reminders of the structural oppression perpetrated by the institution they work for. When a lesbian Haitian staffer—the token diversity face in the video— bemoans her upbringing in a Haiti where 'you don't hear people talking

34. Bedford, *Developing Partnerships*, 30.
35. See Puar, *Right to Maim*, 1–31, for a critique of the original campaign.
36. World Bank GLOBE, 'It Gets Better'.
37. IMF, 'It Gets Better'.
38. FYTA, 'IMF: It Gets Better'.

about gays and lesbians in a very positive way', FYTA remind us that the country's poverty was exacerbated by the devastation of its agricultural sector by IMF policies foisted on it in 1986 as part of loan conditionality.

Little of this comes as news to the informed viewer. Yet the juxtaposition of elite individual distress with widespread social devastation works to evacuate any sympathy we might feel for the individuals featured in the video. Instead, we are invited to marvel at their inability to enlarge their stand against their suffering into a stand against suffering per se—not least the suffering in which they are professionally implicated. There is something apposite about this critique being offered by queer Greek voices in the current conjuncture. In 2013, the IMF admitted to having mishandled the Greek debt crisis by underestimating the damage that its prescriptions of budget cuts and tax increases would do to the Greek economy.[39] Having endured a recession longer than the Great Depression, it does not take much to imagine how self-evidently absurd it must appear to queer Greeks to hear the IMF promise that 'It Gets Better'.

THE COST OF COSTING QUEERPHOBIA

One method by which the World Bank has attempted to persuade its stakeholders of the importance of LGBT rights has been through research seeking to establish the 'economic cost' of queerphobia. The Bank's first initiative in this respect was a 2014 report estimating the cost of exclusion of LGBT people to the Indian economy.[40] The report argues that such exclusion imposes avoidable costs on economies by lowering the productivity of LGBT people through discrimination in employment and education, and by undermining their health by contributing to their disproportionately greater experience of HIV/AIDS, violence, depression, and suicide. The study was first publicised in the very month that the Uganda loan was postponed, making headlines for its estimate that anti-LGBT stigma cost the Indian economy between 0.1% and 1.7% of its 2012 GDP.[41] Another study of thirty-nine countries makes the converse argument that the 'inclusion' of LGBT people as measured by the recognition of rights enumerated by the Global Index on Legal Recognition of Homosexual

39. Elliott and Smith, 'IMF "to Admit Mistakes"'.
40. Badgett, 'Economic Cost of Stigma'.
41. Badgett, 'Economic Cost of Homophobia', 4. The official report, released in October 2014, seems to have retreated from this quantitative claim, citing the lack of sufficient data on LGBT populations in India (Badgett, 'Economic Cost of Stigma').

Orientation (GILRHO) and the Transgender Rights Index correlates positively with increases in per capita GDP and a higher ranking on the Human Development Index. The study found that every additional right on the GILRHO was associated with $1,400 more in per capita GDP.[42] Both studies seek to incentivise governments to combat queerphobia by quantifying the economic growth that they would enjoy as a consequence of doing so. Economist M. V. Lee Badgett, the principal investigator in both studies, has argued that 'the economic argument for LGBT rights is a *complement* to the human rights argument', simply providing another angle from which to view the harms of human rights violations rather than replacing the moral case against them.[43]

I disagree. Wendy Brown has argued that neoliberal reason configures all aspects of life in economic terms, evacuating the subversive and moral content of political categories such as sovereignty, rights, and democracy.[44] When human rights are reconceived as a means to the ends of economic growth and competitive positioning in the global market, they are also subordinated to these ends. In seeking to appeal to constituencies who are more invested in the business bottom line than in rights for their own sake, efforts to cost queerphobia effectively ratify this order of priorities. While the coming together of growth and rights is welcome, this order of priority becomes a problem when they are in tension. In consecrating economic growth as the very basis on which the extension of rights to certain subjects is justified, the argument encourages us to forget the many ways in which the pursuit of limitless growth has undermined social justice and the environment. Moreover, it obscures the possibility that there might be a specifically queer investment in anti-capitalist critique.

For example, in light of the World Bank's turbulent history of involvement in India in development projects that have been destructive of livelihoods and environments,[45] we might legitimately wonder what queer adivasis[46] might make of a Bank project that hailed their participation as queers in the very processes that destroyed their lifeworlds as adivasis. Drawing on ethnographic fieldwork among the adivasis of Attappady, Kerala, Padini Nirmal has argued that the very survival of adivasis in the face of the combined onslaught of colonialism, modernity, capitalism,

---

42. Badgett et al., *LGBT Inclusion and Economic Development*, 2.
43. Badgett, 'Foreword', 15.
44. Brown, *Undoing the Demos*.
45. Roy, *Greater Common Good*.
46. 'Adivasi', meaning original inhabitant, refers to the indigenous peoples of the Indian subcontinent.

and postcolonial development might be read as queer.[47] More particularly, she demonstrates how these processes have transformed adivasi
gender relations, including through the imposition of gender differences
in practices of spirituality, labour, and communality.[48] By illuminating the
heterosexualising character of 'development', Nirmal's work helps to make
visible the ironies implicit in the development industry's determined conflation of queer freedoms and economic progress.

This conflation might account for the Bank's inability to imagine queers
as (wanting to be) anything other than upwardly mobile capitalist subjects.
Shaped by images that would be considered stereotypical even in the
Western contexts from which they are drawn, the Bank's incipient SOGI
research seems inattentive to the complex ways in which sexuality and
gender intersect with class, caste, race, religion, ability, nationality, and
other markers of differentiated belonging. Consider the passing observation in the 2014 report that lesbians in India tend to be pressured into
marrying men and having children. Bemoaning the lack of data on LGBT
employment and wages in India, it gestures at the lesbian 'wage premium'
observed in Western contexts—where research suggests that lesbians earn
9% more than heterosexual women—to speculate that Indian lesbians
might earn considerably more than they currently do if they were freed
from the constraints of compulsory heterosexuality and reproductive labour.[49] While this conclusion is plausible, it is reached through a process
of speculative analogical reasoning with a dissimilar cultural context.
The report seems to insinuate that ending discrimination in India would
have effects on family formation and household decision-making similar to those observed in the Western contexts from which its quantitative data are drawn, evincing little curiosity in the ethnographic literature
documenting the diverse social structures within which lesbian lives are
lived in India.[50] Although it does not discuss the reasons for the lesbian
wage premium observed in the West, in drawing attention to this phenomenon the report implicitly envisions the queer good life as one pursued by
autonomous workers unencumbered by responsibilities to children, extended family, or other community.

Two representations of the queer Indian good life that emerged almost simultaneously with this report suggest that such visions enjoy considerable

47. Nirmal, 'Queering Resistance', 183.
48. Ibid., 190–195.
49. Badgett, 'Economic Cost of Stigma', 31–32.
50. See, for example, Dave, Queer Activism; LABIA, Breaking the Binary; Sharma,
Loving Women.

popularity, despite their unrepresentativeness, within an emerging queer Indian middle class—so much so that it would be inaccurate to lay responsibility for their conception primarily with institutions of international governmentality. In July 2013, the United Nations Human Rights Office launched a global public education campaign for LGBT equality called 'Free & Equal'.[51] As part of the campaign, in April 2014 it released what it described as a 'Bollywood music video' featuring Indian actor Celina Jaitly, which went on to become one of the UN's most watched videos.[52] Titled 'The Welcome', the video depicts a young man bringing his boyfriend home to meet his family for the first time. The family are not expecting a 'special friend' of the same sex and are initially frozen in disbelief. But thanks to a deft and tactful musical intervention from Jaitly, referencing the changing times, the mood shifts decisively and everyone lives happily ever after. Critics of the video queried the elite milieu in which it was set—the pretext for the gay couple's homecoming is their attendance at a lavish wedding at which even the family dog is wearing a silk coat—as evidence of the detachment of mainstream gay activism from the lives of the overwhelming majority of queer Indians.[53] Indeed the choice of setting was puzzling, given that homophobic voices already discredit LGBT rights as an elite issue. Nonetheless, in embedding its pedagogical mission in the familiar cinematic idiom of the 'big wedding'—whose genealogy might be traced back through films such as *Monsoon Wedding* (2001), *Hum Aapke Hain Koun (Who Am I to You?)* (1994), and beyond[54]—the campaign demonstrated a keen awareness, doubtless shaped by the Indian artistes with whom it collaborated, of practices of cinematic spectatorship in contemporary India, where audiences of all classes avidly consume narratives depicting the lives of the super elite in a range of affective modes including identification, aspiration, and escapism. In this sense, what the queer critics were calling 'homonormativity' was also deeply 'authentic', conforming as it did to the genres and consumption practices of mainstream Hindi cinema. Moreover, as Karan Johar's blockbuster *Dostana (Friendship)* (2008) had already confirmed, the gay Indian subject had emerged in mainstream film as rich and consumption oriented—a veritable mannequin for the display of luxury brands, gadgets, and haute couture—rather than as a politically subversive figure in alliance with other subalterns.[55]

51. https://www.unfe.org/.
52. https://www.unfe.org/en/actions/the-welcome.
53. Mowlabocus, 'Homonormativity'.
54. Gopinath, *Impossible Desires*, 93–130.
55. Kapur, 'Unruly Desires', 124. See also Luther, 'Queering Normativity', for an analysis of Johar's oeuvre and impact on middle-class queer life in India.

The prospect of consumption as a route into citizenship was proposed by another early and widely circulated video representation of the queer Indian good life. Titled 'The Visit' and produced for Anouk, a line in contemporary 'ethnic' Indian apparel, the video was described on social media as India's first lesbian advertisement and generated much interest through this frame, judging by the three million views that it notched up within ten days of its release in June 2015.[56] It portrays a cohabiting lesbian couple also preparing for a first encounter with the parents of one of the women. The similarity in narrative premise underlying 'The Welcome' and 'The Visit'—both of which seek to resolve anxieties about the introduction of queerness into the heteronormative family but in ways that reinforce and entrench that family rather than disrupting it—points to the overwhelming homonormativity of such mainstream representations of queerness.[57] Quieter and more quotidian in its setting than 'The Welcome,' 'The Visit' is nonetheless also situated in a comfortably upper middle-class milieu. The women are surrounded by their possessions, many of which signify their cosmopolitan tastes ('tribal' art, a framed poster of A Clockwork Orange). Filling every frame, almost imperceptibly, are the products—clothes, cushion covers, rugs, curtains—that Anouk seeks to market. Produced in a moment in which homosexual conduct was illegal (after having enjoyed a brief period of legality between 2009 and 2013, as a result of a judgement decriminalising homosexuality delivered by the Delhi High Court but subsequently overruled by the Supreme Court), the advertisement offered a seductive reminder of the possibilities for queer self-expression through consumption in the market, notwithstanding legal liminality. In its depiction of this comfortably self-determining existence, the Anouk advertisement, produced by and for an Indian company, provides the perfect visual representation of the lesbian futures contemplated by the World Bank report.

Read together, these representations bring into relief the double-edged nature of consumption as a mode of queer self-expression.[58] On the one hand, queer consumption and visual representations thereof give queers an opportunity to navigate and occupy public space, particularly

56. Inani, 'India's First Lesbian Ad'.
57. An additional exhibit in this archive might be India's first gay matrimonial advertisement in English, published in 2015, which purported to break new ground in its public legitimation of same-sex desire but reinforced caste hierarchies by indicating a preference for a partner of the same caste (Borges, 'This Guy's Mom'). For a critique, see Sircar, 'New Queer Politics', 8–9.
58. Chasin, Selling Out, 24.

in contexts in which queerness is stigmatised.[59] At the same time, the representations through which the market hails queers constitute and consolidate queer subjectivities in what are often deeply elitist ways, rendering other expressions of queerness unintelligible. Beholden to an apparently welcoming market that offers respite from the hostile state, (some) queers acquire a stake in the success of capitalism, given its imbrication with their own liberation, that long outlives their stigmatisation by the state. Moreover, far from being foisted on the nation by international governmentality and capital, the representations through which queer consumers are hailed are co-produced with elite domestic constituencies, attesting to their hegemony as desired and desiring figurations of queer modernity. This hegemony is achieved by clothing these subjectivities in local idioms: this is what makes them *normative* in their respective locales. As such, the new homonormativities congealing in the global South are not simple transplants of Western homonormativity.

Above all, the World Bank's effort to attribute a cost to queerphobia is premised on the assumption that life can be conceived in terms of 'human capital', with injustice or injury being understood as lowering the stock of capital possessed by an individual or inhibiting its efficient utilisation.[60] Brown sees the conceptualisation of human beings as capital as a central feature of neoliberal reason. She argues that the evaluation of persons in terms of their contribution to or detraction from economic growth is regularly invoked to justify strategies of investment in or divestment from them, respectively.[61] Quite simply, those who do not contribute to growth can be sacrificed.[62] The effort to foster respect for rights by illuminating the economic cost of their violation makes respect for the personhood of queers contingent on the promise of their future productivity, were their personhood to be fully recognised. Premising citizenship on productivity disenfranchises those who are unable or unwilling to be productive within the terms of the market—the disabled, the indigenous, the unemployed, the elderly, the alienated. Indeed the consequences of a tightening link between productivity and respect for personhood have been evident in austerity-ridden economies, where public support for welfare for the 'unproductive' (read: undeserving) has become increasingly difficult to sustain.

59. For everyday examples from contemporary Kampala, see Peters, 'Kuchus in the Balance', 102–103, 125–127.

60. Badgett. 'Economic Cost of Stigma', 20; Badgett et al., *LGBT Inclusion and Economic Development*, 14–16.

61. Brown, *Undoing the Demos*, 109.

62. Ibid., 84.

In cleaving potentially productive from unproductive queers, homo-capitalism shares key discursive features of homonationalism, which, as Puar has demonstrated, incorporates within the nation those forms of queerness that have been authorised through processes of race/class/gender-sanitising, while excluding others.[63] But homocapitalism works differently from homonationalism even as it remains closely associated with it. In contexts where queerness is criminalised, homocapitalism offers a persuasive strategy for queer inclusion operative in a moment in which homonationalism has not (yet?) succeeded in drawing recalcitrant societies into its embrace or, worse, has aroused their antipathy. In drawing on the hegemonic logic of neoliberal reason, it offers a powerful and arguably more sophisticated alternative to homonationalism's heavy-handed tropes of civilisation and barbarism that tend to arouse anti-imperialist resistance. Where homonationalism coerces through its discourses of civilisational superiority, homocapitalism elicits consent with its promise of a rosy future of growth and productivity. This is not to suggest that homocapitalism lacks a coercive dimension (the Bank's punitive withdrawal of capital from Uganda is a reminder of this). But it is to suggest that the balance of coercion and consent in homonationalism and homocapitalism is different. Deploying Guha's Gramscian understanding of these terms, we might say that where the former tends toward dominance, the latter tends toward hegemony.[64]

To retain its hegemony, neoliberal reason must tell a story about why the good life that it promises is not yet here. Catherine Rottenberg has argued that strategies of temporal deferment are central to maintaining idealised visions of the good life that are beyond the reach of the vast majority in the present.[65] It is the promise of futurity—the suggestion that the good life is just around the corner, there to be had if only we were to make the requisite sacrifices in the present—that helps neoliberalism to smooth out its inherent contradictions, retaining its appeal even as it fails most people. The 'business case' for LGBT rights relies on a promise of futurity measured in the expectation of higher growth as a consequence of LGBT inclusion and reinforced by the threat of capital withdrawal as punishment for their exclusion. But what contradictions within neoliberalism might these temporal moves conceal? To answer this question, we need to understand how and why neoliberal capitalism nurtures the very phobias against which it also inveighs.

63. Puar, *Terrorist Assemblages*.
64. Guha, *Dominance without Hegemony*.
65. Rottenberg, 'Neoliberal Feminism'.

The Bank's 2014 study of the economic costs of queerphobia understands discrimination as being 'rooted in stigma', which results in the exclusion of LGBT people from full participation in social institutions.[66] Citing the work of psychologist Gregory M. Herek, it defines stigma as 'the negative regard and inferior status that society collectively accords to people who possess a particular characteristic or belong to a particular group or category.'[67] In this, it bears an uncanny resemblance to the theorisation of homophobia offered by Marxist feminist Nancy Fraser.

Fraser has advocated a 'bifocal' understanding of gender as both a class-like differentiation rooted in the economic structure of society, and a status differentiation privileging masculinity over femininity that is rooted in the status order of society.[68] These dimensions, she argues, are analytically distinct and irreducible to one another, even if they may interact with each other. Gender justice, in Fraser's view, requires both an objective redistribution of material resources to ensure that all participants in society can exercise voice, and an intersubjective cultural recognition of equal standing vis-à-vis one another. Although Fraser notes that virtually all injustices perpetrate both maldistribution and misrecognition, she constructs a spectrum of possible proportions in which they might be combined with injustices tilting more heavily in the direction of maldistribution at one end and those entailing primarily misrecognition at the other. Like the Bank, Fraser understands heterosexism primarily as a status injustice of misrecognition.[69]

Judith Butler reads Fraser as thereby relegating oppressions like heterosexism to the derivative and secondary status of the 'merely cultural'.[70] In contrast, Butler argues that in attacking the normative regulation of sexuality by key institutions sustaining the capitalist order—principally, the heteronormative family—movements against heterosexism are also threats to capitalism. She questions the epistemological distinction between recognition and redistribution that lies at the heart of Fraser's argument, noting that homophobic cultural norms that misrecognise queers also have maldistributive effects—for instance, by denying benefits or property to same-sex partners. In her response to Butler, Fraser acknowledges that

66. Badgett, 'Economic Cost of Stigma', 6.
67. Ibid., 12.
68. Fraser, *Fortunes of Feminism*, 162.
69. Ibid., 178.
70. Butler, 'Merely Cultural'.

queers suffer economic harm, but insists that such harm is a maldistributive consequence of a more fundamental injustice of misrecognition (it is here that the resonance with the Bank's view of homophobia as being 'rooted in stigma' is clearest).[71] Moreover, she accuses Butler of an 'Olympian indifference to history',[72] arguing that the relationship between queers and capitalism cannot be settled by definitional fiat. Here Fraser draws attention to the weakening of the links between sexuality and surplus value accumulation in late capitalist society, observing that the contemporary enemies of queers are not multinational corporations determined to extract their labour, but religious conservatives bent on denying their personhood.[73] Capitalism, Fraser concludes, no longer requires the heteronormative family as a stabilising institution.[74] Ergo, attacks on this particular figuration of the family are no longer necessarily anti-capitalist.

Fraser is right to historicise this discussion and to point to the growing rapprochement between capitalism and queerness, which, as I have suggested, is strikingly evident in places like India. But Butler is correct to question her much vaunted distinction between recognition and redistribution. In Lisa Duggan's influential account of LGBT politics in the United States in the 1990s, neoliberals co-opted the LGBT agenda by recognising claims to equality while downplaying demands for redistribution: in essence, they embraced a non-redistributive recognition politics. But crucially in Duggan's telling of this story, far from marking a real separation between different kinds of injustice, as suggested by Fraser, the distinction between recognition and redistribution is a ruse through which neoliberal capitalism pretends to become more inclusive by seizing on a low-cost way of projecting a new queer friendliness.[75] In reifying the distinction between recognition and redistribution, Fraser effectively endorses this ruse while also foreclosing investigations into the possible material roots of misrecognition.

The Fraser-Butler debate and the commentary that it has elicited have been limited in ways that have circumscribed such investigations. For one thing, both debate and commentary have unfolded largely on the terrain of the late capitalist West, begging questions about what the relationship between capitalism and sexuality might look like in other spatiotemporal conjunctures. Moreover, while persuasive in their criticism of her, Fraser's

71. Fraser, *Fortunes of Feminism*, 180.
72. Ibid., 181.
73. Ibid., 182–183.
74. Ibid., 183.
75. Duggan, *Twilight of Equality?*, 83.

critics risk being read as entertaining the voluntarist fantasy that capitalist homonormativity might have been obviated if queer activists had been more successful at refusing the putative distinction between recognition and redistribution. In what follows, I turn back to Uganda, given that developments in that country provided the ostensible pretext for the Bank's interest in queer sexualities. I also move away from the discourse analytic strategy of examining the narratives and counternarratives that constitute contemporary contestations around sexuality in Uganda to think about the structural conditions within which particular narratives acquire salience. In doing so, I make visible the manner in which the Bank is itself implicated in the production of these conditions—a fact that has remained unacknowledged in its pronouncements on the economic cost of stigma.

A focus on enabling conditions, rather than on the narratives of queer activists and their antagonists, also takes our attention away from the elite protagonists in these battles, to whom attention is typically devoted, and redirects it toward their audiences. In recent years, analysts have draws on Stanley Cohen's notion of 'moral panics' to theorise homophobia.[76] Cohen defined moral panics as widespread and volatile concern about the potential or imagined threat posed by a set of actors (folk devils) out of all proportion to any objective harm that they may be likely to cause, that fuels reactions of moral outrage and hostility against those actors.[77] The concept seems especially appropriate as a description of homophobic discourses in Uganda, given the manner in which they portray kuchus as paedophiles 'recruiting' children into homosexuality and as threats to the moral order.[78] In a crucial reorientation of Cohen's work offered in the context of a study of moral panics around 'mugging' in inner city Britain, Stuart Hall et al. suggest that the pivotal question 'is not why or how unscrupulous men [sic] work ... but why audiences respond.'[79] An interest in audiences, in addition to demagogues, might give us a better appreciation for how and why the cultivation of hatred can be populist.

Understanding this in the context of Uganda requires a fuller account of the production and consumption of homophobia than I have provided so far. In Chapter 2, I focused largely on a set of transnational elite relationships between US and Ugandan clergy and politicians forged in the context of frictions within the global Anglican Communion. While

76. Human Rights Watch, 'They Want Us Exterminated'.
77. Cohen, Folk Devils, xxvi.
78. Cheney, 'Locating Neocolonialism'.
79. Hall et al., Policing the Crisis, 156.

useful as an explanation for how homosexuality came to be politicised in Uganda at the time that it did, such an account belies the extent to which what began as an internal battle within Anglicanism resonated with other Christian denominations, especially the country's many Pentecostal Charismatic Churches (PCCs).[80] In recent years, Pentecostal Christianity has registered the single largest increase in adherents amongst all religious denominations in Uganda, rising from 4.7% of the population in 2002 to 11.1% in 2014.[81] Many scholars believe this to be an underestimation, given that such figures do not reflect the reality of simultaneous membership of different churches. Barbara Bompani has argued that Pentecostal moral discourses around sexuality have provided a way of forging unity in the otherwise fragmented Ugandan PCC landscape.[82] As such, paying attention to the forces propelling the rise of Pentecostal Christianity may also give us a better understanding of the reasons for the apparent popularity of homophobic discourses in Uganda.

A Political Economy of Pentecostal Futurity

Three factors have underpinned the impressive growth of Pentecostal Christianity in Uganda from the late 1980s onwards: war, neoliberalism, and HIV/AIDS. Pentecostalism's distinctive promise of temporal rupture and renewal through the experience of being 'born again' that it offers its adherents is central to understanding its appeal in the context of these three factors. After the brutality of the Amin years and the devastation of Museveni's 'bush war' against the government of Milton Obote, Pentecostalism seemed to provide the perfect spiritual complement to the victorious NRM's mission of national reconstruction from 1986 onwards. As Paul Gifford explains, tainted by perceptions of collaboration with or insufficient resistance to previous regimes, the established Anglican and Catholic churches were seen to be part of the old dispensation that needed to be transcended.[83] The new PCCs carried little of this historical baggage.

Taking power in a highly indebted country, the NRM implemented the neoliberal strictures imposed by the Bank and Fund as part of the structural adjustment programme that Uganda underwent in the 1980s and 1990s in return for loan assistance. Indeed, Uganda is widely regarded as

---

80. Ward, 'Anglican and Catholic Churches', 136–137.
81. Uganda Bureau of Statistics, 'National Population and Housing Census', 19.
82. Bompani, '"For God"', 20. See also Valois, 'Scandal Makers'.
83. Gifford, *African Christianity*, 115.

the African country in which the neoliberal project was most enthusiastically embraced.[84] The rise of Pentecostalism is inextricably bound up with the advent of neoliberalism in a number of ways. Structural adjustment created new opportunities for proselytisation for PCCs as they moved into the space vacated by a shrinking state to become major providers of social services such as education and health.[85] In addition, Pentecostalism fostered the 'moral restructuring'[86] necessary for the social embedding of neoliberal norms of individual self-interest and utility maximisation. In contrast to the valorisation of poverty evident in some forms of Christianity, the Pentecostal prosperity gospel encourages the unabashed pursuit of wealth as being part of God's plan for the devout. At the same time, the practice of tithing has become a central pillar of the Pentecostal moral economy and, effectively, a new form of taxation in places where churches rather than governments provide most social services.[87] This has engendered a view of religion as a sort of 'gift exchange', in which paying tithes to the church is believed to unlock divine providence.[88] In an analogy with Max Weber's observation of an elective affinity between the Protestant ethic and the growth of capitalism in the sixteenth and seventeenth centuries, Dana Freeman argues that the Pentecostal ethic has been equally consequential in transforming values and subjectivities in ways that have enabled the embedding and legitimation of neoliberal capitalism.[89]

The distinctive temporality of Pentecostal Christianity is key to understanding its effectiveness in transforming moral subjectivities. Pentecostals insist that being 'born again' entails a 'complete break with the past'.[90] Believers are expected to stop worshipping ancestors and familial gods or relying on native medicine and witch doctors, and to sever connections with kin who continue to do so. Many aspects of this transformation lend themselves to the development of neoliberal subjectivities. Birgit Meyer has found Pentecostal Christianity to be especially popular with urban women in Ghana who struggle to escape the demands of extended families in rural areas. Here, Pentecostalism's emphasis on the nuclear family as a God-given institution and its insistence on breaking with the past seems to give these women permission to sever traditional kin links in their effort to become modern urban individuals, allowing them to sublimate their guilt at

84. Harrison, *Neoliberal Africa*.
85. Gifford, *African Christianity*, 99.
86. Wiegratz, 'Fake Capitalism?'.
87. Freeman, 'Pentecostal Ethic', 13.
88. Meyer, 'Pentecostalism', 18.
89. Freeman, 'Pentecostal Ethic', 20.
90. Meyer, ' "Make a Complete Break" '.

having abandoned poorer relatives into a socially legitimated fear of being bewitched by them.[91] The temporal ruptures that Pentecostal Christianity effects are symbolised in elaborate rituals in which believers strive to recall the past from which they seek deliverance. The effort of doing so often results in their possession by the forces of evil, which are then exorcised through prayer, the laying on of hands, and other gestures of healing. Far from being a one-time occurrence, the act of breaking with the past is continuously reiterated so as to prevent the 'born again' from slipping back into their old ways. These elements of remembrance and repetition lead Meyer to argue that it is too simple to see the break with the past as a neat rupture. Rather, by continuously dwelling on the boundary between past and present, Pentecostalism integrates traditional spirits and deities into the Protestant figure of the Devil, who must constantly be held at bay.[92]

Melinda Cooper draws an intriguing analogy between the temporal rhythms of Pentecostalism and structural adjustment. Both seize upon an event of crisis as an opportunity for the wholesale reconstruction of subjectivity and of time itself. Both command their subjects to sever all links with the past, signified respectively by obligations of extended kinship and rural village life and the welfare mission of the developmental state. Cooper likens the Pentecostal imperative of continuously delivering oneself from a state of sin to the experience of servicing an indefinitely renewed debt: in both, salvation in the future is premised on continuous struggle and sacrifice in the present.[93]

If postwar reconstruction and neoliberal structural adjustment provided openings for Pentecostalism's emergence as a major theopolitical force, Uganda's burgeoning HIV/AIDS epidemic offered the ideal pretext for its interventions in matters of sexuality. As Alessandro Gusman argues, the epidemic encouraged a significant theological reorientation among PCCs from an 'otherworldly' stance focused on saving souls, to more 'this worldly' preoccupations with sociopolitical life.[94] Shifts in HIV prevalence rates from younger to older, often married, individuals generated a discourse in which the older generation was seen to have lost its way, with the reinvigoration of the nation requiring the cultivation of a new morally pure youthful generation. PCCs were especially well positioned to put their conservative sexual morality into practice when they began to receive funds from ideologically like-minded donors such as the US George W. Bush

91. Ibid., 336–337.
92. Ibid., 322; See also Robbins, 'Paradoxes of Global Pentecostalism'.
93. Cooper, 'Theology of Emergency', 67.
94. Gusman, 'HIV/AIDS'.

administration. From 2004 onwards, the President's Emergency Plan for AIDS Relief (PEPFAR) became a major donor to Uganda's HIV/AIDS prevention efforts, accounting for 94% of its total budget at one time.[95] Informed by theological prohibitions on extramarital, commercial, and non-heterosexual sex, PEPFAR diverted funding from progressive public health organisations to faith-based organisations (FBOs), among which US and African PCCs were prominent. As Cooper notes, PEPFAR 'served to institutionalize the presence of Pentecostal-charismatic churches in the very social infrastructure of sub-Saharan Africa, turning them into indispensable conduits to healthcare in the now largely privatized welfare sector.'[96] One consequence for Ugandan HIV prevention efforts was that a programme that had previously pursued a number of complementary strategies, including condom use, shifted abruptly to a biblical emphasis on abstinence. Yet in a curious circularity of influence recalling other moments that I have discussed in this book, Ugandans had themselves helped to steer PEPFAR in the direction of the promotion of abstinence.

Uganda became the focus of intense interest in HIV/AIDS research circles when it registered a dramatic decline in prevalence rates from a high of 18% in 1992 to around 6% in 2001.[97] As Helen Epstein explains, there was little consensus on the reasons for the decline. Public health specialists attributed it to increased condom use, although this had not correlated with declining HIV prevalence in other countries; moreover, condoms were not widely available in Uganda till the mid-1990s.[98] Faith-based advocates attributed it to more widespread abstinence, an explanation that Epstein finds unconvincing given that the average age of sexual debut and the incidence of teen pregnancy hardly changed even as HIV rates fell.[99] Her preferred explanation underscores the importance of grassroots community-based care that encouraged frank conservations about AIDS at all levels and promoted, among other things, a message of partner reduction through slogans such as 'Love Carefully' and 'Zero Grazing'. These messages were premised on an awareness that the overwhelming majority of sexually active adults were involved in multiple concurrent long-term relationships, creating a sexual network whose structure provided ideal conditions for the spread of the virus. By discouraging casual encounters outside of these relationships, 'Zero Grazing' attempted to encourage partner reduction, if not necessarily

95. Cooper, 'Theology of Emergency', 69.
96. Ibid., 58.
97. Gusman, 'HIV/AIDS', 70.
98. Epstein, *Invisible Cure*, 175.
99. Ibid., 188.

monogamy.[100] Robert Thornton has explained the divergent trajectories of HIV/AIDS in Uganda and South Africa by drawing attention to differences in the architecture of their respective sexual networks, which are in turn attributable to their different histories and social structures.[101] He too credits messages like 'Zero Grazing' with breaking key links in the Ugandan network in ways that dramatically lowered HIV prevalence. He provides an illuminating account of both the conceptualisation and distortion of the message in HIV/AIDS policymaking:

> Based on the colloquialisms and metaphors of Museveni's own pastoral tribe, the Hima, this phrase meant, in practice, 'carry on having sex, but keep it local and close to home.' The slogan referred to the practice of tethering a cow to a peg in the middle of a patch of good grazing. As the animal ate the grass that its tether permitted it to reach, it would clear a circular area around the peg. This was the zero of 'zero grazing'. It did not mean abstinence—zero sex—as some earlier researchers, and President Bush's advisors, seemed to think. It simply meant, 'Eat (have sex) as much as you like, but don't roam too widely.'[102]

Yet Ugandans themselves might have had a hand in shaping these misunderstandings, which of course dovetailed nicely with conservative priorities in the United States' own culture wars. Thornton suggests that President Museveni's acceptance of the Bush line on AIDS and sex was the essentially pragmatic consequence of his reliance on US aid. In contrast, as a staunch born-again Christian, it is First Lady Janet Museveni who comes across as the Bush administration's ideological fellow traveller.[103] In a particularly crucial moment during congressional debates over PEPFAR, Janet Museveni flew to Washington, DC, to present a letter to Republican lawmakers attesting that abstinence had been the key to Uganda's success. Epstein credits her intervention with securing the $1 billion that was earmarked for programmes promoting abstinence and faithfulness in the final bill, including of course those that were implemented in Uganda.[104]

Meanwhile, the World Bank was itself promoting the involvement of FBOs in development and humanitarianism. In 1998, then Bank President James Wolfensohn and Archbishop of Canterbury George Carey convened a meeting that produced an advocacy group called the World Faiths and

---

100. Ibid., 176, 196.
101. Thornton, *Unimagined Community*.
102. Ibid., 19.
103. Ibid., 21–22.
104. Epstein, *Invisible Cure*, 187.

Development Dialogue, intended to promote collaboration between international development agencies and FBOs. Bank-commissioned research had found that religious institutions often commanded greater trust among the poor than secular NGOs or governments. The interest in FBOs was also a function of new conceptualisations of 'human development', which no longer saw development in technocratic value-free terms. But above all, the turn to FBOs was a nod to the reality of their increasing importance in an institutional landscape vacated by the state.[105] Virtually ratifying the effects of neoliberalism, the Bank noted that since FBOs provided up to 50% of social services in places like Sub-Saharan Africa, they should be recognised as key partners in development work.[106] To the extent that political homophobia in Uganda has something to do with the colonisation of its public sphere by religious institutions, the Bank has a great deal to answer for.

Money, Morality, and Homophobia

How have ordinary people in Uganda responded to these profound social changes, and how have sexuality and homosexuality come to be implicated in their responses? Joanna Sadgrove et al. have argued that rather than directly reflecting popular concerns, elite homophobic discourses map onto and manipulate other widely felt subaltern anxieties, 'many of which relate directly or indirectly to the profound economic insecurity and fears for the future (especially in the context of the HIV crisis) experienced by ordinary Ugandans.'[107] They find sexual morality to be deeply imbricated with concerns about money in media and popular discourses about homosexuality.[108] Jörg Wiegratz suggests that the precarity engendered by neoliberalism leads poor Ugandans to feel that they have little choice but to prioritise hustling over living a moral life, making it increasingly difficult for them—in their self-perception—to live up to their professed standards, and feeding panics about moral degeneration and decay.[109] In this context, kuchus—not unlike urban women in an earlier historical

---

105. Thomas, 'Faith and Foreign Aid'; Clarke, 'Agents of Transformation?'; Grills, 'Paradox of Multilateral Organizations'.
106. Marshall and Marsh, *Millennium Challenges*, 29.
107. Sadgrove et al., 'Morality Plays', 109.
108. Ibid., 105–106.
109. Wiegratz, 'Fake Capitalism?', 132–134.

moment[110]—provide a visible and vulnerable focal point around which anxieties about the breakdown of moral norms governing kinship and sexuality have coalesced.

One reason why kuchus have so easily been constructed as embodiments of, even scapegoats for, these widespread social anxieties is that in claiming politicised sexual identities they appear to rebel against norms that embed individuals within family networks and that measure their worth in terms of their contribution to those networks through the production of offspring. As Sadgrove et al. explain, such norms are powerful in a society in which marriage and childbearing are understood in economic as much as affective terms.[111] Marriage here, as in many other places, is not only a romantic declaration but also an economic transaction involving the exchange of wealth and establishing material relationships between kin groups. Likewise, the production of children secures inheritance and the transfer of property within kin groups, while also enabling the material sustenance of the family, especially in rural areas, by providing labour and security for parents in their old age. In being seen to reject their reproductive potential, kuchus appear to threaten established networks of exchange and perhaps even to redirect resources into new ones. Moreover, given the imbrication of moral and material considerations in understandings of conventional kinship, their actions are also ascribed material motivations. This explains why money figures so centrally in the stock tropes of homophobic discourse, among which is that of the wealthy kuchu who, backed by Western funding, is able to 'recruit' vulnerable Ugandans into homosexuality. Such perceptions are reinforced by the high visibility of the few kuchus who do succeed in obtaining formal employment in the aid and NGO sectors.

While endorsing this materialist understanding of moral discourses around homosexuality, Peters offers two valuable cautions. First, she warns against understanding Ugandan relationships in purely transactional terms that would deny the spontaneity and pleasure of much erotic life.[112] Second, while accepting that kuchus are *perceived* in homophobic discourse as being disembedded from community networks and plugged into donor flows, she reminds us that such perceptions obscure the actuality of

110. Kintu, *Ugandan Morality Crusade* makes this comparison. That the urban woman continues to arouse such anxieties is evident in recent state efforts to institute dress codes. See Atuhaire, 'Mini-skirts'.
111. Much of the discussion in this section summarises the argument of Sadgrove et al., 'Morality Plays', 117–119. See also Boyd, 'Problem with Freedom'.
112. Peters, '*Kuchus* in the Balance', 20.

their embeddedness in family and community. Indeed much of her work demonstrates how kuchus strive to balance family demands, economic survival, and the production of children with the pursuit of emotionally and sexually fulfilling relationships.[113]

Three theoretical claims are at stake in the political economy of homophobia that I have attempted to offer in this section. First, a political economic analysis of homophobia allows us to account for social antipathy towards figures read as queer, without lapsing into orientalist accounts of a timeless and irredeemable 'African' homophobia. This analysis attends to the contemporary political economic conjuncture within which such affects acquire salience, accounting for their novelty in societies that have rich and socially acknowledged histories of same-sex desire and gender transgression. By taking seriously the material and social anxieties to which the figure of the queer is indexed as an evidentiary scapegoat, as well as the extant normative architecture within which such a move might appear plausible, a political economy of homophobia also resists the tendency to view subalterns as guileless and easily duped by the moral panics produced by wily elites.

In broad strokes, the political economy account that I have offered here makes the following claims. It is hardly controversial to recall that neoliberal capitalism was foisted on highly indebted countries like Uganda in the 1980s and 1990s through punitive structural adjustment programmes. What is less frequently remembered is that these programmes made space for the very social forces that are at the forefront of contemporary moral panics around homosexuality. I have explained how the growing popularity of Pentecostalism in Uganda is inextricable from the entrenchment of neoliberalism in the country. The precarity of everyday life under neoliberalism has exacerbated popular anxieties around the perceived difficulties of making ends meet while living a moral life. Moral panics thrive in the fertile soil of these anxieties, fastening on a range of marginal figures including queers, sex workers, 'witches', women who wear short skirts, and others who appear to disrupt normative kinship, as evidence of the supposed impossibility of managing the tension between money making and morality. A second implication of the analysis, then, is that it suggests a different response to homophobia than that proposed by homocapitalism. If precarity has fed moral panics, we might expect that in circumstances of less profound insecurity, investment in marriage and procreation as mechanisms for assuring welfare and social security would decline, weakening the force

113. Ibid., 21, 184.

of compulsory heterosexuality and the demonisation of those who refuse it. In this sense, the business case for LGBT rights may have its causal story the wrong way around. Rather than the lack of LGBT rights impeding economic growth, it may be material precarity that offers a propitious environment in which moral panics thrive.

Third, this analysis reveals the shallowness and hypocrisy of the current donor discourse on LGBT rights. For reasons that are too obvious to belabour, IFI and donor pronouncements on LGBT rights fail to register the relationship between neoliberalism and homophobia. That these pronouncements are welcomed, even solicited, by local LGBT activists desperate for international support to offset their precarious domestic position[114] should not blind us to their essential disingenuousness. The Bank's adoption of an understanding of homophobia as 'rooted in stigma' (read: 'merely cultural') perpetuates the homonationalist tropes of cultural backwardness through which the attitudes of ordinary Ugandans are viewed, while absolving itself and other agents of global capital of complicity in the production of the conditions in which homophobic moral panics thrive. A generous reading might ascribe this to cognitive failure. More plausibly, we might read this as an ideological move disconnecting the IFIs from the problems they profess to want to alleviate, allowing them to masquerade as agents of benevolence and reinforcing the hegemony of capitalism as an anti-homophobic civilising influence.

RESISTING HOMOCAPITALISM

I call this ideology homocapitalism. The term is not mine, having been in circulation for some time, largely on social media, where it tends to be deployed to criticise gay rapprochement with the market in the United States and Western Europe.[115] The growing propensity of IFIs and multinational corporations to inveigh against 'homophobia' in the global South suggests the emergence of a global homocapitalism that operates through the stick of capital withdrawal as punishment for homophobia, and the carrot of economic growth promised by the business case for LGBT rights. Homocapitalism builds on concepts like homonormativity and

114. See the Joint CSO Letter to the World Bank on Discrimination in Uganda's Health Sector, 23 September 2014, https://www.hrw.org/news/2014/09/23/joint-cso-letter-world-bank-discrimination-ugandas-health-sector, which was supportive of the Bank's decision to postpone the Uganda loan.
115. https://twitter.com/hashtag/homocapitalism.

homonationalism to signify the folding into capitalism of some queers and the disavowal of others, through a liberal politics of recognition that obviates the need for redistribution. Productivity, measured in terms of potential or actual contribution to economic growth, becomes the marker on the basis of which queer inclusion is premised. Selective inclusion widens rifts between queers deemed productive and unproductive, while also threatening to evacuate the anti-capitalist potential of queer movements themselves.

To think through what remains of this potential in the current conjuncture, it is salutary to recall how queers were positioned in relation to capitalism in an earlier moment. Echoing Marx's view of the proletariat as both creature and nemesis of industrial capitalism, John D'Emilio has read gay identity as being both enabled by and potentially antithetical to capitalism.[116] In D'Emilio's account, the proliferation of opportunities for wage labour in the nineteenth century drew people out of the self-sufficient household economy into new capitalist systems of 'free' labour. It was only when people were able to survive outside the structures of normative family, making a living as individuals through the sale of their labour, that they could craft 'personal' lives in which non-normative desire might coalesce into an aspect of identity. Urbanisation, mass migration, and the anonymity of the city enabled the formation of communities organised around such identities. Foucault identifies but does not really account for the discursive shift in the late nineteenth-century understanding of the sodomite from a practitioner of aberrant acts to a distinct 'species' possessing a unique sexual sensibility.[117] D'Emilio more helpfully explains this shift as an ideological response, couched in the language of scientific breakthrough, to the new ways in which people were organising 'sexual' lives.[118]

While D'Emilio's essay is enduringly useful in offering a historical materialist understanding of this originary moment of 'sexuality', it bears the traces of the time and place in which it was written in what, retrospectively, appears to have been the heyday of radical queer liberation politics in the United States. Writing before something that could be called homocapitalism might have been intelligible, D'Emilio finds it possible and necessary to ask how capitalism can both enable the emergence of gay identity and community and perpetuate heterosexism and homophobia.[119] He answers this question by pointing to the contradictory relationship

116. D'Emilio, 'Capitalism and Gay Identity'.
117. Foucault, *Will to Knowledge*, 43.
118. D'Emilio, 'Capitalism and Gay Identity', 105.
119. Ibid., 108.

between capitalism and the family. On the one hand, wage labour and the satisfaction of needs and desires through the market mean that capitalism has taken away the economic functions that once cemented ties between family members. At the same time, the ideology of capitalism enshrines the heteronormative family as the primary locus of love and emotional security in order to perpetuate the unequal gendered division of labour underpinning social reproduction. In short, capitalism drives people into heteronormative families, which it requires in order to reproduce workers, even as it weakens the bonds that once kept families together.[120] Feminists, queers, and others who attack the ideology of heteronormativity become useful scapegoats who can be blamed for the growing instability of the family, for which capitalism is in large measure responsible. Having thus located queers outside the ideology of capitalism, D'Emilio is able to argue that they are well situated to defend and expand the social terrain outside the heteronormative family, and perhaps even to undermine the centrality of that family in organising social reproduction.[121]

Yet the ideological infrastructure[122] of capitalism has proven resilient, deflecting, absorbing, and sometimes even profiting from the contradictions that it generates. Writing two decades after D'Emilio and reflecting on developments in US politics in the 1990s, Duggan traces the rapprochement between mainstream LGBT movements and neoliberal capitalism.[123] As she argues, neoliberals shed their alliance with right-wing culture warriors and embraced an agenda of LGBT 'equality' at the same time as LGBT movements—responding to the defeats of the Reagan/Thatcher era—limited their claims to ones for recognition while downplaying demands for redistribution. Homonormativity is the name for this rapprochement. By this point, it has become clear that queers are not structurally antithetical to capitalism simply by virtue of their gender and sexual non-normativity. In a shockingly brief span of time, queer subjects—once imagined as a quasi-proletariat—have come to be envisaged as human capital in the now ubiquitous business case for LGBT rights.

The trajectory described by the two moments in which D'Emilio and Duggan are writing about the United States does not play out in the global South in the same way. Here, insofar as politics around non-normative

---

120. Ibid., 109.

121. Ibid., 109–111; see also Warner, 'Introduction'.

122. Floyd, *Reification of Desire*, 35, follows Leerom Medovoi in thinking about the norms that legitimate capitalism as 'infrastructural' rather than 'superstructural', that is 'as genuine conditions of possibility for the reproduction of any particular historical form of capitalism.'

123. Duggan, *Twilight of Equality?*

desire and gender is organised in terms of the categories of an imported ontology of sexuality, LGBT movements owe their very origins to the dynamism and reach of neoliberal capitalism. Whether we ascribe those origins to HIV/AIDS funding from IFIs and global philanthropists, or to hegemonic idioms of sex/gender deviance disseminated by global culture industries and human rights movements, the vectors of this ontology flow through the circuits of global capital to which many of the poorest parts of the global South have only recently been opened as a result of coercive processes of structural adjustment.[124] In making this observation, I am less interested in the fact of import than in the material conditions under which it takes place and the constraints that this imposes on the prospects for a queer anti-capitalist politics in the global South.[125] In an ethnographic analysis of transnational organising for LGBTI rights in Uganda, S. M. Rodriguez has demonstrated how the communicative and financial imperatives of working with a transnational 'non-profit industrial complex' have steered local kuchu organisations away from community-based work towards an increasingly narrow agenda focused on the courts, media, and fundraising. More fundamentally, they argue that this complex 'encourages social movements to model themselves after capitalist structures, effectively halting any major critique of those structures.'[126]

Very similarly, the mainstream of the Indian LGBT movement has not been particularly attentive to the depredations of neoliberal capital. This is unsurprising given its origins in the moment of macroeconomic liberalisation unleashed in the early 1990s. Suparna Bhaskaran reminds us that the advent of the movement is inseparable from the development of a late twentieth-century consciousness of 'compulsory individuality', of which sexual subjectivity has been an important component.[127] Surveying a range of sites including the then emerging culture of women's beauty contests and sexual minority activism, Bhaskaran argues that the images of individual choice and consumption that circulated in these sites provided ideological legitimation for wrenching processes of structural adjustment that were beginning to dismantle aspects of the Nehruvian

124. Altman, *Global Sex*.
125. In this regard, my argument is different from that of Joseph Massad, whose fixation with the geographical provenance of the terms in which contemporary queer Arabs imagine their liberation leads him to characterise them as 'native informants' to a 'Gay International' (Massad, 'Re-Orienting Desire'; for a critique, see Rao, *Third World Protest*, 176–179). I am more interested in the class dimensions of this phenomenon than in policing 'culture'.
126. Rodriguez, *Economics of Queer Inclusion*, 83.
127. Bhaskaran, *Made in India*.

developmentalist state around this time. However, this describes only part of the landscape of mobilisation around gender and sexuality. Elite LGBT activism has always coexisted uneasily with other forms of sexual politics—such as those favoured by sex workers—in which the inseparability of concerns around recognition and redistribution has generated collective and more antagonistic stances toward the growing inequalities produced by neoliberal capitalism.[128] Moreover, as Svati Shah has noted, leftist movements that once shied away from concerns around gender and sexuality—hitherto bracketed as elite preoccupations—have increasingly begun to think of these issues as part of their remit.[129] Thus, the critique of homocapitalism marks a schism running through a heterogeneous field of mobilisations around gender and sexuality.[130]

To try to identify the social constituencies that might carry forward such a critique would be to re-enact the persistently futile search for the vanguard revolutionary subject, oblivious to the historical insight that this subject's structural position in relation to capitalism is always shifting so that its antagonism is never guaranteed for all time. As such, rather than looking for the agents in whom we might vest our hopes for the struggle against homocapitalism, I turn in the final section of this chapter to a cinematic text that, drawing on a number of historically situated struggles, powerfully evokes many of the preoccupations of the chapter. My rationale for turning to a work of fiction is straightforward. If, as Dave tells us, normative innovation entails the problematisation of existing norms and the imagination of alternatives prior to their instantiation in creative praxis,[131] then cultural production frequently provides a more conducive terrain for at least the first two of these tasks—particularly when social movements have reached an impasse.

Jayan Cherian's film *Papilio Buddha* tells the story of a Dalit struggle for land, modelled closely on land agitations in Muthanga and Chengara in the south Indian state of Kerala.[132] Set in the fictional Dalit settlement of Meppara and shot in the lush Wayanad forest, the narrative unfolds

128. Kotiswaran, *Dangerous Sex*, 238–239.

129. Shah, 'Queering Critiques', 645–646. See khanna, *Sexualness*, 68, for a brief account of the evolution of the position of the National Alliance of People's Movements on queer issues.

130. For useful accounts of the Indian queer movement that are attentive to its many hierarchies, see Gupta, 'Englishpur ki kothi'; Tellis, 'Disrupting the Dinner Table'; Kapur, 'Unruly Desires'; Kang, 'Casteless-ness'; Baudh, 'Invisibility'; Sircar, 'New Queer Politics'.

131. Dave, *Queer Activism in India*.

132. Cherian (dir.), *Papilio Buddha*. For a useful contextualisation of the film, see Sachindev, 'Papilio Buddha'.

against a landscape that is beautiful but increasingly ravaged by deforestation and resource extraction. At the heart of the story are the Dalit father-son duo, Kariyan and Shankaran. Kariyan is a leading figure in the local Pulaya community's struggle for land and access to the forest. Protesting the increasing alienation of land to multinational corporations and religious institutions, the Pulayas of Meppara have squatted on government land for over a year. Their struggle draws inspiration from the iconography and teachings of Dalit leaders Ambedkar and Ayyankali (a social reformer in the erstwhile princely state of Travancore), as well as of the Buddha himself. Buddhism has been central to Dalit politics ever since Ambedkar led hundreds of thousands of his followers into its fold in a mass conversion shortly before his death in 1956. Buddhism, in his view, provided a vehicle with which to transform moral and spiritual dispositions in a way that Marxism could not, while also valuing reason and deliberation in a way that caste Hinduism did not.[133] The forms and convictions of Ambedkarite neo-Buddhism furnish a key leitmotif that runs through *Papilio Buddha*.

With a degree in zoology and some postgraduate education from the prestigious Jawaharlal Nehru University (JNU)—a bastion of left politics—Shankaran is not inattentive to Dalit struggle. But his initial interests lie elsewhere. In the opening sequences of the film, we see him assisting a visiting American lepidopterist, Jack, in his search for the elusive Papilio Buddha butterfly that is endemic to the region. We witness a moment of physical intimacy between Shankaran and Jack. Kariyan is disapproving of Shankaran's choices, although an early conversation between the two suggests that it is the son's disengagement from politics, rather than his erotic interests, that are the source of the father's vexation. Shankaran's university education gives him access to a different kind of left politics. In a crucial scene, we see him socialising with friends, one of whom runs an NGO that manages welfare projects for Dalits and adivasis with the professed aim of being the 'voice of the voiceless'. Despite the apparent ease with which Shankaran inhabits the spaces of the secular, middle-class, dominant caste, leftist intelligentsia, he soon becomes uneasy with its patronising vision of Dalit upliftment and with the stubborn presence of caste even in spaces ostensibly committed to its effacement. This gives Shankaran a new appreciation for his father's politics in which he begins to immerse himself. His radicalisation is spurred by his arrest, detention, and torture by the police, who allege that the Meppara Dalits

133. Ambedkar, 'Buddha or Karl Marx'.

have been colluding with Maoist rebels in Chhattisgarh in their decades-long armed struggle against dispossession by the Indian state and multi-national capital.[134]

The film portrays the overdetermination of Dalit oppression most clearly in a storyline centred on the character of Manjusree. In addition to running a school in the squat, Manju earns her living by plying an auto rickshaw. Her entry into this male-dominated profession incurs the wrath of her fellow drivers, who spare no effort to intimidate and harass her. One night, she is lured into a deserted area by one of the male drivers posing as a passenger. Unbeknownst to her, he has arranged a rendezvous with the other drivers, who arrive in their own rickshaws, brutally gang rape her, and leave her for dead.

Running through the film is a pointed critique of the ideologies that Dalit struggles have engaged with and found wanting. In our first view of the hut in which Kariyan lives, we see three framed photographs on a high shelf—Ambedkar, Ayyankali, and E. M. S. Namboodiripad, the Communist leader who became the first chief minister of Kerala and head of one of the first elected Communist governments anywhere in the world. Shankaran explains to Jack that his father had once deified EMS, as he has always popularly been called (Shankaran himself is named after the 'S' in EMS). But EMS no longer occupies a place of honour in Kariyan's political con-stellation. Referencing the tendency of the Communist Party of India to relegate the caste question to the superstructural status of what we might call, once again, the 'merely cultural',[135] Kariyan says acerbically, 'When the land reforms started he became a Brahmin and I remained as an untouch-able.' And yet EMS remains on the wall for much of the film, as if to sug-gest acknowledgement of an emancipatory vision, albeit one that remained radically inadequate. Other moments in the film express a more thorough-going disenchantment with Marxism. As the auto rickshaws circle around Manju before she is attacked, the viewer's eye is drawn to the stickers with which drivers often decorate their vehicles. Images of Che and Gandhi come into view, as if to suggest their irrelevance, perhaps even implication, in the fate she is about to suffer. Her own vehicle carries a sticker of Buddha, which is the last image we see before it is engulfed in flames. Towards the end of the film, Kariyan replaces the photograph of EMS in his house with a picture of Buddha. Thus, the film's relationship with Marxism is ambiv-alent, sometimes expressing a disenchanted affiliation and at other times

---

134. On the Maoist struggle in India, see Roy, 'Walking with the Comrades'; Shah, *In the Shadows.*
135. Omvedt, *Ambedkar*, 90–91.

breaking with it in a manner that recalls Ambedkar's own close and critical engagement with Marxism.[136] We might read this cinematic moment in light of queer of colour theorist Rod Ferguson's call for a 'disidentification' with Marxism that would acknowledge both its usefulness and limitations in waging anti-racist and anti-caste struggles.[137]

In contrast with its ambivalence around Marxism, the film's repudiation of Gandhism is categorical and total. The denouement of the film comes when local authorities, anxious to evacuate the squatters with minimal force, solicit the intervention of the local Gandhi Service Society. A Gandhian leader offers to begin a hunger strike to persuade the Dalits to vacate the land they have been squatting. Far from defusing the standoff, the proposal enrages the Dalits, who see it as reprising Gandhi's infamous 1932 hunger strike that blackmailed Ambedkar into renouncing his demand for separate political representation for Dalits.[138] Viewing the Gandhians as the benign face of a coercive state apparatus, the Dalit activists denounce their satyagraha in exactly the terms that Ambedkar did, as 'a foul and filthy act' intended to undermine their own struggle. They demonstrate their contempt by erecting an effigy of Gandhi and garlanding it with slippers before setting fire to it. This elicits a violent response from the police in the course of which the Dalit activists are beaten up and detained and the squat completely destroyed. In the last scene of the film, we see a stream of forest dwellers walking slowly in single file, carrying their possessions across the horizon of a denuded landscape.

In reading *Papilio Buddha* in light of the preoccupations of this chapter, I want to think about the work that gender does in the narrative. The film is laced with moments of homoeroticism—between Shankaran and Jack, between two of their women friends, and possibly between Shankaran and the men with whom he shares a cramped prison cell—without dwelling on these moments in which queer desire is palpable. This might be taken as a statement about the possibilities for the expression of what khanna calls 'sexualness' in the rural lifeworlds in which the film is situated, far from the din around (homo)sexuality that saturates metropolitan Indian spaces.[139] In this regard, *Papilio Buddha* does not quite belong in the new wave of Malayalam films that advocate a politics of sexual identitarian visibility by having their characters claim explicitly queer subject positions,[140]

136. See Omvedt, *Ambedkar* on this question.
137. Ferguson, *Aberrations in Black*.
138. Omvedt, *Ambedkar*, 47; Rao, *Caste Question*. See Chapter 6 for an extended discussion of this important historical episode.
139. khanna, *Sexualness*.
140. Mokkil, 'Shifting Spaces'.

a trend in which we might include Cherian's later film *Ka Bodyscapes*.[141] After being tortured by the police, Shankaran takes refuge in Manju's hut. Broken by the violence which they have both suffered, the two find solace in a moment of deep erotic connection that seems to rejuvenate their revolutionary instincts. As they make love, the Buddha statue at the back of the room rotates to reveal the Tantric Buddhist image of Tara Devi and Buddha embracing one another. Believed to be a female bodhisattva in some variants of Buddhism and a female Buddha in others, Tara is considered the mother of liberation, capable of relieving the distress of ordinary beings.[142] Although Shankaran and Manju embrace in a way that mimics the deities, the film does not gender their qualities in line with this Buddhist iconography. Indeed, after she is raped, Manju shaves her head and takes on an agendered appearance, going on to play an increasingly militant role in the protests with which the film culminates.

How might we think about the relationship between the erotic and the revolutionary? In her attempt to repair what she sees as a disconnect between the cultural and the material in contemporary queer theory, Rosemary Hennessy calls for a conceptualisation of love and affect as vital human needs.[143] She asks, rhetorically:

If the equation that sets human affect against need is somehow wrong, must we not then find ways to understand not only how this realm of who we are as humans is folded into the ways we socially meet—or do not meet—our other human needs, but also figure out how to marshal our human affective capacities in the struggle to redress the inequitable meeting of other human needs? If we no longer ignore affect in the calculus of human needs, then in forging a collective standpoint for oppositional—even revolutionary—forms of consciousness we will need to acknowledge how political agency, practice, and commitment are motivated, complicated, and undermined by our human capacity for affect.[144]

Importantly, Hennessy regards affective capacities as both mediating the social relations through which needs are satisfied and as constituting needs in themselves, thereby blurring the distinction between the two.[145] That is to say, erotic freedoms are both a means to revolutionary ends and revolutionary ends in themselves. Nowhere is this clearer than in Ambedkar's

141. Cherian (dir.), *Ka Bodyscapes*.
142. Sachindev, '*Papilio Buddha*', 145–146.
143. Hennessy, *Profit and Pleasure*, 207–208.
144. Ibid., 208.
145. Ibid., 210–11.

landmark essay calling for the 'annihilation of caste' (about which more in the following chapter), in which he describes intercaste miscegenation as the 'real remedy' for the absence of the 'feeling of kinship, of being kindred' that is both cause and consequence of caste.[146] The great Tamil anti-caste radical E. V. Ramasamy, better known as Periyar, evinced a similar sensibility, pioneering new forms of secular 'Self Respect' marriage in a direct attack on caste Hinduism.[147] We can be in no doubt that the erotic remains a key terrain of struggle in contemporary India, given the violence with which erotic transgressions across lines of caste and religion are routinely punished.[148]

Papilio Buddha pushes us to refuse the many seductions of homocapitalism. Against the instrumentalisation of gender and sexuality for the rehabilitation of capitalism in times of crisis, the film invites us to think about the ways in which the erotic might bring capitalism and caste into crisis. Against the conflation of economic growth with the expansion of rights, the film reminds us of the ways in which these enterprises can be radically antithetical to one another. By forcing us to confront processes of capitalist 'accumulation by dispossession'[149] together with those of caste and gender oppression, it refuses us the fiction that the institutions whose policies have unleashed the former might be allies in struggles against the latter. Instead, it illuminates the necessity of a queer investment in anti-capitalist and anti-caste struggles. Moreover, it does this, not by urging a politics of coalition of separate struggles, but by embodying their intersections in its protagonists. In recent years an exhilarating queer urban Dalit voice has become audible, inaugurated partly through a powerful assertion of visibility performed by Dhiren Borisa, Dhrubo Jyoti, and Akhil Kang at the 2015 Delhi Queer Pride.[150] *Papilio Buddha* offers us a still relatively unusual representation of the intersections of rural, queer, Dalit, and adivasi subjectivities. In its uncompromising bleakness, it gestures at a horizon towards which anti-homocapitalist critique and praxis might aspire.

But this horizon of critique—our very understanding of what queerness *is*—must constantly shift as capitalism and the state apparatus morph to deflect and absorb the antagonisms that they incite. *Papilio Buddha's*

146. Ambedkar, *Annihilation of Caste*, 82.
147. Geetha, 'Periyar'.
148. Rao ed., *Gender and Caste*.
149. Harvey, *New Imperialism*.
150. 'Dalit Queer Pride at Delhi Queer Pride 2015', accessed 16 January 2019, https://www.youtube.com/watch?v=SsQIq2_Di7A. See also Vidya, '(Trans)gender and Caste'; Kang, 'Casteless-ness'; Kang, 'Queering Dalit'; Baudh, 'Invisibility'.

travails with the (Indian) Central Board of Film Certification are a curious testament to this imperative. Initially denied certification on a number of grounds, including its alleged depiction of obscenity and denigration of national leaders, the film was eventually certified for release after the filmmakers agreed to 'mute' extracts from a speech that Ambedkar had made in 1932 criticising the hunger strike that Gandhi had undertaken to deny the Dalit demand for separate representation.[151] In a neoliberal India dominated by a caste Hindu Right, collective Dalit assertion in the terms advocated by Ambedkar is queerer than a same-sex kiss.

151. Prakash, 'Papilio Buddha'.

CHAPTER 6

The Nation and Its Queers

In April 2014, the Supreme Court of India in *National Legal Services Authority (NALSA) v. Union of India* (hereafter *NALSA*),[1] endorsed the demand of trans persons for recognition as a category of 'socially and educationally backward' citizens, entitling them to constitutional guarantees of affirmative action in public employment and education. While the judgement is not without its problems and ambiguities,[2] this aspect of its ruling seemed to promise momentous redistributive gains for trans communities. This may be why it has pointedly been ignored by the executive and legislature in successive attempts to implement the ruling through enabling legislation, including most recently the Transgender Persons (Protection of Rights) Bill 2019.[3]

Readers unfamiliar with the Indian Constitution are likely to balk at the equation of transness with 'backwardness'. After all, this seems to reiterate the ascription of primitiveness to the figure of the queer, who first emerges in the annals of sexology, psychoanalysis, and anthropology as an instance of arrested development, retardation, degeneracy, and decadence,[4] and in international relations discourse as underdeveloped and undevelopable.[5]

1. (2014) 5 SCC 438 (hereafter *NALSA*).
2. For useful critiques, see Dutta 'Contradictory Tendencies'; Semmalar, 'Gender Outlawed'.
3. For a detailed critique of the 2019 Bill, see Sampoorna, 'SPWG Statement'. See also http://orinam.net/resources-for/law-and-enforcement/the-transgender-persons-protection-of-rights-bill-2019/. For critiques of earlier drafts of the Bill see Sampoorna, 'TG Bill 2016 Factsheet'; Semmalar, 'First as Apathy'; Nagpaul, 'Promised Empowerment'.
4. Hoad, 'Arrested Development'.
5. Weber, *Queer International Relations*, 47–71.

Out of Time. Rahul Rao, Oxford University Press (2020). © Oxford University Press.
DOI: 10.1093/oso/9780190865511.001.0001

Moreover, temporal backwardness is a central trope of orientalism—so much so that it is surprising that postcolonial theory has not devoted more attention to the question of how backwardness is inhabited by those deemed backward. In India, where 'backwardness' is understood principally in terms of caste, the struggles of those deemed backward have produced a legal and political framework committed to the amelioration of backwardness through the mechanism of affirmative action. This has meant that the designation of backwardness performs a double function. As Lucinda Ramberg explains, backwardness

> marks a degraded condition that fixes you in the past even as it constitutes the means for your forward mobility by providing a positive basis for claims before the state. To lay claim to those benefits is to mark yourself as backward and therefore to dwell in an oscillation between backwardness and forwardness.[6]

In this chapter, I want to think about what happens when trans persons, through a desire for state recognition of their backwardness, place themselves in this ambivalent temporal location. What sorts of 'backward futures', to borrow Ramberg's evocative phrase, become contemplable from this vantage point? How do these futures differ from those envisaged by homocapitalism? At least one distinction seems clear from the outset. If homocapitalism seeks upward mobility by interpellating queers as model capitalist subjects, the Indian trans movement's desire for backward class status makes common cause with those relegated to the very bottom of the social hierarchy.

Because backwardness has historically been assessed through the lens of caste, in endorsing the trans movement's demand, the Supreme Court was in effect analogising a particular kind of gender identity to caste. Although this move is comprehensible in light of a certain genealogy of governmentality vis-à-vis gender identity that I shall outline, analogical reasoning in social justice struggles is a fraught endeavour. Analogies typically enable temporally subsequent movements to make claims to entitlements based on their putative equivalence with prior movements that have already articulated such claims and made them intelligible. This can sometimes problematically imply that the prior claim has achieved a degree of recognition on which the subsequent movement seeks to trade. At the same time, the very intelligibility of the analogy relies on the persistence—or at least the memory—of the forms

6. Ramberg, 'Backward Futures', 228.

of injustice against which the prior movement struggles. This is why Janet Jakobsen argues that 'the internal structure of analogy . . . makes it particularly effective as a tool to iterate dominations across categories and much less effective in attempts to avoid such (re)iterations'.[7] Claims such as 'queers are the new Jews' or 'queers are the new blacks'[8] paradoxically assume *both* that the prior occupants of these categories have moved on *and* that their status remains relatively unchanged (therefore, familiar) so as to function as a stable ground for the analogy, thereby reiterating their subordinate status even if they have achieved some degree of emancipation.

These problems are evident in some attempts to analogise trans experiences with those of Dalits—groups who were historically considered 'untouchable' in the Hindu caste system. Consider, for example, the following passage from the autobiography of Brahmin hijra activist Laxminarayan Tripathi, one of the petitioners in *NALSA*, who reflects on findings recorded during the conduct of a hijra census:

> The hijras told us that they were no different from the untouchables *of the past*. When they went to the District Civil Hospital in Thane (or to any other hospital for that matter), no one touched them—neither the doctors, nor the nurses, nor *even* the ward boys and ayahs. They were pariah.[9]

Bracketing for a moment the likelihood that many of the hijras counted in this census may have been Dalits or from other subordinate castes, the temporal location of untouchability in the past is problematic. But it is immediately contradicted by Tripathi's surprise that 'even' the ward boys and ayahs do not touch the hijras. Encoded in this slippage is the recognition that these subordinate occupational rungs in the hospital hierarchy tend to be occupied by members of subordinate castes, which then generates her astonishment that 'even' they are capable of being casteist.[10] Thus, Tripathi paradoxically insinuates the passing on of 'untouchability', enabling new

7. Jakobsen, 'Queers Are like Jews', 71.

8. For an account of the deployment of analogies with blackness by white activists in both pro- and anti-LGBT rights campaigns in the US, see Stone and Ward, '"Black People Are Not a Homosexual Act"'.

9. Tripathi, *Me Hijra*, 91, emphasis added. The English term 'pariah' is etymologically derived from the name of the Paraiyar caste, a social group occupying the lowest rungs of the caste hierarchy in southern India and Sri Lanka.

10. Ambedkar, *Annihilation of Caste*, 89–90, reminds us that the durability of the caste system derives from the fact that 'each caste takes its pride and its consolation in the fact that in the scale of castes it is above some other caste. . . .'

subjects to take the place of its historical referents, while also recognising its endurance.

This, however, is only one of many conceptual and political problems. Analogical reasoning invites us to juxtapose and compare categories, placing them side by side as if they were separable. Such juxtaposition obscures the entanglement of gender and caste, the inseparability of which might be understood in three ways. First, gender and caste intersect in a variety of different locations, producing hierarchies within trans communities to which the Supreme Court seems to have been oblivious.[11] The Court regarded trans persons as a homogenous group without considering the ways in which gender identity intersects with categories such as caste (but also class, religion, ability, etc.) to produce differentiated experiences of privilege and marginalisation within the community. This has heightened Dalit trans anxieties that dominant caste trans persons might benefit disproportionately from affirmative action were it to be extended to the trans community as a whole without caste-specific quotas.[12] Second, gender and caste are co-constitutive, in the sense that caste is constituted and reproduced through the regulation of gender and vice versa. As Ambedkar recognised, gender oppressive practices such as sati, compulsory widowhood, and child marriage were mechanisms for the enforcement of endogamy and the reproduction of caste. In his words, 'they create and perpetuate endogamy, while caste and endogamy, according to our analysis of the various definitions of caste, are one and the same thing. Thus the existence of these means is identical with caste and caste involves these means.'[13] Third, gender phobias may be structurally dependent upon caste oppression in a historical sense. Just as racism forges the discursive structures in which subsequent queerphobic moral panics take shape, caste oppression does something similar in the South Asian context. Shamira Meghani provides evidence of this in a reading of recent Indian literary and cinematic texts that demonstrates how the grammar of caste is deployed to represent HIV stigmatisation, revealing 'untouchability' to be foundational to the conceptualisation of HIV stigma in India.[14] Thus, the entanglement of caste and gender might be understood in terms of their intersectionality, co-constitution, and historical path dependence.

11. Dutta, 'Contradictory Tendencies', 234–235.
12. Vidya, '(Trans)gender and Caste'; Sampoorna, 'TG Bill 2016 Factsheet'.
13. Ambedkar, 'Castes in India'. For explorations of the relationship between gender and caste, see Chakravarti, *Gendering Caste*; Rao (ed.), *Gender and Caste*.
14. Meghani, 'HIV Stigma', 2.

None of this is to suggest that the experience of transness cannot be analogised to that of subordinate caste status. Indeed we might expect persons situated at the intersection of these categories to be best placed to comment on the appropriateness of the analogy. In an illuminating interview, Dalit trans actor, director, and writer Living Smile Vidya points out that trans persons sometimes encounter discrimination that is more severe than that experienced by urban Dalits, particularly insofar as housing is concerned. She explains that they can typically secure housing only in Dalit areas, but usually have to pay a higher rent. She suggests that working-class trans persons, for whom begging and sex work are often the only available means of livelihood, are denied a dignity of labour that some Dalits have been able to claim, particularly when engaged in occupations such as agriculture that, they can argue, sustain the wider community. Nonetheless, she points out that both identities have historically been locked into different forms of 'occupational fixity' as a result of social exclusion. Vidya accounts for the differences in constraint and opportunity experienced by these groups with reference to the degree to which they are collectively organised. As she explains, transwomen and hijras (or tirunangais, as they prefer to be called in her native Tamil Nadu), who, like Dalits, have historically had stronger community networks, have been more able to assert themselves in the public sphere than transmen (tirunambis).[15]

Vidya's account suggests that analogies between transness and caste subordination may be sustainable if made with attentiveness to the entanglement of these and other categories. More generally, it is not difficult to appreciate why social movements might feel compelled to make analogies despite their complexities. In a legal system founded on precedent, successful analogies are a means by which citizens lay claim to forms of recognition and redistribution that appear to have advanced the life prospects of others. While recognising the element of pragmatism that underpins analogical reasoning, my interest in this chapter is in the utopian potentials that inhere within the analogy between transness and subordinate caste status. Specifically, I want to consider how the trans appeal to backwardness might import an Ambedkarite politics of futurity into trans and queer politics. What could it mean to strive towards the 'backward futures' that Ambedkar contemplated, in the context of trans and queer politics? Reading Ambedkar through a trans lens, I will argue that he offers a precocious critique of both the assimilationist impulse in what we have come to call homo- and transnormativity, and the separatist

15. Vidya, '(Trans)gender and Caste'; see also Vidya, *I am Vidya*.

impulse in queer liberation politics. And reading trans politics through an Ambedkarite lens, I will tease out the structural resonances between important strands of contemporary trans politics in India and Ambedkar's mission of annihilating caste.

While centring the experiences of trans and gender nonconforming people, I am also interested in this chapter in how regimes of gender normalisation and regulation affect everyone. As such, a second overriding preoccupation of the chapter is a consideration of how its central categories—gender identity and backwardness—have been linked over time in the imagination of the nation itself. In their introduction to a collection of essays, transgender studies scholars Susan Stryker, Paisley Currah, and Lisa Jean Moore express their determination not to 'perpetuate a minoritizing or ghettoizing use of "transgender" to delimit and contain the relationship of "trans-" conceptual operations to "-gender" statuses and practices in a way that rendered them the exclusive property of a tiny class of marginalized individuals.'[16] They suggest that the prefix 'trans' enables 'categorical crossings, leakages, and slips of all sorts,' as illustrated by their non-exhaustive list: 'trans: -gender, -national, -racial, -generational, -genic, -species.'[17] Thus, 'transing' has emerged as a mode of analysis, or what Regina Kunzel calls 'a way of seeing' and 'a way of knowing'[18] that has been taken up in a range of different fields including literary studies,[19] migration studies,[20] and international relations.[21] As Jessica Berman explains, 'when we use the prefix "trans" to mean not just "across, through over . . . or on the other side of" but also "beyond, surpassing, transcending," it represents a challenge to the normative dimension of the original entity or space, a crossing over that looks back critically from its space beyond.'[22] The crossing over that I am interested in here is a shift in the imagination of the Indian nation—particularly by the middle class, dominant caste elites who monopolise the production of its international image—from one of a developing country to that of a great power-in-waiting. The deeply gendered nature of this fantasy suggests a relationship between gender identity and geopolitical backwardness that demands investigation. Turning the question of the first half of the chapter around, I ask how the nation's transness is deployed to reconfigure its backwardness.

16. Stryker, Currah, and Moore, 'Introduction', 11.
17. Ibid.
18. Kunzel, 'Flourishing of Transgender Studies', 289.
19. Berman, 'Trans in Transnational'.
20. Tudor, 'Dimensions of Transnationalism'.
21. Sjoberg, 'Trans-gendering International Relations?'.
22. Berman, 'Trans in Transnational'.

In thinking about the relationship between backwardness and gender identity in the two very different registers of the trans movement and elite imaginaries of the nation, it is not my intention to posit equivalence (if anything, ironic contrast is in greater evidence). Rather, I aim to situate the evolving juridical understanding of the queer and specifically trans subject in the context of the shifting geopolitical positioning of the Indian nation-state.[23] My juxtaposition of the trans movement and the nation draws on a long-standing postcolonial scholarly tendency to theorise the nation from the perspective of what Partha Chatterjee has called its 'fragments'.[24] Gyanendra Pandey has argued that the fragmentary point of view—articulated from the perspective of subordinate religious, caste, class, and gender groups—reveals the Brahminical Hindu 'mainstream' to itself be a fragment, even if frequently elevated to the status of the national culture. The fragment, then, enables a provincialisation of what masquerades as the nation, potentially opening up 'richer definitions of the "nation" and the future political community'.[25]

The argument of this chapter proceeds in four parts. First, I suggest that the Supreme Court's recognition of the trans demand for 'backward class' status in NALSA was enabled in part by a reductionist and specifically temporal understanding of transness, primarily through the figure of the hijra. Reading NALSA alongside three recent judgements that decriminalised, recriminalised, and then definitively decriminalised homosexuality—with a focus on the temporal premises of these judgements—I demonstrate how while the homosexual is construed as a creature of modernity, the (reduced) trans subject is rooted in tradition. This presumption of temporal backwardness subliminally undergirds the Court's finding of socioeconomic backwardness. Yet given the constitutional implications of the recognition of backwardness, this gesture of misrecognition (or partial recognition) opens the door to the possibility of redistribution. The second part of the chapter explores the emancipatory potentials of this recognition of backwardness. Here I contrast a procedural understanding of backwardness and the commitment to its elimination in the Indian Constitution, with the more substantive vision of 'backward futures' expressed by its key architect, the Dalit leader B. R. Ambedkar. Reading a selection of recent trans autobiographical writings, I suggest that we can observe convergences in articulations of Dalit and trans futurity. Third, I situate the judicial recognition of trans backwardness in the current political conjuncture. I suggest

23. A similar intention is evident in Corrêa and khanna, *Emerging Powers*.
24. Chatterjee, *Nation and Its Fragments*.
25. Pandey, 'Defense of the Fragment', 28–29.

that in a putatively Rising India dominated by a neoliberal Hindu Right, the political will to eliminate caste inequality has declined in tandem with a growth in frustration at the country's inability to break into the ranks of great powers. This is particularly evident in a discourse popular among the middle class, dominant caste beneficiaries of neoliberalism, in which distributive justice is seen to detract from the imperatives of growth and greatness. Importantly, this is also a gendered discourse invested in the masculinisation of state and nation. Here, gender reassignment[26] becomes a concomitant of national advancement. Fourth, I attempt to complicate dominant gendered readings of the nation-state by pointing to a range of instances in which gender ambiguity has been politicised. Breaking with approaches that regard such ambiguity as inherently progressive, I point to the productivity of gender trouble on both the right and left of the Indian ideological spectrum. In doing so, I suggest that progressive possibilities inhere not in the fact of gender ambiguity, but in the parameters within which it operates—that is, in the political work that it is allowed to do. By way of illustration, I read Arundhati Roy's novel *The Ministry of Utmost Happiness* as a fable about the coming together of the nation's fragments, paying attention to the centrality of its hijra protagonist with a view to teasing out what, if anything, might distinguish a gender trouble worthy of celebration.

JURIDICAL TEMPORALITIES OF QUEERNESS

In recent years, the higher judiciary in India has been intensely engaged with questions surrounding the constitutional status of rights related to sexual orientation and gender identity. To recapitulate briefly: homosexuality was decriminalised in 2009 by the Delhi High Court in *Naz Foundation v. Government of NCT of Delhi* (hereafter *Naz*),[27] recriminalised in 2013 by the Supreme Court in *Suresh Kumar Koushal v. Naz Foundation* (hereafter *Koushal*),[28] and then definitively decriminalised in 2018 when a larger

26. I use the term 'reassignment' rather than 'affirmation' to underscore the coercive nature of this process.

27. 160 Delhi Law Times 277 (hereafter *Naz*). For an analysis of the judgement, see Narrain and Eldridge, *Right That Dares*; for media and other responses to the judgement, see http://orinam.net/377/background-of-sec-377/delhi-high-court-judgement-2009/.

28. (2014) 1 SCC 1 (hereafter *Koushal*). For an analysis of the judgement, see Narrain, 'We Dissent'; see also http://orinam.net/377/supreme-court-verdict-2013/articles-analysing-verdict/.

bench of the Supreme Court overruled the *Koushal* decision in *Navtej Singh Johar v. Union of India* (hereafter *Navtej*).[29] Two other developments complicated the legal position before this final decision: the *NALSA* judgement's finding that discrimination against trans persons on the basis of sexual orientation or gender identity violated their fundamental rights;[30] and the opinion of four of the nine judges who heard *Puttaswamy v. Union of India*, that the right to choose one's sexual orientation fell within the ambit of a fundamental right to privacy.[31]

While these judgements have attracted extensive media and scholarly commentary, for the most part the temporal moves that animate their reasoning have been left unexamined. Time was central to the arguments advanced by the Naz Foundation, an NGO working on HIV/AIDS and sexual health, in challenging section 377 before the Delhi High Court. Reminding the Court of the law's provenance in traditional Judaeo-Christian morality, Naz argued that its penalisation of 'carnal intercourse' was 'outdated' and had no place in 'modern society'.[32] The government's response was initially ambivalent. The National AIDS Control Organisation maintained that section 377 was an impediment to HIV/AIDS prevention and treatment because it stigmatised vulnerable communities, pushing them beyond the reach of healthcare workers. The Ministry of Home Affairs defended section 377 with the argument that it 'responded to the values and mores [of] Indian society'[33] at the time of its enactment—a breathtakingly disingenuous claim given the undemocratic colonial origins of the provision. It acknowledged that law needed to keep pace with social change, noting that 'changes in public tolerance . . . lead to campaigns to either criminalise some behaviour or decriminalise others', but insisted that 'there is no such tolerance to the practice of homosexuality/lesbianism [*sic*] in Indian society'.[34]

The Delhi High Court rejected this argument, ruling that 'moral indignation, howsoever strong, is not a valid basis for overriding [the] individual's fundamental rights of dignity and privacy.'[35] Fundamental rights might be restricted only on the basis of what it called 'constitutional morality'.[36] The

---

29. WP (Crl) No 76 of 2016 (hereafter *Navtej*); for an archive of resources related to this case see http://orinam.net/377/sc-2018-verdict/.

30. *NALSA*, paras. 55, 77.

31. (2017) 10 SCC 1.

32. *Naz*, para. 7.

33. Counter affidavit on behalf of respondent no. 5 in the matter of *Naz Foundation v. Government of NCT of Delhi*, accessed 29 August 2017, www.lawyerscollective.org/files/MHA%20Affidavit.pdf.

34. Ibid., 12–13.

35. *Naz*, para. 86.

36. Ibid., para. 79.

Court derived its understanding of constitutional morality from a speech that Ambedkar had made to the Constituent Assembly in 1948, when presenting the Draft Constitution for approval. Here Ambedkar quotes the classicist George Grote to explain that constitutional morality is

> a paramount reverence for the forms of the Constitution, enforcing obedience to authority acting under and within these forms yet combined with the habit of open speech, of action subject only to definite legal control, and unrestrained censure of those very authorities as to all their public acts combined too with a perfect confidence in the bosom of every citizen amidst the bitterness of party contest that the forms of the Constitution will not be less sacred in the eyes of his opponents than in his own.[37]

The *Naz* decision was appealed in the Supreme Court by a disparate group of religious and social conservatives. The government did not join the appeal, urging the Court—in a remarkable *volte-face*—to take account of changing social values and to reject the moral views of Victorian Britain which, it now recognised, underpinned section 377.[38] The *Koushal* judgement dealt with the question of time in a perfunctory manner. Acknowledging that the constitutionality of a provision might be affected by the passage of time, it nonetheless concluded from the fact that the legislature had chosen not to amend the provision that it represented the will of the people.[39] It held that unless a clear constitutional violation had been demonstrated, the Court was powerless to strike down a law on account of its incongruence with changed social perceptions.[40] Dismissing the evidence that had been placed before it, it held that queer activists had 'miserably failed' to demonstrate that the State deprived sexual minorities of their fundamental rights.[41] Indeed it seemed to doubt that such a case could ever be made given that sexual minorities constituted a 'miniscule fraction' of the country's population and given also that section 377 had been invoked against fewer than two hundred people in its legislative history.[42]

37. Constituent Assembly Debates, speech by Dr. B. R. Ambedkar, 4 November 1948, https://cadindia.clpr.org.in/constitution_assembly_debates/volume/7/1948-11-04.
38. *Koushal*, para. 21.
39. Ibid., para. 28.
40. Ibid., para. 33.
41. Ibid., para. 40.
42. Ibid., para. 43. This count reflects the number of reported judgements of the higher judiciary rather than the number of times the provision has been invoked to harass or prosecute individuals. For an analysis of the everyday use of section 377, see Puri, *Sexual States*.

This last observation aroused considerable disapproval when a larger bench of the Court reconsidered the *Koushal* decision in *Navtej*.[43] Ruling that the question of numbers had no bearing on the enforcement of fundamental rights, Justice Nariman clarifies that the very purpose of fundamental rights in the Indian Constitution 'is to withdraw the subject of liberty and dignity of the individual and place such subject beyond the reach of majoritarian governments so that constitutional morality can be applied by this Court to give effect to the rights of . . . minorities.'[44] All the judges endorsed the *Naz* court's distinction between popular and constitutional morality, as well as its deployment of the latter as the basis on which the constitutionality of section 377 was to be judged. This makes it imperative to enquire into the temporal dimensions of popular and constitutional morality.

The *Naz* bench mistrusted popular morality because, among other things, it was 'based on shifting and subjective notions of right and wrong.'[45] At first glance, this might suggest that the Court took the view that while popular morality shifts with time, constitutional morality offers a timeless standard against which to make normative judgements. Yet this is not borne out by the extensive discussion in both *Naz*[46] and *Navtej* of how constitutional interpretation must keep pace with the times. In the latter decision, Chief Justice Misra elaborates at length on the principle of 'transformative constitutionalism,' which he understands as 'a pragmatic lens which will help in recognising the realities of the current day' and which enables the Constitution 'to adapt and transform with the changing needs of the times.'[47] This requires the Court, in his view, 'to steer the country and its institutions in a democratic egalitarian direction where there is increased protection of fundamental rights and other freedoms.'[48] The direction of this steer, in turn, is established by a 'doctrine of progressive realisation of rights' and a corresponding 'doctrine of non-retrogression'. As he explains, 'in a progressive and an ever-improving society, there is no place for retreat. The society has to march ahead.'[49] In their concurring judgements, both Justices Nariman and Chandrachud recognise the force of time, the former ruling that the 'Victorian morality' underpinning section 377 'must give way to constitutional morality as has been recognised

43. *Navtej*, per Misra, CJI, paras. 169–172.
44. *Navtej*, per Nariman, J, para. 81.
45. *Naz*, para. 79.
46. Ibid., para. 114.
47. *Navtej*, per Misra, CJI, para. 96. See also per Chandrachud, J, paras. 147–55.
48. *Navtej*, per Misra, CJI, para. 110.
49. Ibid., para. 188.

in many of our judgements'[50] and the latter declaring that the law 'has imposed on [LGBT persons] a morality which is an anachronism.'[51] The dynamic and substantive nature of constitutional morality evidenced in these observations contrasts strikingly with Ambedkar's essentially procedural understanding of the term as entailing a 'reverence for the *forms* of the constitution'.[52]

If the understanding of constitutional morality must constantly expand and transform to enable a progressive realisation of rights, from where do judges obtain the moral content with which they infuse the language of the Constitution—language that, after all, remains static barring explicit amendment? Of course precedent supplies one source of such content. But the judges in these cases were also influenced by their own sense of the trajectory of modernity. The *Naz* Court justified its decision with reference to 'the current scientific and professional understanding',[53] the 'almost unanimous medical and psychiatric opinion that homosexuality is not a disease or a disorder',[54] the 'moral and professional consensus among human rights and equality experts',[55] and the fact that 'a number of open democratic societies have turned their backs to criminalisation of sodomy laws'.[56]

Indeed, *Naz's* extensive reliance on comparative and international law attracted the ire of the Supreme Court in *Koushal*.[57] The *Koushal* bench cites a number of previous Supreme Court decisions that caution against over-reliance on caselaw from other jurisdictions, among which is the case of *Jagmohan Singh v. State of Uttar Pradesh*. In that case, the Supreme Court had been debating the constitutionality of the death penalty. Expressing doubts about the wisdom of transplanting Western experiences of death penalty abolition into the Indian context, the Court observed that 'social conditions are different and so also the general intellectual level.'[58] It is one thing to assert social difference without implying hierarchy; quite another to suggest a difference in *levels* of intellectual attainment. Reiterated in the context of *Koushal*, this otherwise innocuous sentence betrays not so much

50. *Navtej*, per Nariman, J, para. 78.
51. *Navtej*, per Chandrachud, J, para. 3.
52. Mehta, 'What Is Constitutional Morality?', emphasis in original.
53. *Naz*, para. 70.
54. Ibid., para. 67.
55. Ibid., para. 93.
56. Ibid., para. 58.
57. *Koushal*, para. 52.
58. *Jagmohan Singh v. State of Uttar Pradesh*, (1973) 1 SCC 20, para. 14, cited from ibid., para. 52.

a desire to resist modernity or even to perform it differently as an anxiety that one is not yet ready for it.

In a direct riposte to the *Koushal* bench's attitude towards international law, the judges in *Navtej* showed no hesitation in citing international and comparative law. Justice Chandrachud concludes a tour de force of a judgement, sections of which read like a tour around the world,[59] with the clarification that he looks to international and comparative opinion 'not to determine the meaning of the guarantees contained within the Indian Constitution, but to provide a sound and appreciable confirmation of our conclusions about those guarantees.'[60] Yet he cannot suppress an undertone of anxiety in his concluding observation that 'in the march of civilizations across the spectrum of a compassionate global order, India cannot be left behind.'[61]

If the judges fear that India lags behind in its recognition of the homo-sexual subject, this is not the case insofar as the (reductively imagined) trans subject is concerned. The *NALSA* decision also refers extensively to inter-national and comparative law and political philosophy, and it too invokes signifiers of modernity such as 'medical science'[62] and human rights.[63] Yet a very different temporal politics is evident in other parts of the decision, particularly in the lead judgement of Justice Radhakrishnan. In a section purporting to offer a historical overview of transgender communities in India, he begins by noting their 'strong historical presence in our country in Hindu mythology and other religious texts'.[64] He references terms and concepts describing a 'third gender' in Vedic and Puranic literatures, as well as legends from the Ramayana and Mahabharata that feature transgender characters.[65] There are two passing references in the judgement to the fact that hijras historically held positions of responsibility in Muslim royal courts.[66] Both judges suggest that they were treated with 'great respect' till the advent of British colonialism, when they were deemed innately crim-inal and subject to measures of surveillance and punishment under the Criminal Tribes Act, 1871.[67]

---

59. See *Navtej*, per Chandrachud, J, paras. 98–126.
60. *Navtej*, per Chandrachud, J, para. 126.
61. Ibid.
62. *NALSA*, para. 83.
63. Ibid., para. 111.
64. Ibid., para. 12.
65. Ibid., para. 12–15.
66. Ibid., para. 6, 15.
67. Ibid., para. 44, 110.

Gee Imaan Semmalar reads this historical narrative as an instance of what we might call Hindu trans nationalism:

> In a bid to prove rather unnecessarily that transgenders are not western imports, [the judges] end up presenting a golden Hindu period where there was no discrimination and a villainous colonial presence from which the oppression started. This completely ignores the Muslim cultural context within which several hijra gharanas [households] have flourished beyond the restrictions of Hinduism, creating a syncretic culture that respects Islam within the transgender community.[68]

In a useful historical overview, Gayatri Reddy has observed that explicit references to 'eunuchs' in South Asian texts increase dramatically with the advent of Muslim rulers in the eleventh and twelfth centuries, reflecting the positions of responsibility that hijras held in their courts.[69] Moreover, her ethnography of contemporary hijra lives in Hyderabad reveals a remarkable syncretism in which everyday observance of Islamic religious, dietary, and sartorial practices coexists with devotion to the Hindu goddess Bahuchara Mata,[70] suggesting a considerably more complex genealogy than the judgement's potted history is able or willing to provide.

The *NALSA* judgement's recognition of trans subjects through recourse to a selective reading of Indian history generates other problems. Aniruddha Dutta notes a frequent tendency on the part of the judges to conflate trans with hijra, 'making hijras the primary referent of the transgender category despite mentioning a variety of trans identifications and embodiments'.[71] Trans masculine activists were quick to point out that the judgement's emphasis on 'traditional trans feminine communities' had the effect of excluding trans masculine subjects from its purview. Satya observes that

> not a single page carried any of the following words: FTM (Female to Male), Transman, Intergender, Bhaiya, Babu, Kotha, FTK (Female to Kotha), Thirunambi, Genderqueer, Gandabasaka—some common terms used by members of the trans masculine, intersex and inter-gender communities for their identities and/or expressions.[72]

68. Semmalar, 'Gender Outlawed'.
69. Reddy, *With Respect to Sex*, 22.
70. Ibid., 98–108.
71. Dutta, 'Contradictory Tendencies', 230.
72. Satya, 'Transgender Verdict'.

He argues that the judgement's claims to modernity through its references to international law and political thought are hollow because 'the text simultaneously upholds the life and dignity of traditional trans feminine persons primarily because of their historicity and mention in religious scriptures.'[73]

Paradoxically, the Court's reductive reading of trans as hijra may have fostered its willingness to recognise its claim to backward status. To understand this suggestion we have to bear in mind that backwardness has historically been assessed in terms of caste, and also recall an earlier historical moment in which hijras were regarded as a caste. In the colonial census, hijras were frequently enumerated as one of many 'castes and tribes' of India. More specifically, they were classified as a 'criminal caste' and subject to the draconian impositions of the aforementioned Criminal Tribes Act. As Reddy explains, the category of the criminal caste drew on prevailing colonial understandings of Hindu society and of caste in particular, but also on constructions of crime, deviance, and vagrancy in Victorian England. Central to these constructions was the notion of an inborn propensity to crime passed on from one generation to the next, somewhat like caste identity.[74] Premised on the assumption that membership of certain groups predisposed individuals to crime, the 1871 Act called for the 'registration, surveillance and control of certain criminal tribes and eunuchs'. 'Eunuchs' were defined expansively to include an array of gender nonconforming subjects and were regarded as being prone to kidnapping and castrating boys, indulging in the 'unnatural' sexual offences proscribed by section 377, and committing acts of public debauchery. Although the Act was repealed in 1952, it was immediately replaced by the Habitual Offenders Act, which did not mention 'eunuchs' but perpetuated the notion of subjects given to lives of crime among whom hijras remained paradigmatic examples. In recounting this history, Dipika Jain reminds us that as recently as 2011, the state of Karnataka thought fit to empower its police to 'control undesirable activities of eunuchs'.[75]

In her work on intersectionality, Kimberlé Crenshaw argues that the experiences of black women are unthinkable in the law because narratives of gender take as their 'historical base' the experiences of middle-class white

73. Ibid.
74. Reddy, *With Respect to Sex*, 25–28.
75. Jain, 'Shifting Subjects', 45–48. In response to a public interest litigation filed by the Karnataka Sexual Minorities Forum, the NGO Jeeva, and transgender activist Akkai Padmashali, the Government of Karnataka replaced the word 'eunuch' with 'persons' in the relevant provision of the Karnataka Police Act (Deccan Herald News Service, 'Govt to HC').

women, while narratives of race are based on the historical experiences of middle-class black men.[76] I suggest that because hijras are read as the 'historical base' of trans, and because the state has a long history of categorising hijras as a caste, it becomes possible for the *NALSA* judges to think of trans persons as akin to those belonging to subordinate castes despite the ontological non-equivalence of gender identity and caste. This seems borne out by the Court's direction that the 'State is bound to take some affirmative action for their advancement so that the injustice done to them *for centuries* could be remedied'.[77] Here the duration of the injustice, projected backwards in time in the juridical figuration of the trans subject as hijra, is seen to underscore the urgency of remedy.

A collective reading of the *Naz, Koushal, NALSA,* and *Navtej* judgements thus yields some interesting temporal insights. In the judgements dealing with sexual orientation, the homosexual emerges as a figure of modernity, even if the *Koushal* decision evinces a stance towards that modernity different from that espoused in *Naz* and *Navtej*. In contrast, the *NALSA* judgement locates hijras in 'tradition', while barely taking cognisance of trans masculine subjects. Against the presumption in much of the literature on homonationalism that modernity is the primary temporal vehicle for queer legitimation, my reading of these judgements suggests that in the Indian context both tradition and modernity have been deployed as legitimating strategies to render different kinds of queer embodiment and desire intelligible in a juridical register.

THE PROMISE OF BACKWARDNESS

A Brief History of Backwardness

To appreciate the appeal to backwardness as a strategy for emancipation, we need to understand how the category became central to the Indian constitutional vision for socioeconomic advancement. The politics of minority groups in British India were heavily shaped by colonial policies of classification, enumeration, and representation.[78] As the colonial authorities conceded limited forms of representative government from the first decade of the twentieth century onwards, these groups became preoccupied with the question of not only how to represent their interests to the colonial state, but also how to secure them against the threat of Hindu dominance.

76. Crenshaw, 'Demarginalizing the Intersection', 148.
77. *NALSA*, para. 60, emphasis mine.
78. Bajpai, *Debating Difference*, 32.

Anti-caste radicals had long sought to distinguish subordinate castes and 'untouchables' from dominant caste Hindus in an attempt to reject their authority. For its part, the Muslim League complained about the disproportionately low representation of Muslims and demanded separate representation at all levels of government. The British conceded this demand by establishing separate electorates for Muslims, whereby in a certain number of reserved seats, Muslim voters could elect Muslim representatives.

As Anupama Rao explains, Ambedkar initially sought to define Dalits as a political minority similar to Muslims.[79] But the Dalit struggle for adequate representation faced two problems. First, conscious of the power that came with numbers, caste Hindus resisted official recognition of Dalits as non-Hindus, fearing that this would reduce their electoral weight. Moreover, they regarded the caste question as a matter for internal Hindu reform rather than intervention by the colonial state. In 1932, Gandhi successfully thwarted the Dalit demand for separate electorates, advocating an alternative system in which the entirety of the electorate would vote for Dalit candidates in seats reserved for them. Dalits objected that only candidates palatable to the caste Hindu majority would be elected through such a process. Second, while Muslims were able to take advantage of their territorial concentration to transform their minority status into a separate nationality that culminated in the creation of Pakistan, the territorial dispersion of Dalits precluded an analogous nationalist politics.

But in a reversal of their relative positions, when the Constituent Assembly of independent India met to draft its founding document, it placed affirmative action for subordinate caste groups on a firmer footing than special rights for religious minorities. As Rochana Bajpai observes, whereas at the start of the Constituent Assembly Debates the status claimed for groups to denote their entitlement to special treatment was 'minority', by the end of the deliberations this had changed to 'backward', with even Muslim representatives arguing that religious minorities ought to be considered 'backward'.[80] Bajpai argues that the post-independence discourse on group rights in India has been conducted in a legitimating vocabulary comprising a set of interlinked political concepts—secularism, democracy, social justice, national unity, and development—some of which have been more important than others at particular historical junctures.[81] In the immediate aftermath of Partition, national unity took precedence, with all the other concepts being construed through the prism of its

79. Rao, *Caste Question*, 124.
80. Bajpai, *Debating Difference*, 116.
81. Ibid., 14–15.

imperatives. Bajpai suggests that in light of this, Constituent Assembly members took a dim view of political safeguards for religious minorities—of which separate electorates were the paradigmatic example—because they were seen to have culminated in Partition.[82] There was more support for political safeguards for what would come to be called the Scheduled Castes.[83] Affirmative action for those deemed 'backward' was felt to be consistent with the imperative of national unity because it was intended to diminish rather than maintain difference.[84]

The constitutional provisions authorising special measures by the state for the advancement of the 'backward' apply to both the generic category 'socially and educationally backward classes' and the more specific categories of Scheduled Castes (SCs) and Scheduled Tribes (STs).[85] As Marc Galanter explains, the term 'backward' has been used in Indian constitutional law and policy both as an umbrella category encompassing the totality of groups entitled to preferential treatment, and as a more specific label for groups that are marginalised but considered to be more privileged than SCs (defined as those who have historically suffered from the stigma of untouchability) and STs (indigenous peoples or adivasis).[86] In due course, the category 'Other Backward Class' (OBC) came to be used for the latter purpose.

In 1953, the First Backward Classes Commission was charged with establishing criteria for the evaluation of backwardness. Its chairman Kaka Kalelkar took the view that too much of a focus on caste was inimical to the newly independent state's mission of creating a 'classless and casteless society'.[87] Other members of the Commission disagreed, arguing that the evils of caste could only be removed by measures that took caste as their unit of analysis.[88] When the Commission reported its findings in 1955, it reluctantly conceded the impossibility of dissociating caste from backwardness, while also drawing attention to social groups whose marginalisation was irreducible to caste. The Commission expressed concern about sections of the Muslim and Christian communities whose religions were theoretically opposed to caste but who nevertheless suffered its stigma. Moreover,

82. Ibid., 63–68.
83. The term 'Scheduled' comes from the Schedule (appendix) in the Constitution, which lists the communities that are recognised as being entitled to affirmative action at any given time.
84. Bajpai, *Debating Difference*, 125–126.
85. Constitution of India, articles 15(4) and 15(5).
86. Galanter, 'Other Backward Classes'.
87. Government of India, *Backward Classes Commission*, xiv.
88. Ibid., xiii.

the Constitution's use of the phrase 'backward classes', rather than castes, was seen as giving permission for the evaluation of backwardness in terms other than caste, even if prevailing social conditions made this implausible.[89] These and other considerations ultimately produced a set of four criteria for backwardness: low social position in the caste hierarchy; lack of educational advancement; inadequate or no representation in government; and inadequate representation in trade, commerce, and industry.[90] Importantly, the units to which these criteria were applied were caste and sub-caste groups as a whole, rather than individuals therein. Yet the door had been opened to the evaluation of group backwardness on the basis of non-caste criteria.[91]

Trans Claims to Backwardness

Aravani[92] activists in the southern state of Tamil Nadu were among the first trans groups in the country to secure state recognition of their identities. From 2004, they were able to access a number of welfare schemes in respect of housing, employment, and education, targeted at backward classes in the state.[93] In 2010, the Karnataka State Backward Classes Commission (KSBCC) became the first state institution to recommend the inclusion of a range of sexual and gender minorities including 'hijras, kothis, jogappa, F to M, Mangalamukhis, [and] Transgenders' in the state's Backward Classes

89. Ibid.
90. Ibid., 46.
91. The Commission's report was rejected by the then Congress government, which like Kalelkar himself, was opposed in principle to evaluating backwardness through the prism of caste. Galanter, 'Other Backward Classes', explains that the central (federal) government thereafter largely withdrew from the business of identifying OBCs, leaving this to the states till the advent of the 1977 Janata government, whose primary electoral base comprised subordinate castes. See also Galanter, *Competing Equalities*.
92. The term for hijras in Tamil Nadu, although some prefer the term tirunangai. 'Aravani' comes from the origin myth of the community. When Aravan, son of Arjuna, volunteers to sacrifice his life in the Kurukshetra war that is the climactic event of the Mahabharata, Krishna grants him three boons—a heroic death, an opportunity to see the entire war through, and a night of conjugal bliss before his demise. Because no woman wants to marry Aravan, fearing her imminent widowhood, Krishna himself assumes a female form as Mohini and spends the night with Aravan. Aravanis identify with this manifestation of Krishna, with their annual Koovagam festival commemorating the marriage of Aravan and Mohini, followed by ritual mourning of his death.
93. Govindan and Vasudevan, 'Razor's Edge of Oppositionality'.

List.[94] Following a series of public hearings and field visits, the Commission based its recommendation on its findings with regard to the occupations, incomes, access to government employment, educational attainment, and living conditions of the people that it interviewed.

The KSBCC dealt with the question of the caste membership of gender minorities without conflating the two categories. Its report reveals a more explicit, even if occasionally naïve, consideration of the relationship between caste and gender identity than is evident in the *NALSA* judgement. One memorandum submitted to the Commission by the Karnataka Sexual Minorities Forum argues that while hijras originate from different caste locations, 'all of them have been abandoned by their respective castes, tribes and social groups.'[95] Reflecting on data gathered during its field visits, the Commission sums up the condition of the people that it met with the essentially analogical observation that 'what they are facing is nothing but untouchability.'[96] It also notes repeatedly that the hijra households that it surveyed were mixed-caste and multi-religious in their composition and that their members evinced 'no caste feeling'.[97] While this may have been true of the Commission's necessarily limited sample, we should be wary of generalising this claim given that Dalit trans activists have attested to the prevalence of casteism within hijra and trans communities.[98] Nonetheless, the Commission ultimately circumvented the question of caste with the observation that since minority communities that claimed not to have castes, such as Muslims, Christians, Buddhists, and Jains, had been regarded as Backward Classes, the lack of a determinate or unified caste identity was no bar to the inclusion of gender minorities within this category.[99] As Commission Chairperson C. S. Dwarakanath later commented, 'since the Commission addresses backward classes and not only castes, [gender minorities] can be brought under the ambit of backward classes'.[100] Thus, well before the *NALSA* judgement, state institutions had considered and conceded the trans demand for backward class status, in terms that were somewhat more cognisant of the complexity of the relationship between gender identity and caste.

94. Karnataka State Backward Classes Commission (KSBCC), 'Including Transgenders'. Personal communication with Arvind Narrain, 2 October 2017. See also Narrain, 'Gender Identity'.
95. KSBCC, 'Including Transgenders', 11.
96. Ibid., 53.
97. Ibid., 30.
98. Vidya, '(Trans)gender and Caste'; Banu, 'Casteism'.
99. KSBCC, 'Including Transgenders', 56–57.
100. Bageshree, 'BC Panel'.

Because the constitutional mandate for affirmative action for those deemed backward is motivated by a desire to diminish rather than maintain difference, the condition of backwardness and the measures intended to alleviate it were envisaged as being temporary. The expectation was that as castes advanced in socioeconomic terms, they would be removed from the list of groups eligible for assistance. This has tended not to happen, partly because of the glacial pace of change and partly because governments have found it politically inexpedient to withdraw state support given their reliance on caste groups as vote banks. Moreover, the hegemony of 'backwardness' as the basis for accessing political representation and welfare has meant that more and more groups have lobbied to be designated as backward. This has given backwardness as a political category a kind of permanent temporariness in Indian politics.

This temporal ambivalence is visible in radical political thought on the caste question, which strives to bring caste antagonisms into sharper relief while looking forward to their extinction. Referencing the title of Ambedkar's most widely read essay, Rao explains that 'the dual impulse to recognize and to remove caste has produced an agonistic terrain of politics where caste identification is expected to lead to the annihilation of caste'.[101] She identifies the central paradox of Dalit politics as deriving from the fact that 'the term "Dalit" is both analytic and prescriptive: it defines the historical structures and practices of dispossession that experientially mark someone as Dalit and simultaneously identifies the Dalit as someone seeking to escape those same structures.'[102]

In calling for the 'annihilation of caste', Ambedkar pushes against these structures and practices with an attack on the Hindu religious scriptures that authorise them.[103] Locating the root of the evils of caste in Hinduism, Ambedkar searches for an alternative moral foundation on which a society committed to the values of liberty, equality, fraternity, and democracy might be built.[104] He constructs this out of an engagement with Buddhism, counterpoised with and refracted through the claims of Marxism.[105] Insofar as they resemble each other in their antipathy to private property and their understanding of suffering as the result of exploitation, Ambedkar reads

101. Rao, *Caste* Question, 278.
102. Ibid., 16.
103. Ambedkar, *Annihilation of Caste.*
104. Ibid., 64, 97–100.
105. Ambedkar, 'Buddha or Karl Marx'. Omvedt, *Ambedkar*, 161.

Buddhism as a proto-Marxism, while breaking with its more pessimistic and quietist precepts. But he also considers it superior to Marxism in its ability to transform the moral dispositions and not simply the material relations of society.[106] Moreover, by reading Buddhism historically as the original indigenous ethical challenge to Brahminism, and Dalits as the successors of defeated Buddhists, he gives Dalits a consciousness of their distinctive identity in Indian history, providing what Gauri Viswanathan describes as 'a religious framework for a politics of Dalit renewal'.[107] What is significant in all this is that if for the majority of Constituent Assembly members, the amelioration of backwardness required the elimination of difference over time, for Ambedkar the 'annihilation of caste' meant something rather different. Far from simply enabling Dalits to become like caste Hindus, it entailed the production of a new Dalit subjectivity marked by a revolutionary consciousness.[108] In this regard, it is a radically anti-assimilationist project.

At the same time, Ambedkar's politics is not separatist. Despite announcing his intention to renounce Hinduism in 1935 and actually doing so in 1956, as the first law minister of independent India he was deeply invested in reforming Hindu law. The Hindu Code Bill, passed in no small measure due to his efforts (albeit after he had resigned in frustration at its slow progress), significantly improved the position of Hindu women in matters of marriage, divorce, inheritance, and adoption.[109] For several decades the only significant intervention by the state in the personal laws of any religious community, Ambedkar's investment in this legislative initiative is indicative of his determination to disseminate the modernist egalitarian values that he sought to cultivate not only within a Dalit public but throughout the body politic. Thus, his project for the annihilation of caste envisages a future in which a newly reconstituted Dalithood would not simply dissolve into a casteless society, but would serve as a beach-head from which to transform Indian society as a whole. Viewed through the preoccupations of a queer politics, Ambedkar offers a precocious critique of both the assimilationist impulse of homo- and transnormativity and the separatist impulse of queer liberation politics.[110] Both seem insufficiently ambitious, even if in different ways: the former because it deems

---

106. Viswanathan, *Outside the Fold*, 229.

107. Ibid., 232.

108. The same might be said of Tamil anti-caste reformer E. V. Ramasamy (Periyar), with the significant difference that his Suyamariyathai Iyakkam (Self-Respect Movement) was informed by a radical atheism (Geetha, 'Periyar').

109. Zelliot, 'Dr. Ambedkar'; Pardeshi, 'Hindu Code Bill'.

110. On the latter, see Berlant and Freeman, 'Queer Nationality', 175.

revolutionary social transformation to be undesirable, the latter because it too easily resigns itself to its putative infeasibility.

I want to suggest that a similar dialectic between separation and re-engagement, between the sharpening of identity and its dissolution, can be observed in trans and, more specifically, hijra politics. Academic ethnographies of hijra lives have given us thick descriptions of the complex social and kinship arrangements that constitute hijra lifeworlds, at the heart of which are hijra gharanas.[111] They have helped us to understand how the norms that structure these spaces have enabled them to function as places of refuge and sustenance, while also situating them in broader political networks and institutions such as hijra jamaats and panchayats. But this work has tended to convey an impression of time-honoured stasis. In contrast, a striking feature of recent hijra autobiographies—which we might consider insider ethnographies—is an evident willingness on the part of their authors to call out power as it operates in both natal and hijra families.[112] In so doing, they reveal the boundaries between hijra and cis-heteronormative lifeworlds to be more porous than we have tended to suppose. That porosity has a double-edged potential, both threatening to import the hierarchies of cis-heteronormativity into hijra worlds and enabling the latter to infuse and transform the former in revolutionary ways.

In telling the story of her life, hijra activist Revathi offers a poignant account of movement between different kinds of spaces, none of which is free from violence and hardship.[113] Fleeing the oppressions of heteronormativity and transphobia in her native village, she becomes a hijra, only to encounter a different set of conflicts in the hijra networks of the metropolitan cities to which she escapes—conflicts between hijra gurus (teachers) and chelas (disciples), between hijras and their lovers, clients, and the police, and amongst hijras themselves. Finding that she can no longer fully inhabit aravani culture, Revathi throws herself into the work of community organising and professionalised activism when she joins the Bengaluru NGO Sangama.[114] (Interestingly, the English translations of the titles of Revathi's successive books reveal a shift in identification from 'hijra' to 'trans' that may be indicative of this movement.) But Sangama too becomes a space of personal and professional conflicts, many stemming from the difficulties of being a working-class, non-English-speaking person

111. Nanda, *Neither Man nor Woman*; Cohen, 'Pleasures of Castration'; Reddy, *With Respect to Sex*.
112. This is partly why I privilege autobiography over ethnography in this chapter.
113. Revathi, *The Truth about Me*.
114. Ibid., 303–304.

in a leadership position, even in an ostensibly progressive space. Reflecting on this episode of her life, she remarks, 'When I took up activism, I left the hijra jamaat system saying I didn't need it any longer. But now, I feel that it is to this system that I have come back for support.'[115]

These experiences and the ambivalence that they generate underpin Revathi's determination to spare her chelas the rigour of the norms that have traditionally governed guru-chela relations within hijra families in matters of corporeality, desire, residence, livelihood, and filiation. Much to the consternation of more conventional hijras of her generation, Revathi 'allows' her chelas to live independently and does not insist that they hand over their earnings to her. In her words, 'they were the next generation and had their own dreams and aspirations for a better life. If they wished to live like modern girls, who was I to prevent them from doing so?'[116] Thus alongside a critique of the transphobia of everyday life, Revathi also offers a critique of transnormativity. Indeed her determination to rewrite the normative scripts of gender transgression extends outside the hijra world to encompass all aspects of gender identity and expression. Reflecting on a life in activism, Revathi says:

> Today when I look back, I also realize that in my books I had articulated a traditional notion about women—focused on the 3Cs: cooking, cleaning and caring—be it children, husband or in-laws! But that was before I discovered feminism! I then realized how oppressive men have been towards women, forcing us to behave in stereotypically feminine ways—docile, obedient, modest and dress in saris and have long hair with flowers! I then understood how unfair it was. Today I dress in clothes that permit me mobility (salwar kameez, trousers and shirts) and have cut my hair short![117]

The subversiveness of these apparently banal observations becomes clear if we read them as a critique of the traditional hijra investment in an exaggerated and stereotypical femininity. Having journeyed with Revathi through her struggles against both transphobia and hijra normativity towards this transfeminist position, we are not taken by surprise when she says, 'I look forward to a world where there is no gender at all'.[118] In a

---

115. Revathi, *Life in Trans Activism*, 114.
116. Ibid., 41. Although written from the considerably more privileged position of an English-speaking, college-educated Brahmin, we can hear a similar impatience with the conventional ordering of hijra relationships in the autobiography of Laxminarayan Tripathi (*Me Hijra*).
117. Revathi, *Life in Trans Activism*, 85.
118. Ibid., 226.

similar vein, trans scholar activists Sunil Mohan and Rumi Harish advocate a project of 'de-gendering the law'. While recognising the extant social reality in which people gendered female at birth face disproportionate violence and the need for explicit recognition of this reality in the law, they aspire towards the 'elimination of gender as a significant mode of identity that defines a person's selfhood.'[119] We can see here a structural resonance between a transfeminist desire for what might be described as the political annihilation of gender and the Ambedkarite project of annihilating caste.

The annihilation of caste is invoked more pointedly by Gee Imaan Semmalar, a theatre actor, director, and filmmaker, in an autobiographical reflection on how the experience of transition shifts his relationships with those closest to him:

> As I masculinise over the years, I have come to realize that I have also become the child who cannot be 'explained' to many. When you medically transition, the joke is over. The child can no longer be indulged as a tomboy, the 'daughter' will never get married and give you chubby grandchildren, you stumble when you say your kid's name, when you use pronouns, slowly you avoid conversations about that child with friends and family, you panic when someone rings the bell when your child is at home, you cannot ask extended circles to open a few doors of opportunity for your kid. Your erasure is written into family histories as blank spaces where your photograph once was. As someone who is convinced about the need to destroy caste networks, this erasure came as a relief to me. I have begun to understand the erasure as something that is propelled by caste respectability and shame.[120]

In theorising erasure as both deeply painful and 'a relief', Semmalar deploys the queer strategy of transforming an experience of abjection into the grounds of a new agency. What is striking here is the manner in which the destruction of caste becomes imbricated with gender transition. Even as the erasure of trans becoming is driven by the desire of others to preserve caste respectability, this very erasure offers the trans subject the possibility of liberation from caste. Of course this remains only a possibility, a utopian futurity towards which the trans body might (or might not) strive. Semmalar is scrupulously self-reflexive in acknowledging the caste-, class-, and able-bodied privilege that supply the very conditions within which his transition becomes possible. In doing so, he reminds us of the very

119. Mohan et al., *Towards Gender Inclusivity*, 24, 56.
120. Semmalar, 'Emperor Penguins', 198–199.

different kinds of labour that subjects who are differently positioned in the caste hierarchy must undertake to hasten its destruction.

In drawing attention to these narratives, it is not my intention to suggest that they are more authentically trans than others. I am mindful of the critiques of trans studies scholars who have drawn attention to the ways in which queer theorists have tended to conscript trans autobiography to valorise transgressive over reinscriptive narratives of gender or vice versa, effectively deauthorising other ways of being trans.[121] What interests me about the narrative moments to which I have been drawn in the foregoing paragraphs are the ways in which they are structurally homologous with, or explicitly enter into, the project of annihilating caste. These convergences suggest that in at least some strands of trans politics, the claim to recognition as 'backward' is not simply a pragmatic legal and political strategy to access welfare within the terms of the existing constitutional scheme, but also expresses a yearning for the 'backward futures' that Ambedkar and other anti-caste revolutionaries contemplated.

GENDER IDENTITY AND BACKWARDNESS IN THE IMAGINATION OF THE NATION

Recall Jakobsen's caution that one of the perils of analogical reasoning is that it freezes the ground of the analogy in order to make comparison possible, thereby attributing to it a stability that may not be warranted.[122] If we are to avoid this, then in thinking about the relationship between gender identity and caste we need to be alive to the ways in which mobilisations around caste have transformed the prospects of different caste groups while also shifting the professed commitment of the Indian nation-state to ameliorate caste backwardness. Tracking these shifts makes visible crucial transitions in the imagination of the nation over the post-independence period. Of central importance here is the manner in which the nation's purported geopolitical backwardness has been imagined, problematised, and re-envisioned in a certain elite imaginary through the lens of gender. In trying to make sense of these shifts, I suggest that we might begin to recognise the nation's own transness.

A detailed account of the domestic trajectories of caste politics is beyond the scope of this chapter. Suffice to say that the rise of a number of

121. Prosser, *Second Skins*, 14–17; Catherwood, 'Coming *In?*'
122. Jakobsen, 'Queers Are like Jews', 70.

subordinate caste parties by the late 1970s, besides challenging Congress hegemony, enabled the articulation of demands for the extension of caste-based quotas in public employment and education.[123] In 1990, the National Front coalition government led by the Janata Dal recommended a 27% quota for OBCs, provoking a violent backlash from dominant castes.[124] Over time, regional subordinate caste parties have emerged as major players in national politics. Indeed the importance of subordinate caste assertion is attested to by the alacrity with which dominant caste parties such as the now ruling Bharatiya Janata Party (BJP) have begun to court the Dalit and OBC vote, while also attempting to draw these communities more tightly into the Hindu fold by portraying Muslims as a common enemy.

What is striking in all this is that even as caste becomes more en-trenched in the domestic politics of India—as a category of identity, locus of distribution, and basis for electoral mobilisation—it rarely enters into theorisations of Indian foreign policy and international relations. Caste finds little mention in the now extensive literature on India's 'rise' in the international system.[125] It is as if the struggle against caste backwardness, which so dominates domestic politics, has no bearing on the nation-state's attempted extrication of itself from geopolitical backwardness. At one level, this is a function of the success with which the Indian state has thwarted discussions of caste at the international level, most notably at the 2001 World Conference against Racism in Durban, South Africa, at which Dalit groups struggled to obtain recognition of the fact that caste discrimination was a violation of international human rights norms.[126] Caste conflict must be hidden from international scrutiny, not least because its persistence is an embarrassing reminder of the endurance of atavistic social attitudes and the incompleteness of the postcolonial state's developmental mission, both of which undermine its bid for great power status. But the concealment of caste in the international image that India projects also reflects a growing impatience with, perhaps even a repudiation of, its historic commitment to the amelioration of backwardness in the imaginary of the middle-class, dominant-caste elites who play a disproportionate role in the crafting of that image. An examination of this impatience additionally makes visible

123. Bajpai, *Debating Difference*, 225–226.
124. Ibid., 264–268.
125. See, for example, Perkovich, 'Is India a Major Power?'; Narlikar, 'Is India a Responsible Great Power?'; Pardesi, 'Is India a Great Power?'. For an exception, see Guha, *India: The Next Superpower?* The very repetitiveness of these titles tells a story about the preoccupations and anxieties of contemporary foreign policy elites, in which questions about caste remain strikingly absent.
126. Krishna, 'Postcolonial Racial/Spatial Order'; Cabrera, 'Dalit Cosmopolitans'.

the imbrication of gender identity and geopolitical positioning in the very 'idea of India' that animates elite imaginaries.[127]

In 2007, the Times Group—India's largest media conglomerate—launched a campaign called 'India Poised' to mark the sixtieth anniversary of India's independence.[128] The centrepiece of the campaign was an advertisement featuring the Hindi film megastar Amitabh Bachchan. Standing on the then unfinished Sea Link, a bridge connecting the Mumbai suburbs of Bandra and Worli, Bachchan offers us the following narrative in the familiar baritone that has seduced and menaced Indian cinema audiences for the better part of five decades:

> There are two Indias in this country. One India is straining at the leash, eager to spring forth and live up to all the adjectives that the world has been recently showering upon us. The other India is the leash. One India says 'Give me a chance and I'll prove myself.' The other India says 'Prove yourself first, and maybe then, you'll have a chance.' One India lives in the optimism of our hearts. The other India lurks in the scepticism of our minds. One India wants. The other India hopes. One India leads. The other India follows. These conversions are on the rise. With each passing day, more and more people from the other India are coming over to this side. And quietly, while the world is not looking, a pulsating dynamic new India is emerging. An India whose faith in success is far greater than its fear of failure. An India that no longer boycotts foreign made goods, but buys out the companies that make them instead. History, they say, is a bad motorist. It rarely ever signals its intentions when it's taking a turn. This is that 'rarely ever' moment. History is turning a page. For over half a century, our nation has sprung, stumbled, run, fallen, rolled over, got up and dusted herself, and cantered, sometimes lurched on. But now, in our sixtieth year as a free nation, the ride has brought us to the edge of Time's great precipice. And one India, a tiny little voice at the back of the head, is looking down at the bottom of the ravine, and hesitating. The other India is looking up at the sky and saying, 'It's time to fly'.[129]

If the texts through the shared reading of which the nation is imagined are today less the newspapers, journals, and novels that preoccupied Benedict Anderson,[130] than the audiovisual narratives that circulate virally through

127. Khilnani, *Idea of India*.
128. Times Group, 'India Poised'. For an analysis of the Times Group, see Auletta, 'Citizens Jain'.
129. Times Group, 'India Poised'.
130. Anderson, *Imagined Communities*.

social media and messaging services, then it is to ephemeral media such as this video that we must turn to take the pulse of the nation at any given time. In this regard, the video is useful for its very banality, providing what khanna describes as 'one of the most succinct formulations of the ideological frame that enables the current right wing dispensation in India'.[131] In a close reading of the video, Tara van Dijk suggests that it is indicative of the social fantasies that reinforce ideologies of neoliberal urbanism in contemporary India. Drawing on Žižekian ideological analysis and paralleling my own claims about neoliberal futurity in the previous chapter, van Dijk argues that fantasy supports ideology by purporting to explain why its promised outcomes have not yet materialised and by suggesting pathways for overcoming obstacles, thereby sustaining public faith in the ideology despite its self-evident failure.[132]

In characterising the 'other India' as a leash restraining the vanguard sectors of the economy, the advertisement sets up 'backward' sections of society as the scapegoat on whom responsibility for the slowness of economic growth can be displaced. In doing so, it obscures both the contributions of these sections to extant growth for which the 'forward' sections seize credit, as well as the contradictions within capitalism that preclude a more equitable sharing of this growth. The video offers a solution to this impasse in its observation that 'more and more people from the other India are coming over to this side'—although 'coming over' is usefully ambiguous in its coyness about the mechanisms by which this is being achieved. This ambiguity is precisely the point, for it obscures the processes of primitive accumulation by which millions are dragged willy-nilly into the capitalist economy. The transition from backwardness to forwardness is misrepresented as a matter of choice and will—'faith in success' triumphing over 'fear of failure'—transforming questions about the distribution of material power into ones about the development of appropriate mindsets. In a sly evocation of Jawaharlal Nehru's proclamation on the eve of Indian independence that 'at the stroke of the midnight hour, when the world sleeps, India will awake to life and freedom',[133] Bachchan declares that 'quietly, while the world is not looking, a pulsating dynamic new India is emerging.' Declaring their impatience with the temporal drag of backwardness, the writers of this script attempt nothing less than a revision of India's founding ideology, requiring someone of no less than Bachchan's stature to do this. But there is more going on here. khanna

131. khanna, *Sexualness*, 158.
132. Van Dijk, 'World-Class Slum-Free Indian Cities', 25.
133. Nehru, 'Tryst with Destiny'.

astutely draws our attention to the manner in which Bachchan pumps his fist as he proclaims the emergence of the 'pulsating dynamic new India' as if to signify the newfound phallic potency of this reimagined community.[134] Here, gender is mapped onto backwardness and forwardness. The old India is an effete India that must be eliminated or cut down to size through the mystical (and mystifying) process of 'conversion'.[135] The new India is an increasingly masculinising nation that must demonstrate its 'pulsating dynamic' nature in ever more visible ways in order to obtain the international recognition that it seeks.

The Indian nation has been imagined in gendered terms since the very advent of something that could be called 'Indian' political thought. Galled by the British colonial characterisation of Indian men as effeminate,[136] some Indian elites responded by forging a martial and masculine Hinduism. As Sikata Banerjee explains, the discourse of masculine Hinduism typically imagined the nation as embodied in the form of a mother goddess who required the protection of men in the archetypal roles of Hindu soldier and warrior-monk. Women are accorded subordinate roles in this discourse as heroic mother, chaste wife, and exceptionally, celibate masculinised warrior.[137] But the nation has not always been imagined as a woman, even in right-wing Hindu discourse. In his landmark text describing the key tenets of what he called 'Hindutva', V. D. Savarkar frequently refers to the nation as 'pitribhu' (fatherland), betraying his intellectual and political debts to German nationalist and fascist thought.[138] Priya Chacko has suggested that Savarkar's interchangeable and inconsistent use of pitribhu and 'matribhu' (motherland) reveals an unease with the feminine.[139] Indeed, Hindu nationalists' anxiety about the putative effeminacy and degeneracy of Hinduism, which they attribute to the malign influence of pacifist doctrines such as Buddhism, Jainism, Bhakti thought, and Gandhism, fuels a drive towards the masculinisation of both nation and state. The most obvious recent illustration of this can be found in the discourses of phallic potency that accompanied and legitimated the 1998 decision of India's first

134. khanna, *Sexualness*, 158–159.
135. The term 'conversion' also, perhaps unwittingly, evokes the Hindu Right's 'ghar wapsi' ('return home') campaign directed at religious minorities, Dalits, and adivasis, who are exhorted to 'return' to the fold of Hinduism.
136. Sinha, *Colonial Masculinity*.
137. Banerjee, *Make Me a Man!*
138. Savarkar, *Essentials of Hindutva*, 38–44.
139. Chacko, *Indian Foreign Policy*, 179. One other possibility is that the fatherland is imagined as a mother in times of danger. I am indebted to Scott Long and Sonia Corrêa for this insight.

BJP-led government to openly avow nuclear status.[140] BJP ally and leader of the Hindu Shiv Sena party, Bal Thackeray, is said to have applauded the nuclear tests that year with the declaration that 'we have to prove that we are not eunuchs'.[141] Bachchan's pumping fist thus references a familiar discourse in which the nation's transition from geopolitical backwardness to great power status is imagined in deeply gendered terms.

GENDER TROUBLE AND THE NATION

In wanting to prove that he was not a 'eunuch', Thackeray was reiterating a long-standing Hindu nationalist antipathy to the nonviolent politics of Gandhi, who once declared that he wished to be 'God's eunuch'.[142] Uttered in defence of his infamous experiments with sexuality—whereby Gandhi took to sleeping naked with female relatives and companions to test his vow of celibacy, to the consternation of many of his closest associates— this self-description might well serve as a metonym for the androgynous forms of political agency that he crafted. Indeed, Ashis Nandy has read Gandhi's political creativity primarily in gendered terms, arguing that where colonial and nationalist patriarchies both elevated masculinity over femininity in their struggle against one another, Gandhi disabled this binary by drawing on ascetic tropes in Indian thought and praxis for modes of speech, dress, affect, and embodiment that privileged androgeneity.[143] That Gandhi was read in this way in his time is clear from the testimony of his contemporaries. In a remarkable essay on what he calls Gandhi's 'celibate sexuality', Vinay Lal suggests that many of the women who were intimate with Gandhi may have ceased to think of him as a man.[144] Gandhi's assassin Nathuram Godse defended himself in court with the argument that he felt compelled to kill Gandhi because his politics was emasculating the nation. Godse's biography in turn presents a complex tale of gendered becoming. Born to parents who had lost sons in their infancy, he was brought up as a girl for the first years of his life in an attempt to trick fate into sparing him. His very name, Nathuram, is said to have derived from the nose ring (nath) that he was made to wear.[145] It is impossible to say whether this early experience of misgendering might have driven his masculinist Hindu politics.

140. Das, 'Encountering Hindutva'; Chacko, *Indian Foreign Policy*, 178–180.
141. Burns, 'Nuclear Anxiety'.
142. Lal, *Of Cricket*, 127.
143. Nandy, *Intimate Enemy*, 53.
144. Lal, *Of Cricket*, 136–137.
145. Mishra, 'Crisis in Modern Masculinity'.

But more pertinently, what should we make of these stories in which the fact that gender is not what it seems appears to have profound political implications?

Nandy situates his reading of Gandhi within a larger argument that considers the most subversive forms of resistance to be those that refuse, rather than simply reverse, the terms of colonial modernity:

> [I]n every situation of organized oppression, the true antonyms are always the exclusive part versus the inclusive whole—not masculinity versus femininity but either of them versus androgyny, not the past versus the present but either of them versus the timelessness in which the past is the present and the present is the past, not the oppressor versus the oppressed but both of them versus the rationality which turns them into co-victims . . . the opposite of thesis is not the antithesis because they exclude each other. The true 'enemy' of the thesis is seen to be in the synthesis because it includes the thesis and ends the latter's reason for being.[146]

Insofar as Nandy is making a claim here for the progressive possibilities of androgynous political performativity, this reading needs to be complicated. Precisely because Gandhi's authority derived from tropes associating 'bigenderness' with saintliness in Hinduism, these modes of charismatic authority have also been available to the Hindu Right. Paola Bacchetta offers a queer reading of Hindu nationalist icons, arguing that the tropes of celibacy and homosociality through which they are typically represented might appear queer in the colonial gaze, but register as saintly when viewed through the Hindu symbolic imaginary.[147] Yet this queering of Hindu leaders operates within strict limits that constrain its potential subversiveness. As Bacchetta explains, 'otherwise queered gender is acceptable when it can be read in a powerful subject, thus unconnected to weakness, who is also an asexual subject [on account of old age or death], thus unconnected to queer sexuality.'[148] Likewise, Banerjee reads female agency in the Hindu Right as 'transgression within tradition' because the potentially radical implications of women taking on masculine traits to perform public roles in defence of the nation outside the confines of the family are circumscribed by the erasure of their sexuality and a simultaneous valorisation of tradition and gender hierarchy within the home.[149] Thus, it is not the fact of gender

146. Nandy, *Intimate Enemy*, 99.
147. Bacchetta, '(Hindu) Nation Exiles Its Queers', 156–158.
148. Ibid., 158.
149. Banerjee, *Make Me a Man!*, 128–130. For a fascinating contemporary illustration of this argument, see the portrayal of Hindu right-wing women activists in Pahuja

ambiguity per se so much as the domains into which it is channelled—the political work that it is or is not allowed to do—to which we must attend in order to evaluate its broader political implications.

This is necessary, additionally, because gender ambiguity also infuses fantasies of opposition to the Hindu Right. What should we make, for instance, of the centrality of the figure of the hijra in Arundhati Roy's *The Ministry of Utmost Happiness*? In the twenty years since the publication of her first novel, Roy has earned a reputation as one of India's foremost leftist public intellectuals writing in English, principally through her essays on subjects of concern to the Indian Left—nuclear weapons, the appropriation of adivasi land by big dams, the Maoist Naxalite movement, Hindu fundamentalism, caste, and US imperialism, among others.[150] This has made her a polarising and paradoxical figure in Indian public life, at once a global symbol of 'Indian' achievement and a lightning rod for the vitriol of an impatient Rising India whose hubris she is determined to puncture at every opportunity. *The Ministry* gathers together her wide-ranging political preoccupations in the form of a novel, blurring the distinction between her fiction and nonfiction. Its choice of the figure of a hijra as the central node around which the various elements of the narrative cohere (or don't) seems to invest this gendered subject with a progressive potentiality in the current conjuncture that is worth exploring.

Anjum, with whom the novel begins and ends, is at one time 'Delhi's most famous hijra'.[151] A resident of a hijra house that traces its lineage to the days of the Mughal emperor Shah Jahan, she epitomises the fading glory of an Old Delhi whose inhabitants live, cheek by jowl, in a decrepit architectural magnificence that mirrors the rich but endangered Urdu literary tradition in which they remain steeped. Anjum's life takes an ugly turn when she finds herself in the midst of the 2002 anti-Muslim pogrom in Gujarat, from which she escapes only because, in the collective wisdom of the mob, the killing of a hijra is believed to bring bad luck. Traumatised by this experience and, as a consequence, emotionally alienated from everyone, including her adopted daughter, Anjum leaves the hijra house and takes refuge in the graveyard in which her family are buried. Frequented by smack addicts, stray dogs, and homeless people, and used as a dumping ground for hospital waste, it is an unpromising place in which to build a

(dir.), *The World Before Her*; for a useful review of the film, see Mehta, 'The World Before Her'.

150. See, for example, Roy, 'End of Imagination'; *Greater Common Good*; 'Walking with the Comrades'; 'Doctor and the Saint'.

151. Roy, *Ministry*, 26.

new life. Even the gravestones seem to mark the final resting places of a series of drifters and misfits. Yet in its very acceptance of refuse and the refused, it seems to offer Anjum a home. What begins as a shack, built with the assistance of a former client in the construction business, becomes a hut, a house, and ultimately a guesthouse—the Jannat (Paradise) Guest House—that welcomes an ever-expanding cast of eccentric but curiously familiar characters. Much of the rest of the novel tells the story of how three other people come to live in Jannat—Saddam Hussein, a Dalit man masquerading as a Muslim after his father was killed by gau rakshaks[152] enraged by his disposal of cow carcasses; Tilottama (Tilo), a disaffected middle-class architect and writer passionately invested in the struggle for azadi[153] in Kashmir; and Miss Jebeen the Second, a baby abandoned at a protest in Delhi by her Maoist Naxalite mother, whose pregnancy was the result of her being raped by police while in custody. An Indian reading public will recognise in these characters stock subaltern figurations of contemporary political society—the fragments, if you like, of the nation. In the novel, their stories are distinct, even if framed by a common experience of violence at the hands of a Hindu neoliberal state and its social constituencies, intersecting only in the happy contingency of their joint rescue and adoption of Miss Jebeen the Second and their ultimate residence in Jannat. Indeed reviewers have complained that the different stories do not convincingly come together, with one particularly disgruntled critic describing the novel as 'multiple strands of narratives with the merest excuse of a literary scotch tape'.[154]

I want to suggest that if *The Ministry* fails as a novel, it does so in deeply interesting ways that are symptomatic of the challenges of articulation in the political praxis of the Indian Left. Indeed the novel might be read as a parable of these challenges. 'Articulation' is the term that Gramsci used to describe the laborious process of constructing a counter-hegemonic bloc. This entailed not simply a political alliance 'grounded upon a conjunctural coincidence of interests in which the participating sectors retain their

---

152. Literally 'cow protectors', opposed to the slaughter of cows on account of their sacredness in the eyes of dominant caste Hindus. In recent years, moral vigilantism by gau rakshaks has often culminated in the lynching and murder of people (usually Muslims and subordinate castes) on suspicion of eating, storing, or selling beef, or because they have been engaged in the disposal of cow carcases.
153. The term 'azadi' (freedom) has figured centrally in slogans calling for Kashmiri self-determination and has aroused the ire of Indian nationalists who interpret it as a call for secession.
154. Ghoshal, 'Book Review'; see also Sehgal, 'Arundhati Roy's Fascinating Mess'; Walter, 'Ministry of Utmost Happiness'; Mahajan, 'Arundhati Roy's Return'; Hopley, 'Ambiguities among the Cruelties'; Badami, 'Arundhati Roy's The Ministry'.

separate identity', but moral and intellectual leadership that enabled the sharing of 'ideas' and 'values' with a view to forming a '"collective will", which, through ideology, becomes the organic cement unifying a "historical bloc"'.[155] This understanding persists in the thinking of post-Marxists such as Ernesto Laclau and Chantal Mouffe, for whom articulation is not simply about the linkage of dissimilar and fully constituted elements, but establishes 'a relation among elements such that their identity is modified as a result of the articulatory practice'.[156]

When at a political meeting Anjum hears the South Asian Marxist greeting 'Red Salute! Lal Salaam!' (with which she is unfamiliar), she mutters instinctively 'Lal Salaam Aleikum,' inadvertently annexing the Marxist rallying cry to the traditional Urdu greeting 'peace be upon you'. The narrator cannot resist noting in an aside that this 'could have been the beginning of a whole political movement'.[157] It is a joke, but only slightly, because it conjures up the memory of another portmanteau slogan, 'Jai Bhim! Lal Salaam!'—this one bringing the rallying cry of the Ambedkarite Dalit movement ('Victory to Bhim!,' referring to Ambedkar) together with the Marxist call. For a brief moment in early 2016, this slogan rent the air of India's most politicised universities, galvanising Left and Ambedkarite student groups in opposition to the Akhil Bharatiya Vidyarthi Parishad (All India Student Council, ABVP), the student wing of the Hindu Right. The immediate provocations for this mobilisation were ABVP actions that had led to the suicide of Dalit activist Rohith Vemula in Hyderabad and to the prosecution for sedition of the organisers of a Kashmir solidarity event at JNU in New Delhi.[158] Yet the attempt to forge unity between Marxist and Ambedkarite groups against the Hindu Right has been a fraught endeavour, given the long history of suspicion and mutual recrimination between these groups.[159] I am not sure whether *The Ministry*'s disinclination to do more by way of connecting its various narrative strands should be understood as a lapse or a conscious choice. My point is that this characteristic of the novel allows us to reflect on the vexed problem of articulation that has bedevilled an Indian Left to which the book holds up a mirror.

In *The Ministry*, Anjum plays a central articulating role, producing the very space—the Jannat Guest House—in which the nation's fragments

---

155. Laclau and Mouffe, *Hegemony and Socialist Strategy*, 66–67.
156. Ibid., 87, 105.
157. Roy, *Ministry*, 426.
158. Shankar et al., 'Two Colours'.
159. For commentary sceptical of the attempted Marxist-Ambedkarite alliance, see Prasad, '"Jai Bhim"'; Jessie, 'Lal Salaam'; Kumar, '"Jai Bhim, Lal Salaam"'.

gather. This is, as Anjum describes it, 'the place of falling people',[160] a funeral parlour for those whom no one else will bury, 'a Noah's ark of injured animals'.[161] Its consolations are also temporal. For Tilo, living with the agonising uncertainty of whether the man she loves has been consumed by the struggle in Kashmir,

> the battered angels in the graveyard that kept watch over their battered charges held open the doors between worlds (illegally, just a crack), so that the souls of the present and the departed could mingle, like guests at the same party. It made life less determinate and death less conclusive. Somehow everything became a little easier to bear.[162]

What is it about Anjum that makes it possible for her to produce the utopian spacetime that is Jannat? More generally, what is it about hijra subjectivity that infuses it with a progressive potentiality that appeals to a certain radical leftist imaginary in India? Two related characteristics stand out as being crucial here: a capaciousness of subjectivity, and an agonistic refusal to resolve the contradictions of this subjectivity. Early in the novel, when Anjum is living as a boy named Aftab, one of the hijras in the house that she eventually joins asks:

> *Arre yaar*, think about it, what are the things you normal people get unhappy about? I don't mean *you*, but grown-ups like you—what makes them unhappy? Price-rise, children's school admissions, husbands' beatings, wives' cheatings, Hindu-Muslim riots, Indo-Pak war—*outside* things that settle down eventually. But for us the price-rise and school-admissions and beating-husbands and cheating-wives are all *inside* us. The riot is *inside* us, the war is *inside* us. Indo-Pak is *inside* us. It will never settle down. It *can't*.[163]

Nimmo Gorakhpuri's words are a counsel of despair, purporting to explain why the hijra is 'a living creature that is incapable of happiness'.[164] But Anjum does something different with these irresolvable contradictions. She is once told (incorrectly) by a sweet-talking client that her name

160. Roy, *Ministry*, 84.
161. Ibid., 399.
162. Ibid., 398. Other temporal connotations attach to the name Jannat, meaning 'paradise'. Everyone in *The Ministry*, including the Islamist separatists in Kashmir, wants a place in Jannat, whether in this life or the hereafter. In this sense, 'jannat' is a placeholder analogous to the Aristotelian 'good life', even if invested with very different content.
163. Ibid., 23.
164. Ibid.

written backwards in English spells Majnu, like the famous lover of Persian lore. When he corrects his mistake in a moment of sobriety, Anjum says:

> It doesn't matter. I'm all of them. I'm Romi and Juli, I'm Laila and Majnu. *And Mujna*, why not? Who says my name is Anjum, I'm Anjuman.[165] I'm a *mehfil*,[166] I'm a gathering. Of everybody and nobody, of everything and nothing. Is there anyone else you would like to invite? Everyone's invited.[167]

What might come across as self-aggrandising in another character are, here, the very qualities that enable Anjum to produce the spacetime of Jannat. It is the non-resolution of the contradictions in her subjectivity that underpins the radical democracy of this space. 'Augmented by her ambiguity',[168] even her voice with its 'peculiar, rasping quality . . . sounded like two voices quarrelling with each other instead of one'.[169] This refusal to resolve two voices into one grounds a condition that Mouffe describes as 'agonistic pluralism'.[170] Where Habermasian deliberative democracy postulates an idealised public sphere in which power and antagonism have been eliminated and where a rational consensus can be reached, agonistic pluralism views the task of politics as that of 'domesticating hostility', thereby enabling the creation of unity in a context of conflict and diversity.[171] Within an emerging counterhegemonic bloc, the commitment to agonistic pluralism might assist the difficult work of articulation. Between this bloc and its antagonists, it might transform relations of enmity into ones of adversity—a condition in which political disagreement is underpinned by a 'shared adhesion to the ethico-political principles of democracy',[172] or what Ambedkar might have called constitutional morality.

In this chapter, I have tried to think about the relationship between gender identity and backwardness on two registers. In the first half of the chapter, I contextualised the trans movement's demand for backward class status in light of the legal and political understanding of backwardness in India. I suggested that the analogy between gender identity and caste that

---

165. Association.
166. An evening of poetry or music performed for a small audience in an intimate setting, typically featuring ghazals and Urdu poetry.
167. Roy, *Ministry*, 4.
168. Ibid., 122.
169. Ibid., 29.
170. Mouffe, 'Deliberative Democracy'.
171. Ibid., 754–755.
172. Ibid., 755.

underpins this claim is simultaneously plausible, problematic, and potent in its promise to infuse trans and queer struggles with an Ambedkarite sensibility that envisions the annihilation of all forms of hierarchy. In the second half of the chapter, I offered a parallel reading of a middle-class, dominant-caste discourse that, while dismissive of the state's historic responsibility to ameliorate backwardness, is intensely preoccupied with what it experiences as the geopolitical backwardness of the Indian state. I suggested that this discourse is itself a gendered one, so much so that its desire for great power status might also be understood as a project of gender transition—albeit one underpinned by a radically different politics.

Having surveyed the productivity of gender trouble on both the right and left of the Indian political spectrum, it should be obvious that the crossing or transcending of the gender binary does not, by itself, promise wider progressive effects. Much depends on how struggles around gender identity are articulated, in the Gramscian sense of that word, with other movements and demands.[173] These articulations might take any number of forms. To return to a figure with whom this chapter began, Brahmin hijra activist Tripathi has incurred the wrath of many trans, gender nonconforming, and intersex collectives on account of her support for the Hindu Right's mission of building a temple dedicated to the god Rama on the site of the Babri mosque demolished by Hindu mobs in 1992.[174] Analogously, Anjana Raghavan has drawn attention to the conservative and normalising discourses of some tirunangai activists and artists in Tamil Nadu, who seek recognition for transwomen by underscoring their potential to perform as exemplary capitalist subjects and patriotic citizens.[175] These manifestations of transnormativity exist in tension with a strong Dalit bahujan[176] sensibility, particularly among working-class, subordinate caste sections of the trans movement who strive towards the 'backward futures' envisaged by Ambedkar and other anti-caste radicals.

Despite the contingency of actually existing trans politics, a certain utopian figuration of the trans and especially hijra subject continues to exercise a hold over leftist imaginaries. Drawing on her ethnographic work with hijras and in particular on her observation of their syncretic gender, religious, and caste performativity, Reddy speculates that this is because

---

173. Laclau and Mouffe, *Hegemony and Socialist Strategy*, 87.
174. Trans, Gender Nonconforming and Intersex Collectives, 'Strongly Condemn'.
175. Raghavan, *Towards Corporeal Cosmopolitanism*, 108–110.
176. The term 'bahujan' means 'people of the majority' and is used to refer collectively to Dalits and subordinate castes, adivasis, and religious minorities who together comprise the majority of India's population.

'hijras, whether "real" or symbolic . . . embody the only transcendent position in a world of categorical absolutes in contemporary (Hindu) India—the very violence of their becoming locating them indelibly as the ultimate border agents of humanity in contemporary South Asia.'[177] They seem to epitomise what Gloria Anzaldúa, writing about the US-Mexico borderlands, has called a mestiza consciousness. 'A borderland', Anzaldúa explains, 'is a vague and undetermined place created by the emotional residue of an unnatural boundary.'[178] It is a zone of tension and danger, but also one that is generative of the tolerance for ambiguity that we will all need to learn in order to live together. In her prophetic words, 'the future will belong to the mestiza.'[179] If we are transfixed by utopian representations of these border figures, it should not be because we think of them as revolutionary vanguards, but because we have come to understand their capaciousness and irreducible ambivalence as prerequisites for the constitutional morality that is not yet here.

177. Reddy, *With Respect to Sex*, 120.
178. Anzaldúa, *Borderlands*, 3.
179. Ibid., 80.

Epilogue

Conjugating like a State

Why does queerness appear anticolonial in the time of Kabaka Mwanga, but complicit with imperialism in the eyes of the contemporary Ugandan state and church? What accounts for its elision with whiteness in the gaze of the British state? Why do international financial institutions hail queers as harbingers of capitalist success? How has the Indian state come to think of trans persons as a 'backward class', akin to a subordinate caste? The answers to these questions lie partly in the way they are framed, referring us as they do to the fields of visibility of particular states and institutions.

In his account of 'seeing like a state', James Scott argues that statecraft is premised on the ability of states to make 'legible' the societies over which they rule.[1] This entails reducing the array of detail that they confront to a set of categories that might facilitate summary description, comparison, and aggregation, with a view to simplifying the quintessential state functions of taxation, conscription, and order maintenance.[2] Scott's argument is somewhat functionalist in its claim that the categorical abstractions through which states apprehend their societies depend on the particular interests at stake.[3] History seems to play little part in the choice, fashioning, or deployment of these categories. This may be because Scott has a particular

1. Scott, *Seeing like a State*.
2. Ibid., 77.
3. Ibid., 13.

interest in high modernism—an ideological sensibility infused with a confidence in the possibility of progress and perfectibility and that seeks temporal rupture in the service of the rational reordering of society. As Scott describes it, high modernism takes the view that 'a planned social order is better than the accidental, irrational deposit of historical practice.'[4]

Contrast this with Hortense Spillers's account of an 'American grammar'.[5] In the article in which she introduces this notion, Spillers explores the exclusion of black men and women from a dominant symbolic order, in particular through what she calls the 'ungendering' of the female African subject under conditions of enslavement. Criticising the pathologisation of the 'Negro family' in dominant narratives that purport to account for its variance from the structures of white patriarchal society, Spillers seeks to reclaim the insurgent potential inherent in its position of externality to this order. While the gender dimensions of this argument have been deeply influential,[6] what interests me here is the notion of an 'American grammar'. What does it mean for a state or society to have a grammar? Where does it come from, and what does it do? If we take grammar to refer to the system of rules that define how words change their form and combine with other words to make sentences, Spillers is similarly interested in the rules that define the relations of affiliation, descent, and consanguinity that can and cannot be entered into by certain bodies rendered as 'flesh' under conditions of enslavement. In doing so, she makes visible the structure of a dominant American grammar and the lifeworlds that are (dis)allowed by it. As she explains:

> Even though the captive flesh/body has been 'liberated,' and no one need pretend that even the quotation marks do not *matter*, dominant symbolic activity, the ruling episteme that releases the dynamics of naming and valuation, remains grounded in the originating metaphors of captivity and mutilation so that it is as if neither time nor history, nor historiography and its topics, shows movement, as the human subject is 'murdered' over and over again by the passions of a bloodless and anonymous archaism, showing itself in endless disguise.[7]

We might think of the grammar of the state, then, as its dominant symbolic order, 'the ruling episteme' that is forged in the originary foundational violence to which it owes its existence, a violence that marks a beginning but

---

4. Ibid., 94.
5. Spillers, 'Mama's Baby'.
6. See, for example, Spillers et al., '"Whatcha Gonna Do?"'.
7. Spillers, 'Mama's Baby', 68.

'is really a rupture and a radically different kind of cultural continuation.'[8] The question of how the categories of this grammar relate to the conceptual abstractions through which states apprehend 'their' societies is a complex one. In Scott's account, high modernist state planning seeks to leave behind the 'accidental, irrational deposit of historical practice'. But this break is not easily achieved. Scott's project is to explain 'how certain schemes to improve the human condition have failed'. The story of failure that he tells is largely the result of a clash between two forms of knowledge—the thin, schematic, abstract knowledge of universal planning imposed from above (techne) that is impervious to criticism and oblivious of the ways in which it is parasitic on more local, divergent, and adaptable forms of knowledge (metis) developed within communities over time. What he does not consider is that the utopian aspirations of techne may be thwarted by the tenacity—the 'temporal drag',[9] if you like—of the foundational political grammar in which the state is grounded and that endlessly reproduces its traumatic birth.

The endurance of this foundational grammar might account in large measure for the queer metonymic mutations occasioned by the encounters between queer difference and state institutions that we have witnessed in the foregoing chapters. Confronted with the fact of queerness, institutions respond in ways that betray the persistence of their dominant grammars. Puar explains US homonationalism as a momentary sanctioning of some homosexualities, 'often through gendered, racial, and class sanitizing, in order to produce "monster-terrorist-fags".'[10] One way of understanding this is to think of the grammar of the state as performing a sorting function, establishing the mechanisms of incorporating/quarantining, setting the terms of recognition, and undergirding the patterns of inclusion and exclusion that are foundational to its institutions. Much of the argument in the preceding chapters has been devoted to explicating the grammars through which different institutions apprehend queerness and the materialisations of queerness that result from what we might think of as operations of 'conjugating like a state.' The homophobic Ugandan state responds to queer difference quite differently from the homonationalist US state, but its response is likewise revealing of the structure of a grammar forged, in its case, through the ruptures of colonisation, decolonisation, civil war, structural adjustment, and HIV/AIDS. Likewise, the apprehension of queerness through the lenses of race, caste, and class by the British

8. Ibid.
9. Freeman, *Time Binds*, 65.
10. Puar, *Terrorist Assemblages*, 46.

and Indian states and IFIs, respectively, reveal these to be foundational categories of their respective grammars, forged in the originary violence to which these institutions owe their existence.

Queer activists frequently approach institutions in the terms of the grammars in which they anticipate being hailed by them. Thus, mindful of the IFIs' mission as guardians of global capitalism, some queer activists enlist them as allies in the struggle for recognition by presenting themselves and their constituencies as model capitalist subjects whose liberty might unleash untapped potential for growth and productivity. In quite a different way, mindful of the Indian state's constitutional commitment to the amelioration of caste backwardness, trans activists present themselves and their constituencies as 'backward', drawing subliminally on the reading of hijras as a caste in the colonial episteme. I hope to have shown, however, that one can work with the dominant grammar in ways that both reinforce and undermine it. Thus, while elite LGBT activists present themselves as an entrepreneurial class-in-waiting in a bid for upward mobility in a capitalist system that they have no intention of dismantling, trans activists who speak the language of caste do so in solidarity and identification with those at the bottom of a caste hierarchy in the destruction of which they might be co-participants.

To note this correspondence between the grammars of states and activists is to think of their engagements as being what Achille Mbembe calls 'convivial'.[11] Mbembe introduces this notion in the context of his claim that to understand postcolonial hegemony, 'we need to go beyond the binary categories used in standard interpretations of domination, such as resistance vs. passivity, autonomy vs. subjection, state vs. civil society, hegemony vs. counter-hegemony, totalization vs. detotalization' to consider the ways in which power and its subjects 'share the same living space' or, more precisely, 'the same episteme.'[12] Mbembe illustrates this claim with a discussion of the use that both the putative dominators and dominated make of the grotesque and the obscene by drawing on the body as a locus for both the display of power and its ridicule. The very strategies and metaphors favoured by the postcolonial clientelist state for cultivating authority and exacting obedience—the extravagant display of power as personified in the body of the despot who delights in the consumption of food, drink, and sex—are, with the slightest turn of phrase or subtly modified affect, amenable to travesty. Unpacking key tropes of what he calls the 'aesthetics of

11. Mbembe, *On the Postcolony.*
12. Ibid., 103–104, 110.

vulgarity', Mbembe notes an obsession with orifices, odours, and genital organs in political speech and humour. As he remarks, 'the image of, say, the president's anus is not of something out of this world—although, to everyone's amusement, the official line may treat it as such; instead, people see it as it really is, capable of defecating like any commoner's.'[13]

Mbembe's remarks are astonishingly prescient as a description of the contemporary Ugandan public sphere, which offers numerous examples of convivial engagement within a shared aesthetics of vulgarity. Take the case of the country's leading queer theorist Stella Nyanzi, whose interventions as a public intellectual are often made in this idiom. Nyanzi has cultivated an impressive following on social media in her multiple capacities as feminist, anthropologist, single mother, writer of erotica, and leading activist of the Ugandan opposition party Forum for Democratic Change. Even as the Ugandan public sphere has become saturated with a discourse that routinely politicises sexuality, often through the use of graphic descriptions and imagery of queer sex intended to elicit disgust, Nyanzi has responded with a sexualisation of politics as it relates to issues well beyond the realm of sexuality. Her social media posts criticise President Museveni and his wife Janet Museveni (in her capacity as a minister in the government) for the despotism and corruption of the regime in defiantly vulgar language laced with references to menstrual blood, shit, masturbation, farting, fucking, and ejaculating, earning her the distinction of being, in the words of one admirer, 'Uganda's best vulgarist of the modern time.'[14] Likening political leadership to sexual intercourse in the sense that both must be consensual to be pleasurable, Nyanzi elaborates in her inimitable style:

> How can the fucker enjoy if the fucked receive no pleasure from the fucking? Oh God, this fuck from Museveni is bitterly painful! . . . Misruling us in perpetuity after stealing our votes, is as treacherous as raping our neglected unwashed pussies. Miiaaaooowww, our dry pussies recoil from the rape epitomised by Museveni's unwanted misgovernance. . . . Leaving his aged erection grinding away inside the dry depths of Uganda's vagina is painful and gross. Surely, the dictatorship cannot be enjoying the bitter rape of Uganda![15]

It is tempting to note here the short semantic distance between conjugation as an operation of grammar and as a sexual act. In the absence of legitimacy, conjugating like a state in the sense of regulating what combinations

13. Ibid., 108.
14. Serunkuma, 'Stella Nyanzi–Museveni Family'.
15. *Edge*, 'Stella Nyanzi'.

and associations are (and are not) permissible might take the form of what Teemu Ruskola describes, albeit in the slightly different context of colonial international legal discourse, as 'raping like a state'.[16]

What can the sexualisation of politics do? Mbembe reminds us that what is significant about the sharing of the aesthetics of vulgarity is that it allows the dominated to simulate adherence to the official forms while saying the unsayable. Where the despot might wish for the sacralisation and fetishisation of his person, the dominated might—in the very act of paying excessive obeisance—reveal it for the sham that it is, transforming it into mere artefact.[17] Mbembe is cautious not to claim too much on behalf of subversion. Indeed he argues that the very entanglement of the apparently dominant and dominated in this discourse produces not revolutionary rupture but something like 'mutual zombification' so that, at best, the dominated produce 'potholes of indiscipline on which the *commandement* may stub its toe.'[18]

And yet Nyanzi has clearly rattled the Museveni regime. In January 2017, outraged by remarks that Museveni had made in the course of a speech declaring that he was not a public servant but a freedom fighter, Nyanzi declared in a Facebook post that 'Museveni is just another pair of buttocks. Rather than being shocked at what the *matako* [buttocks] said . . . Ugandans should be shocked that we allowed these buttocks to continue leading our country.'[19] The following month, she criticised Janet Museveni for failing to implement an NRM campaign pledge to provide sanitary pads to Ugandan schoolgirls, and declared: 'I should visit her without protection during my next menstruation period, sit in her spotless sofas and arise after staining her soul with my menstrual blood!'[20] Calling for public donations, Nyanzi began her own campaign to supply sanitary pads to girls.[21] In September 2018, Nyanzi wrote a satirical poem in honour of Museveni's birthday, ruing his birth in language that was seen as having insulted his mother: 'I wish the poisoned uterus sitting just above Esiteri's dry clitoris had prematurely miscarried a thing to be cast upon a manure pit / Prematurely miscarried just like you prematurely aborted

16. Ruskola, 'Raping like a State'. Weber, *Faking It*, is the classic work in IR that takes seriously the sexualisation of interstate relations.

17. Mbembe, *On the Postcolony*, 108.

18. Ibid., 104, 111.

19. Stella Nyanzi, 'Museveni matako nyo!', public Facebook post, 28 January 2017, https://www.facebook.com/stella.nyanzi/posts/10154878225000053.

20. Stella Nyanzi, 'I despise people', public Facebook post, 7 November 2018, https://www.facebook.com/stella.nyanzi/posts/10154932446045053.

21. Lule, 'Stella Nyanzi's Tongue'.

any semblance of democracy, good governance and rule of law.'[22] For her pains, Nyanzi has been arrested and charged with 'cyber harassment' and 'offensive communication', imprisoned, subjected to a travel ban, and had her employment at Makerere University terminated.[23] In August 2019, she was sentenced to 18 months in prison.[24] In cultivating a reputation for outrage and excess at tremendous personal cost, Nyanzi has created a space in which not only she but countless others might say the unsayable, as the long comment threads on her social media posts attested. She has found, in the words of a sympathetic commentator, 'the right packaging and expression of Kampala's anger in a place where teargas cannot reach.'[25] Only time will tell whether her exposure of the brittleness of the Museveni regime can bring it into terminal crisis.

DISORIENTING ORIENTALISM

Much of this book has been preoccupied with the global frictions that anticipated, precipitated, and followed in the wake of the Ugandan Anti Homosexuality Act. I have been particularly invested in disrupting narratives that purport to account for these frictions by locating agency in actors and spaces outside Uganda and predominantly in the global North. Instead, I have tried to demonstrate how a number of processes central to our understanding of the law—the colonial institutionalisation of 'homophobia' as well as contemporary memory of this moment, the crafting of theological doctrine as much as of HIV/AIDS policy, the production of global financial governmentality in relation to LGBTI rights—have been the result of collaboration and transaction across the North/South divide, in which participants have converged momentarily in projects of various kinds while acting from disparate, even contradictory, motivations. In doing so, I have adopted the quintessentially postcolonial strategy of countering orientalism by demonstrating the mutual constitution of core and periphery.[26] In telling stories of contemporary US evangelical conservatives whose intellectual genealogies might be traced back to the East African Revival Movement of the 1930s, or of putatively US-originated AIDS policies that were shaped by Ugandan readings of the Ugandan experience

22. *Uganda Mirror*, 'Stella Nyanzi's Poem'.
23. For a discussion of the legal issues raised by Nyanzi's prosecution, see Rukundo, '"My President"'.
24. BBC News, 'Uganda's Stella Nyanzi'.
25. Serunkuma, 'Stella Nyanzi's Rebel Speech'.
26. Said, *Culture and Imperialism*.

with the disease, my aim has been to *disorient* the reader in the sense of making it impossible to answer with certainty the question of who is singularly responsible for the state of affairs that we now confront. Here I am inspired by Sara Ahmed's reading of the potentials of disorientation in her meditations on queer phenomenology.[27] To disorient is to cause someone to lose their bearings; to dis-orient might also be to dislocate something that has hitherto been placed in the 'orient'. Merleau-Ponty describes disorientation as involving not only 'the intellectual experience of disorder, but the vital experience of giddiness and nausea, which is the awareness of our contingency, and the horror with which it fills us.'[28] If in tacking back and forth between here, there, and elsewhere in telling the story of the AHA, I have induced a feeling of giddiness and nausea in the reader, I hope this might unsettle both the supremacist narratives of orientalism and the revanchist impulses of a postcolonial nativism that mark global conversations about queer rights today.

The geographical disorientation that I have offered here nonetheless hews to a long-standing postcolonial preoccupation with entanglements between core and peripheries, between North and South. A different kind of work might have told a story of lateral friction between the locations with which this book is concerned.[29] Such a story would not be difficult to tell, given the rich history of interaction between South Asia, East Africa, and Britain.[30] But what might a queer account of this connectivity look like? For a start, it might need to be less attentive to a history and politics of *sexuality*, given the manner in which such a preoccupation invariably directs our attention to the flow of knowledge, funding, and idioms of political organising and solidarity between North and South.[31] Conversely, it may need to be more attuned to desire, intimacy, affect, and movement in those everyday realms in which the state, law, and its genealogies are not overwhelming preoccupations.

In his ethnographic work on gay nightlife in Bangalore, Kareem Khubchandani offers us a glimpse of what such work might look like.[32] Taken aback by a bravura performance of voguing at a gay party in the

---

27. Ahmed, *Queer Phenomenology*.
28. Cited from ibid., 4.
29. For works that explore the horizontal relations between 'peripheral' movements, see Bose and Manjapra, *Cosmopolitan Thought Zones*; Manjapra, *M. N. Roy*; Slate, *Colored Cosmopolitanism*; Shilliam, *Black Pacific*.
30. Alibhai-Brown, *The Settler's Cookbook*; Parmar, 'Reading the Double Diaspora'; Aiyar, *Indians in Kenya*.
31. Meghani, 'Queer South Asian Muslims'.
32. Khubchandani, 'Voguing in Bangalore'.

city, which he finds unusual on account of the fact that 'black femininities do not have much erotic or cultural currency in gay Indian spaces', Khubchandani is compelled to enquire into the discourses, histories, and political economies that enable the proximity, legibility, and intimacy of black and brown bodies vis-à-vis one another. He tells the story of Andy, a gay Tamil Christian working in one of the city's many business-process outsourcing companies, the growth of which has enabled the recent entry of many into the middle classes. Andy's desire for African men, expressed through stereotypical tropes that fetishise black male sexuality, drives his appropriation and embodiment of black femininity, which he performs through a devout emulation of black female musical and dance forms. But this appropriation is not routed through the white gay cultural references that tend to dominate India's middle-class gay scene. Moreover, Andy's conviviality with black folks in the city contrasts starkly with the everyday experiences of racism, discrimination, sexual harassment, and violence that African migrants in urban India routinely encounter. Troubling as some of the drivers of his desire are, Andy's intimacies with black men and his movements through African spaces of pleasure and community-making in Bangalore give Khubchandani a precious archive with which to imagine blackness and black people as part of the quotidian fabric of a global Indian city. Gesturing at what might be at stake in such investigations, Khubchandani's work evinces a curiosity in the 'subaltern resources that can be shared between marginal black and brown subjects so that they may become legible to each other and foster intimacies where there have been centuries-long socio-political cleavages.'[33]

On other dance floors, it has occurred to me that some black and brown bodies may become so powerful that they cease to be racialised as such. Another way of telling a queer story about South Asia, East Africa, and Britain might be through the biography of the man the world knows as Freddie Mercury. Born Farrokh Bulsara into a Parsi family in what was then the British protectorate of Zanzibar and schooled in India before moving to Britain at the age of seventeen, the geographical coordinates of Mercury's life track a well-worn itinerary shaped by trade, migration, colonialism, and postcolonial ferment. Appropriately, no superlative has been spared to describe Mercury's genius in matters of musical range, style, versatility, composition, and showmanship. What remains consistently inexplicable is the fact that a semi-closeted queer, ambiguously racialised, HIV positive man could have become the world's greatest rock star in a decade in which any

33. Ibid.

one of those identities, let alone their intersection, might have sunk another talent. It seems too reductive to insist that the comprador position of large sections of the Parsi bourgeoisie under British colonialism facilitated Mercury's whitening or, conversely, that the admittedly gobsmacking majesty of Queen's oeuvre blinded its fans to everything else. Additionally, one of the dangers of narratives of exceptional migrant success is their amenability to instrumentalisation in ways that deploy the achievements of a fortunate few to shore up the racist capitalist structures that immigrants must battle to make their way in the world. Yet Mercury's story is too idiosyncratic to permit assimilation into model minority narratives. Indeed it may well be the impossibility of appropriating him *in toto* that accounts for the fact that he can be celebrated as easily in the repertoire of a Christian a cappella group in Bangalore as in a karaoke bar in Kampala or at the closing ceremony of the London Olympics.

TIME AND THE UNCANNY

In 2016, as if to vindicate her role in my sexual formation and my use of *Cloud 9* as a point of departure for this book, Caryl Churchill wrote a play about the Ugandan Anti Homosexuality Act.[34] Its title, *Pigs and Dogs*, references former Zimbabwean President Mugabe's infamous rhetorical question, 'If dogs and pigs don't do it why must human beings?'[35] Casting instructions inform us that the play's three unnamed characters may be performed by actors of any gender and race, but cannot be alike. Their lines are crisp, almost curt, delivered as if they were newspaper headlines or fragments of a telegram. We hear the homophobic claims of African elites juxtaposed with vignettes from the archive attesting to the existence of same-sex desire and transgender identification across broad swathes of African history. We are reminded of the English law of buggery, its importation into the colonies, its repeal in Britain, its persistence in the postcolony. This, together with the nefarious activities of American evangelists in Kampala, throws into relief for the audience the irony of Museveni's claim that 'This Act that we have passed / shows our independence / independence in the face of western pressure.'[36] In short, the play covers virtually the same ground as this book—*very* short, for it does so in a piece that is only ten minutes long.

34. Churchill, *Pigs and Dogs*.
35. Ibid., 5.
36. Ibid., 17.

What work is time doing in a play whose audience is likely to spend more time travelling to and from the theatre than at the show itself? Is its bite-sized duration a sardonic nod to attention spans in the Twitter age? Might it imply that the play's truths are so simple as to be self-evident, so that the mission of the play is simply to remind? Or might it suggest, much like this book, that we spend far more time in the temporal modes of anticipation and recollection than we do in that moment that we call the present? I am not sure. But the brevity of the piece makes me think of it as a coda to *Cloud 9*. Here Churchill ventures offstage to where the 'natives' and 'stable boys' are being flogged, to work through the afterlives of imperialism with which their spectres and descendants now contend.

A few months after watching the play, I developed a crick in my neck—to which the labour of writing this book contributed in some measure—that took me to two osteopaths. The first was also a geologist. When I asked her what the connection between her two professions was, she thought for a moment and then replied that joints in both bones and rocks told her something about stresses accumulated over long periods. When the first osteopath retired, I found a second, who engaged me in conversation about my work at our first session. I was grateful for the contours of his massage table, which came fitted with a cradle into which I could place my head when lying face down while still being able to breathe and speak comfortably. This meant that there was room for my jaw to drop when he said, 'My mother has just written a ten-minute play about homosexuality in Africa.'

BIBLIOGRAPHY

Abdy, Dora C. *The Martyrs of Uganda*. London: Sheldon Press, 1928.

Achebe, Chinua. *Hopes and Impediments: Selected Essays*. New York: Anchor Books, 1990.

Adichie, Chimamanda Ngozi. 'The Danger of a Single Story.' *TED*. Accessed 25 July 2016. https://www.ted.com/talks/chimamanda_adichie_the_danger_of_a_single_story?language=en.

Adong, Judith. *Just Me, You and the Silence*. Play reading, Old Vic Theatre, London, 4 November 2012.

Advocate. 'Maddow Uganda Be Kidding Me,' 4 December 2009. http://www.advocate.com/news/daily-news/2009/12/04/maddow-uganda-be-kidding-me.

Agathangelou, Anna M., and Kyle D. Killian. 'Introduction: Of Time and Temporality in World Politics.' In *Time, Temporality and Violence in International Relations: (De)fatalizing the Present, Forging Radical Alternatives*, edited by Anna M. Agathangelou and Kyle D. Killian, 1–22. Abingdon: Routledge, 2016.

Ahmed, Sara. *Queer Phenomenology: Orientations, Objects, Others*. Durham, NC: Duke University Press, 2006.

Aiyar, Sana. *Indians in Kenya: The Politics of Diaspora*. Cambridge, MA: Harvard University Press, 2015.

Aldrich, Robert. *Colonialism and Homosexuality*. Abingdon: Routledge, 2003.

Alibhai-Brown, Yasmin. *The Settler's Cookbook: A Memoir of Love, Migration and Food*. London: Granta, 2010.

All Party Parliamentary Group on Global LGBT Rights. 'The UK's Stance on International Breaches of LGBT Rights' (April 2016). Accessed 4 December 2016. http://www.appglgbt.org/publications.

Altman, Dennis, and Jonathan Symons. *Queer Wars: The New Global Polarization over Gay Rights*. Cambridge: Polity Press, 2016.

Altman, Dennis. 'Global Gaze/Global Gays.' *GLQ: A Journal of Lesbian and Gay Studies* 3, no. 4 (1997): 417–436.

Altman, Dennis. *Global Sex*. Chicago: University of Chicago Press, 2001.

Amadiume, Ifi. *Male Daughters, Female Husbands: Gender and Sex in an African Society*. London: Zed Books, 1987.

Amar, Paul. *The Security Archipelago: Human-Security States, Sexuality Politics, and the End of Neoliberalism*. Durham, NC: Duke University Press, 2013.

Ambedkar, B. R. *Annihilation of Caste: An Undelivered Speech*, edited by Mulk Raj Anand. New Delhi: Arnold, 1990 [1936].

Ambedkar, B. R. 'Buddha or Karl Marx.' Accessed 13 January 2019. http://www. ambedkar.org/ambcd/20.Buddha%20or%20Karl%20Marx.htm.

Ambedkar, B. R. 'Castes in India: Their Mechanism, Genesis and Development.' *Indian Antiquary* 41 (1917): 81–95.

Amoko, Apollo. 'Casting Aside Colonial Occupation: Intersections of Race, Sex, and Gender in *Cloud Nine* and *Cloud Nine* Criticism.' *Modern Drama* 42, no. 1 (1999): 45–58.

Amos, Valerie, and Pratibha Parmar. 'Challenging Imperial Feminism.' *Feminist Review* 17 (1984): 3–19.

Anderson, Benedict. *Imagined Communities: Reflections on the Origin and Spread of Nationalism*. London: Verso, 1983.

Anderson, John. 'Conservative Christianity, the Global South and the Battle over Sexual Orientation.' *Third World Quarterly* 32, no. 9 (2011): 1589–1605.

Anzaldúa, Gloria. *Borderlands/La Frontera: The New Mestiza*. San Francisco: Aunt Lute Books, 1987.

Arendt, Hannah. *The Origins of Totalitarianism*. Cleveland, OH: Meridian Books, 1958.

Arondekar, Anjali. *For the Record: On Sexuality and the Colonial Archive in India*. New Delhi: Orient BlackSwan, 2010.

Ashe, Robert Pickering. *Two Kings of Uganda; Or, Life by the Shores of Victoria Nyanza, Being an Account of a Residence of Six Years in Eastern Equatorial Africa*. London: Sampson Low, Marston, Searle & Rivington, 1890.

Associated Press. 'African Nations Attempt to Suspend UN's LGBT Rights Monitor.' *Guardian*, 7 November 2016. https://www.theguardian.com/global-development/2016/nov/07/african-nations-attempt-suspend-un-united-nations-lgbt-rights-monitor-vitit-muntarbhorn.

Atuhaire, Patience. 'Mini-skirts and Morals in Uganda.' *BBC News*, 9 July 2017. https://www.bbc.co.uk/news/world-africa-40507843.

Augé, Marc. *Oblivion*. Translated by Marjolijn de Jager. Minneapolis: University of Minnesota Press, 2004.

Auletta, Ken. 'Citizens Jain.' *The New Yorker*, 8 October 2012. https://www.newyorker.com/magazine/2012/10/08/citizens-jain.

Awondo, Patrick, Peter Geschiere, and Graeme Reid. 'Homophobic Africa? Toward a More Nuanced View.' *African Studies Review* 55, no. 3 (2012): 145–168.

Bacchetta, Paola. 'When the (Hindu) Nation Exiles Its Queers.' *Social Text* 61 (1999): 141–166.

Badami, Sunil. 'Arundhati Roy's *The Ministry of Utmost Happiness* Lost in a Crowd.' *The Australian*, 15 July 2017. http://www.theaustralian.com.au/arts/review/arundhati-roys-the-ministry-of-utmost-happiness-lost-in-a-crowd/news-story/91d9e87c7f0c81310fdd2864e2362506.

Badgett, M. V. Lee. 'The Economic Cost of Homophobia and the Exclusion of LGBT People: A Case Study of India.' Last modified February 2014. https://www.worldbank.org/content/dam/Worldbank/document/SAR/economic-costs-homophobia-lgbt-exlusion-india.pdf.

Badgett, M. V. Lee. 'The Economic Cost of Stigma and the Exclusion of LGBT People: A Case Study of India.' Washington, DC: World Bank Group, 2014. http://documents.worldbank.org/curated/en/527261468035379692/The-economic-cost-of-stigma-and-the-exclusion-of-LGBT-people-a-case-study-of-India.

Badgett, M. V. Lee. 'Foreword.' In *Open for Business: The Economic and Business Case for Global LGB&T Inclusion*, edited by Jon Miller and Lucy Parker, 14–15. Open for Business, 2015. Accessed 7 March 2017. https://static1.squarespace.

com/static/5bba53a8ab1a62771504d1dd/t/5c6425a671c10b7fdcaa141b/
1550067113397/Open+For+Business_Report_2015.pdf.

Badgett, M. V. Lee, Sheila Nezhad, Kees Waaldijk, and Yana van der Meulen Rodgers. *The Relationship between LGBT Inclusion and Economic Development: An Analysis of Emerging Economies*. Los Angeles, CA: The Williams Institute, 2014. http://williamsinstitute.law.ucla.edu/wp-content/uploads/lgbt-inclusion-and-development-november-2014.pdf.

Bageshree S. 'BC Panel to Submit "Open" Report in Kannada.' *The Hindu*, 3 July 2010. http://www.thehindu.com/todays-paper/tp-national/tp-karnataka/BC-panel-to-submit-lsquoopen-report-in-Kannada/article16183151.ece.

Baguma, Arthur. 'How Would You Have Handled the Martyrs' Case Today?' *New Vision*, 3 June 2009.

Baguma, Arthur. 'My Grandpa Survived Martyrdom—Nkoyooyo.' *New Vision*, 4 June 2004.

Baguma, Raymond. 'Nyerere Fit to Be a Saint—Museveni.' *New Vision*, 2 June 2009.

Bajpai, Rochana. *Debating Difference: Group Rights and Liberal Democracy in India*. New Delhi: Oxford University Press, 2011.

Banerjee, Sikata. *Make Me a Man! Masculinity, Hinduism, and Nationalism in India*. Albany: State University of New York Press, 2005.

Banu, Grace. 'Casteism Very Much Exists among Trans* People: Video Interview with Grace Banu.' *Dalit Camera*, 24 July 2016. http://www.dalitcamera.com/grace-banu-challenges-dalit-transperson-education/.

Barkawi, Tarak, and Mark Laffey. 'The Postcolonial Moment in Security Studies.' *Review of International Studies* 32, no. 2 (2006): 329–352.

Baudh, Sumit. 'Invisibility of "Other" Dalits and Silence in the Law.' *Biography* 40, no. 1 (2017): 222–243.

BBC News. 'Blair "Sorrow" over Slave Trade.' 27 November 2006. http://news.bbc.co.uk/2/hi/6185176.stm.

BBC News. 'David Cameron Rules Out Slavery Reparation during Jamaica Visit.' 30 September 2015. http://www.bbc.com/news/uk-34401412.

BBC News. 'Ghana Refuses to Grant Gays' Rights Despite Aid Threat.' 2 November 2011. http://www.bbc.co.uk/news/world-africa-15558769.

BBC News. 'Obama Condemns Uganda Anti-Gay Bill as "Odious".' 4 February 2010. http://news.bbc.co.uk/2/hi/africa/8498836.stm.

BBC News. 'Royal Pardon for Codebreaker Alan Turing.' 24 December 2013. http://www.bbc.com/news/technology-25495315.

BBC News. 'Transcript Philip Hammond Interview.' *The Andrew Marr Show*, 30 October 2011. http://news.bbc.co.uk/1/hi/programmes/andrew_marr_show/9627898.stm.

BBC News. 'Uganda Fury at David Cameron Aid Threat over Gay Rights.' 31 October 2011. http://www.bbc.co.uk/news/world-africa-15524013.

BBC News. 'Uganda's Stella Nyanzi Bares Breasts in Protest at Jail Sentence.' 2 August 2019. https://www.bbc.co.uk/news/world-africa-49210281.

BBC News. 'World Bank Postpones $90 Million Uganda Loan over Anti-Gay Law.' 28 February 2014. http://www.bbc.co.uk/news/world-africa-26378230.

Beckford, Robert, and Bindu Mathur (directors). *The Empire Pays Back*. 2005.

Beckles, Hilary McD. *Britain's Black Debt: Reparations for Caribbean Slavery and Native Genocide*. Kingston: University of West Indies Press, 2013.

Bedford, Kate. *Developing Partnerships: Gender, Sexuality, and the Reformed World Bank*. Minneapolis: University of Minnesota Press, 2009.

Benjamin, Walter. 'On the Concept of History.' Translated by Dennis Redmond. Accessed 18 August 2018. https://www.marxists.org/reference/archive/benjamin/1940/history.htm.

Bennett, Jane. 'Subversion and Resistance: Activist Initiatives.' In *African Sexualities: A Reader*, edited by Sylvia Tamale, 77–100. Cape Town: Pambazuka Press, 2011.

Berlant, Lauren, and Elizabeth Freeman. 'Queer Nationality.' *boundary 2* 19, no. 1 (1992): 149–180.

Berlant, Lauren. *Cruel Optimism*. Durham, NC: Duke University Press, 2011.

Berman, Jessica. 'Is the Trans in Transnational the Trans in Transgender?' *Modernism/modernity* 2, no. 2 (2017). https://modernismmodernity.org/articles/trans-transnational.

Bhaskaran, Suparna. *Made in India: Decolonizations, Queer Sexualities, Trans/national Projects*. New York: Palgrave, 2004.

Binnie, Jon. *The Globalization of Sexuality*. London: Sage, 2004.

Bisiika, Asuman. 'Bishop Hannington, the Unnamed Martyr.' *New Vision*, 2 June 2005.

Bisiika, Asuman. 'Namugongo: Place of Hope Even in Death.' *New Vision*, 3 June 2004.

Bleys, Rudi C. *The Geography of Perversion: Male-to-Male Sexual Behaviour outside the West and the Ethnographic Imagination 1750–1918*. London: Cassell, 1996.

Bob, Clifford. *The Global Right Wing and the Clash of World Politics*. Cambridge: Cambridge University Press, 2012.

Boisvert, Donald L. *Sanctity and Male Desire: A Gay Reading of Saints*. Cleveland, OH: Pilgrim Press, 2004.

Bompani, Barbara, and Caroline Valois. 'Sexualizing Politics: The Anti-Homosexuality Bill, Party-Politics and the New Political Dispensation in Uganda.' *Critical African Studies* 9, no. 1 (2017): 52–70.

Bompani, Barbara. ' "For God and for My Country": Pentecostal-Charismatic Churches and the Framing of a New Political Discourse in Uganda.' In *Public Religion and the Politics of Homosexuality in Africa*, edited by Adriaan van Klinken and Ezra Chitando, 19–34. Abingdon: Routledge, 2016.

Borges, Andre. 'This Guy's Mom Wanted to Find Him a Husband, So He Placed India's First Gay "Groom Wanted" Ad.' *Buzzfeed*, 19 May 2015. https://www.buzzfeed.com/andreborges/first-gay-matrimonial-groom-wanted-ad.

Bose, Sugata, and Kris Manjapra, eds. *Cosmopolitan Thought Zones: South Asia and the Global Circulation of Ideas*. Basingstoke: Palgrave Macmillan, 2010.

Boyd, Lydia. 'The Problem with Freedom: Homosexuality and Human Rights in Uganda.' *Anthropological Quarterly* 86, no. 3 (2013): 697–724.

Brierly, Jean, and Thomas Spear. 'Mutesa, The Missionaries, and Christian Conversion in Buganda.' *The International Journal of African Historical Studies* 21, no. 4 (1988): 601–618.

Brown, Gordon. 'Gordon Brown: I'm Proud to Say Sorry to a Real War Hero.' *The Telegraph*, 10 September 2009. http://www.telegraph.co.uk/news/politics/gordon-brown/6170112/Gordon-Brown-Im-proud-to-say-sorry-to-a-real-war-hero.html.

Brown, Wendy. *Politics Out of History*. Princeton, NJ: Princeton University Press, 2001.

Brown, Wendy. *Undoing the Demos: Neoliberalism's Stealth Revolution*. New York: Zone Books, 2015.

Browne, Victoria. *Feminism, Time, and Nonlinear History*. New York: Palgrave Macmillan, 2014.

Bryan, Austin. 'Kuchu Activism, Queer Sex-Work and "Lavender Marriages," in Uganda's Virtual LGBT Safe(r) Spaces.' *Journal of Eastern African Studies* 13, no. 1 (2019): 90–105.

Bunting, Madeleine. 'African Homophobia Has Complex Roots.' *Guardian*, 21 May 2010. https://www.theguardian.com/commentisfree/2010/may/21/complex-roots-africa-homophobia.

Burack, Cynthia. *Because We Are Human: Contesting US Support for Gender and Sexuality Human Rights Abroad*. Albany: State University of New York Press, 2018.

Burns, John F. 'Nuclear Anxiety: The Subcontinent; India Glows with Pride as Outrage Rises Abroad.' *New York Times*, 13 May 1998. https://www.nytimes.com/1998/05/13/world/nuclear-anxiety-the-subcontinent-india-glows-with-pride-as-outrage-rises-abroad.html.

Burton, Richard F. 'Terminal Essay.' In *A Plain and Literal Translation of the Arabian Nights Entertainments*, vol. 10. London: The Burton Club, 1886.

Butler, Judith. *Gender Trouble: Feminism and the Subversion of Identity*. Abingdon: Routledge, 1999 [1990].

Butler, Judith. 'Merely Cultural.' *Social Text* 52/53 (1997): 265–277.

Butler, Judith. *Undoing Gender*. New York: Routledge, 2004.

Cabrera, Luis. 'Dalit Cosmopolitans: Institutionally Developmental Global Citizenship in Struggles against Caste Discrimination.' *Review of International Studies* 43, no. 2 (2016): 280–301.

Cameron, David. 'Troubled Families Speech.' 15 December 2011. https://www.gov.uk/government/speeches/troubled-families-speech.

Carastathis, Anna. *Intersectionality: Origins, Contestations, Horizons*. Lincoln: University of Nebraska Press, 2016.

Carbone, Nick. 'Top 10 Viral Videos.' *Time*, 4 December 2012. http://entertainment.time.com/2012/12/04/top-10-arts-lists/slide/kony-2012/.

Castelli, Elizabeth A. *Martyrdom and Memory: Early Christian Culture Making*. New York: Columbia University Press, 2004.

Catherwood, Rhiannon. 'Coming *In*? The Evolution of the Transsexual Memoir in the Twenty-First Century.' *Genre* 48, no. 1 (2015): 35–71.

Chacko, Priya. *Indian Foreign Policy: The Politics of Postcolonial Identity from 1947 to 2004*. Abingdon: Routledge, 2012.

Chakrabarty, Dipesh. *Provincializing Europe: Postcolonial Thought and Historical Difference*. Princeton, NJ: Princeton University Press, 2000.

Chasin, Alexandra. *Selling Out: The Gay and Lesbian Movement Goes to Market*. New York: Palgrave, 2000.

Chatterjee, Partha. *The Nation and Its Fragments: Colonial and Postcolonial Histories*. Princeton, NJ: Princeton University Press, 1993.

Cheney, Kristen. 'Locating Neocolonialism, "Tradition," and Human Rights in Uganda's "Gay Death Penalty".' *African Studies Review* 55, no. 2 (2012): 77–95.

Cherian, Jayan K. (director). *Ka Bodyscapes*. 2016.

Cherian, Jayan K. (director). *Papilio Buddha*. 2013.

Chinweizu. 'Reparations and a New Global Order: A Comparative Overview.' Paper presented at the Second Plenary Session of the First Pan-African Conference on Reparations, Abuja, Nigeria, 27 April 1993. ncobra.org/resources/pdf/Chinweizu-ReparationsandANewGlobalOrder1.pdf.

Churchill, Caryl. *Cloud 9*. London: Nick Hern Books, 1989 [1979].

Churchill, Caryl. *Pigs and Dogs*. London: Nick Hern Books, 2016.

Clarke, Gerard. 'Agents of Transformation? Donors, Faith-Based Organisations and International Development.' *Third World Quarterly* 28, no. 1 (2007): 77–96.

Cohen, Lawrence. 'The Pleasures of Castration: The Postoperative Status of Hijras, Jankhas and Academics.' In *Sexual Nature, Sexual Culture*, edited by Paul R. Abramson and Steven D. Pinkerton, 276–304. Chicago: University of Chicago Press, 1995.

Cohen, Stanley. *Folk Devils and Moral Panics: The creation of the Mods and Rockers*. Abingdon: Routledge, 2011 [1972].

Colpani, Gianmaria. 'Queer Hegemonies: Politics and Ideology in Contemporary Queer Debates.' PhD diss., University of Verona, 2017.

Combahee River Collective Statement. Reprinted in *This Bridge Called My Back: Writings by Radical Women of Color*, edited by Cherríe Moraga and Gloria Anzaldúa, 210–18. Albany: State University of New York Press, 1977.

Conrad, Joseph. *Heart of Darkness*. London: Penguin, 1976 [1899].

Cooper, Melinda. 'The Theology of Emergency: Welfare, Reform, US Foreign Aid and the Faith-Based Initiative.' *Theory, Culture & Society* 32, no. 2 (2015): 53–77.

Corrêa, Sonia, and akshay khanna. *Emerging Powers, Sexuality and Human Rights: 'Fumbling around the Elephant?'* Rio de Janeiro: Sexuality Policy Watch, 2015.

Crenshaw, Kimberlé. 'Demarginalizing the Intersection of Race and Sex: A Black Feminist Critique of Antidiscrimination Doctrine, Feminist Theory and Antiracist Politics.' *University of Chicago Legal Forum* 1 (1989): 139–167.

Crenshaw, Kimberlé. 'Mapping the Margins: Intersectionality, Identity Politics, and Violence against Women of Color.' *Stanford Law Review* 43 (1991): 1241–1299.

Croome, Philippa. 'Sweden Suspends Some Aid to Uganda over Anti-Gay Law.' *Reuters*, 6 March 2014. http://www.reuters.com/article/us-uganda-aid-sweden-idUSBREA2509720140306.

Currier, Ashley, and Thérèse Migraine-George. 'Queer Studies/African Studies: An (Im)possible Transaction?' *GLQ: A Journal of Lesbian and Gay Studies* 22, no. 2 (2016): 281–305.

D'Emilio, John. 'Capitalism and Gay Identity.' In *Powers of Desire: The Politics of Sexuality*, edited by Ann Snitow, Christine Stansell, and Sharon Thompson, 100–113. New York: Monthly Review Press, 1983.

Das, Runa. 'Encountering Hindutva, Interrogating Religious Nationalism and (En)gendering a Hindu Patriarchy in India's Nuclear Policies.' *International Feminist Journal of Politics* 8, no. 3 (2006): 370–93.

Dave, Naisargi N. *Queer Activism in India: A Story in the Anthropology of Ethics*. Durham, NC: Duke University Press, 2012.

Davis, Angela. *The Prison Industrial Complex*. Chico, CA: AK Press, 1977.

De Las Casas, Bartolomé. *A Brief Account of the Destruction of the Indies*. 1542. http://www.gutenberg.org/cache/epub/20321/pg20321-images.html.

Deccan Herald News Service. 'Govt to HC: Word "Eunuch" Removed from Police Act.' *Deccan Herald*, 7 February 2017. http://www.deccanherald.com/content/595200/govt-hcamp8200word-eunuch-removed-police.html.

Derrida, Jacques. *Spectres of Marx: The State of the Debt, the Work of Mourning and the New International*. New York: Routledge, 1994.

Deutsche Welle. 'Germany to Pay Convicted Gays 30 Million Euros—Media.' 8 October 2016. http://www.dw.com/en/germany-to-pay-convicted-gays-30-million-euros-media/a-35996592.

Dollen, Charles. *African Triumph: The Life of Charles Lwanga and Other Martyrs of Uganda*. Boston: Daughters of St. Paul, 1986.

Douglass, Frederick. *Narrative of the Life of Frederick Douglass, an American Slave / Written by Himself*. Blacksburg: Virginia Tech, 2001 [1845].

Du Plessis, Max. 'Historical Injustice and International Law: An Exploratory Discussion of Reparation for Slavery.' *Human Rights Quarterly* 25, no. 3 (2003): 624–659.

Duffy, Nick. 'How Many People Have Been Pardoned under Turing's Law?' *Pink News*, 10 July 2018. https://www.pinknews.co.uk/2018/07/10/gay-sex-pardons-turings-law/.

Duffy, Nick. 'Theresa May Tells Commonwealth Leaders: We "Deeply Regret" Colonial-Era Anti-Gay Laws.' *Pink News*, 17 April 2018. https://www.pinknews.co.uk/2018/04/17/theresa-may-commonwealth-anti-gay-laws/.

Duggan, Lisa. *The Twilight of Equality? Neoliberalism, Cultural Politics, and the Attack on Democracy*. Boston: Beacon Press, 2003.

Dutoya, Virginie. 'Defining the "Queers" in India: The Politics of Academic Representation.' *India Review* 15, no. 2 (2016): 241–271.

Dutta, Aniruddha. 'Contradictory Tendencies: The Supreme Court's *NALSA* Judgment on Transgender Recognition and Rights.' *Journal of Indian Law and Society* 5 (Monsoon 2014): 225–236.

Dutta, Aniruddha, and Raina Roy. 'Decolonizing Transgender in India: Some Reflections.' *TSQ: Transgender Studies Quarterly* 1, no. 3 (2014): 320–337.

Economist. 'Pride and Prejudice New York.' Accessed 25 February 2017. https://www.youtube.com/watch?v=BHeibAzHcBM.

Economist. 'The World Bank: Right Cause, Wrong Battle.' 12 April 2014. http://www.economist.com/news/leaders/21600684-why-world-banks-focus-gay-rights-misguided-right-cause-wrong-battle.

Edelman, Lee. *Homographesis: Essays in Gay Literary and Cultural Theory*. New York: Routledge, 1994.

Edelman, Lee. *No Future: Queer Theory and the Death Drive*. Durham, NC: Duke University Press, 2004.

Edge. 'Stella Nyanzi Praises Besigye, Likens Politics to Sex.' 9 December 2017. https://edge.ug/2017/12/09/stella-nyanzi-praises-besigye-likens-politics-to-sex/.

Ekine, Sokari, and Hakima Abbas, eds. *Queer African Reader*. Dakar: Pambazuka Press, 2013.

Eleveld, Kerry. 'White House Condemns Uganda Bill.' *Advocate*, 12 December 2009. http://www.advocate.com/news/daily-news/2009/12/12/white-house-condemns-uganda-bill.

Elias, Juanita. 'Davos Woman to the Rescue of Global Capitalism: Postfeminist Politics and Competitiveness Promotion at the World Economic Forum.' *International Political Sociology* 7, no. 2 (2013): 152–169.

Elliott, Larry, and Helena Smith. 'IMF "to Admit Mistakes" in Handling Greek Debt Crisis and Bailout.' *Guardian*, 5 June 2013. https://www.theguardian.com/business/2013/jun/05/imf-admit-mistakes-greek-crisis-austerity.

Eng, David L. *The Feeling of Kinship: Queer Liberalism and the Racialization of Intimacy*. Durham, NC: Duke University Press, 2010.

Epprecht, Marc. 'Black Skin, "Cowboy" Masculinity: A Genealogy of Homophobia in the African Nationalist Movement in Zimbabwe to 1983.' *Culture, Health & Sexuality* 7, no. 3 (2005): 253–266.

Epprecht, Marc. *Heterosexual Africa? The History of an Idea from the Age of Exploration to the Age of AIDS.* Athens: Ohio University Press, 2008.

Epstein, Helen. *The Invisible Cure: Africa, the West, and the Fight against AIDS.* New York: Farrar, Straus and Giroux, 2007.

Equiano, Olaudah. *The Interesting Narrative of the Life of Olaudah Equiano, or Gustavus Vassa, the African/Written by Himself,* edited by Angelo Constanzo. Peterborough, ON: Broadview Press, 2001 [1789].

European Parliament. *Resolution on Uganda: Anti-Homosexual Draft Legislation,* 16 December 2009, RC-B7-0259/2009. http://www.europarl.europa. eu/sides/getDoc.do?pubRef=-//EP//TEXT+MOTION+P7-RC-2009-0259+0+DOC+XML+V0//EN.

Fabian, Johannes. *Time and the Other: How Anthropology Makes Its Object.* New York: Columbia University Press, 2014 [1983].

Fanon, Frantz. *Black Skin, White Masks.* Translated by Charles Lam Markmann. London: Pluto Press, 1986 [1952].

farajajé-jones, elias. 'Holy Fuck.' In *Male Lust: Pleasure, Power, and Transformation,* edited by Kerwin Kay, Jill Nagle, and Baruch Gould, 327–335. Binghamton, NY: Haworth Press, 2000.

Farris, Sara R. *In the Name of Women's Rights: The Rise of Femonationalism.* Durham, NC: Duke University Press, 2017.

Faupel, John F. *African Holocaust: The Story of the Uganda Martyrs.* London: Geoffrey Chapman, 1965.

Feder, Lester. 'Ugandan President Denounces Anti-Homosexuality Bill—But Stops Short of Blocking It—In Letter to Parliament.' *BuzzFeed,* 17 January 2014. https://www.buzzfeed.com/lesterfeder/ugandan-president-denounces-anti-homosexuality-bill-but-stop?utm_term=.yhr7GMMV2#.spvGkyyr4.

Feder, Lester. 'World Bank President: Our Efforts Have Slowed Rise of Anti-LGBT Laws.' *BuzzFeed,* 9 April 2015. https://www.buzzfeed.com/lesterfeder/ world-bank-president-our-efforts-have-slowed-rise-of-anti-lg?utm_term=. vaQvbak6Z#.oe6DLW6XY.

Feder, Lester. 'World Bank Review Team to Recommend Approving Loan to Uganda Despite Anti-Homosexuality Act.' *BuzzFeed,* 23 April 2014. https://www. buzzfeed.com/lesterfeder/world-bank-review-team-to-recommend-approving-loan-to-uganda?utm_term=.hhzaBe1dQ#.xiD5ljVpY.

Ferguson, Roderick A. *Aberrations in Black: Toward a Queer of Color Critique.* Minneapolis: University of Minnesota Press, 2004.

Floyd, Kevin. *The Reification of Desire: Toward a Queer Marxism.* Minneapolis: University of Minnesota Press, 2009.

Foucault, Michel. *The Will to Knowledge: The History of Sexuality,* vol. 1. Translated by Robert Hurley. London: Penguin, 1981 [1976].

Fraser, Nancy. *Fortunes of Feminism: From State-Managed Capitalism to Neoliberal Crisis.* London: Verso, 2013.

Fraser, Nancy. 'Rethinking the Public Sphere: A Contribution to the Critique of Actually Existing Democracy.' *Social Text* 25/26 (1990): 56–80.

Freeman, Dana. 'The Pentecostal Ethic and the Spirit of Development.' In *Pentecostalism and Development: Churches, NGOs and Social Change in Africa,* edited by Dana Freeman, 1–38. Basingstoke: Palgrave Macmillan, 2012.

Freeman, Elizabeth. *Time Binds: Queer Temporalities, Queer Histories*. Durham, NC: Duke University Press, 2010.

Freud, Sigmund. 'Negation.' In *The Ego and the Id and Other Works*, vol. 19, *The Standard Edition of the Complete Psychological Works of Sigmund Freud*, edited by James Strachey, 235–239. London: Hogarth Press, 1925.

Freud, Sigmund. 'The Uncanny.' In *An Infantile Neurosis and Other Works*, vol. 17, *The Standard Edition of the Complete Psychological Works of Sigmund Freud*, edited by James Strachey, 219–253. London: Hogarth Press, 1919.

Frosh, Stephen. *Hauntings: Psychoanalysis and Ghostly Transmissions*. Basingstoke: Palgrave Macmillan, 2013.

Fry, Stephen. *Out There* (episode 1). BBC Two, 14 October 2013. https://www.youtube.com/watch?v=HCp_5-CsYuM.

Fuss, Diana. 'Interior Colonies: Frantz Fanon and the Politics of Identification.' *Diacritics* 24, nos. 2–3 (1994): 19–42.

FYTA. 'IMF: It Gets Better (Pinkwashing Version).' Accessed 28 February 2017. https://www.youtube.com/watch?v=SZ00OGUgEu4.

Galanter, Marc. *Competing Equalities: Law and the Backward Classes in India*. Berkeley: University of California Press, 1984.

Galanter, Marc. 'Who Are the Other Backward Classes?: An Introduction to a Constitutional Puzzle.' *Economic & Political Weekly* 13, nos. 43–44 (1978): 1812–1828.

Gallagher, Julia. 'Can Melanie Klein Help Us Understand Morality in IR? Suggestions for a Psychoanalytic Interpretation of Why and How States Do Good.' *Millennium: Journal of International Studies* 38, no. 2 (2010): 295–316.

Geetha, V. 'Periyar, Women and an Ethic of Citizenship.' *Economic & Political Weekly* 33, no. 17 (1998): 9–15.

Gettleman, Jeffrey. 'Americans' Role Seen in Uganda Anti-Gay Push.' *New York Times*, 3 January 2010. http://www.nytimes.com/2010/01/04/world/africa/04uganda.html?_r=0.

Gevisser, Mark. 'Human Rights vs Homophobia: Who Is Winning Africa's Cultural Wars.' *Open Society Initiative for Southern Africa*, 20 June 2013. http://www.osisa.org/openspace/regional/human-rights-vs-homophobia-who-winning-africas-cultural-wars.

Ghoshal, Somak. 'Book Review: The Ministry of Utmost Happiness by Arundhati Roy.' *HuffPost India*, 2 June 2017. http://www.huffingtonpost.in/2017/06/01/book-review-the-ministry-of-utmost-happiness-by-arundhati-roy_a_22121017/.

Gifford, Paul. *African Christianity: Its Public Role in Uganda and Other African Countries*. Kampala: Fountain, 1999.

Gilroy, Paul. *After Empire: Melancholia or Convivial Culture?* Abingdon: Routledge, 2004.

Gledhill, Ruth. 'For God's Sake.' *Times*, 5 July 2007. https://virtueonline.org/abuja-nigeria-gods-sake-ruth-gledhill-interviews-peter-akinola.

Gluck, Carol. 'Operations of Memory.' In *Ruptured Histories: War, Memory, and the Post-Cold War in Asia*, edited by Sheila Miyoshi Jager and Rana Mitter, 47–77. Cambridge, MA: Harvard University Press, 2007.

Gopal, Priyamvada. 'Redressing Anti-Imperial Amnesia.' *Race & Class* 57, no. 3 (2016): 18–30.

Gopinath, Gayatri. *Impossible Desires: Queer Diasporas and South Asian Public Cultures*. Durham, NC: Duke University Press, 2005.

Gordon, Avery F. *Ghostly Matters: Haunting and the Sociological Imagination.* Minneapolis: University of Minnesota Press, 1997.

Gosine, Andil. 'The World Bank's GLOBE: Queers In/Queering Development.' In *Development, Sexual Rights and Global Governance*, edited by Amy Lind, 67–85. London: Routledge, 2010.

Government of India. *Report of the Backward Classes Commission*, vol. 1. Simla: Government of India Press, 1955. https://dspace.gipe.ac.in/xmlui/handle/10973/33678.

Govindan, Padma, and Aniruddhan Vasudevan. 'The Razor's Edge of Oppositionality: Exploring the Politics of Rights-Based Activism by Transgender Women in Tamil Nadu.' In *Law like Love: Queer Perspectives on Law*, edited by Arvind Narrain and Alok Gupta, 84–112. New Delhi: Yoda Press, 2011.

Griffin, Penny. 'Gendering Global Finance: Crisis, Masculinity, and Responsibility.' *Men and Masculinities* 16, no. 1 (2012): 9–34.

Griffin, Penny. *Gendering the World Bank: Neoliberalism and the Gendered Foundations of Global Governance.* Basingstoke: Palgrave Macmillan, 2009.

Grills, Nathan. 'The Paradox of Multilateral Organizations Engaging with Faith-Based Organizations.' *Global Governance* 15, no. 4 (2009): 505–520.

Gross, Aeyal. 'Sex, Love, and Marriage: Questioning Gender and Sexuality Rights in International Law.' *Leiden Journal of International Law* 21, no. 1 (2008): 235–253.

Grosz, Elizabeth. *Volatile Bodies: Toward a Corporeal Feminism.* Crows Nest, NSW: Allen & Unwin, 1994.

Guha, Ramachandra. *India: The Next Superpower?: Will India Become a Superpower?* London: LSE IDEAS, 2012. http://eprints.lse.ac.uk/43442/.

Guha, Ranajit. *Dominance without Hegemony: History and Power in Colonial India.* Cambridge, MA: Harvard University Press, 1998.

Guha, Ranajit. *Elementary Aspects of Peasant Insurgency in Colonial India.* Delhi: Oxford University Press, 1992 [1983].

Guma, Prince Karakire. 'Narratives of "Saints" and "Sinners" in Uganda: Contemporary (Re)presentations of the 1886 Story of "Queer" Mwanga and "Ganda" Martyrs.' In *Public Religion and the Politics of Homosexuality in Africa*, edited by Adriaan van Klinken and Ezra Chitando, 197–209. Abingdon: Routledge, 2016.

Gupta, Alok. 'Englishpur ki Kothi: Class Dynamics in the Queer Movement in India.' In *Because I Have a Voice: Queer Politics in India*, edited by Arvind Narrain and Gautam Bhan, 123–142. New Delhi: Yoda Press, 2005.

Gusman, Alessandro. 'HIV/AIDS, Pentecostal Churches, and the "Joseph Generation" in Uganda.' *Africa Today* 56, no. 1 (2009): 66–86.

Halberstam, Judith. *The Queer Art of Failure.* Durham, NC: Duke University Press, 2011.

Hall, Catherine. 'Persons Outside the Law.' *London Review of Books* 40, no. 14 (2018): 3–5.

Hall, Stuart, Brian Roberts, John Clarke, Tony Jefferson, and Chas Critcher. *Policing the Crisis: Mugging, the State, and Law and Order.* Basingstoke: Palgrave Macmillan, 1978.

Halperin, David. *How to Do the History of Homosexuality.* Chicago: University of Chicago Press, 2004.

Hamilton, Kenneth Lewis. 'The Flames of Namugongo: Postcolonial, Queer, and Thea/ological Reflections on the Narrative of the 1886 Ugandan Martyrdom.' Accessed 27 July 2016. https://www.academia.edu/1404802/The_flames_of_Namugongo_Postcolonial_queer_and_thea_ological_reflections_on_the_narrative_of_the_1886_Ugandan_martyrdom.

Han, Enze, and Joseph O'Mahoney. 'British Colonialism and the Criminalization of Homosexuality.' *Cambridge Review of International Affairs* 27, no. 2 (2014): 268–288.

Han, Enze, and Joseph O'Mahoney. *British Colonialism and the Criminalization of Homosexuality: Queens, Crime and Empire*. London: Routledge, 2018.

Harrison, Graham. *Neoliberal Africa: The Impact of Global Social Engineering*. London: Zed Books, 2010.

Hartman, Saidiya V. *Lose Your Mother: A Journey along the Atlantic Slave Route*. New York: Farrar, Straus and Giroux, 2008.

Hartman, Saidiya V. *Scenes of Subjection: Terror, Slavery, and Self-Making in Nineteenth-Century America*. New York: Oxford University Press, 1997.

Hartman, Saidiya V. 'The Time of Slavery.' *The South Atlantic Quarterly* 101, no. 4 (2002): 757–777.

Harvey, David. *Cosmopolitanism and the Geographies of Freedom*. New York: Columbia University Press, 2009.

Harvey, David. *The New Imperialism*. Oxford: Oxford University Press, 2005.

Hassett, Miranda K. *Anglican Communion in Crisis: How Episcopal Dissidents and Their African Allies Are Reshaping Anglicanism*. Princeton, NJ: Princeton University Press, 2007.

Hennessy, Rosemary. *Profit and Pleasure: Sexual Identities in Late Capitalism*. New York: Routledge, 2000.

Hoad, Neville. *African Intimacies: Race, Homosexuality, and Globalization*. Minneapolis: University of Minnesota Press, 2007.

Hoad, Neville. 'Arrested Development or the Queerness of Savages: Resisting Evolutionary Narratives of Difference.' *Postcolonial Studies* 3, no. 2 (2000): 133–158.

Hodges, Andrew. *Alan Turing: The Enigma*. London: Vintage, 2014.

Hom, Andrew, Christopher McIntosh, Alasdair McKay, and Liam Stockdale, eds. *Time, Temporality and Global Politics*. Bristol: E-International Relations, 2016.

Hook, Derek. 'White Privilege, Psychoanalytic Ethics, and the Limitations of Political Silence.' *South African Journal of Philosophy* 30, no. 4 (2011): 494–501.

hooks, bell. 'Feminism as a Persistent Critique of History: What's Love Got to Do with It?' In *The Fact of Blackness: Frantz Fanon and Visual Representation*, edited by Alan Read, 76–85. London: Institute of Contemporary Arts, 1996.

Hooper, Charlotte. *Manly States: Masculinities, International Relations, and Gender Politics*. New York: Columbia University Press, 2001.

Hopgood, Stephen. *The Endtimes of Human Rights*. Ithaca, NY: Cornell University Press, 2013.

Hopgood, Stephen. *Keepers of the Flame: Understanding Amnesty International*. Ithaca, NY: Cornell University Press, 2006.

Hopley, Claire. 'Ambiguities among the Cruelties of the Caste System.' *Washington Times*, 6 July 2017. https://www.washingtontimes.com/news/2017/jul/6/book-review-the-ministry-of-utmost-happiness/.

Howell, Alfred Ernest. *The Fires of Namugongo*. London: Samuel Walker, 1948.

Hozić, Aida A., and Jacqui True. 'Making Feminist Sense of the Global Financial Crisis.' In *Scandalous Economics: Gender and the Politics of Financial Crises*, edited by Aida A. Hozić and Jacqui True, 3–20. New York: Oxford University Press, 2016.

Human Dignity Trust. 'Human Dignity Trust Launches Criminalisation in the Commonwealth 2015 report.' Last modified 22 November 2015. http://www.humandignitytrust.org/pages/NEWS/News?NewsArticleID=470.

Human Dignity Trust. 'Legal Cases Challenging the Criminalisation of Homosexuality Supported by the Human Dignity Trust.' Accessed 4 December 2016. http://www.humandignitytrust.org/pages/OUR%20WORK/Cases.

Human Dignity Trust. 'Should the UK Government Appoint a Special Envoy to Work towards Ending the Persecution of the LGBT Community across the Globe?' Accessed 4 December 2016. http://www.humandignitytrust.org/uploaded/Library/Other_Material/Special_Envoy_Six_Reasons_-_3_July_2015_FINAL.pdf.

Human Rights Watch. *'They Want Us Exterminated': Murder, Torture, Sexual Orientation and Gender in Iraq*. New York: Human Rights Watch, 2009. https://www.hrw.org/report/2009/08/17/they-want-us-exterminated/murder-torture-sexual-orientation-and-gender-iraq.

Human Rights Watch. *This Alien Legacy: The Origins of 'Sodomy' Laws in British Colonialism*. New York: Human Rights Watch, 2008. https://www.hrw.org/report/2008/12/17/alien-legacy/origins-sodomy-laws-british-colonialism.

Hutchings, Kimberly. *Time and World Politics: Thinking the Present*. Manchester: Manchester University Press, 2008.

Hyam, Ronald. *Empire and Sexuality: The British Experience*. Manchester: Manchester University Press, 1990.

ICG (International Crisis Group). *Uganda: No Resolution to Growing Tensions*. Nairobi/Brussels: ICG, 2012. https://www.crisisgroup.org/africa/horn-africa/uganda/uganda-no-resolution-growing-tensions.

ILGA (International Lesbian, Gay, Bisexual, Trans and Intersex Association). 'The ILGA-RIWI 2016 Global Attitudes Survey on LGBTI People in Partnership with Logo.' Accessed 14 February 2019. https://ilga.org/downloads/07_THE_ILGA_RIWI_2016_GLOBAL_ATTITUDES_SURVEY_ON_LGBTI_PEOPLE.pdf.

ILGA (International Lesbian, Gay, Bisexual, Trans and Intersex Association). 'Maps—Sexual Orientation Laws.' Accessed 28 November 2018. https://www.ilga.org/maps-sexual-orientation-laws.

IMF (International Monetary Fund). 'It Gets Better.' Accessed 28 February 2017. https://www.youtube.com/watch?v=rwuR85gRjnk.

Inani, Rohit. 'India's First Lesbian Ad Goes Viral.' *Time*, 11 June 2015. http://time.com/3917400/india-lesbian-ad-lgbt-anouk/.

Invisible Children (dir. Jason Russell). *Kony2012*. Accessed 14 February 2019. http://invisiblechildren.com/kony-2012/.

Jain, Dipika. 'Shifting Subjects of State Legibility: Gender Minorities and the Law in India.' *Berkeley Journal of Gender, Law & Justice* 32, no. 1 (2017): 39–72.

Jakobsen, Janet R. 'Queers Are like Jews, Aren't They? Analogy and Alliance Politics.' In *Queer Theory and the Jewish Question*, edited by Daniel Boyarin, Daniel Itzkovitz, and Ann Pellegrini, 64–89. New York: Columbia University Press, 2003.

Jessie, Jashwanth. 'Lal Salaam to Jai Bhim: Why Rohith Vemula Left Indian Marxists.' *Hindustan Times*, 22 January 2016. http://www.hindustantimes.

com/india/lal-salaam-to-jai-bhim-why-rohith-vemula-left-indian-marxists/
story-Ut2xjokyFWae30oQiJZOxJ.html.

Jones, Jason. 'We Won in Trinidad. Now It's Time to End All
   Homophobic Laws in the Commonwealth.' *Guardian*, 14 April
   2018. https://www.theguardian.com/commentisfree/2018/apr/13/
   trinidad-homphobic-laws-win-case-commonwealth.

Kabuye, Kalungi. 'Did You Know Muslims Are among the Uganda Martyrs?' *New
   Vision*, 3 June 1996.

Kadden, Jeremy. 'World Bank Releases Disappointing Third "Safeguards" Draft;
   Omits LGBTQ Community.' Last modified 27 July 2016. http://www.hrc.org/
   blog/world-bank-releases-disappointing-third-safeguards-draft-omits-lgbtq-
   commun.

Kagolo, Francis. 'Museveni Warns on Dangers of Sodomy.' *New Vision*, 3
   June 2010.

Kagwa, Apolo. *The Customs of the Baganda*. Translated by Ernest B. Kalibala, edited by
   May Mandelbaum Edel. New York: Columbia University Press, 1934.

Kahyana, Danson Sylvester. 'Shifting Marginalities in Ham Mukasa and Sir Apolo
   Kagwa's *Uganda's Katikiro in England*.' *Journal of African Cultural Studies* 30, no.
   1 (2018): 36–48.

Kajoba, Nicholas. 'Catholics Pray for Nyerere.' *New Vision*, 3 June 2008.

Kaleidoscope Trust. 'Kaleidoscope Trust Launches Parliamentary Friends Group.' Last
   modified 28 February 2013. http://kaleidoscopetrust.com/news/36.

Kalibbala, Gladys. 'Bravery Kept Him from Martyrdom.' *New Vision*, 3 June 2008.

Kang, Akhil. 'Casteless-ness in the Name of Caste.' *Roundtable India*, 4 March 2016.
   http://roundtableindia.co.in/index.php?option=com_content&view=article&i
   d=8491%3Acasteless-ness-in-the-name-of-caste&catid=119%3Afeature&Itemi
   d=132&fbclid=IwAR0hmagFuXKxEHO7l_HCuphY0hh4mPMuPMMq5TYP8l5
   q4TjeaBg9sPCGT2o.

Kang, Akhil. 'Queering Dalit.' *Tanqeed*, October 2016, http://
   www.tanqeed.org/2016/10/queering-dalit-tq-salon/?fbclid
   =IwAR1DSHgrb2lQE1n6vNlVFjL7Vf7X2OHFDJFejJHr-HtkjEC9b2vmrRzGCvc.

Kaoma, Kapya. 'An African or Un-African Sexual Identity? Religion, Globalisation
   and Sexual Politics in Sub-Saharan Africa.' In *Public Religion and the Politics of
   Homosexuality in Africa*, edited by Adriaan van Klinken and Ezra Chitando, 113–
   129. Abingdon: Routledge, 2016.

Kaoma, Kapya. *Colonizing African Values: How the US Christian Right Is Transforming
   Sexual Politics in Africa*. Somerville, MA: Political Research Associates, 2012.
   http://www.politicalresearch.org/resources/reports/full-reports/colonizing-
   african-values/#sthash.f7FQWWC9.dpbs.

Kaoma, Kapya. *Globalizing the Culture Wars: US Conservatives, African Churches, and
   Homophobia*. Somerville, MA: Political Research Associates, 2009. http://
   www.politicalresearch.org/2009/12/01/globalizing-the-culture-wars-u-s-
   conservatives-african-churches-homophobia/#sthash.MhVSoJ4Q.dpbs.

Kapur, Ratna. 'Unruly Desires, Gay Governance and the Makeover of Sexuality in
   Postcolonial India.' In *Global Justice and Desire: Queering Economy*, edited by
   Nikita Dhawan, Antke Engel, Christoph F. E. Holzhey, and Volker Woltersdorff,
   115–131. Abingdon: Routledge, 2015.

Karnataka State Backward Classes Commission. 'Including Transgenders, Hijras,
   Kothis and Other Sexual Minorities in the List of Backward Classes.'
   Suggestion No. 25 (Dwarakanath Report), 2010. On file with author.

Kassimir, Ronald. 'Complex Martyrs: Symbols of Catholic Church Formation and Political Differentiation in Uganda.' *African Affairs* 90 (1991): 357–382.

Kato, Chris M. 'Sheikh Muzaata Should Apologise,' Letter to *The Observer*, 30 March 2016. http://www.observer.ug/component/content/archive?year=2016&month=3.

Kaufman, Will. 'On the Psychology of Slavery Reparation: A Kleinian Reading.' *Atlantic Studies* 4, no. 2 (2007): 267–284.

Kennedy, Dane. *The Highly Civilized Man: Richard Burton and the Victorian World.* Cambridge, MA: Harvard University Press, 2005.

khanna, akshay. *Sexualness.* New Delhi: New Text, 2016.

khanna, akshay. 'Us "Sexuality Types": A Critical Engagement with the Postcoloniality of Sexuality.' In *The Phobic and the Erotic: The Politics of Sexualities in Contemporary India*, edited by Brinda Bose and Subhabrata Bhattacharyya, 159–200. London: Seagull, 2007.

Khilnani, Sunil. *The Idea of India.* London: Penguin, 2012.

Khubchandani, Kareem. 'Voguing in Bangalore: Desire, Blackness, and Femininity in Globalized India.' *S&F Online* 14, no. 3 (2018). http://sfonline.barnard.edu/feminist-and-queer-afro-asian-formations/voguing-in-bangalore-desire-blackness-and-femininity-in-globalized-india/.

Kincaid, Timothy. 'Sweden Responds to Uganda's Proposed "Kill Gays" Bill.' *Box Turtle Bulletin*, 28 November 2009. http://www.boxturtlebulletin.com/2009/11/28/16968.

Kintu, Deborah. *The Ugandan Morality Crusade: The Brutal Campaign against Homosexuality and Pornography under Yoweri Museveni.* Jefferson, NC: McFarland, 2018.

Kirby, Michael. 'The Sodomy Offence: England's Least Lovely Criminal Law Export?' In *Human Rights, Sexual Orientation and Gender Identity in the Commonwealth: Struggles for Decriminalisation and Change*, edited by Corinne Lennox and Matthew Waites, 61–82. London: Institute of Commonwealth Studies, 2013.

Kivumbi, Kikonyogo (director). *Gay Love in Pre-colonial Africa: The Untold Story of the Uganda Martyrs.* Kampala: Uganda Health and Science Press Association, 2012.

Kleitz, Gilles. 2000. 'Why Is Development Work So Straight?' Last modified 27 January 2000. https://www.ids.ac.uk/files/dmfile/whystraight.pdf.

Kotiswaran, Prabha. *Dangerous Sex, Invisible Labor: Sex Work and the Law in India.* Princeton, NJ: Princeton University Press, 2011.

Krishna, Sankaran. 'A Postcolonial Racial/Spatial Order: Gandhi, Ambedkar, and the Construction of the International.' In *Race and Racism in International Relations: Confronting the Global Colour Line*, edited by Alexander Anievas, Nivi Manchanda, and Robbie Shilliam, 139–156. Abingdon: Routledge, 2015.

Kumar, Vinod. '"Jai Bhim, Lal Salaam": Myth and Reality.' *Round Table India*, 27 June 2016. https://roundtableindia.co.in/index.php?option=com_content&view=article&id=8653:jai-bhim-lal-salam-myth-and-reality&catid=119:feature&Itemid=132.

Kumarakulasingam, Narendran. 'Introduction.' *Contexto Internacional* 38, no. 3 (2016): 755–61.

Kunzel, Regina. 'The Flourishing of Transgender Studies.' *TSQ: Transgender Studies Quarterly* 1, nos. 1–2 (2014): 285–297.

LABIA (Lesbians and Bisexuals in Action). *Breaking the Binary: Understanding Concerns and Realities of Queer Persons Assigned Gender Female at Birth across a Spectrum*

of Lived Gender Identities. Mumbai: LABIA, 2013. https://sites.google.com/site/
labiacollective/we-do/research/report_btb.

Laclau, Ernesto, and Chantal Mouffe. *Hegemony and Socialist Strategy: Towards a
Radical Democratic Politics*. Translated by Winston Moore and Paul Cammack.
London: Verso, 1985.

Lal, Vinay. *Of Cricket, Guinness and Gandhi: Essays on Indian History and Culture*. New
Delhi: Penguin, 2005.

Lane, Christopher. *The Ruling Passion: British Colonial Allegory and the Paradox of
Homosexual Desire*. Durham, NC: Duke University Press, 1995.

Lauder, Simon. 'Commonwealth Leaders to Be Confronted on Homophobia.' *ABC
News*, 18 October 2011. http://www.abc.net.au/am/content/2011/s3341950.
htm.

Lavers, Michael. 'US Official Declines to Criticize Anti-LGBT Religious Figures.'
Washington Blade, 11 August 2016. https://www.washingtonblade.com/2016/
08/11/us-official-declines-criticize-anti-lgbt-religious-figures/.

Lee, Jia Hui. 'The Extraversion of Homophobia: Global Politics and Sexuality in
Uganda.' In *Public Religion and the Politics of Homosexuality in Africa*, edited by
Adriaan van Klinken and Ezra Chitando, 130–145. Abingdon: Routledge, 2016.

Lennox, Corinne, and Matthew Waites. 'Human Rights, Sexual Orientation and
Gender Identity in the Commonwealth: From History and Law to Developing
Activism and Transnational Dialogues.' In *Human Rights, Sexual Orientation and
Gender Identity in the Commonwealth: Struggles for Decriminalisation and Change*,
edited by Corinne Lennox and Matthew Waites, 1–59. London: Institute of
Commonwealth Studies, 2013.

Love, Heather. *Feeling Backward: Loss and the Politics of Queer History*. Cambridge,
MA: Harvard University Press, 2007.

Low, D. A. 'Converts and Martyrs in Buganda.' In *Christianity in Tropical Africa*, edited
by C. B. Baëta, 150–164. Oxford: Oxford University Press, 1968.

Lugones, María. 'Heterosexualism and the Colonial/Modern Gender System.' *Hypatia*
22, no. 1 (2007): 186–209.

Lukwago, Juliet, and Juliet Waiswa. 'Mukajjanga: Murderer or King's Obedient
Servant?' *New Vision*, 3 June 2009.

Lule, Baker Batte. 'Stella Nyanzi's Tongue May Be Acidic, but Her Sanitary Pads
Campaign Is Real.' *The Observer*, 5 April 2017. https://observer.ug/lifestyle/
52162-stella-nyanzi-s-tongue-may-be-acidic-but-her-sanitary-pads-campaign-
is-real.

Lusimbo, Richard, and Austin Bryan. '*Kuchu* Resilience and Resistance in Uganda: A
History.' In *Envisioning Global LGBT Human Rights: (Neo)colonialism,
Neoliberalism, Resistance and Hope*, edited by Nancy Nicol, Adrian Jjuuko,
Richard Lusimbo, Nick J. Mulé, Susan Ursel, Amar Wahab, and Phyllis Waugh,
323–345. London: Institute of Commonwealth Studies, 2018.

Luther, Danny. 'Queering Normativity: Uncovering the Invisible Working of Norms in
South Asian Public Culture.' PhD diss., SOAS University of London, 2018.

Lwanga-Lunyiigo, Samwiri. *Mwanga II: Resistance to Imposition of British Colonial Rule
in Buganda 1884–1899*. Kampala: Wavah Books, 2011.

Lynch, Andrea. *Sexuality and the Development Industry*, edited by Susie Jolly and
Andrea Cornwall. Brighton: Institute of Development Studies, 2008.

Macharia, Keguro. 'Frantz Fanon and White Queer Studies.' Last modified 22
February 2016. https://gukira.wordpress.com/2016/02/22/frantz-fanon-
white-queer-studies/.

Macharia, Keguro. 'Homophobia in Africa Is Not a Single Story.' *Guardian*, 26
    May 2010. https://www.theguardian.com/commentisfree/2010/may/26/
    homophobia-africa-not-single-story.

Macharia, Keguro. 'On Being Area-Studied: A Litany of Complaint.' *GLQ: A Journal of
    Lesbian and Gay Studies* 22, no. 2 (2016): 183–189.

Macharia, Keguro. 'Queer Genealogies (Provisional Notes).' Last modified 13 January
    2013. https://bullybloggers.wordpress.com/2013/01/13/queer-genealogies-
    provisional-notes/.

Mahajan, Karan. 'Arundhati Roy's Return to the Form That Made Her Famous.'
    New York Times, 9 June 2017. https://www.nytimes.com/2017/06/09/books/
    review/arundhati-roys-return-to-the-form-that-made-her-famous.html.

Mahmood, Saba. *Politics of Piety: The Islamic Revival and the Feminist Subject.*
    Princeton, NJ: Princeton University Press, 2012 [2005].

Malaba, Tom. *The Story of the Uganda Martyrs and Namugongo.* Kampala: Tourguide
    Publications, 2006.

Mamdani, Mahmood. 'Kony: What Jason Did Not Tell the Invisible Children.' *Al
    Jazeera*, 14 March 2012. https://www.aljazeera.com/indepth/opinion/2012/
    03/20123138139642455.html.

Mandell, Sean. 'Elton John: The Queen Could Change Anti-Gay Laws in the
    Commonwealth "With One Wave of Her Hand"—WATCH.' *Towleroad*, 5
    November 2015. http://www.towleroad.com/2015/11/elton-john-the-queen-
    could-change-anti-gay-laws-in-the-commonwealth-with-one-wave-of-her-
    hand-watch/.

Mani, Lata. *Contentious Traditions: The Debate on Sati in Colonial India.*
    Berkeley: University of California Press, 1998.

Manjapra, Kris. *M. N. Roy: Marxism and Colonial Cosmopolitanism.* New
    Delhi: Routledge, 2010.

Marion, Francis. *New African Saints: The Twenty-two Martyrs of Uganda.* Milan: Ancora
    Publications, 1964.

Marshall, Katherine, and Richard Marsh, eds. *Millennium Challenges for Development
    and Faith Institutions.* Washington, DC: The World Bank, 2003.

Marx, Karl, and Friedrich Engels. *The Communist Manifesto.* London: Penguin, 2004
    [1848].

Massad, Joseph. 'Re-Orienting Desire: The Gay International and the Arab World.'
    Public Culture 14, no. 2 (2002): 361–385.

Massey, Doreen. *Space, Place and Gender.* Cambridge: Polity Press, 1994.

Mbabazi, Hamlet Kabushenga. *Leadership under Pressure: The Authorized Biography
    of the Most Rev. Dr. Livingstone Mpalanyi Nkoyoyo, Archbishop Church of the
    Province of Uganda (Anglican), 1995–2004.* Kampala: African Christian Research
    Literature Institute, 2004.

Mbembe, Achille. *On the Postcolony.* Berkeley: University of California Press, 2001.

Mbuthia, Richard. 'Tanzania: Africa, Want Aid? Recognise Gay Rights!' *Tanzania Daily
    News*, 26 December 2011. http://allafrica.com/stories/201112271071.html.

McEwan, Ian. *Atonement.* London: Vintage, 2010.

Meghani, Shamira. 'HIV Stigma, Gay Identity, and Caste "Untouchability": Metaphors
    of Abjection in *My Brother . . . Nikhil*, *The Boyfriend*, and "Gandu Bagicha".'
    Journal of Medical Humanities (2017): 1–15. https://doi.org/10.1007/
    s10912-017-9437-5.

Meghani, Shamira. 'Queer South Asian Muslims: The Ethnic Closet and Its Secular
    Limits.' In *Imagining Muslims in South Asia and the Diaspora: Secularism, Religion,*

Representations, edited by Claire Chambers and Caroline Herbert, 172–184. Abingdon: Routledge, 2015.

Mehta, Akanksha. 'The World Before Her: A Review.' *Feminist Dissent* 1 (2016): 139–143.

Mehta, Pratap Bhanu. 'What Is Constitutional Morality?' *Seminar* 615 (2010). http://www.india-seminar.com/2010/615/615_pratap_bhanu_mehta.htm.

Mercer, Kobena. 'Decolonisation and Disappointment: Reading Fanon's Sexual Politics.' In *Frantz Fanon and Visual Representation*, edited by Alan Read, 114–130. London: Institute of Contemporary Arts, 1996.

Meyer, Birgit. '"Make a Complete Break with the Past": Memory and Post-Colonial Modernity in Ghanaian Pentecostalist Discourse.' *Journal of Religion in Africa* 28, no. 3 (1998): 316–349.

Meyer, Birgit. 'Pentecostalism and Neo-Liberal Capitalism: Faith, Prosperity and Vision in African Pentecostal-Charismatic Churches.' *Journal for the Study of Religion* 20, no. 2 (2007): 5–28.

Mikdashi, Maya, and Jasbir K. Puar. 'Queer Theory and Permanent War.' *GLQ: A Journal of Lesbian and Gay Studies* 22, no. 2 (2016): 215–222.

Mills, Scott. *The World's Worst Place to Be Gay?* BBC Three, 13 May 2011. https://www.youtube.com/watch?v=fV0tS6G8NNU.

Miti, James Kibuka. *A Short History of Buganda, Bunyoro, Busoga, Toro and Ankole.* Translated by G. K. Rock, 1939. Makerere University archives, box number AR/BUG/66/2.

Mohan, Sunil, and Sumathi Murthy, *Towards Gender Inclusivity: A Study on Contemporary Concerns around Gender*, edited by Alok Vaid-Menon. Bangalore: Alternative Law Forum, 2013.

Mohanty, Chandra Talpade. *Feminism without Borders: Decolonizing Theory, Practicing Solidarity*. Durham, NC: Duke University Press, 2003.

Mohanty, Chandra Talpade. 'Under Western Eyes: Feminist Scholarship and Colonial Discourses.' *boundary 2* 12, no. 3 (1984): 333–358.

Mokkil, Navaneetha. 'Shifting Spaces, Frozen Frames: Trajectories of Queer Politics in Contemporary India.' *Inter-Asian Cultural Studies* 10, no. 1 (2009): 12–30.

Morgan, Ruth, and Saskia Wieringa, eds. *Tommy Boys, Lesbian Men and Ancestral Wives: Female Same-Sex Practices in Africa*. Johannesburg: Jacana Media, 2005.

Mouffe, Chantal. 'Deliberative Democracy or Agonistic Pluralism?' *Social Research* 66, no. 3 (1999): 745–758.

Mowlabocus, Sharif. 'Homonormativity Gets a Musical Makeover.' Last modified 30 April 2014. http://sharifmowlabocus.com/2014/04/30/homonormativity-gets-a-musical-makeover/.

Mugisa, Anne, and Juliet Waiswa. 'Family of Martyrs Killer Apologises.' *New Vision*, 4 June 2008.

Mukasa, Victor. 'Spreading Lies in Kampala.' Last modified 5 March 2009. http://iglhrc.wordpress.com/2009/03/05/spreading-lies-in-kampala/.

Mullins, Rev. J. D. *The Wonderful Story of Uganda. To Which Is Added the Story of Ham Mukasa, Told by Himself*. London: Church Missionary Society, 1904.

Muñoz, José Esteban. *Cruising Utopia: The Then and There of Queer Futurity*. New York: New York University Press, 2009.

Muñoz, José Esteban. *Disidentifications: Queers of Color and the Performance of Politics*. Minneapolis: University of Minnesota Press, 1999.

Murray, Stephen O., and Will Roscoe, eds. *Boy-Wives and Female Husbands: Studies of African Homosexualities*. New York: St. Martin's Press, 1998.

Mutua, Makau. 'Savages, Victims, and Saviors: The Metaphor of Human Rights.'
    Harvard International Law Journal 42 (2001): 201–245.
Nagpaul, Satya Rai. 'Promised Empowerment of Trans People and the New Dealers
    of a False Liberty.' Last modified 15 August 2017. https://sampoornaindiablog.
    wordpress.com/2017/08/15/promised-empowerment-of-trans-people-and-the-
    new-dealers-of-a-false-liberty/.
Najmabadi, Afsaneh. *Women with Mustaches and Men without Beards: Gender and
    Sexual Anxieties of Iranian Modernity*. Berkeley: University of California
    Press, 2005.
Namutebi, Joyce. 'Fight Homos—Odoki.' *New Vision*, 4 June 2004.
Nanda, Serena. *Neither Man nor Woman: The Hijras of India*. Belmont,
    CA: Wadsworth, 1990.
Nandy, Ashis. *The Intimate Enemy: Loss and Recovery of Self under Colonialism*. New
    Delhi: Oxford University Press, 1988 [1983].
Nannyonga-Tamusuza, Sylvia A. *Baakisimba: Gender in the Music and Dance of the
    Baganda People of Uganda*. New York: Routledge, 2005.
Nannyonga-Tamusuza, Sylvia A. 'Female-Men, Male-Women, and
    Others: Constructing and Negotiating Gender among the Baganda of Uganda.'
    Journal of Eastern African Studies 3, no. 2 (2009): 367–380.
Narlikar, Amrita. 'Is India a Responsible Great Power?' *Third World Quarterly* 32, no. 9
    (2011): 1607–1621.
Narrain, Arvind. *Queer: Despised Sexuality, Law and Social Change*. Bangalore: Books
    for Change, 2004.
Narrain, Arvind, and Gautam Bhan. 'Introduction.' In *Because I Have a Voice: Queer
    Politics in India*, edited by Arvind Narrain and Gautam Bhan, 1–30. New
    Delhi: Yoda Press, 2005.
Narrain, Arvind, and Marcus Eldridge. *The Right That Dares to Speak Its Name: Naz
    Foundation vs. Union of India and Others*. Bangalore: Alternative Law
    Forum, 2009.
Narrain, Arvind, and Alok Gupta. 'Introduction.' In *Law like Love: Queer Perspectives
    on Law*, edited by Arvind Narrain and Alok Gupta, xi–lvi. New Delhi: Yoda
    Press, 2011.
Narrain, Siddharth. 'Gender Identity, Citizenship and State Recognition.' *Socio-Legal
    Review* 8, no. 2 (2012): 106–115.
Narrain, Siddharth. 'We Dissent.' Last modified 12 December 2013. https://kafila.
    online/2013/12/12/we-dissent-siddharth-narrain/.
Navtej Singh Johar v. Union of India, WP (Crl) No. 76 of 2016.
Naz Foundation v. Government of NCT Delhi, 160 Delhi Law Times 277.
Nehru, Jawaharlal. 'A Tryst with Destiny.' Available at https://www.theguardian.com/
    theguardian/2007/may/01/greatspeeches.
Nelson, Maggie. *The Argonauts*. Minneapolis, MN: Graywolf Press, 2015.
Neumann, Daniel (director). *Getting Out*. 2011.
Nirmal, Padini. '*Queering* Resistance, *Queering* Research: In Search of a Queer
    Decolonial Feminist Understanding of Adivasi Indigeneity.' *Journal of
    Resistance Studies* 2, no. 2 (2016): 167–204.
Noll, Stephen. 'The Handwriting on the Wall.' Accessed 3 August 2016. http://www.
    virtueonline.org/handwriting-wall-stephen-noll.
Nora, Pierre. 'Between Memory and History: Les Lieux de Memoire.' *Representations*
    26 (1989): 7–24.
Nsambu, Jean-Marie. 'Acholi Boys Head for Sainthood.' *New Vision*, 3 June 2002.

Nyanzi, Stella. 'Dismantling Reified African Culture through Localised Homosexualities in Uganda.' *Culture, Health & Sexuality* 15, no. 8 (2013): 952–967.

Nyanzi, Stella. 'LGBTIQ Ugandans Mourn Orlando Victims.' Last modified 19 June 2016. https://76crimes.com/2016/06/19/lgbtiq-ugandans-mourn-orlando-victims/.

Nyanzi, Stella. 'Queer Pride and Protest: A Reading of the Bodies at Uganda's First Gay Beach Pride.' *Signs* 40, no. 1 (2014): 36–40.

Nyanzi, Stella, and Andrew Karamagi. 'The Social-Political Dynamics of the Anti-Homosexuality Legislation in Uganda.' *Agenda: Empowering Women for Gender Equity* 29, no. 1 (2015): 24–38.

Ogenga-Latigo, Morris. 'Anti-Homosexuality Bill: Where Is Our Honesty?' *The Observer*, 13 December 2012. http://www.observer.ug/index.php?option=com_content&view=article&id=22603:-anti-homosexuality-bill-where-is-our-honesty-&catid=37:guest-writers&Itemid=66.

Ogle, Vanessa. *The Global Transformation of Time 1870–1950*. Cambridge, MA: Harvard University Press, 2015.

Okello, Benson. *History of East Africa: 1000 AD to Independence*. Kampala: Fountain, 2011.

Oliver, Marcia. 'Transnational Sex Politics, Conservative Christianity, and Antigay Activism in Uganda.' *Studies in Social Justice* 7, no. 1 (2013): 83–105.

Oliver, Roland. *The Missionary Factor in East Africa*. London: Longman, 1965.

Omvedt, Gail. *Ambedkar: Towards an Enlightened India*. New Delhi: Penguin, 2008.

Onen, James. 'FBUP Episode 012: Evaluating the Case against Homosexuality in Uganda.' Accessed 13 December 2012. http://fatboyunplugged.files.wordpress.com/2012/04/fbup-episode-012-evaluating-the-case-against-homosexuality-in-uganda.mp3.

Orford, Anne. *Reading Humanitarian Intervention: Human Rights and the Use of Force in International Law*. Cambridge: Cambridge University Press, 2004.

Orombi, Henry Luke. 'The Church Cannot Heal This Crisis of Betrayal.' Accessed 4 August 2016. http://www.virtueonline.org/kampala-church-cannot-heal-crisis-betrayal-henry-orombi.

Orombi, Henry Luke. 'What Is Anglicanism?' Accessed 4 August 2016. http://www.firstthings.com/article/2007/08/001-what-is-anglicanism.

Oyěwùmí, Oyèrónké. *The Invention of Women: Making an African Sense of Western Gender Discourses*. Minneapolis: University of Minnesota Press, 1997.

Pahuja, Nisha (director). *The World Before Her*. 2012.

Pambazuka News. 'Statement on British "Aid Cut" Threats to African Countries That Violate LGBTI Rights.' Last modified 27 October 2011. http://www.pambazuka.org/activism/statement-british-aid-cut-threats-african-countries-violate-lbgti-rights.

Pan-Afrikan Reparations Coalition in Europe. 'PARCOE Position Paper in Response to Discussion Points Generated by Our July 2013 Open Letter to Caribbean Heads of Government on Reparations.' Last modified 23 August 2013. https://oyeseyie.wordpress.com/caricom-reparations-commission-parcoe-position-paper/.

Pandey, Gyanendra. 'In Defense of the Fragment: Writing about Hindu-Muslim Riots in India Today.' *Representations* 37 (1992): 27–55.

Pardeshi, Pratima. 'The Hindu Code Bill for the Liberation of Women.' In *Gender and Caste*, edited by Anupama Rao, 346–362. New Delhi: Kali for Women, 2003.

Pardesi, Manjeet S. 'Is India a Great Power? Understanding Great Power Status in Contemporary International Relations.' *Asian Security* 11, no. 1 (2015): 1–30.

Parker, Trey, Robert Lopez, and Matt Stone. *The Book of Mormon.* New York: Newmarket Press, 2011.

Parkinson, Angus. 'Mwanga's Ghost: An Analysis of Anti-Sodomy Discourse in 19th Century and Modern Uganda.' LLM diss., Keele University, UK, 2010.

Parmar, Maya. 'Reading the Double Diaspora: Representing Gujarati East African Cultural Identity in Britain.' *Atlantis: Journal of the Spanish Association of Anglo-American Studies* 35, no. 1 (2013): 137–155.

Perkovich, George. 'Is India a Major Power?' *The Washington Quarterly* 27, no. 1 (2003): 129–144.

Peters, Melissa Minor (Olive Melissa Minor). '*Kuchus* in the Balance: Queer Lives under Uganda's Anti-Homosexuality Bill.' PhD diss., Northwestern University, Evanston, IL, 2014.

Picq, Manuela Lavinas, and Markus Thiel, eds. *Sexualities in World Politics: How LGBTQ Claims Shape International Relations.* Abingdon: Routledge, 2015.

Polgreen, Lydia, and Laurie Goodstein. 'At Axis of Episcopal Split, an Anti-Gay Nigerian.' *New York Times*, 25 December 2006. http://www.nytimes.com/2006/12/25/world/africa/25episcopal.html?pagewanted=print&_r=0.

Prakash, Asha. 'Papilio Buddha Gets Censor Certification.' *The Times of India*, 14 January 2013. http://timesofindia.indiatimes.com/entertainment/malayalam/movies/news/Papilio-Buddha-gets-censor-certification/articleshow/18016634.cms.

Prasad, Archana. ' "Jai Bhim" and "Lal Salaam" and How the Twain Shall Meet.' *Sabrang*, 21 April 2016. https://sabrangindia.in/article/%E2%80%98jai-bhim%E2%80%99-and-%E2%80%98lal-salaam%E2%80%99-and-how-twain-shall-meet.

Prashad, Vijay. *The Darker Nations: A People's History of the Third World.* New York: The New Press, 2007.

Prosser, Jay. *Second Skins: The Body Narratives of Transsexuality.* New York: Columbia University Press, 1998.

Prügl, Elisabeth. 'Lehman Brothers and Sisters: Revisiting Gender and Myth after the Financial Crisis.' In *Scandalous Economics: Gender and the Politics of Financial Crises*, edited by Aida A. Hozić and Jacqui True, 21–40. New York: Oxford University Press, 2016.

Puar, Jasbir K. 'Citation and Censorship: The Politics of Talking about the Sexual Politics of Israel.' *Feminist Legal Studies* 19 (2011): 133–142.

Puar, Jasbir K. ' "I Would Rather Be a Cyborg than a Goddess": Becoming-Intersectional in Assemblage Theory.' *philoSOPHIA* 2, no. 1 (2012): 49–66.

Puar, Jasbir K. 'Mapping US Homonormativities.' *Gender, Place and Culture* 13, no. 1 (2006): 67–88.

Puar, Jasbir K. *The Right to Maim: Debility, Capacity, Disability.* Durham, NC: Duke University Press, 2017.

Puar, Jasbir K. *Terrorist Assemblages: Homonationalism in Queer Times.* Durham, NC: Duke University Press, 2007.

Puar, Jasbir K. 'Transnational Sexualities: South Asian (Trans)nation(alism)s and Queer Diasporas.' In *Q&A: Queer in Asian America*, edited by David L. Eng and Alice Y. Hom, 405–422. Philadelphia: Temple University Press, 1998.

Puri, Jyoti. *Sexual States: Governance and the Struggle over the Antisodomy Law in India.* Durham, NC: Duke University Press, 2016.

Puttaswamy v. Union of India, (2017) 10 SCC 1.

Quesada, Andrea, Bisi Alimi, Hasan Abdessamad, Miroslawa Makuchowska, and Xiaogang Wei. 'The World Bank: Why It Should Consider Gay Rights.' Last modified 25 April 2014. http://www.economist.com/blogs/feastandfamine/ 2014/04/world-bank.

Raghavan, Anjana. *Towards Corporeal Cosmopolitanism: Performing Decolonial Solidarities*. London: Rowman & Littlefield, 2017.

Ramberg, Lucinda. 'Backward Futures and Pasts Forward: Queer Time, Sexual Politics, and Dalit Religiosity in South India.' *GLQ: A Journal of Lesbian and Gay Studies* 22, no. 2 (2016): 223–248.

Rao, Anupama. *The Caste Question: Dalits and the Politics of Modern India*. Berkeley: University of California Press, 2009.

Rao, Anupama, ed. *Gender and Caste*. New Delhi: Kali for Women, 2003.

Rao, Rahul. 'Before Bandung: Pet Names in Telangana.' In *Meanings of Bandung: Postcolonial Orders and Decolonial Visions*, edited by Quỳnh N. Phạm and Robbie Shilliam, 85–94. London: Rowman & Littlefield, 2016.

Rao, Rahul. 'On "Gay Conditionality", Imperial Power and Queer Liberation.' *Kafila*, 1 January 2012. https://kafila.online/2012/01/01/on-gay-conditionality-imperial-power-and-queer-liberation-rahul-rao/.

Rao, Rahul. 'Recovering Reparative Readings of Postcolonialism and Marxism.' *Critical Sociology* 43, nos. 4–5 (2017): 587–598.

Rao, Rahul. 'Review Article: One Time, Many Times.' *Millennium: Journal of International Studies* 47, no. 2 (2019): 299–308.

Rao, Rahul. 'Staying Positivist in the Fight against Homophobia.' *Sexuality Policy Watch Newsletter* no. 14, 3 July 2014. http://sxpolitics.org/article-newsletter-n14-rahul-rao/9411.

Rao, Rahul. 'The State of "Queer IR".' *GLQ: A Journal of Lesbian and Gay Studies* 24, no. 1 (2018): 139–149.

Rao, Rahul. *Third World Protest: Between Home and the World*. Oxford: Oxford University Press, 2010.

Reddy, Gayatri. *With Respect to Sex: Negotiating Hijra Identity in South India*. Chicago: University of Chicago Press, 2005.

Reid, Richard. 'Ghosts in the Academy: Historians and Historical Consciousness in the Making of Modern Uganda.' *Comparative Studies in Society and History* 56, no. 2 (2014): 351–380.

Reid, Richard. 'Images of an African Ruler: Kabaka Mutesa of Buganda, 1857–1884.' *History in Africa* 26 (1999): 269–298.

Revathi, A. *A Life in Trans Activism*. Translated by Nandini Murali. New Delhi: Zubaan, 2016.

Revathi, A. *The Truth about Me: A Hijra Life Story*. Translated by V. Geetha. New Delhi: Penguin, 2010.

Reynolds, Andrew. 'The UK Just Elected a Record Number of LGBTQ People to Parliament.' *Pink News*, 9 June 2017. https://www.pinknews.co.uk/2017/06/ 09/the-uk-just-elected-a-record-number-of-lgbtq-people-to-parliament/.

Rice, Xan. 'Ugandan Gay Rights Activist David Kato Found Murdered.' *Guardian*, 27 January 2011. https://www.theguardian.com/world/2011/jan/27/ ugandan-gay-rights-activist-murdered.

Richter-Montpetit, Melanie. 'Everything You Always Wanted to Know about Sex (in IR) But Were Afraid to Ask: The "Queer Turn" in International Relations.' *Millennium: Journal of International Studies* 46, no. 2 (2017): 220–240.

Robbins, Joel. 'On the Paradoxes of Global Pentecostalism and the Perils of Continuity Thinking.' *Religion* 33 (2003): 221–231.

Robinson, Colin. *Decolonising Sexual Citizenship: Who Will Effect Change in the South of the Commonwealth?* London: Commonwealth Advisory Bureau, 2012.

Rodriguez, S. M. *The Economics of Queer Inclusion: Transnational Organizing for LGBTI Rights in Uganda*. Lanham, MD: Lexington Books, 2019.

Roscoe, John. *The Baganda: An Account of Their Native Customs and Beliefs*. London: Macmillan, 1911.

Rosenberg, Jordy, and Amy Villarejo, eds. 'Queer Studies and the Crises of Capitalism.' *GLQ: A Journal of Lesbian and Gay Studies* 18, no. 1 (2012): 1–210.

Rottenberg, Catherine. 'Neoliberal Feminism and the Future of Human Capital.' *Signs* 42, no. 2 (2017): 329–348.

Roy, Arundhati. 'The Doctor and the Saint.' *Caravan*, 1 March 2014. https://caravanmagazine.in/essay/doctor-and-saint.

Roy, Arundhati. 'The End of Imagination.' *Outlook*, 3 August 1998. https://www.outlookindia.com/magazine/story/the-end-of-imagination/205932.

Roy, Arundhati. *The Greater Common Good*. Bombay: India Book Distributors, 1999.

Roy, Arundhati. *The Ministry of Utmost Happiness*. London: Hamish Hamilton, 2017.

Roy, Arundhati. 'Walking with the Comrades.' *Outlook*, 29 March 2010. https://www.outlookindia.com/magazine/story/walking-with-the-comrades/264738.

Rubenstein, Mary-Jane V. 'Anglicans in the Postcolony: On Sex and the Limits of Communion.' *Telos* 143 (2008): 133–160.

Rukundo, Solomon. ' "My President Is a Pair of Buttocks": The Limits of Online Freedom of Expression in Uganda.' *International Journal of Law and Information Technology* 26, no. 3 (2018): 252–271.

Ruskola, Teemu. 'Raping like a State.' *UCLA Law Review* 57 (2010): 1477–1536.

Sachindev P. S. '*Papilio Buddha*: Exploring Ecological Connectedness.' In *Culture and Media: Ecocritical Explorations*, edited by Rayson K. Alex, S. Susan Deborah, and P. S. Sachindev, 141–156. Newcastle: Cambridge Scholars, 2014.

Sadgrove, Joanna, Robert M. Vanderbeck, Johan Andersson, Gill Valentine, and Kevin Ward. 'Morality Plays and Money Matters: Towards a Situated Understanding of the Politics of Homosexuality in Uganda.' *Journal of Modern African Studies* 50, no. 1 (2012): 103–129.

Said, Edward W. *Culture and Imperialism*. London: Vintage, 1994.

Said, Edward W. *Orientalism: Western Conceptions of the Orient*. London: Penguin, 1995 [1978].

Said, Edward W. *Reflections on Exile and Other Literary and Cultural Essays*. London: Granta, 2001.

Sampoorna. 'SPWG Statement on Transgender Persons (Protection of Rights) Bill 2019.' Last modified 19 July 2019. https://sampoornaindiablog.wordpress.com/2019/07/19/spwg-statement-on-transgender-persons-protection-of-rights-bill-2019/.

Sampoorna. 'TG Bill 2016 Factsheet: Bill Provisions and Community Demands.' Last modified 23 November 2017. https://sampoornaindiablog.wordpress.com/2017/11/23/tg-bill-2016-factsheet-bill-provisions-community-demands/.

Satya. 'Why the Transgender Verdict Is an Incomplete One.' *LiveMint*, 18 April 2014. http://www.livemint.com/Leisure/Nv9Azw4bFA30CGbyCWSXUJ/LOUNGE-OPINION-Why-the-transgender-verdict-is-an-incomplete.html.

Savarkar, V. D. *Essentials of Hindutva*. 1923. http://savarkar.org/en/encyc/2017/5/23/2_12_12_04_essentials_of_hindutva.v001.pdf_1.pdf.

Schotten, C. Heike. *Queer Terror: Life, Death, and Desire in the Settler Colony*. New York: Columbia University Press, 2018.

Scott, James C. *Seeing like a State: How Certain Schemes to Improve the Human Condition Have Failed*. New Haven, CT: Yale University Press, 1998.

Seckinelgin, Hakan. 'Global Activism and Sexualities in the Time of HIV/AIDS.' *Contemporary Politics* 15, no. 1 (2009): 103–118.

Sedgwick, Eve. *The Epistemology of the Closet*. Berkeley: University of California Press, 2008 [1990].

Sedgwick, Eve. *Touching Feeling: Affect, Pedagogy, Performativity*. Durham, NC: Duke University Press, 2003.

Segal, Lynne. *Out of Time: The Pleasures and the Perils of Ageing*. London: Verso, 2013.

Sehgal, Parul. 'Arundhati Roy's Fascinating Mess.' *The Atlantic*, July/August 2017. https://www.theatlantic.com/magazine/archive/2017/07/arundhati-roys-fascinating-mess/528684/.

Semmalar, Gee Imaan. 'Emperor Penguins.' In *A Life in Trans Activism*, edited by A. Revathi, 194–203. New Delhi: Zubaan, 2016.

Semmalar, Gee Imaan. 'First as Apathy, Then as Farce: The Transgender Persons (Protection of Rights) Bill, 2016.' Last modified 14 August 2017. https://sampoornaindiablog.wordpress.com/2017/08/14/first-as-apathy-then-as-farce-the-transgender-persons-protection-of-rights-bill-2016/.

Semmalar, Gee Imaan. 'Gender Outlawed: The Supreme Court Judgment on Third Gender and Its Implications.' *Round Table India*, 19 April 2014. https://roundtableindia.co.in/index.php?option=com_conten t&view=article&id=7377:because-we-have-a-voice-too-the-supreme-court-judgment-on-third-gender-and-its-implications&catid=120&Ite mid=133.

Serunkuma, Yusuf. 'Of Stella Nyanzi's Rebel Speech and Politics.' *The Observer*, 13 March 2017. https://observer.ug/viewpoint/51729-of-stella-nyanzi-s-rebel-speech-and-politics.

Serunkuma, Yusuf. 'Revisiting the Stella Nyanzi–Museveni Family Affair.' *The Observer*, 7 November 2018. https://observer.ug/viewpoint/59122-revisiting-the-stella-nyanzi-museveni-family-affair.

Shah, Alpa. *In the Shadows of the State: Indigenous Politics, Environmentalism, and Insurgency in Jharkhand, India*. Durham, NC: Duke University Press, 2010.

Shah, Nayan. 'Sexuality, Identity, and the Uses of History.' In *A Lotus of Another Color: An Unfolding of the South Asian Gay and Lesbian Experience*, edited by Rakesh Ratti, 113–132. Boston: Alyson Publications, 1993.

Shah, Svati P. 'Queering Critiques of Neoliberalism in India: Urbanism and Inequality in the Era of Transnational "LGBTQ" Rights.' *Antipode* 47, no. 3 (2015): 635–651.

Shah, Svati P. *Street Corner Secrets: Sex, Work, and Migration in the City of Mumbai*. Durham, NC: Duke University Press, 2014.

Shankar, Aranya, Sreenivas Janyala, Chandan Haygunde, Johnson T. A., Dipti Singh, and Arun Janardhanan. 'Two Colours: How "Common Enemy" in University Campuses United Jai Bheem, Lal Salaam.' *Indian Express*, 10 April 2016. http://indianexpress.com/article/india/india-news-india/jai-bheem-lal-saalam-b-r-ambedkar-campus-violence-jnu-hcu-ftii-tiss-iit-b-protest/.

Sharlet, Jeff. 'Straight Man's Burden: The American Roots of Uganda's Anti-Gay Persecutions.' *Harper's Magazine*, September 2010. http://harpers.org/archive/2010/09/straight-mans-burden/.

Sharma, Maya. *Loving Women: Being Lesbian in Underprivileged India*. New Delhi: Yoda Press, 2006.

Shepherd, Verene. 'David Cameron, You Still Owe Us for Slavery.' *Guardian*, 30 September 2015. https://www.theguardian.com/commentisfree/2015/sep/30/david-cameron-slavery-caribbean.

Shepherd, Verene. 'Slavery, Shame and Pride: Debates over the Marking of the Bicentennial Trans-Atlantic Trade in Africans in 2007.' *Caribbean Quarterly* 56, nos. 1–2 (2010): 1–21.

Shilliam, Robbie. *The Black Pacific: Anti-Colonial Struggles and Oceanic Connections*. London: Bloomsbury, 2016.

Simwogerere, Haji Ashraf (director). *Mukajanga: The Passion of the Uganda Martyrs*. Kampala: Pearl Afric Pictures, 2009.

Sinani, Nezir. 'Can the World Bank Take Pride in Its Defense of the LGBT Community?' *Huffington Post*, 25 April 2016. http://www.huffingtonpost.com/nezir-sinani/can-the-world-bank-take-p_b_9771078.html.

Sinha, Mrinalini. *Colonial Masculinity: The 'Manly Englishman' and the 'Effeminate Bengali' in the Late Nineteenth Century*. Manchester: Manchester University Press, 1995.

Sircar, Oishik. 'New Queer Politics in the New India: Notes on Failure and Stuckness in a Negative Moment.' *Unbound* 11, no. 1 (2017): 1–36.

Sjoberg, Laura. 'Toward Trans-gendering International Relations?' *International Political Sociology* 6, no. 4 (2012): 337–354.

Slate, Nico. *Colored Cosmopolitanism: The Shared Struggle for Freedom in the United States and India*. Cambridge, MA: Harvard University Press, 2012.

Smith, Anna Marie. *New Right Discourse on Race and Sexuality: Britain, 1968–1990*. Cambridge: Cambridge University Press, 1994.

Smith, David. 'Why Africa Is the Most Homophobic Continent.' *Guardian*, 23 February 2014. https://www.theguardian.com/world/2014/feb/23/africa-homophobia-uganda-anti-gay-law.

Smith, Nicola. 'Toward a Queer Political Economy of Crisis.' In *Scandalous Economics: Gender and the Politics of Financial Crises*, edited by Aida A. Hozić and Jacqui True, 231–247. New York: Oxford University Press, 2016.

SMUG (Sexual Minorities Uganda). *'And That's How I Survived Being Killed': Testimonies of Human Rights Abuses from Uganda's Sexual and Gender Minorities*. April 2016. https://sexualminoritiesuganda.com/wp-content/uploads/2016/04/And-Thats-How-I-Survived_Report_Final.pdf.

SMUG (Sexual Minorities Uganda). *From Torment to Tyranny: Enhanced Persecution in Uganda Following the Passage of the Anti-Homosexuality Act 2014*. 9 May 2014. https://sexualminoritiesuganda.com/wp-content/uploads/2014/11/SMUG-From-Torment-to-Tyranny.pdf.

Spillers, Hortense J. 'Mama's Baby, Papa's Maybe: An American Grammar Book.' *Diacritics* 17, no. 2 (1987): 64–81.

Spillers, Hortense, Saidiya Hartman, Farah Jasmine Griffin, Shelly Eversley, and Jennifer L. Morgan. '"Whatcha Gonna Do?": Revisiting "Mama's Baby, Papa's Maybe: An American Grammar Book": A Conversation with Hortense Spillers, Saidiya Hartman, Farah Jasmine Griffin, Shelly Eversley and Jennifer L. Morgan.' *Women's Studies Quarterly* 35, nos. 1–2 (2007): 299–309.

Spivak, Gayatri Chakravorty. 'Can the Subaltern Speak?' In *Marxism and the Interpretation of Culture*, edited by Cary Nelson and Lawrence Grossberg, 271–313. Basingstoke: Macmillan, 1988.

Ssebaggala, Richard. 'Straight Talk on the Gay Question in Uganda.' *Transition* 106 (2011): 44–57.

Ssejjengo, Emmanuel. 'Mwanga Judged Too Harshly?' *New Vision*, 3 June 2004.

Ssempa, Martin. 'When Faith, State and State-Inspired Homosexuality Clash.' *New Vision*, 3 June 2005.

Ssemuwemba, Abbey Kibirige. 'Do the Uganda Martyrs Deserve the Hype?' *New Vision*, 8 June 2009.

Statement of the African Group on the Presentation of the Annual Report of the United Nations Human Rights Council. 71st Session of the United Nations General Assembly, New York, November 4, 2016. http://www.groundup.org.za/media/uploads/documents/AfricanGroupLetterToUNHRC.pdf.

Stockton, Kathryn Bond. *The Queer Child: Or Growing Sideways in the Twentieth Century*. Durham, NC: Duke University Press, 2009.

Stoler, Ann Laura. *Race and the Education of Desire: Foucault's History of Sexuality and the Colonial Order of Things*. Durham, NC: Duke University Press, 2000.

Stone, Amy L,. and Jane Ward. 'From "Black people Are Not a Homosexual Act" to "Gay Is the New Black": Mapping White Uses of Blackness in Modern Gay Rights Campaigns in the United States.' *Social Identities* 17, no. 5 (2011): 605–624.

Strey, Jacquelyn. 'Queer Moments, Queer Imaginings: Everyday Queer and an Ethics of Liveability.' PhD diss., SOAS University of London, 2018.

Stryker, Susan, Paisley Currah, and Lisa Jean Moore. 'Introduction: Trans-, Trans, or Transgender?' *Women's Studies Quarterly* 36, nos. 3–4 (2008): 11–22.

Stychin, Carl. *A Nation by Rights: National Cultures, Sexual Identity Politics, and the Discourse of Rights*. Philadelphia: Temple University Press, 1998.

Stychin, Carl. 'Same-Sex Sexualities and the Globalization of Human Rights Discourse.' *McGill Law Journal* 49 (2004): 951–968.

Sunderland, Ruth. 'The Real Victims of This Credit Crunch? Women.' *Guardian*, 18 January 2009. https://www.theguardian.com/lifeandstyle/2009/jan/18/women-credit-crunch-ruth-sunderland.

Suresh Kumar Koushal v. Naz Foundation, (2014) 1 SCC 1.

Tamale, Sylvia. 'Confronting the Politics of Nonconforming Sexualities in Africa.' *African Studies Review* 56, no. 2 (2013): 31–45.

Tamale, Sylvia. *Homosexuality: Perspectives from Uganda*. Kampala: Sexual Minorities Uganda, 2007.

Tamale, Sylvia. 'Out of the Closet: Unveiling Sexuality Discourses in Uganda.' *Feminist Africa* 2 (2003). http://www.awdflibrary.org/bitstream/handle/123456789/361/13%20Tamale_OutoftheCloset_FemAfrica.pdf?sequence=2&isAllowed=y.

Tamale, Sylvia. 'Researching and Theorising Sexualities in Africa.' In *African Sexualities: A Reader*, edited by Sylvia Tamale, 11–36. Oxford: Pambazuka Press, 2011.

Tatchell, Peter. 'David Cameron Urged: Apologise for Anti-Gay Laws Imposed by UK.' Last modified 27 October 2011. http://www.petertatchellfoundation.org/david-cameron-urged-apologise-for-anti-gay-laws-imposed-by-uk/.

Taylor, Adam. 'Britain's Parliament Might Be the Most LGBT in the World.' *Washington Post*, 13 January 2016. https://www.washingtonpost.com/news/worldviews/wp/2016/01/13/britains-parliament-might-be-the-most-lgbt-in-the-world/?utm_term=.ee6ecbb45705.

Taylor, Jerome. 'Gay Activists in India Want British Apology for Sex Law.' *Independent*, 16 August 2008. https://www.independent.co.uk/news/world/asia/gay-activists-in-india-want-british-apology-for-sex-law-898979.html.

Tellis, Ashley. 'Disrupting the Dinner Table: Re-thinking the "Queer Movement" in Contemporary India.' *Jindal Global Law Review* 4, no. 1 (2012): 142–156.

Thomas, Kendall. '"Ain't Nothin' like the Real Thing": Black Masculinity, Gay Sexuality, and the Jargon of Authenticity.' In *Traps: African American Men on Gender and Sexuality*, edited by Rudolph P. Byrd and Beverly Guy-Sheftall, 327–341. Bloomington: Indiana University Press, 2001.

Thomas, Scott M. 'Faith and Foreign Aid: How the World Bank Got Religion, and Why It Matters.' *The Brandywine Review of Faith & International Affairs* 2, no. 2 (2004): 21–29.

Thompson, Janna. 'Apology, Justice, and Respect: A Critical Defense of Political Apology.' In *The Age of Apology: Facing Up to the Past*, edited by Mark Gibney, Rhoda E. Howard-Hassmann, Jean-Marc Coicaud, and Niklaus Steiner, 31–44. Philadelphia: University of Pennsylvania Press, 2008.

Thoonen, J. P. *Black Martyrs*. London: Sheed & Ward, 1941.

Thoreson, Ryan Richard. 'Troubling the Waters of a "Wave of Homophobia": Political Economies of Anti-Queer Animus in Sub-Saharan Africa.' *Sexualities* 17, nos. 1–2 (2014): 23–42.

Thornton, Robert J. *Unimagined Community: Sex, Networks, and AIDS in Uganda and South Africa*. Berkeley: University of California Press, 2008.

Times Group. 'India Poised.' Accessed 12 October 2017. https://www.youtube.com/watch?v=MiItWDN2Cs8.

Tinsley, Omise'eke Natasha. 'Black Atlantic, Queer Atlantic: Queer Imaginings of the Middle Passage.' *GLQ: A Journal of Lesbian and Gay Studies* 14, nos. 2–3 (2008): 191–215.

Trans, Gender Nonconforming and Intersex Collectives. 'Strongly Condemn Kinnar Akhara's Support for Ram Temple at Ayodhya, India.' *Round Table India*, 24 November 2018. http://roundtableindia.co.in/index.php?option=com_content&view=article&id=9509%3Atrans-gender.

Tripathi, Laxminarayan. *Me Hijra, Me Laxmi*. Translated by R. Raj Rao and P. G. Joshi. New Delhi: Oxford University Press, 2015.

Trouillot, Michel-Rolph. *Silencing the Past: Power and the Production of History*. Boston: Beacon Press, 1995.

True, Jacqui. 'The Global Financial Crisis's Silver Bullet: Women Leaders and "Leaning In".' In *Scandalous Economics: Gender and the Politics of Financial Crises*, edited by Aida A. Hozić and Jacqui True, 41–56. New York: Oxford University Press, 2016.

Tsing, Anna Lowenhaupt. *Friction: An Ethnography of Global Connection*. Princeton, NJ: Princeton University Press, 2005.

Tudor, Alyosxa. 'Dimensions of Transnationalism.' *Feminist Review* 117 (2017): 20–40.

Uganda Bureau of Statistics. *The National Population and Housing Census 2014—Main Report*. March 2016. https://www.ubos.org/onlinefiles/uploads/ubos/NPHC/NPHC%202014%20FINAL%20RESULTS%20REPORT.pdf.

Uganda Mirror. 'Stella Nyanzi's Poem on President Museveni's Birthday, You Won't Like What She wrote!!' 17 September 2018. https://ugmirror.com/index.php/2018/09/17/stella-nyanzis-poem-on-president-musevenis-birthday-you-wont-like-what-she-wrote/.

UK Ministry of Justice. 'Press Release: Thousands Officially Pardoned under "Turing's Law".' Last modified 31 January 2017. https://www.gov.uk/government/news/thousands-officially-pardoned-under-turings-law.

Valois, Caroline. 'Scandal Makers: Competition in the Religious Market among Pentecostal-Charismatic Churches in Uganda.' In *Christianity and Controversies over Homosexuality in Contemporary Africa*, edited by Ezra Chitando and Adriaan van Klinken, 38–50. Abingdon: Routledge, 2016.

Van Dijk, Tara. 'The Impossibility of World-Class Slum-Free Indian Cities and the Fantasy of "Two Indias".' In *Urban Utopias: Excess and Expulsion in Neoliberal South Asia*, edited by Tereza Kuldova and Mathew A. Varghese, 19–36. Basingstoke: Palgrave, 2017.

Van Klinken, Adriaan. *Kenyan, Christian, Queer: Religion, LGBT Activism, and Arts of Resistance in Africa*. State College: Penn State University Press, 2019.

Van Zandt, Cynthia J. *Brothers among Nations: The Pursuit of Intercultural Alliances in Early America, 1580–1660*. New York: Oxford University Press, 2008.

Vanita, Ruth, and Saleem Kidwai, eds. *Same-Sex Love in India: Readings from Literature and History*. Basingstoke: Palgrave, 2001.

Vidya, Living Smile. *I Am Vidya: A Transgender's Journey*. New Delhi: Rupa, 2013.

Vidya, Living Smile. '(Trans)gender and Caste Lived Experience—Transphobia as a Form of Brahminism: An Interview of Living Smile Vidya,' transcript of a conversation with Kaveri Karthik and Gee Ameena Suleiman. *Round Table India*, 2 March 2013. https://roundtableindia.co.in/index.php?option=com_content&view=article&id=6254:transgender-and-caste-lived-experience-transphobia-as-a-form-of-brahminism-an-interview-of-living-smile-vidya&catid=120&Itemid=133.

Viswanathan, Gauri. *Outside the Fold: Conversion, Modernity, and Belief*. Princeton, NJ: Princeton University Press, 1998.

Waites, Matthew. 'LGBTI Organizations Navigating Imperial Contexts: The Kaleidoscope Trust, the Commonwealth and the Need for a Decolonizing, Intersectional Politics.' *The Sociological Review* 65, no. 4 (2017): 644–662.

Walter, Natasha. '*The Ministry of Utmost Happiness* by Arundhati Roy: Review—A Bright Mosaic.' *Guardian*, 2 June 2017. https://www.theguardian.com/books/2017/jun/02/ministry-utmost-happiness-arundhati-roy-review.

Ward, Kevin. 'A History of Christianity in Uganda.' In *From Mission to Church: A Handbook of Christianity in East Africa*, edited by Zablon Nthamburi, 81–112. Nairobi: Uzima Press, 1991.

Ward, Kevin. 'The Role of the Anglican and Catholic Churches in Uganda in Public Discourse on Homosexuality and Ethics.' *Journal of Eastern African Studies* 9, no. 1 (2015): 127–44.

Ward, Kevin. 'Same-Sex Relations in Africa and the Debate on Homosexuality in East African Anglicanism.' *Anglican Theological Review* 84, no. 1 (2002): 81–111.

Warner, Michael. 'Introduction.' In *Fear of a Queer Planet: Queer Politics and Social Theory*, edited by Michael Warner, vii–xxxi. Minneapolis: University of Minnesota Press, 1993.

Warner, Michael. 'Publics and Counterpublics.' *Public Culture* 14, no. 1 (2002): 49–90.

Waters, Chris. 'Turing in Context: Sexual Offences in Cheshire in the 1950s.' Public lecture as part of *Queer Lives Past and Present: Interrogating the Legal*, Birkbeck College, London, 29 November 2017.

Waterton, Emma. 'Humiliated Silence: Multiculturalism, Blame, and the Trope of "Moving on".' *Museum and Society* 8, no. 3 (2010): 128–157.

Watt, Nicholas. 'Fury at Uganda Proposal for Gay Executions.' *Guardian*, 27 November 2009. https://www.theguardian.com/world/2009/nov/27/uganda-bill-proposes-gay-executions.

Weber, Cynthia. *Faking It: US Hegemony in a 'Post-Phallic' Era*. Minneapolis: University of Minnesota Press, 1999.

Weber, Cynthia. *Queer International Relations: Sovereignty, Sexuality and the Will to Knowledge*. New York: Oxford University Press, 2016.

Weiss, Meredith L. 'Prejudice before Pride: Rise of an Anticipatory Countermovement.' In *Global Homophobia: States, Movements, and the Politics of Oppression*, edited by Meredith L. Weiss and Michael J. Bosia, 149–173. Urbana: University of Illinois Press, 2013.

Wesaka, Anthony. 'Minister Wins Gays Case.' *Daily Monitor*, 24 June 2014. http://www.monitor.co.ug/News/National/Minister-wins-gays-case/-/688334/2359266/-/focv8tz/-/index.html.

Wiegman, Robyn, and Elizabeth A. Wilson. 'Introduction: Antinormativity's Queer Conventions.' *differences: A Journal of Feminist Cultural Studies* 26, no. 1 (2015): 1–25.

Wiegratz, Jörg. 'Fake Capitalism? The Dynamics of Neoliberal Moral Restructuring and Pseudo-Development: The Case of Uganda.' *Review of African Political Economy* 37, no. 124 (2010): 123–137.

Wieringa, Saskia. 'Women Marriages and Other Same-Sex Practices: Historical Reflections on African Women's Same-Sex Relations.' In *Tommy Boys, Lesbian Men and Ancestral Wives: Female Same-Sex Practices in Africa*, edited by Ruth Morgan and Saskia Wieringa, 281–307. Johannesburg: Jacana Media, 2005.

Williams, Joe. 'Stephen Fry Attempted Suicide after Interviewing "Frothing" Homophobic Politician.' *PinkNews*, 9 February 2016. http://www.pinknews.co.uk/2016/02/09/stephen-fry-attempted-suicide-after-interviewing-frothing-homophobic-politician/.

Williams, Matt. 'Kony 2012 Campaigner Jason Russell: "I Wasn't in Control of My Mind or Body."' *Guardian*, 8 October 2012. https://www.theguardian.com/world/2012/oct/08/kony-2012-jason-russell-interview-nbc.

Williams, Zoe. 'Gay Rights: A World of Inequality.' *Guardian*, 13 September 2011. https://www.theguardian.com/world/2011/sep/13/gay-rights-world-of-inequality.

Wintemute, Robert. 'From "Sex Rights" to "Love Rights": Partnership Rights as Human Rights.' In *Sex Rights: The Oxford Amnesty Lectures 2002*, edited by Nicholas Bamforth, 186–224. Oxford: Oxford University Press, 2005.

Woodward, Vincent. *The Delectable Negro: Human Consumption and Homoeroticism within US Slave Culture*. New York: New York University Press, 2014.

World Bank. 'Directive: Addressing Risks and Impacts on Disadvantaged or Vulnerable Individuals or Groups.' 4 August 2016. https://policies.worldbank.org/sites/ppf3/PPFDocuments/e5562765a5534ea0b7877e1e775f29d5.pdf.

World Bank. 'Environmental and Social Framework: Setting Environmental and Social Standards for Investment Project Financing.' 4 August 2016. http://consultations.worldbank.org/Data/hub/files/consultation-template/review-and-update-world-bank-safeguard-policies/en/materials/the_esf_clean_final_for_public_disclosure_post_board_august_4.pdf.

World Bank. 'World Bank Announces New Advisor on Sexual Orientation and Gender Identity Issues.' Last modified 27 October 2016. http://www.worldbank.org/en/news/press-release/2016/10/27/

world-bank-announces-new-advisor-on-sexual-orientation-and-gender-identity-issues.

World Bank GLOBE. 'It Gets Better.' Last modified 14 March 2011. https://www.youtube.com/watch?v=HZMdv24W-sk.

Wright, Katherine Fairfax, and Malika Zouhali-Worrall (directors). *Call Me Kuchu*. 2013.

Younis, Musab. 'Race, the World and Time: Haiti, Liberia and Ethiopia (1914–1945).' *Millennium: Journal of International Studies* 46, no. 3 (2018): 352–370.

Yukhananov, Anna. 'World Bank Postpones Uganda Loan over Anti-Gay Law.' *Reuters*, 27 February 2014. http://www.reuters.com/article/us-uganda-worldbank-idUSBREA1Q2C320140227.

Zakaria, Fareed. 'The Rise of Illiberal Democracy.' *Foreign Affairs* 76, no. 6 (November/December 1997): 22–43.

Zelliot, Eleanor. 'Dr. Ambedkar and the Empowerment of Women.' In *Gender & Caste*, edited by Anupama Rao, 204–217. New Delhi: Kali for Women, 2003.

INDEX

For the benefit of digital users, indexed terms that span two pages (e.g., 52–53) may, on occasion, appear on only one of those pages.

CPSIA information can be obtained
at www.ICGtesting.com
Printed in the USA
BVHW031022081222
653654BV00002B/4